**W9-ATZ-315**

TOKYO

Mayumi Yoshida Barakan and Judith Conner Greer

NEW

CITY

GUIDE

TOKYO CITY GUIDE

Mayumi Yoshida Barakan & Judith Connor Greer

CHARLES E. TUTTLE COMPANY
Rutland, Vermont & Tokyo, Japan

First published by Ryuko Tsushin Co., Ltd., 1985

Published by the Charles E. Tuttle Company, Inc.
of Rutland, Vermont & Tokyo, Japan
with editorial offices at
2-6 Suido 1-chome, Bunkyo-ku, Tokyo 112

© 1996 by Charles E. Tuttle Publishing Co., Inc.

LCC Card No. 94-60932
ISBN 0-8048-1964-5

First revised and updated edition, 1996

Printed in Japan

INTRODUCTION

June 1996

Fifteen years ago, when I first came to Japan from America, I didn't buy a guidebook to the city. The books available directed the tourist to bus tours, expensive imported designer boutiques in Ginza, to ancient nightclubs and cabarets. It was just intuition at the time, but I knew there must be more than that going on in Tokyo, and I decided to find out what it was.

Over the years Mayumi and I have guided hundreds of friends through the city. We became experts at drawing maps and running off copied handouts on where to go, what to do, and where to find what. It was always fun, always great to see people get as excited about the city as we were. Still, we often wished that there was a single volume, collecting all the information, that we could give to visitors. The book should have been published long ago, and when no one else did it, we decided to do it ourselves.

In the past few years Tokyo has received more good PR overseas than any other city in the world. More and more people are coming to the city, most of them with different reasons and expectations from those that people came with ten or even five years ago. For some, the city is disappointingly westernized; for others, it's a super-technopolis of the future. For yet others it's simply frustrating. But few people fail to be intrigued, if not captivated, by the curious combination of new technology, internationalism, traditional behavior and aesthetics, and the cross-cultural kitsch that make up Tokyo's special brand of urban life.

The city casts its spell over even the most adamantly unhappy of its foreign residents. Conversations here turn with an almost predictable frequency to Japan and the Japanese. Much of the talk consists of complaints, accusations, stories about silly Mr. Suzuki, or games of one-upmanship as to who has read the most hysterical, the most bizarre, or the most obscene misprinted English phrase of the day. But whether arising from love or hate, the fascination never dies.

The repertoire of complaints is fairly standardized: the ugliness of the city; people rudely pushing and shoving their way through crowds; the noise pollution; the difficulty of getting around with no consistent system of addresses or street names; the constant pointing and staring at foreigners and the audible *"gaijin da!"* ("It's a foreigner!"); the pervasive belief that foreigners can't learn the impossible Japanese language. But most vehemently criticized is the general sense of regimentation and the overall lack of individuality in the people—the inability to do anything that doesn't go by the rules or isn't decided after lengthy discussion with the "group."

The criticisms are at least partially justified, the frustrations undeniable. You can go into a coffee shop and order a ham and cheese sandwich, hold the ham (or even just the mustard), and it provokes a major crisis. If you're feeling assertive, you'll get angry, wondering why something so simple can't be done. But that's how things work here so eat your sandwich ham and all, quietly take it off yourself, or leave Japan.

The aggressive individuality most foreigners were raised to believe in doesn't figure in the Japanese scheme of things. The Japanese do not believe in individuality, but in the concept of a group where every single person has his place, duties, and responsibilities. This one basic difference leads to more misunderstanding and frustration than any of the multitude of other cultural differences. Individualism is great and makes for a vibrant and actively creative society. But it's not the only way to organize life, and certainly not the Japanese way. To their credit, the Japanese have managed to work out a system that keeps most of the population healthy, happy, and prosperous—if lacking in individuals. For skeptics it's worth noting that the state of Japan is analogous to a hypothetical situation where half the population of the United States would be squeezed into Southern California. All those American individuals would probably end up killing each other off within the week. You pay one way or the other.

The bad parts of the city are the most blatantly obvious, while the good parts are often found in the easily overlooked small things—the careful wrapping of the most humble purchase, the hot *oshibori* towel before a meal, the safety, the back streets swept spotlessly clean by the local residents—all of which are just day-to-day manifestations of the general Japanese attitude toward life. It may sound simplistic, but for us, the good parts of the city are a more than equal trade-off for the bad.

We both came to the city as temporary residents. Mayumi arrived as a college student in 1977 from Sapporo, a city in northern Japan. Her reactions were at first similar to those of any tourist and she often thought of leaving. But after spending a year in London, she returned with a new interest in things Japanese and an objective appreciation for Tokyo.

I came from Seattle, a provincial city on the West Coast of America. Tokyo was to be the first stop on a trip around the world. I stayed and learned the language. Curiosity kept me here as three months turned into four years, and I'm still curious.

We both have a great time in Tokyo. We like the technopolitan city that's built on an unshakably Japanese foundation. Tokyo lacks the glamour and sophistication of New York and Paris, but the combination of new and old, the ceaseless input of new cultural variables from around the world, the friction between what gets accepted and what doesn't, give the city an energy—the excitement of a contemporary urban culture constantly in the process of creation.

The Tokyo City Guide has been out of print since about 1990 and the question of updating or not updating has cast its shadow over our lives for about that much time. We were not really sure we wanted to take it on again, and more-or-less hoped that someone who had the spirit we had in 1984 would come out with something new and better. Every time we went to a party and were asked when the new edition was coming out—we cringed. After years of cringing and a few false starts, it finally happened.

In some ways, the revision has resulted in a more conservative book than its predecessors. This has been a hard thing to accept, but aside from the fact that we are no longer the wild and free young women we were in 1984, experience has taught us that too many of the new places go under and that no one wants to search out a place that maybe was interesting three years ago, but no longer even exists.

For better or for worse, this new version is perhaps more personal than our first edition. With so many new and good clubs, restaurants, and shops—we have had to make our selections based on personal choice. And, predictably, we have included a section on children which was missing from our earlier book and our art and architecture sections have grown.

Tokyo has changed since the first edition of the *Tokyo City Guide* was released in 1984, and so have our lives. With two children each, we no longer find ourselves at bars, discos, and restaurants after midnight. In our mid- to late thirties, we no longer shop on the back streets of Harajuku. For better or for worse, we experience the city in a different way.

When people hear I've been in Tokyo for more than a decade, the almost inevitable response is "So, you must love it!" I never quite know what to say. In some ways Yes, in others No. Mayumi feels the same. But I suspect that someday, when we both live in some other city, in some other part of the world, we'll both remember Tokyo as the city where we spent the most interesting and exciting years of our lives.

HOW TO USE THIS BOOK

Cross-referencing

The book is divided into three main sections. The beginning covers the history of the city, its districts, and neighborhoods. The middle section is divided into guide chapters covering specific topics: accommodation, restaurants, shopping, arts, etc. The book ends with the map sections. There are fifty maps charting most of the listings found in the guide sections and covering the districts described in the first chapter. Next to each map is a list of its contents with the text-page reference number for each entry.

Our intention was to provide a complete cross-referencing system. Ideally, you should browse through the entire book. But if you're in a hurry and are looking for something specific, e.g., a sushi restaurant, then you can look one up in the restaurant chapter under sushi. If you want to spend a day in a particular district, read about the history and description of the district in the first chapter, then turn to the map to see what the area has to offer in terms of shops, restaurants, etc.

How We Selected

Even with a book this size, only a fraction of what the city has to offer can be included. But then, we didn't intend to compile a phone directory. We have selected and included things we know, things we like, and things we would like others to know about. Our selection covers a broad range of prices, and a huge range of possibilities. Convenience figured to some extent. Some places we couldn't include because their Japanese owners didn't want to be made public.

While the decisions were basically our own, we consulted various local "experts" to discover new places, and to reconfirm that our decisions were not made purely on the basis of sentimental association. Our "experts" included born and bred Tokyoites aged sixty-plus, foreign residents of all ages and nationalities, journalists, artists, shop owners, etc. Many of the older shops and restaurants are famous Japanese institutions; the newer places are often those less known among both Japanese and the international community.

How You Can Select
There is a great deal of information in this book. For a future resident or long-term visitor this may be useful, but for a short-term tourist possibly confusing. For short-term visitors, our suggestion is to pick one new and one historical district to explore—for example the Aoyama–Harajuku area or Shinjuku for contemporary Tokyo and Asakusa for old Tokyo. Spend the evening in Roppongi. From our listings for restaurants (or accommodation), you can choose according to price range. All offer excellent quality, if not quantity, for the price.

Listings
The shops, restaurants, hotels, etc., listed in this book, with few exceptions, correspond to a number on one of the maps in the map section. The map reference number is marked after each entry as, for example, [M-3], meaning "Map Number Three." The exceptions are not located on any of our maps and are marked [off Map]. Sometimes we have included instructions for how to get to these "mapless" entries, other times we have just listed the nearest station.

The prices and addresses are valid as of publication, but Tokyo changes very quickly. Some of our favorite places closed down while we were writing the book, and more will doubtless close within the next year. In most cases it won't be necessary, but if you are planning to go out of your way to visit a particular shop or restaurant, we suggest that you call ahead just to make certain that it is still in business and in the same location.

Most addresses have been written in English, but for some of the more difficult-to-locate entries we have included the names and addresses written in Japanese so you can show the book to someone if and when you get lost.

When an entry appears more than once in the text, the address, hours, etc., have been noted with the main entry.

Proper Names
Japanese proper names have been written in the Japanese manner with the family name first.

Place Names
Place names have been written in the Japanese form. For example Yoyogi Koen means Yoyogi Park, but if you ask a Japanese person where Yoyogi

Park is, few people will understand you. The same goes for museums, gardens, temples, etc. Sometimes we have listed an entry as, for examples, "Senso-ji temple." The "ji" means temple, so the entry literally translates as Senso Temple temple. There is no practical way around this.

Italics

In all but a few isolated cases, all words in italics—that are not personal or place names—are Japanese terms.

Pronunciation

We recommend that you consult the pronunciation guide in the language section before attempting to use any Japanese language. In most places throughout the book, where Japanese words appear in the text long vowels have been indicated.

Romanizations of Japanese words in the text are slightly different from those normally used for teaching Japanese, but we have attempted to make them as easy to read as possible for those not acquainted with the Japanese language.

Language Section

The chapter on the Japanese language was written by Peter Barakan, a resident of Tokyo since 1974 who speaks flawless Japanese and holds a university degree in the language. He is British, which is important for non-British speakers of the English language to remember when following the instructions for pronunciation.

In addition to endless researching and telephoning, we have walked the streets of Tokyo trying to make this book as error free as possible. But in spite of our efforts, there will be mistakes: hours and prices change; shops open and close; the maps may have omissions. You may hate our selections. For this we would like to apologize.

CONTENTS

14 CONTENTS

東京

TOKYO

TOKYO

THE CITY

It is often said, by Japanese and foreigners alike, that Tokyo is not the "real" Japan. What they mean is that it's not the "ideal" Japan, the Japan of a people unspoiled by the West, where the descendants of the sun goddess live in spiritual harmony with nature in the Land of the Rising Sun.

The nostalgia is understandable. With a population of nearly twelve million, Tokyo reads at times like a lexicon of the problems confronting Japan today. But the ideal Japan, like all objects of nostalgic devotion, is part of an irretrievable past. With barely 125 years of modern history, the Japanese still suffer from growing pains. The events of those one hundred years, the greatest successes and the greatest defeats, were first felt in Tokyo.

Kyoto was the center of the country during the golden days of Japan. There in the rarefied air of the emperor's presence, a court aristocracy pursued a life of aesthetic sensitivity and refinement. What was most important was the turn of a phrase in a cryptic poem, the perfect harmony found in twelve layers of subtly shaded kimono, the just-so sweep of a brush across a sheet of immaculate paper. The present site of Tokyo was then called Musashi no Kuni, a land of fields and thickly forested hills.

Tokyo came of age with Tokugawa Ieyasu's rise to power in 1600. The *daimyo* (feudal lords) were brought to submission and the country was ruled for 250 years of domestic peace and isolation from the world under the Tokugawa shogunate based in Edo.

Edo had prospered since the mid-fifteenth century as a castle town built by the minor daimyo Ota Dokan. Throughout Japan, the daimyo consolidated their power in castle towns that grew into provincial capitals of cultural and economic activity centered on the needs of the lord and the samurai aristocracy. Primarily constructed for defense, the castles were surrounded by concentric circles of moats and ramparts, the streets laid out in irregular zigzag patterns to surprise and confuse an attacking enemy. The seemingly random pattern of Tokyo streets today is a survival of this early urban planning.

Edo became the greatest castle in the land. The city grew rapidly as the daimyo built homes within the castle walls, alternating residence between their provincial domains and mandatory attendance on the shogun in Edo. With the influx of daimyo and samurai troops, the need for a service class increased. Tokugawa Ieyasu invited merchants and artisans to the city, assigning them quarters in the eastern marshes by the sea, now the lands stretching west and southwest from Hibiya. Dirt from the top of Surugadai, one of Tokyo's larger hills, was provided to start the process of reclamation from the sea that continues today. By the 1700s, the population of Edo was close to a million, making it possibly the largest city in the world at the time.

The conservative Edo period government legally enforced a strict division of classes, placing the samurai at the top and the theoretically unproductive merchant at the bottom. But the urban samurai had become utterly dependent, and increasingly indebted to, the merchant class. Despite government efforts to enforce the status quo, the merchants continued to prosper. Restricted to *shitamachi,* the crowded downtown districts, from the merchant and artisan classes emerged a culture that was as vibrantly creative as it was unabashedly vulgar. In the amusement quarters of the city, the merchants escaped from the pressures of the rigid social system and the demands of business. Under their patronage, the arts flourished—the Bunraku and Kabuki theaters, geisha, and *ukiyoe*-style prints were all products of the time.

Tokugawa rule ended shortly after the arrival in Tokyo Bay of Commodore Matthew Perry and the United States Navy in 1953. Unable to protect the country from the "Southern Barbarians," the government lost its claim to legitimacy. A coalition of powerful families from the southern and western provinces seized power from the shogunate, and in the 1868 Meiji Restoration reestablished Imperial rule. The Emperor was moved to Edo castle and the city renamed Tokyo—the "eastern capital."

The new government quickly realized that national security could best be achieved by meeting the West on its own terms, and a program was undertaken to promote rapid modernization. Things Western were adopted and praised as far superior to Japanese. Foreign experts were sought and extravagantly paid. Tokyo took on a new air as brick buildings, trains, and tailored suits came into vogue.

Patterns of urban use also changed. The daimyo packed up and moved back to the provinces leaving vast stretches of vacant land in the castle areas. No longer confined to shitamachi, the wealthy merchants moved to the western, hilly parts of town. Without their patronage, the arts and entertainment forms of Edo popular culture lost their major source of support. The old pleasure quarters and theaters fell on hard times and shitamachi was left to the poor.

Tokyo continued to grow, and by the 1920s had a population of over two million. Then in 1923 came the Great Kanto Earthquake. The earthquake, and the fires and tidal waves that followed, left nearly 140,000 people dead and half of the city destroyed. Tokyo was rebuilt and in less than ten years the population was again at pre-earthquake levels. In 1932, the city limits were expanded to the current twenty-three wards, boosting the population another two million.

The city has suffered over the years from a variety of natural and unnatural disasters—in the Edo period from over five hundred major fires, from floods, typhoons, earthquakes, and in 1945 from the fire bombings of World War II. Each time, the people reconstructed the city and resumed their lives with a stoic resilience. Tokyo has never had a tradition of permanence.

Now the second largest city in the world, Tokyo sprawls across more than eight hundred square miles of the Kanto Plain. As an urban environment, the capital shows little concern for outward appearances, and evokes neither the alien exoticism of an Asian city, nor the sense of wonder and awe one expects from a city of its size and international importance. But while Westerners build monuments to the future, the Japanese have built and rebuilt for the present. The chaos of the city today is the function of an attitude that puts the exigencies of survival above all other concerns. A major earthquake has been predicted in Tokyo. They happen every sixty years or so; the last one was in 1923, and the next is already overdue. The city keeps building its functional modern high-rises and just waits.

Yet the "technopolitan" Tokyo of first impressions is really just a thin veneer that hides what remains in essence a city of villages. Within walking distance of almost any of the city's major districts are back-street neighborhoods where life operates pretty much the same as in any small suburban community. Shops and homes line the narrow wandering streets where children play and grandmothers chat at the corner fruit stand. The man next door waters his street-side garden in his pajamas each morning and the tofu seller tours the neighborhood in the evening by bicycle, calling out to the local housewives with his distinctive horn.

The districts and neighborhoods that divide Tokyo make it a city of varied pleasures and endless discovery. Each has a history, each growing up at a different stage in the life of the city. Some, aging, are museums of the past; others are still in the first neon flush of youth.

THE DISTRICTS
Roppongi

The most international district in Tokyo, Roppongi is famous as one of the city's major nightlife districts. Less expensive and established than Ginza and Akasaka, more sophisticated than Shinjuku and Shibuya, Roppongi claims some of the best restaurants, bars and nightclubs, and a crowd with more blond hair and blue eyes than any other part of town.

It is also one of the city's high-rent residential areas, a reputation the area has had since the Edo period. One theory on the original of the district's "six trees" name claims that six Edo-period samurai, whose names included the character for tree, lived in the neighborhood. In the Meiji period the area was inhabited by wealthy Japanese and foreigners connected with the newly established embassies. Later the military set up camp toward Nogizaka where the Self-Defense Force headquarters are located today. After the war more foreigners moved in as embassies relocated to the area, and the U.S. military established a base on part of the former Japanese Army lands. It was still a quiet district, notable for a street car running along the main thoroughfare and a few Western-style bars and restaurants serving burgers and pizza.

During the late fifties and early sixties, as the post-war prosperity took hold, the Japanese began to look beyond the need for survival, and the traditional values propagated by the nationalistic wartime government. Roppongi, with its international air, attracted the new cosmopolitan Japanese. In a few cafes and bars—Nicola's, Gino's, and the still famous Chianti—gathered the liberal elite of intellectuals, entertainers, fashion designers, and other notables. The district's popularity grew, more bars and restaurants opened, and the young Japanese who frequented the area were dubbed the *Roppongi-zoku*— the Roppongi people.

Life in Roppongi starts at the Roppongi crossing and its tribute to the Japanese love of coffee shops and kitsch architecture—the famous Almond (pronounced *amando*)—a multi-story pink coffee shop with some of the worst coffee and cakes in town. This is, however, a major landmark and the corner in front a favorite rendezvous spot.

By day, Roppongi is relatively quiet—nothing seems to be open before 11:00 A.M. Worth visiting are the Axis Building, full of shops specializing in contemporary interior goods, and Wave, one of the first high-tech record shops in the world.

A short walk down the hill from the main crossing is Azabu-juban, a neighborhood shopping area that grew up as a textile center producing linen cloth, *asa*, from which the area gets its name. Restaurants, bars, and discos are moving to this area in increasing numbers although it remains a cozy shopping street by day.

Nishi Azabu—Hiro-o

As Roppongi reached a virtual nightclub saturation point in the early eighties, the fallout from the its burgeoning prosperity drifted into some of the city's residential and warehouse districts. At one point it seemed that nearly every really hip bar was located in Nishi Azabu. It is still a neighborhood rich in great restaurants and bars.

More residential than the Kasumi-cho area, Hiro-o has typically had the rather dubious reputation of being the "*gaijin* ghetto" (*gaijin* means "foreigner") of the city. Expensive company-subsidized apartment complexes are full of foreign executives and their families, while two large Western-style supermarkets help comfort the homesick. One street near the station is a more traditional Japanese-style shopping area, and Arisugawa Park is a short walk away.

Shibuya

One of the first things anyone should know about Shibuya is the heartwarming story of Hachi, a dog of the native Japanese Akita breed. Hachi would escort his master, a professor at Tokyo University, to Shibuya Station each morning and return in the evening to meet him on his way home from work. One day the professor suffered a stroke and never came home, but the faithful Hachi returned to the station each evening to wait. This went on for seven years. When Hachi finally died in 1935, he was on the front page of all the major newspapers. Gifts and letters poured in from around the country, and a bronze statue of Hachi was erected in the plaza in front of the station. Hachiko Square (North Exit) is probably the most famous meeting place in the city. The real Hachi was stuffed and is part of the collection of the Tokyo Metropolitan Museum of Art.

As a district, Shibuya fits somewhere between the wildness of Shinjuku, the kids of Harajuku, and the sophistication of Roppongi. There is an abundance of department stores, boutiques, record shops, and theaters. In the evening the area draws crowds of students and young office workers to its inexpensive discotheques and *nomiya* (Japanese-style bars). Since the 1980s, its development has been spurred by the "store wars" between competing department store chains: Seibu and its Parco, Seed, Prime, and Loft Buildings; Tokyu with its Tokyu Plaza, Tokyu Hands, 109, and Bunkamura; Marui with its several fashion buildings.

Until recently, Shibuya was a quiet residential area. Named after the

Shibuya family whose castle was located here, during the Edo period the district was just one step up from the provinces. After the Meiji Restoration, the samurai residents vacated and the lands were used for tea fields and grazing. When the earthquake destroyed much of Tokyo in 1923, people moved from the center of town and undeveloped, almost rural districts like Shibuya, Meguro, and Setagaya became heavily residential. After the war, Shibuya housed one of the city's largest black markets.

Daikanyama—Ebisu

A short distance from Shibuya, Daikanyama has been a model for the development of Tokyo's peripheral residential districts. Since the seventies when the Maki Fumihiko-designed Hillside Terrace complex was first opened, the area has grown slowly and gracefully with shops, restaurants, and the occasional gallery. Like many of the recently developed, or soon to be developed, neighborhoods, public transportation is limited making them favorite destinations for weekend drivers. The streets are lined with foreign imported cars and their fashionably dressed passengers.

Benefiting from this popularity, Ebisu has followed suit and is now positioned to become one of the next hip areas. Already restaurants, clubs, and shops are filling the back streets and the major Sapporo Beer development is guaranteed to change the face of the neighborhood.

Harajuku

Dedicated to youth, fashion trendiness, and the belief that all consumers under twenty-five are created equal, Harajuku thrives as the kid's capital of Tokyo. The district swarms with the well-dressed pampered youth of Japan, raised in an era of post-war prosperity and carefree consumerism. But the rigorous school system, the pressures for conformity applied to the salary-man, and the satisfied-housewife pattern of life have their young victims. Many of the dancers who have filled Harajuku's Yoyogi Park every Sunday for the past decade or so are the ones who can't make it in the system or simply don't care to try. In an ironic display of rebellious behavior, the kids dance in well-choreographed, polite groups—usually boys with boys, girls with girls. The original dancers in the later 70s were named the *Takenoko-zoku,* or "bamboo-shoot-people," after the bright Asian-style costumes made by a boutique called Takenoko. In the eighties James Dean was the role model and fifties nostalgia reigned. Since the nineties, the dancers have been joined by growing crowds of foreign, often Middle Eastern, laborers who gather nearby.

The spirit of Harajuku is as infectious as it is insipid. For young fashion, the district beats any other part of Tokyo. Most of the big designers' boutiques are in nearby Aoyama and Shibuya, but cheap knock-offs and play clothes overflow from the hundreds of shops near the central crossing and lining the back streets. The main landmark is the La Foret fashion building, and down the street toward Togo Jinja shrine is Takeshitadori, famous for its bargains in trendy fashions.

North of the district is Yoyogi Park, the Meiji Jingu shrine, and its outer gardens. The park attracts some of Tokyo's more individualistic inhabitants—dancers and street performers of all kinds, and toward the north end of the park a few saxophonists or trumpeters will invariably be practicing their instruments in the bushes.

Aoyama

The post-Harajuku generation finds more of interest in the neighboring Aoyama district, where life moves at a more sophisticated, expensive pace. The main street, Aoyama-dori, stretches from Shibuya to Akasaka, meeting along the way a number of side streets that spawn ever growing numbers of boutiques, specialty shops, and restaurants. Kotto-dori, on the Shibuya end, is famous for its antique shops. The road to the Nezu Museum nearby has boutiques by Tokyo's top fashion designers and many top European designers as well. It also boasts Tokyo's first major building by Osaka-based architect Ando Tadao—La Collectione.

Aoyama has more good design and architecture than any other district. The Spiral and Tepia buildings by Maki Fumihiko, Collectione by Ando Tadao, the Mori Hanae Building, and Sogetsu Hall by Tange Kenzo, and dozens of other smaller buildings by young and emerging Japanese architects as well as work by well-known western architects such as Mario Botta and Aldo Rossi.

The Edo period Aoyama daimyo family lived here, leaving for posterity their name and the family graveyard, now the Aoyama-bochi, a great place for a quiet stroll or for viewing the spring cherry blossoms.

On the Akasaka end of Aoyama-dori is a huge walled-in green spot that hides the Akasaka detached palace, the latter being an official state guest house modeled after Buckingham Palace on the outside and Versailles on the inside.

Shinjuku

A showcase for all the worst aspects of the city's chaos, Shinjuku has, at the same time, a stronger, more vibrant spirit than any other part of town. Much of the spirit borders on sleaze. Shinjuku is the latest of the late night districts, and one of the cheapest. It's here that night-time revelers come to escape the sophistication and civility of the city's chic southwest districts.

Shinjuku has always had a rather questionable reputation. During the Edo period it was a small lodging town, not even within the city limits. A fight between a local brothel owner and the younger brother of an influential samurai official led to the area's disappearance. But fifty years later it grew up again and became a major pleasure quarter frequented by the lower classes.

In 1889 Shinjuku Station was built with a new train line servicing the western suburbs. The area immediately prospered. The residential population increased, as did the number of pleasure houses. When courtesans were liberated in 1872, the formalities of the geisha entertainments were abandoned, and most of the former geisha houses became simple houses of prostitution with rooms for rent. Shinjuku was notorious for having more such rooms than any other part of town. Plans to clean up the neighborhood and relocate the pleasure quarter were drawn up but never put into effect.

The area continued to grow and in 1920 part of it was annexed into the city's Yotsuya Ward. The rest of the district became a part of Tokyo in 1932 when the city limits were redrawn. The station became increasingly important as a commuter transfer point and is now the largest in the country, handling over two million passengers a day.

Shinjuku has prospered. Around the station are found some of the highest rents in Japan. Department stores, boutiques, fashion buildings, and the huge Shinjuku Station underground arcade serves commuters on their way home or suburbanites in for the weekends when the major thoroughfare becomes a pedestrian "paradise" (or "hell" depending on how much you like mobs). Students from the surrounding universities form another big part of the crowd.

But life in Shinjuku really begins after dark. Kabukicho is the center of the action. The Kabuki theater originally planned as a cultural focus for the neighborhood never materialized, but gave the district its name. In its place a modern pleasure quarter flourished after the war. The area has numerous movie theaters, and the surrounding streets are famous for their x-rated establishments and "pink" cabaret (in Japan "pink" is the symbolic x-rated color). This is where you're most likely to spot *yakuza* types—the Japanese mafia who are easily recognized by their gangster-style dress, their squared-off crew cuts or short perms, and the notable absence of fingers.

Goruden-gai, another famous neighborhood now threatened by the forces of redevelopment, is a street full of quirky, tiny closet-sized bars and is one of the few parts of town where a little caution is advised. Shomben-yokocho, near the train tracks on the west side of the station, is yet another drinking area. Full of cheap *nomiya,* the name literally translates as "piss alley." Ni-chome is the gay bar district.

The Nishi-guchi (west-side) of Shinjuku claims more skyscrapers than any other part of Tokyo. Built on land that was formerly a water and sewage treatment plant, the area is properly antiseptic. The oldest building dates from 1971. In 1991 after years of planning, the Tokyo Metropolitan Government opened its new city hall. The controversial, almost gothic architecture of this huge Tange Kenzo-designed building has become Shinjuku's proud new landmark and a rather thought-provoking symbol of 1980's Japan.

Ikebukuro

Ikebukuro is basically a less interesting version of Shinjuku. A commuter's town, the district lacks specific character. The major attractions are the sprawling Seibu Department Store (at one time the largest in the world) and the sixty-story Sunshine City complex.

Until the Meiji period the district was one of farm and forest lands, famous as a spot for viewing the summer fireflies. A small bag-shaped pond in the area gave the district its name—Ikebukuro means literally "pond bag." A train station was built in 1903 and served, at the time, about thirty passengers a day. Now it's second only to Shinjuku.

In the thirties, Ikebukuro was a haunt of artists and writers, and the area was dubbed, in all seriousness, "Ikebukuro Montparnasse." The district later became the site of Tokyo Prison. After World War II, the prison was renamed Sugamo by the Occupation Authorities and was used to hold Japanese war criminals. Seven men, including Field Marshal Tojo Hideki, were hung in the prison. In 1958 the name was changed back to Tokyo Prison, but the building was torn down in 1972 to build a new cultural center for the area. The Sunshine City Building now stands on the site.

The west side of Ikebukuro Station is similar in flavor to Shinjuku's Kabukicho. Here and behind the Bungei-za Theater on the east side are two "dangerous" areas with the reputation for being the scene of an occasional gun battle between rival yakuza gangs.

Until recently the area was known for its inexpensive accommodations and was favored by students but now is home for huge numbers of predominantly Asian resident foreigners.

Akasaka—Nagatacho

The side streets in Akasaka are lined with Japanese-style buildings of a uniform sand color, with discreet signs giving the name of the restaurant. These are not places that the ordinary foreigner can enter, nor the ordinary

Japanese for that matter. Most of these *ryotei* restaurants require an introduction. In the evening geisha are called, and over bottles of saké (rice wine)
and meals in the best Japanese tradition, politicians, and big business types
cement those bonds of friendship so important in the greater world of
economic and governmental affairs. On a back street hill nearby is a row of
empty rickshaw. In the mid-Meiji period there were over fifty thousand in
the city, but the rickshaw are now used only by geisha on their way to a
party.

Yet the discreet ryotei seem somehow anomalous in an area now dominated by the glitz and glamour of the entertainment scene centered around
the hundreds of tiny restaurants, noisy *nomiya,* hostess bars, cabarets, and
TBS Television, which since 1960 has ensured a steady flow of TV personalities and their fans into the neighborhood.

Hotels give the district an added international dimension. The major
ones are the New Otani, the Akasaka Prince, the Akasaka Tokyu (otherwise
known as the "Pajama Hilton" for its pink and white striped exterior), the
Capitol Tokyu, and the remains of the ill-fated New Japan Hotel, which
burned up along with a number of tourists in a fire that led to a wave of new
safety regulations for hotels.

Top level Edo period daimyo had lived in the area during the Tokugawa
reign. The neighboring Hie Jinja shrine was one of the big three shrines of
the time. In the early Meiji period, the daimyo moved away and the
government confiscated the lands, turning them to agricultural uses. Akasaka became a hill of tea bushes and *akane,* plants that produced a red dye,
giving the district the name which translates to "red slope." The military
moved in later, while the Nagatacho area north of Akasaka became the
center of Meiji period state government. The reputation of the "Akasaka
ryotei," and their tradition of serving power and politics, dates from this
time. The "Akasaka geisha," the lowest class of geisha during the Edo
period, were upgraded to entertain the important clientele and are still
considered some of the city's best.

Ginza

Ginza used to be synonymous with the glamour of big city life in Tokyo.
Elegant, expensive, and at one time the most international part of the city,
Ginza inspired a string of hit songs in the first half of the century. Best
remembered are songs like "Ginza Rhapsody," or "Ginza Can-Can Girl."
Even the American surf-rock band The Ventures wrote a song called "Ginza
for Two" (an interesting bit of trivia—The Ventures were a big success here
in the early sixties and, until recently, toured Japan every year). The name

Ginza has now become another way of saying "shopping street"—there are some 450 "Ginza streets" throughout Japan and the number is still growing.

Originally little more than a swamp, Ginza was among the first areas reclaimed from the sea during the reign of Tokugawa Ieyasu. Overshadowed by the more prosperous Nihombashi area, Ginza grew as a town of artisans and craftsmen. In 1612 the Tokugawa silver mint was moved to the area. *Gin* mean silver and *za* means a licensed association of craftsmen; the district earned its name from the numbers of craftsmen working in the metal. When the mint was moved during the Meiji period, the name remained.

The Tokugawa (Edo) period ended with the challenge from the West and Ginza was one of the first parts of the city to feel the effects of the Meiji government's modernization program. When the area was destroyed by fire in 1872, the government hired the British architect Josiah Conder and planned a model Western-style urban center. Nearly one thousand brick buildings were constructed, tiled pavements laid, and willow trees planted. The first horse trolley in Tokyo passed through Ginza to Nihombashi and Shimbashi. The first gas lights in the city were installed, turning Ginza into a night life area. A single lamp post remains across the street from the Matsuya Department Store.

Ginza-dori in 1928. Courtesy of Shiseido Co., Ltd.

While the brick buildings created quite a stir, most remained vacant long after completion. Though fireproof in theory, the buildings were badly ventilated and believed to be hazardous to health. Still, crowds of people turned out to see the novelty, and the commercial success of Ginza dates from this time. Shopping in Ginza by day, with evening strolling by gaslight, became a fad that led to the coining of a new term *ginbura* meaning "wandering around in Ginza."

Another term coined in the Meiji era was *haikara,* or "high collar," a reference to Western-style shirts that became the Meiji era equivalent of the modern "trendy." At the time this meant "Western" and Ginza more than any other part of Tokyo was the center for all that was Western and new—men's suits, watches, meat eating, and coffee drinking.

The area was full of new ideas and entrepreneurs. The famous cosmetics company Shiseido was started in a small Ginza pharmacy in 1872 by Fukuhara Akinobu, a former pharmacist for the navy. The Seiko watch company began as a retail and repair shop opened by Hattori Kintaro. By the Taisho period all the major department stores had opened branches in the area. The Ginza Matsuzakaya was the first department store in the country that didn't require its customers to take off their shoes.

After the war Ginza was the first place to which prosperity returned. The department stores were crowded again, exclusive boutiques began to fill the back streets, and Ginza was called the "Fifth Avenue" of Tokyo. The neighborhood became a treasury of expensive Japanese restaurants and clubs catering to the businessman of the future economic miracle. Even now Ginza claims the largest number of public establishments in Tokyo.

Expensive and conservative, for the postwar generation Ginza has less shopping appeal than the newer districts to the West. Yet somewhat incongruously, the area has Tokyo's largest concentration of art galleries, many of which specialize in the young and avant-garde.

Hibiya—Kasumigaseki—Yurakucho

Like Ginza, Hibiya was part of the marshland reclaimed from the sea during the early Edo period. Close to the central part of the castle, daimyo mansions occupied the grounds. With the early Meiji period exodus of daimyo families from the city, the area was left an empty wasteland. Part of the land was used as the first parade ground for the new Western-style military. Nearby were built the Rokumeikan in 1883 and in 1890 the original Imperial Hotel.

The Rokumeikan was a state-owned guest house designed by Josiah Condor. One of the more idealistic endeavors of the Meiji period establishment, it was believed that, by inviting foreign diplomats to parties given at the ornate western-style building, Japan would be placed on the roster of civilized nations.

The Imperial Hotel was built on the site of the present hotel building. Originally designed by a Japanese, the second building was the work of American architect Frank Lloyd Wright. The Wright building was torn down in 1968 and the third and present hotel constructed.

The military gave its parade ground to the city in 1893. The initial plan was to build a concentration of government office buildings on the site, but when the land proved unable to support the weight of the proposed constructions, the area was made into the city's first western-style park and opened in 1903. If you happen to take a bus tour that passes through the area, the tour guide is likely to make some slightly risqué joke about Hibiya Park's reputation as a favorite spot for lovers. As early as 1908, the police were raiding the park and fining indiscreet couples.

Hibiya is now the home of numerous theaters and movie houses, as well as the famous Takarazuka Theater.

The neighboring Yurakucho area is known for its cheap *yakitoriya* beneath the elevated train tracks. During the first five years after the war, General McArthur's headquarters were located in the Yurakucho Daiichi Seimei Building (the room remains, though you can't enter). The area had a large black market and was full of U.S. soldiers, prostitutes, orphans, and shoeshine boys. Even today, there are several blocks near the station with a slight postwar air about them.

Kasumigaseki is a short walk through Hibiya Park. In this district of government offices, there are ministries of just about everything—MITI (Ministry of International Trade and Industry), the National Diet building, and the Prime Minister's Official residence. The thirty-six story Kasumigaseki Building, constructed in 1968, was proudly known as the first Japanese skyscraper.

Marunouchi

Marunouchi is as prestigious as business addresses come in Japan, and most major corporations are located here. Typically, little of the corporate income, however, has been spent on image and the area remains architecturally one of the least interesting in the city.

Marunouchi's reputation was set in the early part of the century. Like many of the city's central areas, the land had been vacated by the samurai at the start of the Meiji period and had been taken over by the new government. Owned by the military, the lands were left unused by all but rickshaw pullers and other Meiji period lowlife characters and became known as "Gambler's Field." The land was put up for sale and first offered to the imperial family, who were unable to raise sufficient funds. In 1889 it was bought by the already powerful Mitsubishi Company.

Plans were made for the Mitsubishi purchase to become a new business district and Josiah Condor was commissioned to build a brick office center modeled on London's Lombard Street. The first building was completed in 1894, and about twenty-five years and twenty-seven brick buildings later the development was completed and became known as Tokyo's "Little London." The buildings were torn down after the war and the area took on its current middle-of-the-road modern air.

The strategic location of Tokyo Station was largely responsible for the success of the new development. Built as the main terminal for trains from the south, the main entrance faced toward the palace and the Mitsubishi buildings, rather than the more established Nihombashi and Kyobashi districts. The Mitsubishi gamble paid off (whether someone else was paid off to ensure the pay-off is another story), and by 1922 over half of Japan's major corporations had already relocated there.

Tokyo Station, home base of the famous Shinkansen "Bullet Train," was built in 1914, and is the oldest remaining station in the city. The Japanese had just beaten the Russians in war and, full of pride and patriotism, decided to build a station to shock the world. Amsterdam Station was chosen as the unlikely model and a vaguely post-Victorian red brick building was erected. The old building can still be seen from the west side of the station. Uninspiring though the building may be, it was the site of two famous political assassinations: that of Prime Minister Hara Takashi by a nineteen-year-old youth in 1877, and in 1930 that of Prime Minister Hamaguchi Osachi by a right-wing terrorist.

Shimbashi—Shiba—Hamamatsu-cho

Situated at the southern end of Ginza, Shimbashi has always been the less illustrious neighborhood of the two. The station was one of the first in the city, and the original terminal for trains from the south. The surrounding area was known for its shopping arcades, bazaars, and cheap drinking spots. The "Shimbashi geisha" quarter was one of the two great geisha districts of the Meiji period.

Ginza was centered closer toward Shimbashi during the early Meiji period. But, with the opening of Tokyo Station, Shimbashi lost its prominence and the center of Ginza moved north to the crossing where it remains today. The old station was closed and a new one built on the old drinking area. The shops moved to the side and the district is still known for its tiny restaurants, *nomiya,* and salaryman clientele.

South from Shimbashi is Shiba, an important Edo period temple district protecting the castle from the south, a direction that, according to superstition, was a potentially dangerous one. Zojo-ji, a Tokugawa family temple, was the area's greatest.

The sea reached as far as the Zojo-ji *daimon* (main gate) at the beginning of the Edo period. A port served merchant vessels, and salt was made on the beaches. Hamarikyu, a villa of the Tokugawa shogun, and its extravagant gardens stretched along the Shiba coast. Now only the gardens remain. Reclamation projects moved the sea far away, and by the Meiji period Shiba became one of the city's industrial districts.

Now Hamamatsu-cho to the west of Shiba borders the sea, its coast lined with warehouses and piers. Takeshiba Sanbashi pier serves ships to the islands lying off the Izu Peninsula. Hamamatsu-cho is best known for its World Trade Center, built in 1970, which became the second tallest skyscraper in Japan. The terminal for the monorail to Haneda Airport is connected to the Trade Center. A copy of the Brussels Manniken-Pis is in the Hamamatsu-cho Station building. Since 1956 this statue of a small naked boy has collected an extensive wardrobe of clothing donated by concerned women passengers. The wardrobe now includes over two hundred outfits that may make the statue one of the best dressed works of public art in the world.

Another famous neighborhood copy is the Tokyo Tower. Built as a tourist attraction in 1958, the tower unfortunately fails to lend the area the hoped for European flair.

Nihombashi—Kyobashi

Old money and conservatism usually go hand-in-hand, and Nihombashi is no exception. Nihombashi has been the center of big money in Japan since the Edo period, and most of the country's big mercantile families started off in this neighborhood.

Nihombashi was the first of the merchant neighborhoods designated by the shogun to be reclaimed from the sea. With the construction of the Nihombashi Bridge in 1603, it became the official last stop on the famous Tokaido route from Kyoto and the point from which all roads in Japan were measured. Rebuilt in 1911, the Nihombashi and the nearby Tokiwa are the oldest bridges in the city.

The district grew up as the heart of commercial Edo with a fish market, the shops of craftsmen and artisans, and offices of money-changers. One of the most densely populated districts of the city, wooden houses were cramped together along the narrow alleys and backstreets. The homes of wealthy merchants and a few of the samurai aristocracy lined the banks of the river.

Nearby was the Kyobashi district, named for its "capital bridge" (the Chinese character for the *kyo* in Kyobashi is the same *kyo* as in Tokyo and Kyoto). Next to the bridge was the first Kabuki theater, built in 1624 by Nakazawa Kanzaburo.

The Nihombashi and Kyobashi areas had, in the early days, been full of theaters and temples, while neighboring Ningyo-cho was famous for its pleasure quarters. By the late Edo period all were moved to the northern outskirts of town by the conservative shogunate. The wealthy downtown merchants then traveled north for their pleasures, and the trip was usually by boat from the Kyobashi bridge.

With the changes that came during the Meiji period, the wealthy merchants moved away from the area to the prestigious residential districts to the south and west. Not as receptive to change as Ginza and Marunouchi, Nihombashi was slow to catch up with the modernism of the new era. But by the end of the Meiji period, the district had come into its own with a series of monumental buildings of an architectural style that blended European classical elements with traditional Japanese. The Bank of Japan opened its new building in 1896, and more banks and government offices followed. The department stores—Mitsukoshi and Takashimaya—expanded and added floors.

Little remains from the early days—a few Edo period shops and some bridges and buildings from the Meiji and Taisho periods. The commercial banks are still there as is the stock exchange. But among the major business districts in Tokyo, Nihombashi retains the greatest sense of history and a quiet dignity.

Tsukiji

Tsukiji is one of Tokyo's more offbeat tourist attractions. At the main fish market for the city, buying and selling starts at about 5:00 A.M. and finishes shortly after noon. An early morning trip to the market for a fresh sushi breakfast is a great way to start off a day of sightseeing in Tokyo.

Until the 1923 earthquake, the fish market was located in the heart of Nihombashi, near the Bank of Japan and Mitsukoshi Department Store. When nearly four hundred people died there during the post-earthquake fires, the market was torn down and rebuilt on its present site.

Tsukiji, formerly the mouth of the Sumida River, was a major Edo period reclamation project, the name meaning "constructed land."

When the country was opened to the West during the Meiji period, Tsukiji was built as a foreign settlement to isolate and protect the citizens and foreigners from each other. The area was never much liked, except by the Christian missionaries who built St. Luke's Hospital and St. Paul University. The Hoterukan Hotel was built nearby, an early attempt at Western architecture with over two hundred rooms. In 1869 the Tokyo government opened the Shibaura pleasure quarter in Tsukiji in an attempt to please the foreign population. The quarter had over two hundred houses with nearly two thousand geisha and courtesans, but the Shibaura was more than most of the prudish foreigners could take. The quarter never prospered and was shut down shortly afterward.

At the end of the nineteenth century when the treaties with foreign powers were revised and autonomy returned to Japan, foreigners were permitted to live where they chose in the city. Most moved from the settlement and the remaining buildings burned down in the earthquake.

Kanda—Jimbocho

It was with dirt from the top of Kanda's Surugadai hill that the marshlands of early Edo were reclaimed. Nearly half of the hill was carried off over the years and by the late Tokugawa era the hill had a large flat plateau on the top.

Kanda means "god's field," the land having originally belonged to Ise Jingu shrine, the oldest in Japan. The area developed as a town for workers and craftsmen; its fruit and vegetable market provisioned the castle. Edo Period gangsters frequented the district and its bath houses, known for their rather tough breed of women.

The Meiji-period *haikara* liberals and intellectuals found a home here. The Nikoraido Russian Cathedral was an impressive foreign monument for the neighborhood; there were bookstores and the highest concentration of universities in the city.

The district now has the feel of a classic university town. The nearby Jimbocho secondhand book district adds to the general intellectual atmosphere and over sixty percent of Japan's publishers are in the neighborhood. The district also has many sporting goods stores catering to the average student who, once through the "examination hell" that comes before acceptance into university, spends more time drinking, playing sports, or going to mah-jongg parlors than studying.

Also in the Kanda district are a number of restaurants that date from the Edo period, including Tokyo's most famous noodle shop—Yabu Soba.

Ochanomizu—Hongo—Yushima

With Kanda, these areas make up the major students' districts of Tokyo. Always fond of foreign analogies, the Japanese like to call this the city's "Quartier Latin." The district's real name Ochanomizu means "tea water," a reference to the waters of a nearby spring that were used by Tokugawa Ieyasu for the tea ceremony.

The district's reputation for education dates from the Edo period with the construction of the official Confucian Academy for the shogunate. The Yushima Seido shrine, formerly part of the school, still survives.

Hongo's Tokyo University, popularly known as "Todai," is the most prestigious university in the country. In January and February each year, hundreds of hopeful junior high and high school students make a pilgrimage to the area, walking from Yushima Seido, to Yushima Shrine (dedicated to a famous Heian period scholar) and finally ending up at the gates of "Todai heaven." Complementing the district's overall educational atmosphere is a nearby concentration of love hotels.

Akihabara

The electronics discount district of Tokyo, Akihabara is a good place to go to experience the productiveness of the country. Besides the electrical goods that interest most foreigners, the selection of home appliances built for the Japanese domestic market is also fun to browse through.

The district was formerly the grounds of an Edo period shrine called the Akiba, or "autumn leaf." When the shrine was destroyed in one of Kanda's frequent fires, the lands were cleared as a fire break and became known as the field of Akiba or Akibagahara. The land was later used as a freight depot by the Meiji government, and the name took on its current form.

Korakuen

Korakuen is best known among the Japanese for its baseball stadium, the site of the yearly Japan Series. From 1871 until the end of World War I, the stadium grounds had been occupied by a government munitions factory that was then moved to Kyushu. The stadium was built in 1934 with Babe Ruth invited as the honored guest at the opening ceremony.

The Korakuen Station was torn down and replaced by the "Big Egg" stadium in 1988. Like the Kasumigaseki Building, the "Egg" has become a standard of measurement and comparison for things of overwhelming size—the annual amount of garbage produced by a particular ward will be likened to filling the "Big Egg" three times, or a new development will be a mere half.

The name Korakuen comes from the Koishikawa Korakuen Gardens that date from the early Edo period. One of the most famous and most beautiful in the city, the garden offers a striking contrast to its namesake stadium and the surrounding amusement park that now dominates the area.

Shinagawa

The original Shinagawa Station, located nearer to the sea than the present one, served the first Japanese rail line that ran from here to Yokohama (Kanagawa Prefecture). The line was later extended to Shimbashi. One of the most striking of Meiji period modernization efforts, the first trains were expensive and used only by the wealthy, government officials, and foreigners. A story is told of how when the Japanese first boarded the trains, they politely removed their shoes on the platform before entering the cars. Upon arrival, the Japanese passengers disembarked, astonished to find that their shoes were not waiting outside the door where they had left them.

Shinagawa had been a major stop on the Edo-period Tokaido route to the south, growing up as a way station with inns and a pleasure quarter that was second only to the famous Yoshiwara. The pleasure quarter declined in the later Meiji period when the station was moved to its current site.

Meiji-period Shinagawa was part of the city's industrial zone, though now little remains of the district's early flavor. The station is still an important transfer point, but the surrounding area is best known for its hotels and for being the location of the Sony headquarters.

Ningyocho

Ningyocho is a quiet neighborhood, known to most foreigners as the location of TCAT, the Tokyo City Air Terminal, with its bus service to Narita Airport. Close to the central Edo period business districts, Ningyocho was a major amusement center with kabuki theaters, and the famous Yoshiwara geisha district. The area was named "doll town" for the number of shops selling dolls to the theater audiences.

Ningyocho lost its geisha, and later its theaters, to Asakusa in the north. The city's doll shops are now in Asakusabashi. On the outer fringes of the Meiji period downtown development, Ningyocho escaped the era's modernization madness and settled into the quiet *shitamachi* (downtown) neighborhood it remains today.

Along the main crossing is a shopping area. Some shops are historical. Kotobuki sells the same traditional sweets they've been famous for since the late 1800s. Suitengu Shrine is still visited by expectant mothers and those with newborn babies.

Asakusa

Tokyo passed through various stages of growth, and the districts of the city followed along, or were left behind, as modernization and new modes of transportation changed the patterns of urban life. The original shitamachi areas—Nihombashi and Ginza—moved with the city into its Meiji period growth, and are, now, more memorable as districts from the early modern era. But the feeling of the shitamachi era remains in a district that was, in the early Edo period, a very distant neighborhood of marginal interest to the central downtown populace.

Asakusa flourished after the Edo period Tempo Reforms enacted by the financially unstable Tokugawa government. The theaters and pleasure quarters were moved here from the downtown districts in an attempt to encourage the merchants to lead more frugal lives, while the samurai class as a whole was slowly sinking into poverty. Asakusa thrived through the Meiji and Taisho periods, but when the railroads became important, Asakusa Station remained a minor stop, and the modernization that changed the real downtown areas never affected it. Today Asakusa retains more of the old Tokyo shitamachi character than any other part of town.

The district is centered around Senso-ji temple, popularly known as the Asakusa Kannon-dera. Dating from the eighth century, the temple enshrines a small golden statue of Kannon, the Buddhist Goddess of Mercy, found by local fishermen in 628. At least that's how the legend goes. The statue is never on view and no one ever seems to have seen it, but its existence has never been questioned by the millions of pilgrims who flocked to the area and continue to come today.

This northern tip of the city was originally underwater, and later became a fishing village. As the temple attracted ever greater crowds of worshippers, the surrounding area filled up with shops, and the sometimes bawdy forms of entertainment typical of many Edo period temples. When the theaters and pleasure quarters entered the area its amusements increased and so did the crowds.

Moved from its original Ningyocho home, Yoshiwara to the north was the most famous of Edo and Meiji period geisha districts. The downtown merchants traveled by boat from the southern parts of the city along the Sumida River, often finishing the trip on foot through the cherry-tree-lined park that stretches from the main Asakusa bridge north on both sides of the river.

At the start of the twentieth century, Asakusa was still largely rural in character, and much of the city's rice land was found in the area. But by the end of the Meiji era, the district claimed the highest population density in the city. The Yoshiwara geisha quarter had declined with the advance of modernization, and was destroyed in the fire of 1911. When the district was rebuilt, its days of glory were clearly over.

Asakusa continued to prosper through the Taisho and early Showa periods. The Kabuki theaters moved back to their original downtown homes as the new day made the old popular culture respectable. Movie houses took their place and the first film showing in Japan was held in Asakusa in the early thirties.

The district was badly scarred by the war. Fire bombing destroyed most of its monuments. Asakusa and its temples were rebuilt, but the postwar city looked more to the western districts and Asakusa was gradually left behind.

Asakusa is one of the last strongholds of the Edokko, the born and bred child of Edo. The shitamachi spirit and sensibilities remain here. Craftsmen work in their traditional shops, in the traditional way, maintaining the sense of pride for which the Edokko was famous.

Ueno

When the fabled cherry blossoms burst out in spring, the favorite viewing spot for the average Tokyoite is Ueno Park. Since the Edo period, Ueno Hill was famous for its blossoms, but, surrounded by the Tokugawa family temple complex, the viewing was kept fairly sedate. Things have changed and now Ueno draws huge crowds to frolic beneath the blossoms.

It is quite a spectacle, though not nearly as poetic as might be imagined. On approximately four tatami mat-sized sheets of plastic (about eight square meters), cardboard or cloth, the parties gather. A row of shoes fringe the sides of the mat and each area is separated from its neighbor by ropes and strings tied between the trees. By day things remain quiet, with families making up the greater part of the crowd. But after dark, thousands of office workers make a mad rush for the little plot saved by a junior co-worker whose assignment was to sit in the park and hold that space. Until 10:00 P.M. when the park closes, the crowds will eat, drink, and sing songs, getting for the most part absolutely plastered and feeling very Japanese. Stray foreigners are almost always invited to join a group—which can be amusing for a while. When the crowd disperses, the park is left quiet, filled with the pink blossoms and mountains of garbage deposited by the nature loving revelers. This is one cultural experience you shouldn't miss.

During the Edo period, Ueno was one of the city's main temple districts. Being in the northeast quarter of town, the temples served to protect the castle from this traditionally dangerous direction (demons were believed to favor this route of attack). The temples were also planned to double as forts in the event of a military attack on the city. The main temple was Kan'eiji, where six of the fifteen Tokugawa shoguns were buried.

In of the Meiji Restoration, the city of Edo was turned over to the new government without a fight. The few remaining Tokugawa loyalists retreated to the hills surrounding the temple and a final battle was fought. The loyalists were soon defeated, but most of the temple complex was burned.

In early Meiji, plans were drawn up to build a medical school on the former temple grounds. When a German doctor was consulted about the project he suggested that the medical school be located elsewhere and the hill be turned into a park. His suggestion was followed and in 1873 Ueno became the first public park in the city. Officially named the Ueno Royal Park, the land was transferred to the royal family in 1890, and on the marriage of the Showa emperor in 1924, was returned to the city. The renaissance-style building of the National Museum in the park was a gift from the citizens of Tokyo in commemoration of the emperor's wedding.

The park was the first place in Japan to have a museum and a zoo. It now has four major museums and the zoo that is famous for its pandas and the rather sad condition in which the animals are kept. Shinobazu Pond in the western portion of the park was originally part of the marshlands that covered most of the downtown districts. Annexed to the park in 1885, it was a favorite spot for viewing waterlilies.

Aside from its cultural attractions, Ueno is known for the large numbers of country people who stream into its station from the north. Less sophisticated than downtown Tokyo, old shops and restaurants remain from the Edo period when its main street was one of the busiest shopping areas in the city. After the war a large black market flourished beneath the railroad tracks. The market is still there and, though no longer a black market, Ameyoko retains much of the flavor of one.

Further north of Ueno is Yanaka, a continuation of the Ueno temple district. This area escaped the fires of the earthquake and World War II; numerous small temples, shrines, and old shops remain. The Yanaka cemetery is another famous spot for cherry blossom viewing.

Asakusabashi—Kuramae—Ryogoku

Asakusabashi is a wholesale district known for its shops selling dolls, toys, novelties, and seasonal decorations. The district is named for the Asakusa bridge that crosses the narrow Kanda River.

Yanagibashi, the "Willow Bridge," crosses the Kanda further down, close to the point where it meets the Sumida River. The bridge was famous for its geisha quarter and as a departure point for boat passage to the northern Yoshiwara. The Yanagibashi area was the more conservative geisha district of the two. At its peak in the late Edo and early Meiji periods, it faithfully maintained the traditional ways. The boathouses later became *ryotei,* the most exclusive type of Japanese restaurant. A few ryotei remain in the neighborhood today, and boats can still be rented near the bridge.

Kuramae was a rice warehouse district in the Edo period. Since 1954, sumo tournaments had been held in the area's Kokugikan. But sumo really belongs to the other side of the Sumida River, to Ryogoku. In 1985 a new sumo stadium was opened and the tournaments returned to their true home.

Ryogoku literally translates as "both countries," the Sumida River having long separated the districts on either side. In the Edo period, bridge building was restricted by the government in order to make an attack on the capital more difficult for potential invaders. But when hundreds of people were trapped and killed on the banks of the river during one of the many Edo fires, the shogunate permitted a bridge to be constructed in the area.

Ryogoku remains the center of sumo. Many of the stables where sumo wrestlers live and train are located in the area. During the Tokyo sumo tournaments the wrestlers wander around the streets in all their enormous glory.

Fukagawa—Kiba—Tsukudajima

Fukagawa lies on the east side of the Sumida River, south of Ryogoku, bordering Tokyo Bay. The district and the neighboring Kiba were known through the Edo period for their lumberyards. The skills of the early lumber-yard workers are now commemorated in a yearly festival in Kiba. Both areas often suffered damage from the frequent floods of the Sumida. Flood control banks have been built along the river's edge, protecting the lands but destroying much of the neighborhood's atmosphere.

Until the early Meiji period, Fukagawa was one of the less densely populated districts in the city. Convenient to cheap water transportation, it became one of the major industrial districts of Meiji-period Tokyo.

Tsukudajima lies to the southwest. The island has grown with postwar reclamation projects, but the original part of the island escaped from the constant fires of the downtown district as well as those of World War II. In spite of recent development and an increasing number of tall buildings, the back streets remain closer to those of the Edo period city than any other part of town.

Tokyo Bay and the Developing City

One tends to forget that Tokyo has a waterfront. Tokyo Bay and the Sumida River that were so important to Edo Tokyo have long been lost to the people of this city. For years laws have restricted the use of the Tokyo waterfront to industries that depended upon the sea. Only relatively recent-ly were these laws repealed.

In the 1980s Tokyo began a vigorous program of planned development along the waterfront—its last remaining, undeveloped resource. Initial stages of planning seemed to offer a hope that the people of Tokyo would soon be able to breathe the sea air, that restaurants and shops could face out on something more than a gray street. Bold plans were discussed, great hopes rose, but the forces that be seem to have swayed the tide in their favor and the waterfront risks being lost to the people once again.

Spurred on by the property boom of the eighties, huge developments grow along the banks of the river and bay. In a city gasping for breath, only token parks—strips of uninviting concrete walkways and plazas have been left in exchange. A public golf course built on an island created from a garbage fill gives off so much methane gas that smoking is forbidden for fear that the greens might explode. And, while the recession that hit Japan in the late eighties has slowed this "progress" down a bit, it is hard to know what the long-term affects will be.

Throughout Tokyo, old neighborhoods have been unceremoniously decimated by the omnipresent and seemingly omnivorous machines that push down and crush the fragile old wooden houses as a child might smash a tiny wooden fort. What replaces these remains of the past offers the promise of a mediocre future. Aging wooden homes are replaced by multi-unit "kit" houses or antiseptic apartment blocks. The aggressive, monumental architecture characteristic of new development sites never seems to work.

Of course, there are some exceptions. There is more good contemporary architecture in Tokyo now than there was in the early eighties, there is better art. There are new neighborhoods blossoming in former warehouse or residential areas. There is a new form of contemporary life emerging from the chaos of the city.

It is difficult to guess what this rapidly and radically changing metropolis will be like in a few years. But the real life of Tokyo will not emerge from the big developments planned by Japan, Inc. It will emerge from the individual creativity and energy of the people who live here. It will flourish in funny little pockets here and there, in overlooked neighborhoods where, as in the past, the traditional and the avant-garde will coexist, on a human and intimate scale, each playing off the other in that fascinating, sometimes whimsical way that will always make Tokyo an exciting place to be.

宿

ACCOMMODATION

ACCOMMODATION

Your hotel in Tokyo is about the only place where you'll get away from the city's nearly twelve million inhabitants. Obviously, this should be a subject for serious consideration. Unless you have a friend or relative in town, your choices will fall into four main categories: major hotels, business hotels, Japanese-style lodgings, and hostels.

Which category you choose will most likely be a matter of budget. Your second criterion should be convenience to where you'll be doing most of your work or play. Equally important is accessibility to public transport. The train and subway systems are so efficient that even if you don't mind paying for a taxi, public transport can save you time. If you're a "night person," consider staying in a hotel close to one of the night life districts. During the day you can travel by transit system, but after midnight the trains and subways go home to rest and you're left with your legs or taxis with a thirty percent surcharge after 11:00 P.M.

HOTELS

We have selected what we consider the best of the major and business hotels, then divided them by districts. Best is defined here as good quality and service for the price, convenience, and accessibility to public transport. A list of "other" second choice hotels is supplied in the event that our recommended hotels are booked up. All hotels are safe and clean. Most provide cotton *yukata* robes. Distance on foot to the nearest station has been noted. Rates listed are basic room charges (tax inclusive prices have been noted). In addition, you will pay a service charge of ten to fifteen percent and taxes that run around thirteen percent. In mid-February when the university entrance exams are held in Tokyo, it is almost impossible to find a room—book early.

Major Hotels—Like anywhere in the world, these range from first class to not particularly distinguished. Price is usually a good indication of quality.

The number of rooms has not been noted, but most are large. According to most surveys, the three best hotels in Tokyo are the **Okura**, the **Imperial,** and the **Capitol Tokyu.**

Business Hotels—Theoretically for the "businessman," these are relatively low-priced hotels with minimal but efficient service. Most hotels with singles under ¥12,000 fall into this category. Rooms are generally quite small and rather Spartan. Bathrooms are strictly utilitarian molded-in-one-piece units. Televisions are usually provided, though sometimes they're coin-operated with extra-charge "adult" video channels.

Ginza—Shimbashi—Hibiya

IMPERIAL HOTEL—In Japanese called the "Teikoku Hotel." Established in 1980, new tower completed in 1983. Considered one of the best, but some feel it is too big and impersonal. Good location, best views of Imperial Palace are from upper floors in the new tower.

帝国ホテル　千代田区内幸町 1-1-1

1-1-1 Uchisaiwai-cho, Chiyoda-ku. Tel: 3504-1111. Fax: 3581-9146.
Rates: Sgl. from ¥30,000, Dbl. from ¥34,000.
—Swimming pool, executive salon, good shopping arcade, excellent restaurants, two minutes from Hibiya and Yurakucho Stations. [M-10]

HOTEL SEIYO GINZA—Without a doubt this late-eighties hotel offers the ultimate in Tokyo luxury—at a price few are willing to pay. Sophisticated, elegant, and discreet, there is no reception desk but "personal secretaries" who pamper you from check in throughout your stay.

ホテル西洋銀座　中央区銀座 1-11-2

1-11-2 Ginza, Chuo-ku. Tel: 3535-1111. Fax: 3535-1110.
Rates: Sgl. from ¥40,000, Dbl. from ¥48,000.
—Excellent but pricey restaurants, health facilities, business center. Two minutes from Kyobashi and Ginza Itchome Stations. [M-8]

GINZA DAI-ICHI HOTEL—Respected business hotel.

銀座第一ホテル　中央区銀座 8-13-1

8-13-1 Ginza, Chuo-ku. Tel: 3542-5311. Fax: 3542-3030.
Rates: Sgl. from ¥17,000, Dbl. from ¥24,000.
—Five minutes from Shimbashi Station. [M-8]

GINZA TOBU HOTEL—Opened in 1987, it is very convenient and the rooms are relatively spacious (largest are those on the concierge floor).

銀座東武ホテル　中央区銀座 6-14-10

6-14-10 Ginza, Chuo-ku. Tel: 3546-0111. Fax: 3546-8990.
Rates: Sgl. from ¥16,000, Dbl. from ¥ 30,000.
—One minute from Higashi Ginza Station. [M-8]

MITSUI URBAN HOTEL GINZA—Mitsui Urban chain hotel. Has a very good reputation. Typical small rooms but very convenient.

三井アーバンホテル　中央区銀座 8-6-15

8-6-15 Ginza, Chuo-ku. Tel: 3572-4131. Fax: 3572-4254.
Rates: Sgl. from ¥11,800, Dbl. from ¥17,500.
—One minute from Shimbashi Station. [M-8]

HOTEL ATAMISO—Formerly a *ryokan,* opened as a Western-style hotel in 1984. Rooms often a curious blend of Japanese and Western styles.

ホテル熱海荘　中央区銀座 4-14-3

4-14-3 Ginza, Chuo-ku. Tel: 3541-3621. Fax: 3541-3262.
Rates: Sgl. from ¥9,403, Twin from ¥18,354, Japanese style from ¥19,374 double occupancy, Japanese and Western-style ¥18,241 (incl. tax).

—Two minutes from Higashi Ginza Station. [M-8]

SHIMBASHI DAI-ICHI HOTEL—Newly reconstructed hotel with excellent services for business-people.

新橋第一ホテル　中央区新橋 1-2-6

1-2-6 Shimbashi, Minato-ku. Tel: 3501-4411. Fax: 3595-2634.

Rates: Twin from ¥34,000, Dbl. from ¥30,000.

—Three minutes from Shimbashi Station. [M-11]

• **Other Hotels**

GINZA TOKYU HOTEL

銀座東急ホテル　中央区銀座 5-15-9

5-15-9 Ginza, Chuo-ku. Tel: 3541-2411. Fax: 3541-6622.

Rates: Sgl. from ¥16,800, Dbl. from ¥26,800, Japanese style: ¥42,000.

—One minute from Higashi Ginza Station. Close to the Kabuki-za. [M-8]

KYOBASHI KAIKAN—Inexpensive business hotel with good service and convenient location for the price; best to book one month in advance.

京橋会館　中央区銀座 1-26-1

1-26-1 Ginza, Chuo-ku. Tel: 3564-0888. Fax: 3561-8080.

Rates: Sgl. from ¥6,500, Twin from ¥11,000. Japanese-style ¥27,500 five persons per room.

— Indoor swimming pool, three minutes from Kyobashi, five minutes from Ginza Itchome Stations. [M-8]

GINZA MARUNOUCHI HOTEL

銀座丸ノ内ホテル　中央区銀座 8-13-1

8-13-1 Ginza, Chuo-ku. Tel: 3543-5431. Fax: 3543-6006.

Rates: Sgl. from ¥17,000, Dbl. from ¥24,000.

—Two minutes from Higashi Ginza Station. [M-22]

GINZA NIKKO HOTEL

銀座日航ホテル　中央区銀座 8-4-21

8-4-21 Ginza, Chuo-ku. Tel: 3571-4911. Fax: 3571-8379.

Rates: Sgl. from ¥15,742, Dbl. from ¥30,316 (incl. tax).

—Four minutes from Shimbashi Station. [M-8]

Tokyo—Marunouchi

PALACE HOTEL—Quiet and subdued atmosphere, ask for a room overlooking the Imperial Palace moats and gardens.

パレスホテル　千代田区丸ノ内 1-1-1

1-1-1 Marunouchi, Chiyoda-ku. Tel: 3211-5211. Fax: 3211-6987.

Rates: Sgl. from ¥20,000, Dbl. from ¥30,000.

—Three minutes from Otemachi and seven minutes from Tokyo Station. [M-10]

YAESU FUJIYA HOTEL—Good, basic hotel.

八重洲富士屋ホテル　中央区八重洲 2-9-1

2-9-1 Yaesu, Chuo-ku. Tel: 3273-2111. Fax: 3273-2180.

Rates: Sgl. from ¥12,100, Dbl. from ¥16,500.

—Two minutes from Tokyo Station. [M-9]

HOTEL KOKUSAI KANKO

ホテル国際観光　千代田区丸ノ内 1-8-3

1-8-3 Marunouchi, Chiyoda-ku. Tel: 3215-3281. Fax: 3215-3186.

Rates: Sgl. from ¥13,500, Dbl. from ¥20,500.

—One minute from Tokyo Station. [M-9]

TOKYO STATION HOTEL—Built in 1915 at the same time as Tokyo Station itself.

東京ステーションホテル　千代田区丸ノ内 1-9-1

1-9-1 Marunouchi, Chiyoda-ku. Tel: 3231-2511. Fax: 3231-3513.

Rates: Sgl. from ¥8,720 (w/o bath), Dbl. from ¥19,000 (w/o bath).

—Above Tokyo Station. [M-10]

• Other Hotels

TOKYO MARUNOUCHI HOTEL

東京丸ノ内ホテル　千代田区丸ノ内 1-6-3

1-6-3 Marunouchi, Chiyoda-ku. Tel: 3215-2151. Fax: 3215-8036.

Rates: Sgl. from ¥15,000, Dbl. from ¥24,000.

—Five minutes from Tokyo Station. [M-10]

TOKYO CITY HOTEL

東京シティーホテル　中央区日本橋本町 1-5-4

1-5-4 Nihombashi Honcho, Chuo-ku. Tel: 3270-7671. Fax: 3270-8930.

Rates: Sgl. from ¥7,004, Dbl. from ¥18,015 (incl. tax).

—Two minutes from Mitsukoshi-mae Station, five minutes by taxi from Tokyo City Air Terminal. [M-9]

Akasaka—Nagatacho

CAPITOL TOKYU HOTEL—Formerly the Tokyo Hilton. Comfortable and relaxing atmosphere, the interiors are a blend of Japanese and Western design.

キャピトル東急ホテル　千代田区永田町 2-10-3

2-10-3 Nagatacho, Chiyoda-ku. Tel: 3581-4511. Fax: 3581-5822.

Rates: Sgl. from ¥24,500, Dbl. from ¥33,000, Japanese-style: ¥80,000.

—Outdoor pool, excellent restaurants, two minutes from Kokkaigijido-mae Station. [M-6]

HOTEL NEW OTANI—One of the largest hotels in Asia. A new tower and old building combined in a sprawling and somewhat confusing fashion.

ホテルニューオータニ　千代田区紀尾井町 4-1

4-1 Kioi-cho, Chiyoda-ku. Tel: 3265-1111. Fax: 3221-2619.

Rates: Sgl. from Y24,000, Dbl. from ¥31,500.

—Four-hundred-year-old Japanese garden, health facilities, rooms for women only and handicapped, twenty-four-hour child-care, four minutes from Akasaka-mitsuke Station. [M-6]

AKASAKA PRINCE HOTEL—Prince chain hotel. New Tange Kenzo building opened in March 1983. Ultra-modern, some say "cold" interior.

赤坂プリンスホテル　千代田区紀尾井町 1-2

1-2 Kioi-cho, Chiyoda-ku. Tel: 3234-1111. Fax: 3262-5163.

Rates: Sgl. from ¥23,000, Dbl. from ¥34,000, Japanese-style from ¥85,000.

—Rooms have great views. Executive salon. Four minutes from Akasaka-mitsuke Station. [M-6]

ANA HOTEL TOKYO—"Zen-Nikku Hotel." In the center of a recent development complex, the busy and noisy lobby feels not unlike a shopping mall. Convenient location.

全日空ホテル　港区赤坂 1-12-33

1-12-33 Akasaka, Minato-ku. Tel: 3505-1111. Fax: 3505-1155.

Rates: Sgl. from ¥21,000, Dbl. from ¥29,000.

—Gym, outdoor pool, ten minutes from Roppongi or Toranomon Stations. [M-11]

HOTEL KAYU KAIKAN—Hotel Okura chain. Nice and quiet, smaller hotel.

ホテル霞友会館　千代田区三番町 8-1

8-1 Sanban-cho, Chiyoda-ku. Tel: 3230-1111. Fax: 3230-2529.

Rates: Sgl. from ¥12,000, Dbl. from ¥16,000, Japanese-style ¥20,000.

—Five minutes from Hanzomon Station. [M-17]

DIAMOND HOTEL—Good central location in quiet residential area.

ダイヤモンドホテル　千代田区一番町 25

25 Ichiban-cho, Chiyoda-ku. Tel: 3262-2211. Fax: 3263-2222.

Rates: Sgl. from ¥11,660, Dbl. from ¥16,428 (incl. tax).

Diamond Hotel Annex: Sgl. from ¥10,000, Dbl. from ¥14,500.

—One minute from Hanzomon Station. [M-6]

HOTEL YOKO AKASAKA

ホテル陽光赤坂　港区赤坂 6-14-12

6-14-12 Akasaka, Minato-ku. Tel: 3586-4050. Fax: 3586-5944.

Rates: Sgl. from ¥8,500, Twin from ¥15,000.

—Four minutes from Akasaka Station. [M-6]

Roppongi—Toranomon—Shiba

HOTEL OKURA—One of the most highly-rated hotels in the world, its quiet Japanese elegance and efficiency is impressive. Best rooms are in main building overlooking inner garden.
ホテルオークラ　港区虎の門 2-10-4
2-10-4 Toranomon, Minato-ku. Tel: 3582-0111. Fax: 3582-3707.
Rates: Sgl. from ¥27,500, Dbl. from ¥37,500, Japanese-style from ¥38,000.
—Full health facilities, executive salon, excellent restaurants, five to seven minutes from Kamiyacho and Toranomon Stations. [M-11]

TOKYO PRINCE HOTEL—Prince chain hotel. Located next to Zojo-ji temple. Large but comfortable-quality hotel that's starting to show its age.
東京プリンスホテル　港区芝公園 3-3-1
3-3-1 Shiba-koen, Minato-ku. Tel: 3432-1111. Fax: 3434-5551.
Rates: Sgl. from ¥23,000, Dbl. from ¥24,000.
—Swimming pool (summer only), three minutes from Onarimon and six minutes from Kamiyacho Stations. [M-11]

SHIBA PARK HOTEL—Pleasant smaller hotel.
芝パークホテル　港区芝公園 1-5-10
1-5-10 Shiba-koen, Minato-ku. Tel: 3433-4141. Fax: 5470-7519.
Rates: Sgl. from ¥14,000, Dbl. from ¥20,000.
—Three minutes from Onarimon Station. [M-11]

ROPPONGI PRINCE HOTEL—Designed by Kurokawa Kisho, a glass-sided swimming pool forms the focal point of the central court and the stares of visiting businessmen.
六本木プリンスホテル　港区六本木 3-2-7
3-2-7 Roppongi, Minato-ku. Tel: 3587-1111. Fax: 3587-0770.
Rates: Sgl. from ¥19,500, Dbl. from ¥23,500.
—Swimming pool, five minutes from Roppongi Station [M-1]

• **Other Hotels**

TOKYO GRAND HOTEL
東京グランドホテル　港区芝 2-5-3
2-5-3 Shiba, Minato-ku. Tel: 3456-2222. Fax: 3454-1022.
Rates: Sgl. from ¥14,574, Dbl. from ¥18,128 (incl. tax).
—Two minutes from Shiba-koen Station. [M-11]

HOTEL IBIS
ホテルアイビス　港区六本木 7-14-4
7-14-4 Roppongi, Minato-ku. Tel: 3403-4411. Fax: 3479-0609.
Rates: Sgl. from ¥13,000, Dbl. from ¥19,500.
—One minute from Roppongi station. [M-1]

SHIBA YAYOI KAIKAN
芝弥生会館　港区海岸 1-10-27
1-10-27 Kaigan, Minato-ku. Tel: 3434-6841. Fax: 3432-2505.
Rates: Sgl. from ¥5,700, Twin from ¥9,100.
—Older hotel on the waterfront, seven minutes from Hamamatsu-cho Station. [M-11]

Shibuya—Harajuku—Aoyama

THE PRESIDENT HOTEL AOYAMA—One of the best medium-priced hotels in town. Extremely convenient, efficiently small rooms have been described as "like a kit."
プレジデントホテル青山　港区南青山 2-2-3
2-2-3 Minami Aoyama, Minato-ku. Tel: 3497-0111. Fax: 3401-4816.
Rates: Sgl. from ¥11,000, Dbl. from ¥16,000.
—One minute from Aoyama Itchome Station. [M-5]

SHIBUYA TOBU HOTEL—In the middle of the Shibuya shopping area.
渋谷東武ホテル　渋谷区宇田川町 3-1
3-1 Udagawa-cho, Shibuya-ku. Tel: 3476-0111. Fax: 3476-0903.

Rates: Sgl. from ¥12,826, Dbl. from ¥16,995 (incl. tax).
—Six minutes from Shibuya Station. [M-3]

CRESTON HOTEL—Business hotel, somewhat inconvenient but well-equipped for business.
渋谷クレストンホテル　渋谷区神山町 10-8
10-8 Kamiyama-cho, Shibuya-ku. Tel: 3481-5800. Fax: 3481-5515.
Rates: Sgl. from ¥12,000, Dbl. from ¥18,000.
—Ten minutes from Shibuya Station. [M-3]

ASIA CENTER OF JAPAN—A cross between a business hotel and student lodgings, this is one of the best deals in town.
アジア会館　港区赤坂 8-10-32
8-10-32 Akasaka, Minato-ku. Tel: 3402-6111. Fax: 3402-0738.
Rates: Sgl. w/o bath ¥4,500, w/bath ¥5,400, Dbl. w/o bath ¥6,000, w/bath ¥9,120.
—Five minutes from Aoyama Itchome, eight minutes from Roppongi Stations. [M-5]

• **Other Hotels**

HILLPORT HOTEL
ヒルポートホテル　渋谷区桜ケ丘 23-19
23-19 Sakuragaoka, Shibuya-ku. Tel: 3462-5171. Fax: 3496-2066.
Rates: Sgl. from ¥9,700, Twin ¥15,600, Japanese-style ¥37,000.
—Four minutes from Shibuya Station. [M-3]

SHIBUYA SUNROUTE
渋谷サンルートホテル　渋谷区南平台町 1-11
1-11 Nampeidai-cho, Shibuya-ku. Tel: 3464-6411. Fax: 3464-1678.
Rates: Sgl. from ¥6,911, Dbl. from ¥13,821 (incl. tax).
—Five minutes from Shibuya Station. [off Map]

HOTEL HARAJUKU TRIMM
ホテル原宿トリム　渋谷区神宮前 6-28-6
6-28-6 Jingumae, Shibuya-ku. Tel: 3498-2101. Fax: 3498-1777.
Rates: Sgl. from ¥7,700, Twin from ¥12,200. No credit cards/foreign exchange.
—Sports facilities, three minutes from Harajuku or Meiji-Jingumae Stations. [M-4]

NIHON SEINENKAN
日本青年館　渋谷区霞岳町 15
15 Kasumigaoka-machi, Shibuya-ku. Tel: 3401-0101. Fax: 3404-0611.
Rates: Twin from ¥6,100 per person.
—Ten minutes from Sendagaya Station. [M-5]

Shinjuku

TOKYO HILTON HOTEL—Standard Hilton Hotel. If you must stay in Shinjuku, this is perhaps the best choice.
東京ヒルトンホテル　新宿区西新宿 6-6-2
6-6-2 Nishi Shinjuku, Shinjuku-ku. Tel: 3344-5111. Fax: 3342-6094.
Rates: Sgl. from ¥26,000, Dbl. from ¥32,000, Japanese-style from ¥55,000.
—Executive salon, good sports facilities, eight minutes from Shinjuku Station. [M-7]

KEIO PLAZA HOTEL—An undistinguished forty-five-story concrete and glass skyscraper. Interiors are more of the same.
京王プラザホテル　新宿区西新宿 2-2-1
2-2-1 Nishi Shinjuku, Shinjuku-ku. Tel: 3344-0111. Fax: 3345-82-69.
Rates: Sgl. from ¥21,000, Dbl. from ¥26,000, Japanese style from ¥70,000.
—Health facilities, executive salon, six minutes from Shinjuku Station. [M-7]

HOTEL CENTURY HYATT—Another monolithic Shinjuku hotel, average service and interior.
ホテルセンチュリーハイアット　新宿区西新宿 2-7-2
2-7-2 Nishi Shinjuku, Shinjuku-ku. Tel: 3349-0111. Fax: 3344-5575.
Rates: Sgl. from ¥21,000, Dbl. from ¥30,000, Japanese style ¥60,000.
—Good sports facilities, discothèque, nine minutes from Shinjuku Station. [M-7]

PARK HYATT TOKYO—Luxury hotel occupying the top fourteen floors of Tange Kenzo's fifty-two story Shinjuku Park Tower. Just 178 rooms, but each equipped with fax, CD, laser disc, etc., and breathtaking contemporary design. The New York Grill, on the top floor, offers a panoramic view of the city.

パークハイアット東京　新宿区西新宿 3-7-1-2

3-7-1-2 Nishi Shinjuku, Shinjuku-ku. Tel: 5322-1234. Fax: 5322-1288.

Rates: Sgl. from ¥36,000, Dbl. from ¥41,000.

—Ten minutes from Shinjuku Station. [off Map]

HOTEL SUNROUTE TOKYO—Sunroute Chain Hotel.

ホテルサンルート東京　渋谷区代々木 2-3-1

2-3-1 Yoyogi, Shibuya-ku. Tel: 3375-3211. Fax: 3379-8757.

Rates: Sgl. from ¥11,310, Dbl. from ¥15,862 (incl. tax).

—Two minutes from Shinjuku Station. [M-7]

WASHINGTON HOTEL—High-tech eighties hotel with computerized check in and human clerks to show you how to use it.

ワシントンホテル　新宿区西新宿 3-2-9

3-2-9 Nishi Shinjuku, Shinjuku-ku. Tel: 3343-3111. Fax: 3340-1804.

Rates: Sgl. from ¥11,024, Dbl. from ¥16,480 (incl. tax). No foreign exchange, accepts Visa.

—Eight minutes from Shinjuku Station. [M-7]

• **Other Hotels**

SHINJUKU PRINCE HOTEL

新宿プリンスホテル　新宿区歌舞伎町 1-30-1

1-30-1 Kabukicho, Shinjuku-ku. Tel: 3205-1111. Fax: 3205-1952.

Rates: Sgl. from ¥13,500, Dbl. from ¥15,000.

—Five minutes from Shinjuku Station. [M-7]

HOTEL RISTEL SHINJUKU

ホテルリステル新宿　新宿区新宿 5-3-20

5-3-20 Shinjuku, Shinjuku-ku. Tel: 3350-0123. Fax: 3350-0444.

Rates: Sgl. from ¥8,000, Dbl. from ¥15,000.

—Five minutes from Shinjuku Gyoen Station. [M-7]

Ikebukuro—Mejiro

FOUR SEASONS HOTEL CHINZAN-SO TOKYO—Opened in 1992, this Tokyo branch of the famous Four Seasons Hotel is located on the grounds of the beautiful Chinzan-so Gardens. A bit inconvenient to the central city, it is beautifully designed and elegantly discreet.

フォーシーズンズホテル　文京区関口 2-10-8

2-10-8 Sekiguchi, Bunkyo-ku. Tel: 3943-2222. Fax: 3943-0909.

Rates: Sgl. from ¥20,000, Dbl. from ¥33,000, Japanese-style ¥36,000 for one, ¥40,000 for two.

—Luxurious health club with swimming pool, saunas, beauty center, etc., ten minutes from Edogawa-bashi Station, eight minutes by car from Mejiro Station. [off Map]

SUNSHINE CITY PRINCE HOTEL—Prince Hotel chain. Linked to the Sunshine City building, huge and rather impersonal.

サンシャインシティプリンスホテル　豊島区東池袋 3-1-5

3-1-5 Higashi Ikebukuro, Toshima-ku. Tel: 3988-1111. Fax: 3988-7878.

Rates: Sgl. from ¥13,000, Dbl. from ¥20,000.

—Ten minutes from Ikebukuro Station. [M-18]

HOTEL METROPOLITAN—A newer hotel trying to bring a touch of elegance to Ikebukuro.

ホテルメトロポリタン　豊島区西池袋 1-6-1

1-6-1 Nishi Ikebukuro, Toshima-ku. Tel: 3980-1111. Fax: 3980-5600.

Rates: Sgl. from ¥14,000, Dbl. from ¥18,500.

—Three minutes from Ikebukuro Station. [M-18]

• **Other Hotels**

IKEBUKURO CENTER CITY HOTEL

池袋センターシティホテル　豊島区池袋 2-62-14

2-62-14 Ikebukuro, Toshima-ku. Tel: 3985-1311. Fax: 3980-7001.

Rates: Sgl. from ¥5,500, Dbl. from ¥9,500.
—Four minutes from Ikebukuro Station. [M-18]

Shinagawa

TAKANAWA PRINCE HOTEL—Prince Hotel chain. Considered discreetly elegant by the Japanese. Quiet atmosphere, lovely garden.
高輪プリンスホテル　港区高輪 3-13-1
3-13-1 Takanawa, Minato-ku. Tel: 3447-1111. Fax: 3446-0849.
Rates: Sgl. from ¥19,000, Dbl. from ¥23,000, Japanese-style from ¥44,000.
—Swimming pool (summer only), ten minutes from Shinagawa Station. [M-36]

NEW TAKANAWA PRINCE HOTEL—Recent addition to the Takanawa Prince.
新高輪プリンスホテル　港区高輪 3-13-1

3-13-1 Takanawa, Minato-ku. Tel: 3442-1111. Fax: 3444-1234.
Rates: Sgl. from ¥20,000, Dbl. from ¥27,000.
—All rooms have a private balcony, swimming pool (summer only), five minutes from Shinagawa Station. [M-36]

SHINAGAWA PRINCE HOTEL— Prince Hotel chain. This hotel adjoins a sports center that includes tennis courts and bowling facilities. A new thirty-nine story annex, with 1,736 rooms, dwarfs the original building now.
品川プリンスホテル　港区高輪 4-10-30
4-10-30 Takanawa, Minato-ku. Tel: 3440-1111. Fax: 3441-7092.
Rates: Sgl. from ¥8,400, Dbl. from ¥13,000.
—Five minutes from Shinagawa Station. [M-36]

TAKANAWA KEIKYU HOTEL—Convenient, new business hotel.
高輪京急ホテル　港区高輪 4-10-8
4-10-8 Takanawa, Minato-ku. Tel: 3443-1211. Fax: 3443-1221.
Rates: Sgl. from ¥10,000, Dbl. from ¥14,000.
—Two minutes from Shinagawa Station. [M-36]

•Other Hotels

HOTEL PACIFIC
ホテルパシフィック　港区高輪 3-13-3
3-13-3 Takanawa, Minato-ku. Tel: 3445-6711. Fax: 3445-5137.
Rates: Sgl. from ¥20,500, Dbl. from ¥23,000.
—Five minutes from Shinagawa Station. [M-36]

KEIHIN HOTEL
京品ホテル　港区高輪 4-10-20
4-10-20 Takanawa, Minato-ku. Tel: 3449-5711. Fax: 3441-7230.
Rates: Sgl. from ¥8,415, Dbl. from ¥14,300.
—One minute from Shinagawa Station. [M-36]

HOTEL SANJOEN
ホテル三條苑　品川区上大崎 2-23
2-23 Kami-osaki, Shinagawa-ku. Tel: 3779-1010. Fax: 3779-4070.
Rates: Sgl. from ¥10,000, Dbl. from ¥18,000.
—Two minutes from Meguro Station. [M-19]

NEW OTANI INN TOKYO
ニューオータニイン東京　品川区大崎 1-6-2
1-6-2 Osaki, Shinagawa-ku. Tel: 3779-9111. Fax: 3779-9181.
Rates: Sgl. from ¥13,000, Dbl. from ¥27,000.
—One minute from Osaki Station. [off Map]

Meguro—Ebisu

MIYAKO HOTEL TOKYO—Affiliated with the famous Miyako Hotel in Kyoto, not particularly convenient but quiet and nice.

都ホテル東京　港区白金台 1-1-50
1-1-50 Shiroganedai, Minato-ku. Tel: 3447-3111. Fax: 3447-3133.
Rates: Sgl. from ¥18,000, Dbl. from ¥23,000, Japanese-style ¥22,000.
—Health facilities, twenty minutes from Meguro Station. [M-19]

THE WESTIN TOKYO—Newly opened in Yebisu Garden Place. Classical European-style interiors, big rooms with high ceilings.
ウェスティンホテル東京　目黒区三田 1-4-1
1-4-1 Mita, Meguro-ku. Tel: 5423-7000. Fax: 5423-7600.
Rates: Sgl. from ¥28,000, Dbl. from ¥30,000.
—Five minutes from Ebisu Station. [M-20]

MEGURO GAJOEN—The old Gajoen Ryokan was rebuilt as a super-spacious luxury hotel. Remaining of the old building are the Japanese baroque wedding hall and meeting rooms.
目黒雅叙園　目黒区下目黒 1-8-1
1-8-1 Shimo-meguro, Meguro-ku. Tel: 3491-4111. Fax: 5434-3931.
Rates: Dbl. from ¥70,000, Japanese rooms from ¥90,000, double occupancy.
—Three-minute walk from Meguro Station. [M-19]

GAJOEN KANKO HOTEL—An eccentric older hotel with an interesting blend of Western and Japanese interiors. Formerly associated with the Meguro Gajoen Ryokan next door.
雅叙園観光ホテル　目黒区下目黒 1-8-1
1-8-1 Shimo-meguro, Meguro-ku. Tel: 3491-0111. Fax: 3495-2450.
Rates: Sgl. ¥10,197, Dbl. ¥17,926 (incl. tax).
—Five minutes from Meguro Station. [M-19]

Ochanomizu—Kudan

HILLTOP HOTEL—Called *Yama no ue* or "Top of the hill," this charming older hotel is famous for its history of being a favorite of writers and artists.
山の上ホテル　千代田区神田駿河台 1-1
1-1 Kanda Surugadai, Chiyoda-ku. Tel: 3293-2311. Fax: 3233-4567
Rates: Sgl. from ¥13,000, Dbl. from ¥21,000.
—Five minutes from Ochanomizu Station. [M-15]

KUDAN KAIKAN HOTEL—This Meiji-period building houses a hotel and concert hall. Ask for a room facing the Imperial Palace.
九段会館ホテル　千代田区九段南 1-6-5
1-6-5 Kudan-minami, Chiyoda-ku. Tel: 3261-5521. Fax: 3221-7238.
Rates: Sgl. from ¥8,034, Dbl. from ¥14,935, Japanese-style ¥12,296 for one, ¥17,304 for three (incl. tax).
—Two minutes from Kudanshita Station. [M-17]

• **Other Hotels**

HOTEL GRAND PALACE
ホテルグランドパレス　千代田区飯田橋 1-1-1
1-1-1 Iidabashi, Chiyoda-ku. Tel: 3264-1111. Fax: 3230-4985.
Rates: Sgl. from ¥18,000, Dbl. from ¥27,000.
—One minute from Kudanshita Station. [M-17]

FAIRMONT HOTEL
フェアモントホテル　千代田区九段南 2-1-17
2-1-17 Kudan-minami, Chiyoda-ku. Tel: 3262-1151. Fax: 3264-2476.
Rates: Sgl. from ¥11,310, Dbl. from ¥20,394 (incl. tax).
—Six minutes from Kudanshita Station. [M-17]

Asakusa—Ueno

ASAKUSA VIEW HOTEL—The only major hotel in this old downtown area. Convenient for sightseeing in "old Tokyo." A public Japanese cedar bath overlooks a small garden.
浅草ビューホテル　台東区西浅草 3-17-1
3-17-1 Nishi Asakusa, Taito-ku. Tel: 3842-2111. Fax: 3842-2117.

Rates: Sgl. from ¥15,000, Dbl. from ¥21,000, Japanese-style from ¥40,000 for one, each additional person is ¥3,000.
—Good sports facilities, seven minutes from Tawaramachi Station. [M-12]
TOURIST HOTEL—Small business hotel, but very convenient.
ツーリストホテル　台東区東上野 3-19-11
3-18-11 Higashi Ueno, Taito-ku. Tel: 3831-0237. Fax: 3837-1218.
Rates: Sgl. from ¥7,500, twin from ¥13,000.
—Two minutes from Ueno Station. [M-13]
SUIGETSU HOTEL—Inexpensive hotel with a large number of Japanese rooms, some Western rooms, and a large Japanese bath. On the grounds is the former home of the famous novelist Mori Ogai (1862–1922) that the hotel's owner has tried to preserve.
水月荘ホテル　台東区池之端 3-3-21
3-3-21 Ikenohata, Taito-ku. Tel: 3822-4611.
Rates: Sgl. from ¥7,800, Twin from ¥14,000.
—Three-minute walk from Nezu Station, ten minutes from Ueno. [M-13]

Tokyo City Air Terminal

HOLIDAY INN—Just like in America.
ホリディイン　中央区八丁堀 1-13-7
1-13-7 Hatchobori, Chuo-ku. Tel: 3553-6161. Fax: 3553-6040.
Rates: Sgl. from ¥16,906, Dbl. from ¥24,486 (incl. tax).
—Swimming pool (summer only), one minute from Hatchobori Station, three minutes by taxi to TCAT. [M-25]
•**Other Hotels**
HOTEL KITCHO
ホテル吉晁　中央区日本橋人形町 2-32-8
2-32-8 Nihombashi Ningyocho, Chuo-ku. Tel: 3666-6161. Fax: 3661-6162.
Rates: Sgl. from ¥8,755, Dbl. from ¥13,190 (incl. tax).
—Two minutes from Hamacho Station. [M-23]
KAYABACHO PEARL HOTEL
茅場町パールホテル　中央区新川 1-2-5
1-2-5 Shinkawa, Chuo-ku. Tel: 3553-2211. Fax: 3555-1849.
Rates: Sgl. from ¥8,000, Twin from ¥13,000.
—Three minutes from Kayaba-cho Station. [off Map]

Narita Airport

NARITA VIEW HOTEL
成田ビューホテル　千葉県成田市小菅 700
700 Kosuge, Narita City, Chiba Prefecture. Tel: (0476) 32-1111. Fax: (0476) 32-1193.
Rates: Sgl. from ¥15,158, Dbl. from ¥20,394 (incl. tax).
—Health facilities, next to Narita Airport, and ten minutes by taxi to Narita Station. [off Map]
NARITA U CITY HOTEL
成田ユーシティホテル　千葉県成田市囲護台 1-1-2
1-1-2 Igodai, Narita City, Chiba Prefecture. Tel: (0476) 24-0101. Fax: (0476) 24-0160.
Rates: Sgl. from ¥9,000, Twin from ¥16,000.
—One minute from Narita Station (West Exit), twenty to thirty minutes from hotel to Narita Airport, and free hourly bus service. [off Map]

RYOKAN

A Japanese inn *ryokan* may be the closest you'll get to staying in a traditional Japanese home. You'll sleep in a tatami (straw-matted) room, in place of a bed, there will be a futon. Baths are Japanese-style and often communal (sexes are segregated). Privacy and excellent service are another plus. Morning and evening meals will be served in your room and your futon laid out at night. Good *ryokan* are expensive. Prices range from ¥20,000 to ¥60,000 or more, but two meals are included and the cuisine is often excellent.

Unfortunately, the best inns are not found in Tokyo. With land prices skyrocketing in the city, most innkeepers have opted for high-rise hotels. If you are planning to travel outside of Tokyo, you should perhaps save your *ryokan* experience until then. On page fifty-six, we have listed a few top-rated *ryokan* located a short distance from the city. Any of these places would make an ideal weekend trip out of Tokyo.

Because the few exceptional *ryokan* in Tokyo will accept only "introduced" guests, we have listed one medium-class *ryokan* and five inexpensive, somewhat tourist-oriented inns that can give you a taste of this tradition. Major hotels often have Japanese-style rooms. Most are expensive, but a few, like the **Kudan Kaikan** and the **Suigetsu Hotel,** are very affordable.

KIMI RYOKAN—Japanese-style rooms all with bath, meals not included.
貴美旅館　豊島区池袋 2-36-8
2-36-8 Ikebukuro, Toshima-ku. Tel: 3971-3766.
Rates: One person ¥4,300, ¥7,500 for two.
—Six minutes from Ikebukuro station (West Exit). [M-18]

SANSUISO—Communal bath and showers, meals not included.
山水荘　品川区東五反田 2-9-5
2-9-5, Higashi Gotanda, Shinagawa-ku. Tel: 3441-7475. Fax: 3449-1944.
Rates: Up to three people per room. Single occupancy from ¥4,300, ¥3,700 per person if three to a room.
—Five minutes from Gotanda Station. [off Map]

SAWANOYA—Close to Ueno Park, meals not included.
澤の屋　台東区谷中 2-3-11
2-3-11 Yanaka, Taito-ku. Tel: 3822-2251. Fax: 3822-2252.
Rates: One person ¥4,000 (w/o bath), for two ¥7,000 (w/o bath) or ¥8,000 (w/bath).
—Seven minutes from Nezu Station. [M-13]

INABASO—Japanese or Western-style rooms all with baths, meals not included.
稲葉荘　新宿区新宿 5-6-13
5-6-13 Shinjuku, Shinjuku-ku. Fax: 3354-3332.
Rates: One person ¥5,000, for two ¥8,755 (incl. tax).
—Three minutes from Shinjuku San-chome Station. [M-7]

MIKAWAYA BEKKAN—Located in the center of Asakusa. Communal baths, meals not included.
三河屋別館　台東区浅草 1-31-11
1-31-11 Asakusa, Taito-ku. Tel: 3843-2345. Fax: 3843-2348.
Rates: One person ¥5,200, for two ¥9,600.
—Five minutes from Asakusa Station. [M-12]

Out of Town *Ryokan*

We have listed five excellent *ryokan* located in the Hakone and Izu areas. As with most good *ryokan*, morning and evening meals are included in the price. The rates listed here are per person, double occupancy, only a few places will accept single guests—and if they do the price goes up. The rates also generally go down if you want to stay four to a room.

Hakone

NARAYA—Established in the Edo period, the current building dates from over one hundred years ago. There is one main building and eight smaller ones all surrounded by a beautiful garden on Mt. Hakone.

奈良屋　神奈川県足柄下郡箱根町宮ノ下 162

162 Miyanoshita, Hakone-cho, Ashigarashimo-gun, Kanagawa-ken. Tel: (0460) 2-2411. Fax: (0460) 7-6231.
Rates: Rooms from ¥30,000.

RYUGUDEN (HAKONE PRINCE HOTEL WAFU-BEKKAN)—Every room faces Lake Ashinoko and Mt. Fuji.

龍宮殿　神奈川県足柄下郡箱根町元箱根 139

139 Moto Hakone, Hakone-cho, Ashigarashimo-gun, Kanagawa-ken. Tel: (0460) 3-7111. Fax: (0460) 3-7011.
Rates: Rooms from ¥24,000 per person for two or more.

TSUBAKI—Located between Hakone and Atami, this famous *ryokan* is noted for its excellent Kyoto-style *kaiseki* cuisine.

海石榴　神奈川県足柄下郡湯河原町宮上 776

776 Miyakami, Yugawara-cho, Ashigarashimo-gun, Kanagawa-ken. Tel: (0465) 63-3333. Fax: (0465) 63-6640.
Rates: Rooms from ¥56,000 per person, for two or more.

Izu

HOURAI—The hot spring here was founded in the eighth century Manyo period and is one of the oldest in Japan. There are beautiful views of the sea and wonderful *kaiseki* cuisine.

蓬莱　静岡県熱海市伊豆山 750-6

750-6 Izusan, Atami-shi, Shizuoka-ken. Tel: (0557) 80-5151. Fax: (0557) 80-0205.
Rates: Rooms from ¥40,000 per person for two or more.

ASABA—This 350-year-old *ryokan* is distinguished by its *Noh* theater where special performances of *Noh* plays are given three times a year.

あさば旅館　静岡県田方郡修善寺町 3450-1

3450-1 Shuzenji, Shuzenji-cho, Tagata-gun, Shizuoka-ken. Tel: (0558) 72-0700. Fax: (0558) 72-7077.
Rates: Rooms from ¥25,000 per person for two or more.

CHEAP ACCOMMODATIONS

If you're on a budget, there are a number of inexpensive alternatives to hotels. In addition to being cheap, most are inconveniently located, lacking in privacy, and offer only minimal service. They are, however, safe, and they maintain reasonable standards of cleanliness. Choices include the YMCA and other youth hostels, public lodges (*kokumin shukusha*), *minshuku* "family-run lodging," and Buddhist temples. We have listed a few, but for further confirmation, contact one of the organizations listed below.

Youth Hostels

Rates average ¥3,500, including two meals. There is usually a central kitchen so you can cook for yourself. Rules are rather strict—including a 9:00 P.M. curfew. To enter a youth hostel, you must be a member of the "International Youth Hostel Federation." They sell memberships at the Tokyo International Youth Hostel office for ¥2,000 plus one passport photo.

TOKYO INTERNATIONAL YOUTH HOSTEL
東京国際ユースホステル　新宿区神楽河岸 21-1 セントラルプラザ 18 階
Central Plaza, 18F, 21-1 Kaguragashi, Shinjuku-ku. Tel: 3235-1107. Fax: 3267-4000. Most rooms are shared by four people at about ¥3,840 per person. [Near Iidabashi Station, off map.]
—New, clean, and liberal by Japanese standards. (They even serve beer in the dining room!) The average guests here are between the ages of fourteen and twenty-four. There are also a fair number of bargain-hunting businessmen, and a few Japanese-style rooms for families.

JAPAN YOUTH HOSTELS ASSOCIATION
日本ユースホステル協会　新宿区市ヶ谷砂土原町 1-2 保険会館 3 階
Hoken Kaikan, 3F, 1-2 Ichigaya Sadohara-cho, Shinjuku-ku. Tel: 3269-5831/3. Fax: 3235-0629.

Minshuku

The average rate is ¥5,000 a day. There are over 27,000 of these lodgings throughout the country. Make your reservations through one of the following organizations:

JAPAN MINSHUKU CENTER
日本民宿センター　千代田区有楽町 2-10-1 交通会館ビル
Kotsu Kaikan Bldg., B1, 2-10-1 Yurakucho, Chiyoda-ku. Tel: 3216-6556. Fax: 3216-6557.

JAPAN MINSHUKU ASSOCIATION
日本民宿協会　新宿区高田馬場 1-29-5
1-29-5 Takadanobaba, Shinjuku-ku. Tel: 3232-6561. Fax: 3232-6405.

Others

Japan Travel Bureau can reserve lodgings in Buddhist temples and People's Lodges. TIC also has a pamphlet titled *Reasonable Accommodations in Japan.* Listings of other inexpensive lodgings can be found in the *Tour Companion* and the *Tokyo Journal.*

TOKYO YMCA
千代田区神田美土代町 7
7 Kanda Mitoshiro-cho, Chiyoda-ku. Tel: 3293-1911.
Rates: Sgl. from ¥10,300, twin from ¥18,540.
—Communal bath, one minute from Shin-ochanomizu Station. [M-14]

YMCA ASIA YOUTH CENTER
千代田区猿楽町 2-5-5
2-5-5 Sarugaku-cho, Chiyoda-ku. Tel: 3233-0611.
Rates: Sgl. ¥6,500, Dbl. ¥11,000, Triple ¥15,000.
—Private bath, five minutes from Suidobashi Station. [M-15]

TOKYO YWCA SADOHARA HOSTEL
新宿区市ケ谷砂土原町 3-1-1
3-1-1 Ichigaya Sadohara-cho, Shinjuku-ku. Tel: 3268-7313.
Rates: Sgl. from ¥5,360, twin from ¥10,000. Room with kitchenette for married couples ¥11,000.
—Communal bath, seven minutes from Ichigaya Station. [off Map]

TOKYO INTERNATIONAL HOUSE: Has various rooms around the center of Tokyo. Shared kitchen, living room and bath. Tel: 3945-1699.
Rates: From ¥60,000 per month.

KOTANI HOUSE: Two locations, both just outside of Ikebukuro, Shin-Okubo, Tel: 3962-4979.

Rates: Sgl. from ¥2,000, Dbl. ¥1,800 (per person). Monthly rates: ¥60,000 for a shared room, ¥40,000 (per person) for a couple. [off Map]

APPLE HOUSE: The largest guest house in Japan, this new facility is geared for foreigners, and offers inexpensive daily, weekly, and monthly rates. Located about twenty minutes from Shinjuku. Contact them for further information: Tel: (0422) 51-2277. Fax: (0422) 51-4499. [off Map]

CAPSULE HOTELS

The capsule hotel phenomenon provides an amusing insight into city life in Japan. Located in night life areas and near the major commuter train stations, these hotels have hundreds of tiny sleeping capsules stacked one on top of the other. The average capsule size is 1.1 meters wide, 1.2 meters high, and 2.2 meters long. Standard equipment includes color television with porn channel, radio, alarm clock, air conditioner, emergency button, and sprinkler system. The clients are predominantly intoxicated businessmen who missed the last train back to their suburban homes (women aren't allowed). The occupancy rate is very high, with the busiest check in hours being between 12:00 P.M. and 3:00 A.M. The check-out rush comes between 8:00 A.M. and 9:00 A.M. when the hundreds of very serious faced and bluesuited businessmen scurry off to work.

GREEN PLAZA SHINJUKU—This huge capsule hotel boasts 660 "rooms."
グリーンプラザ新宿　新宿区歌舞伎町1-29-3
1-29-3, Kabukicho, Shinjuku-ku. Tel: 3207-5411.
Rates: ¥4,100 per capsule (male only), for an afternoon nap the rate is ¥1,000 for two hours, 10:00 A.M.–5:00 P.M.
—Huge sauna, gym, and massage, two minutes from Shinjuku Station. [M-7]

HOTEL WHITE CITY
ホテルホワイトシティ　豊島区東池袋1-11-11
1-11-11 Higashi Ikebukuro, Toshima-ku. Tel: 3987-3011.
Rates: Same as above, but they also have normal rooms from ¥7,210.
—Sauna, two minutes from Ikebukuro Station. [M-18]

CAPSULE INN AKASAKA
カプセルイン赤坂　港区赤坂6-14-1
6-14-1 Akasaka, Minato-ku. Tel: 3588-1811.
Rates: ¥4,000 between 5:00 P.M.–10:00 A.M. Men only. [M-6]

CAPSULE HOTEL ASAKUSA—This one also has a floor for women.
カプセルホテル浅草　台東区寿4-14-9
4-14-9 Kotobuki, Taito-ku. Tel: 3847-4477.
—Three minutes from Tawaramachi station. [M-12]

APARTMENT HOTELS

For people planning a longer stay, residential hotels with maid service and kitchenettes are ideal, though not particularly inexpensive. Besides the few listed below, they are often advertised in the local newspapers under "Apartments for Rent." The larger real estate companies often manage places for short-term lease (see "Housing" in the Appendix).

KITANO ARMS—2-16-15 Hirakawa-cho, Chiyoda-ku. Tel: 3265-2371. The most popular and respected of Tokyo residential hotels, you will have to reserve far in advance to insure a room. Rooms are from ¥345,000 a month. [M-6]

AZABU COURT—4-5-39 Minami Azabu, Minato-ku. Tel: 3446-8610. Close to Hiro-o Station, this hotel leases rooms by the day, the week, or the month. A single room will cost from about ¥150,000 to ¥230,000 a month, a studio will cost about ¥9,000 a day. [M-2]

ASAHI HOMES—Several apartment hotels in Tokyo with monthly rates ranging from ¥350,000 for a single room (¥90,000 weekly). Tel: 3583-7551.

食

EATING OUT

EATING OUT

Japanese food is one of the truly great achievements of the Japanese. Its current popularity overseas is no surprise to the locals who even when traveling abroad will search out the neighborhood sushi bar (which is never quite as good as in Japan). But there is a lot more to Japanese cuisine than sushi and tempura. Most versions, however, do not appear outside of the country. For anyone interested in food, Tokyo can be a source of endless culinary experimentation.

For more than two thousand years the Japanese diet has been based on rice, a fact often pointed out by the Japanese as a reason for the myriad differences between "us" and "them," meaning Western meat-eaters. For the common people, expensive white rice was never a main part of the meal. Rather a mixture of white and brown rice, millet, and greens was consumed while the white rice crop was paid in land rents to the aristocracy. It wasn't until after World War II that perfectly white rice was democratized and became standard fare for all.

As meat consumers, the Japanese have a history of only just over one hundred years. Considered unclean by the adopted Buddhist religion, meat eating was outlawed in 675 by the emperor Temmu. Hunted animals such as deer and wild boar were allowed on occasion as a sort of medicinal food. In the Edo period, the practice of eating meat to increase strength became somewhat more common, though it was still disliked by the general public. In 1872, the emperor Meiji made headlines by declaring publicly, "I shall eat meat." In the country's attempt to become as powerful as the invading Westerners, meat eating seemed like a possible means of increasing Japanese strength. *Gyunabeya*, beef restaurants, suddenly became popular especially among the Meiji-period liberals. The beef was prepared Japanese style, boiled in a broth with vegetables.

The basic diet of the people remained as before, the main part of every meal being the rice, miso soup and pickles served with side dishes of cooked vegetables and sometimes fish. Meals have always been seasonal in Japan. Today, one of the most difficult parts of ordering in restaurants is keeping up with the ever-changing menu of what is particularly great at a particular time of the year.

EATING OUT IN TOKYO

There are almost too many restaurants in Tokyo, over 80,000 at the last official counting. The majority of these establishments tend to be small and moderately priced. The best of them, as anywhere in the world, are the most expensive.

Aside from the sheer numbers, the variety of types of food is mind-boggling. Not only are there the numerous styles of Japanese cooking, but every imaginable kind of international cuisine is represented in some form somewhere in the city. We've concentrated on Japanese food and tried to provide good explanations of the food, how to order, and where to eat. Hopefully, after using this book at one of these recommended restaurants, you can venture off on your own. Restaurants included here range in price from dirt cheap to top of the line, but all offer good, if not excellent, quality for the price.

For international cuisine, we've primarily selected restaurants with a good reputation for quality. While excellent Japanese food can be had in a broad range of prices, Western food doesn't come cheap. It is, however, generally quite refined.

While French and Italian restaurants have been plentiful for years now, other non-Western and more exotic cuisine flourished in the late eighties. African, Mexican, Balinese, Middle Eastern—just about every country with an embassy here has restaurants to match. Much of the food is excellent and inexpensive.

The average seating capacity of Japanese restaurants is somewhere around fourteen persons, which accounts in part for the astonishing numbers. Many of the less expensive restaurants do not take reservations or credit cards. The more expensive ones, Japanese and Western, often require reservations, and most accept at least American Express, Visa, and Diners' Club. Travelers' checks are only rarely accepted. Many restaurants close early, often by 9:00 or 10:00 P.M.

Following is a brief description of the general categories of eating places in Tokyo.

• Very Expensive but High Quality
Ryotei—offering full course Tokyo- or Kyoto-style cooking, usually accompanied by traditional Japanese geisha entertainment, these are the most

expensive places to dine, with the prices easily ¥40,000 or more per person. Sand-colored Japanese style buildings with discreet signs, shuttered windows, and a pervasive air of secrecy, *ryotei* are frequented by parties of politicians and businessmen. One wonders what goes on behind those walls—unfortunately, an introduction is usually required.

Kaiseki-ryori is a meal traditionally served at the tea ceremony. The most expensive restaurants, as with *ryotei*, are patronized mainly by businessmen with expense accounts. There are also several moderately-priced *kaiseki* restaurants that attract a more average crowd.

•Expensive to Medium-Priced

Tempura, sushi, *sukiyaki, shabu-shabu,* etc., can be quite expensive or reasonably priced depending on the restaurant, what part of town it's located in, the decor, and the service.

•Cheap Food

Katei-ryori—Most restaurants in this category are called *shokudo* or *meshiya* (*meshi* means rice and, by implication, the meal itself). These places serve food just like mom used to make. Students and ordinary working people are the main clientele. Many of the smaller home-cooking restaurants have an actual mother figure, who both cooks for and entertains the often-regular customers.

Nomiya—*Yakitori, robatayaki,* and *oden* restaurants usually fit into this category. These restaurants are usually small places located near train stations so the businessmen who stop off after work don't have to stumble too far to catch a train back to the suburbs. *Nomiya* literally means "drinking place." Theoretically, what they serve are snacks to go along with the drinks, but the snacks can be a full meal depending on how much you order.

Noodle Restaurants—Serving *soba, udon,* and Chinese *ramen,* another inexpensive type of food. Even the best noodle restaurants are still relatively cheap.

Yoshokuya—These are restaurants serving Japanese-style Western food. Many of these places started in the Meiji period (1868–1912) when the country was reopened to Western influences. Because English food was the first official import, much of the food is typically British. Other favorites were food from Holland, Portugal, Spain, and France. This kind of food is also popular for home cooking. The food is very basic, but can be quite good. Typical items are hamburger steak and various kinds of croquettes.

Department Store and Arcade Restaurants—Perhaps the easiest and the cheapest way of eating in Tokyo is to go to one of the big underground arcades or the department store restaurant floors. The restaurants all have plastic food models which make ordering ever so simple. There is usually a wide variety of restaurants to choose from, all in one concentrated location. Although generally not *haute cuisine,* these places are sometimes worth it for the sheer simplicity.

Street Food—*Yatai* are small moving carts equipped with a stove and counter. Serving *yaki-imo* (roasted sweet potatoes), *yakitori, oden, ramen, okonomi-yaki, yakisoba,* or *tako-yaki,* the stalls are always set up at festival sites, and on weekends and holidays at the major parks. At night they're found in busy night club areas like Ginza, Roppongi, Akasaka, and Shinjuku.

Fast Food—Aside from McDonald's and its various Japanese spinoffs, there are forms of fast food indigenous to Japan. *Tachigui-soba* and *tachigui-udon* (stand-up noodle restaurants) are the main ones for people who want to "slurp and go" on a budget. Another favorite is *kaiten-zushi,* or sushi restaurants where a moving belt carries plates of very cheap sushi along in front of a counter. Take-out sushi shops are also popular.

Hoka-hoka bento is another recent fast food hit. A home-made meal packed in the shop, it's still warm when you get it home. And the price is a mere ¥300–¥500. A photo display panel will show the variations available. The big customers here are office workers, students, and housewives.

Another common packaged meal is the *eki-ben,* a packaged meal available at most train stations. The larger stations, Shinjuku, Tokyo, Ueno, and Shinagawa have their own name-brand *eki-ben.*

•International Cuisine

There are an increasingly wide range of choices for non-Japanese food. Restaurants specializing in Western cuisine such as Italian and French are plentiful, but the best are not cheap. Other restaurants specializing in Asian and non-Asian cuisine are now proliferating and are often surprisingly reasonable in price.

Districts

While restaurants can be found in every Tokyo neighborhood, they tend to be concentrated in the major commuter train station areas. These are just a few of the most important areas:

Roppongi is the most international dining area of Tokyo. Some of the best Japanese and foreign food is found in this area. Restaurants here tend to stay open later than in other parts of town. Just southwest of Roppongi are the Hiro-o and Azabu neighborhoods where more and more restaurants are locating.

Ginza is one of the traditional places to go for a nice dinner. Many of the oldest and most prestigious restaurants are found here. But since Ginza land price are among the highest in Tokyo, you're helping pay the rent with the considerable extra cost attached to the price of your meal.

Akasaka is where you'll find the largest concentration of *ryotei* in the city. Other Japanese-style restaurants cater to the night clubs and nearby Tokyo Broadcasting System television crowd.

Yurakucho is notable mainly for the rows of tiny *yakitori-ya* (*nomiya* serving *yakitori*) found along the back streets near the train tracks.

Downtown areas such as Asakusa and Ueno are full of restaurants with a *shitamachi* (downtown) feeling and atmosphere, good food, and prices that are very reasonable. The distance is intimidating to many foreigners who tend to keep to the south-western fringes of the city. Surprisingly, once you get there, you begin to wonder why it seemed like such a problem in the first place.

Etiquette

Strict rules of dining etiquette do exist in Japan, but as in the West they are rarely followed in real life. The saying "ignorance is bliss" is doubly true here where as a foreigner you're forgiven for almost any embarrassing breach of etiquette you might unwittingly commit. The best policy is to watch the people around you, but here are a few generalizations:

- The Japanese do not usually put sauces (particularly soy sauce) on their rice.
- Do not rest your chopsticks vertically in your rice. This is associated with death.
- Do not pass food to each other from chopsticks to chopsticks. Put the food on a plate. At Buddhist funerals, the bones of the cremated deceased person are passed this way.
- Sauces often come with condiments such as sliced green onions, grated radish, etc., which are meant to be mixed in, not eaten separately.
- Sauces are generally intended for dipping, not dunking and soaking the food. Doing so risks destroying the flavor of the often delicate Japanese cooking.
- When drinking beer or saké, one person will usually pour for the others, who will hold up their glasses while the drink is being poured. People take turns, which can sometimes become a bothersome ritual. As the night wears on, and the level of intoxication rises, it's everyone for themselves.
- When starting your meal say *Itadakimasu,* which means "I receive." At the end you can say *Gochiso-sama deshita,* which means "That was a lovely meal, thank you."

JAPANESE FOOD
Ordering

Ordering Japanese food can be a rather intimidating job. English menus are rare, and even when you know the main type of food being served (or can at least order by the "show and tell" method), ordering appetizers and side dishes is always difficult. The simplest solution is to order a set menu, called a *kosu* (course) or *teishoku*. Most restaurants will offer some sort of course. Ordering this way also gives you a general idea of how much your meal will cost.

If you want to order a la carte, the general practice is first to order an appetizer (often *sashimi*), then a few side dishes, followed by the entree, with soup and rice finishing the meal. We have listed a few common appetizer and side-dish menu items, and explained some general cooking terms. Following is a list of seasonal fish.

The restaurants have been divided by type of food. We've included entree menus and listed a few side dishes common to that particular type of cooking. Restaurant prices are as of Summer 1993.

•General Menu

Kosu	A full-course meal, as in Western restaurants.
Teishoku	Set menu—including a main dish with rice, soup, and pickles. Home cooking, *tempura, tonkatsu,* and *unagi* are usually offered this way. *Teishoku* sometimes is offered in three grades: *nami* (regular), *jo* (choice), and *tokujo* (deluxe).
Tsumami	Starters and side dishes.
morokyu	Cold cucumber served with a thick miso sauce.
itawasa	Sliced fish cake, served with soy sauce (add *wasabi*—green horseradish, if you wish).
sashimi	Raw fish
kinpira	Fried burdock root and carrots in a sauce seasoned with soy, sugar, and red pepper.
hijiki	Seaweed simmered in a soy and sugar sauce.
hiyayakko	Cold tofu served with chopped leeks, grated ginger, and soy sauce.
Gohan	Rice
onigiri	Rice balls (often triangular in shape) wrapped in dried seaweed. The center will be filled with *ume* (pickled sour plum), *sake* (salmon), or *tarako* (cooked codfish roe).

yaki-onigiri	Grilled *onigiri* seasoned with soy sauce.
ochazuke	A bowl of rice with tea or sometimes fish stock poured over it. Comes with *sake, tsukemono* (pickles), or *nori* (dried seaweed).
kamameshi	Steamed and seasoned rice with vegetables and a choice of chicken, crab, salmon, etc.
zosui	Rice that has been boiled in a seasoned soup, with *kani* (crab), *kaki* (oysters), egg, and various vegetables mixed in.

Shiru — Soup, usually with chopped leeks, bean curd, and seaweed.

misoshiru	Made with yellow (white) or brown (red) fermented soybean paste.
osuimono	Clear soup made with dried bonito flakes and *konbu* (seaweed.)

Yakimono — Fried or grilled foods.

robata-yaki	Usually, food cooked over an open grill.
sumibi-yaki	Food grilled over a charcoal hearth.
teppan-yaki	Food grilled over a flat grill.
ishi-yaki	Food cooked on hot stones.
shio-yaki	A grilling method using salt.
teriyaki	A grilling method for meat or fish that has been marinated and basted with sweet sauce.

Nimono — Usually fish or vegetables that have been boiled with soy sauce, sugar, and saké.

Mushimono — Foods that have been steamed.

chawan-mushi	Steamed egg with fish stock, similar to a custard.

-don (or *-donburi*) — *Don* means a pottery bowl, and by association any meal served in a bowl with rice. These are common lunch meals: *tendon* (tempura on rice) or *oyako-donburi* (chicken and egg on rice).

-ju — Means food served in a lacquered box, usually a small box with rice and something on top, such as *tenju* (tempura on rice).

• Seasonal Fish

Spring

hirame	halibut/flounder
mutsu	bluefish
hamachi	yellowtail (young)
sayori	halfbeak
tai	sea bream
shira-uo	whitebait
nishin	herring

Summer

kuruma-ebi	large prawn
isaki	grunt
aji	horse mackerel
kisu	sillago/smelt
awabi	abalone
anago	conger eel
ayu	river trout
masu	trout
ainame	rock trout
ika	squid
katsuo	bonito

Autumn

saba	mackerel
iwashi	sardine
sanma	mackerel/pike
sake	salmon

Winter

ise-ebi	spiny lobster/crayfish
karei	turbot
tako	octopus
sawara	spanish mackerel
kani	crab
akagai	red clam
kaki	oyster
buri	yellowtail (mature)
maguro	tuna
aoyagi	round clam
tara	haddock/cod
hatahata	sandfish

JAPANESE RESTAURANTS
Kaiseki-ryori

When the tea ceremony became popular in Kyoto during the Ashikaga period, *kaiseki-ryori* was a light meal of three or four dishes served to help protect the stomach from the strong green tea. *Kaiseki* literally means a "warm stone on the stomach," a reference to the heated stones monks placed in their robes during meditation to help them forget their hunger pains.

Kaiseki is one of the most expensive kinds of Japanese cooking with *haute cuisine* prices that can be easily over ¥15,000 per person. Some restaurants do offer less expensive courses, others have a *bento* box that will give you the general idea of what *kaiseki* is like. While the best *kaiseki* meals in Tokyo are extremely expensive, for just a little more money you can stay in a beautiful *ryokan* an hour or so outside of the city where a fabulous *kaiseki* meal will be included with the room charge.

Menu—*Kaiseki* restaurants usually serve a set menu.

How to Order

- Since *kaiseki* usually comes as a set meal, you can order according to the price.
- There is a set of very formal rules for eating *kaiseki-ryori*, but since even most Japanese don't know them, you should just follow the basic rules we mentioned before.

Asakusa's Tatsumiya. The restaurant's *noren* is hung out in front of the door announcing to customers that it's open for business. © 1984 Tobias Pfeil

KOCHO 胡蝶　千代田区有楽町 1-12 新有楽町ビル

Shin Yurakucho Bldg., B1-2, 1-12-1 Yurakucho, Chiyoda-ku. Tel: 3214-4741 (B-2), 3214-4746 (B-1). Hours: 11:00 A.M.–2:00 P.M., 5:00–9:00 P.M., closed Sun. & hol. If you can't manage to wrangle the introduction necessary for dining at the prestigious, exclusive and very expensive **KITCHO** (8-17-4 Ginza, Chuo-ku. Tel: 3541-8228.), Kocho is a very acceptable alternative. Deep in the basement of a central Tokyo building, your excellent *kaiseki* meal will be served in a thatch-roofed dining area surrounded by bamboo groves and a pond full of majestic carp. Here lunch is from ¥25,000, dinner from ¥52,000. On the B1 floor is a more casual area serving slightly less refined *kaiseki* cuisine. [M-10]

TAKAMURA 篁　港区六本木 3-4-27

3-4-27 Roppongi, Minato-ku. Tel: 3585-6600. Hours: noon–3:00 P.M. (reservations only, four people or more), 5:00–10:30 P.M., closed Sun. Lunch courses from ¥10,000. Dinner courses from ¥15,000. With an absolutely wonderful and very Japanese atmosphere, this restaurant looks and feels like a teahouse in the mountains. There is a lovely garden and each room has a hearth. [M-1]

TSUKIJI TAMURA つきじ田村　中央区築地 2-12-11

2-12-11 Tsukiji, Chuo-ku. Tel: 3541-1611. Hours: noon–3:00 P.M., 6:00–10:00 P.M. daily. This famous restaurant has recently been rebuilt, and is now in a seven-story building. On the first floor you can have *kaiseki-ryori* at a table with chairs: lunch from ¥6,000, dinner from ¥8,000. On the second and third floors you can sit on tatami mats and have lunch from ¥10,000, dinner from ¥30,000. [M-22]

HANNYAEN 般若苑　港区白金台 2-20-10

2-20-10 Shirogane-dai, Minato-ku. Tel: 3441-1256. Hours: 6:00–10:00 P.M., closed Sun. & hol. In lovely grounds shared with the Hatakeyama Collection, **Hannyaen** is a sprawling, traditional Japanese-style estate. Your *kaiseki* meal will be served in a room overlooking the garden and an evening will include a performance by *koto* players. Although the food is not absolutely top grade, the atmosphere is suitably intriguing to justify the costs. ¥40,000 per person. Lunches are possible for groups of over five people. [M-19]

HOUMASA 庖正　港区元麻布 3-2-21 ルミエール元麻布

3-2-21 Moto-azabu, Minato-ku. Tel: 3479-2880. Hours: 6:00–10:30 P.M., closed Sun & hol. Houmasa is ideal for perfect *kaiseki* cuisine without the formality of most top-ranked restaurants. You can sit at the counter and watch the chef, or on tatami at the two tiny tables along one wall. It's best if you can order a la carte in Japanese, but they also offer an *omakase* course (chef's choice) for ¥13,000. [M-2]

KISSO 吉左右　港区六本木 5-17-1 アクシスビル

Axis Bldg., 5-17-1 Roppongi, Minato-ku, B1. Tel: 3582-4191. Hours: 11:30 A.M.–2:00 P.M., 5:30–10:00 P.M., closed Sun. **Kisso** serves excellent, but simple *kaiseki* in one of the most pleasant contemporary settings in Tokyo, which probably explains why this restaurant is a favorite with the local design elite. Lunch from ¥2,500, dinner from ¥8,000. [M-1]

Shojin-ryori

A traditional form of vegetarian cuisine, *shojin-ryori* was developed in Buddhist temples where eating meat, fish, or any animal product was against the tenets of the religion. The style of cooking was brought from China to Japan by the *Zen* monk Dogen (1200–53) after his training in the Chinese monasteries. The meal was rearranged to suit Japanese tastes and is now rather like a humble version of *kaiseki*.

Shojin-ryori is served in restaurants or at temples, where it is a special meal for guests. The monks themselves usually eat one bowl of rice in the morning, a bowl of rice and one of soup for lunch, and nothing for dinner.

Menu

• *Shojin-ryori* is usually as a set course of several dishes with rice and soup.

- In place of meat and fish, they have devised numerous ways of preparing soybeans, one of the main ones being tofu.

How to Order—Just ask for *kaiseki*.

DAIGO　醍醐　港区愛宕 2-4-2
2-4-2 Atago, Minato-ku. Tel: 3431-0811. Hours: noon–3:00 P.M., 5:00–9:00 P.M., closed Thurs. Charming building and gardens in this restaurant attached to a Buddhist temple. Meals served in traditional private rooms. Lunch from ¥12,000, dinner from ¥14,000 [M-11]

BON　梵　台東区竜泉 1-2-11
1-2-11 Ryusen, Taito-ku. Tel: 3872-0375. Hours: noon–1:00 P.M., 5:00–8:00 P.M., closed Tue. This is a wonderful restaurant, but slightly out of the way. Lunch from ¥6,000, dinner from ¥7,000, prepared in a style that originated in Manpuku-ji temple in China. Tables are all in simple, Japanese-style semi-private rooms. [M-40]

SANKOIN TEMPLE　三光院　小金井市本町 3-1-36
3-1-36 Honcho, Koganei-shi. Tel: (0423) 81-1116. Hours: noon–2:00 P.M., 2:00–4:00 P.M., closed Tues., Aug. 1–31, and Dec. 25–Jan 10. (Located a ten-minute walk from the north exit of Musashi Koganei Station on the Chuo Line.) This convent, built in 1934, is the most famous temple serving *shojin-ryori*. Reservations are accepted up to one month in advance; during the busy spring and autumn seasons, you should book early. Courses from ¥2,000 [off Map]

MURYOAN　無量庵　港区赤坂 6-9-17
6-9-17 Akasaka, Minato-ku. Tel: 3585-5829. Hours: noon–3:00 P.M., 5:00–9:00 P.M., closed Mon. Like **Bon**, **Muryoan** offers a type of monk's food that originated in China: *fucha-ryori*. All meals are served in private *tatami* rooms. Lunch ¥11,000, dinner ¥17,000 [M-6]

Sushi

A favorite question of the Japanese to the foreigner used to be "Can you eat raw fish?" While in years past about seventy-five percent of the answers were a definitive (if not disgusted) No, most visitors now look forward to their first real Japanese sushi meal. Raw fish has been demystified, and chances are that now you'll be asked "Can you eat *natto?*" which is a sticky kind of fermented soybean that half of the Japanese population won't eat themselves.

During the Heian period, a primitive form of sushi was a favorite delicacy of the aristocracy. Sliced raw fish was soaked in a salt brine that naturally fermented and preserved it. The slightly sour sushi became so popular that demand for the fermented fish exceeded supply. The solution was to put fresh sliced fish on vinegared rice. In the Edo period the art of sushi reached its current form as *nigiri-zushi* and became the favorite meal of the city-wise *Edokko*.

Ideally, sushi is prepared by thinly slicing only the choicest parts of the freshest of fish, and serving it on a bed of specially prepared, vinegar-flavored rice. Sometimes a dab of *wasabi*, green horseradish, is spread between the two. The sushi chef trains for years, spending two or three on just the rice balls, before he is considered a master.

Menu–These are the types of fish most commonly served as *sushi*:

maguro	tuna
toro	tuna belly

hamachi	yellowtail (young)
ika	squid
tako	octopus (boiled)
anago	conger eel (cooked & served with a sweet sauce)
ikura	salmon roe
uni	sea urchin roe
katsuo	bonito
ebi	shrimp (boiled)
ama-ebi	shrimp (raw)
awabi	abalone
akagai	red clam
hotate	scallop
tamago	cooked egg
norimaki	raw fish and various fillings rolled in dried seaweed
kappamaki	*norimaki* with cucumber
tekkamaki	*norimaki* with tuna
chirashi-zushi	raw fish with various other ingredients scattered on top of a bowl of rice (good for lunch)
gari	pickled ginger served as a sushi condiment
wasabi	green horseradish that is mixed in with the soy sauce when eating *sashimi* (use sparingly or you lose the flavor of the fish).

How to Order

- As an hors d'oeuvre, *sashimi* is usually eaten with saké before the sushi.
- If you sit at the counter, you can order your sushi by pointing at or naming the fish. At a table you can also order piece by piece, but the best and easiest way is to order a set course such as *matsu* (expensive), *take* (medium), or *ume* (inexpensive). If you want more after the course, you can then order more of your favorites.
- When you make an order, the sushi will usually come in a pair.
- Certain fish are particularly good at certain times of the year. See the list of seasonal fish, or order by asking for "*Shun no sakana.*"
- To eat the sushi, use your hands and dip it, fish side down, in soy sauce you've poured into a small dish. Cooked fish such as *anago* shouldn't be dipped since they will already be sauced.

TSUKIJI FISH MARKET   Go early in the morning and have the freshest fish possible at one of the sushi shops in the area. [M-22]

KIYOTA   きよ田　中央区銀座 6-3-15
6-3-15 Ginza, Chuo-ku. Tel: 3572-4854. Hours: 11:30 A.M.–8:00 P.M., closed Sun. & hol. If you

checked in any Japanese restaurant guide, this famous sushi bar would probably be given top ratings for food, service, and atmosphere. There is no need to order here, the chef will just present you with possibly the best fish in town. Its list of regulars is also impressive: assorted politicians, captains of industry, and other celebrities. A minimal sushi meal will start at ¥25,000. [M-8]

FUKUZUSHI 福鮨し　港区六本木 5-7-8
5-7-8 Roppongi, Minato-ku. Tel: 3402-4116. Hours: 11:30 A.M.–2:00 P.M., 5:30–11:00 P.M., closed Sun. Considered by some to be the best sushi restaurant in town. Very good sushi in a sleek, modern setting. Courses from ¥6,000. [M-1]

ICHIKAN 市勘　渋谷区代官山町 10-5
9-5 Daikanyama-cho, Shibuya-ku. Tel: 3461-2002. Hours: 11:30 A.M.–2:00 P.M., 5:00–11:00 P.M., closed Mon. An excellent classic sushi bar, rather on the spacious side, so it is particularly good for larger groups (it gets crowded so try to make reservations). A meal here will cost upward of ¥10,000. [M-20]

KIKAKUZUSHI きかく寿司　港区南青山 3-7-2
3-7-2 Minami Aoyama, Minato-ku. Tel: 3401-3880. Hours: noon–3:00 P.M., 5:00–10:00 P.M., closed Mon. Small and intimate, Kikakuzushi has the feel of a friendly neighborhood sushi bar. A basic meal here runs from about ¥5,000. [M-5]

SUSHI SEI 寿司清　中央区銀座 8-2-13 第 7 金井ビル／青山ベルコモンズ／港区六本木 5-9-20
Ginza: Dainana Kanai Bldg., 1F, 8-2-13 Ginza, Chuo-ku. Tel: 3572-4770. Hours: 11:45 A.M.– 2:00 P.M., 4:45–10:40 P.M., closed Sun. & hol. [M-8] Aoyama: Bell Commons, 5F, Tel: 3475-8053. Hours: 11:30 A.M.–2:30 P.M., 5:30–10:30 P.M. Sat., Sun., & hol.: 11:30 A.M.–9:30 P.M. [M-5] Roppongi: 3-2-9 Nishi Azabu, Minato-ku. Tel: 3401-0578. Hours: 11:45 A.M.–2:30 P.M., 4:45–10:45 P.M., Sun. & hol.: 11:45 A.M.–9:30 P.M., closed second and third Wed. [M-1] A reputable, medium-priced sushi restaurant, there are numerous branches throughout the city. The restaurants have good basic sushi-bar interiors and good food. About ¥4,000 per person.

TSUKIJI EDOGIN 築地江戸銀　中央区築地 4-5-1
4-5-1 Tsukiji, Chuo-ku. Tel: 3542-4401. Hours: 11:00 A.M.–9:30 P.M., closed Sun. This old shop, located near the fish market, is famous for the size of their sushi as well as its taste and low prices. Their *tamago-yaki* is huge. About ¥3,000 per person. [M-22]

MATSUKAN まつ勘　港区麻布十番 3-4-12
3-4-12 Azabu-juban, Minato-ku. Tel: 3455-4923. Hours: noon–2:00 P.M., 5:00–11:00 P.M. (Sat.: noon–10:30 P.M., Sun. & hol.: noon–9:00 P.M.), closed Mon. The food, service, and interior is just like a sushi bar should be. Cost is about ¥7,000 per person. For a side dish, try their *hotate no shioyaki* (grilled scallop) or other *shioyaki*-style fish. [M-1]

SAKAEZUSHI HONTEN 栄寿司本店　新宿区新宿 3-6-2
3-6-2 Shinjuku, Shinjuku-ku. Tel: 3351-2525. Hours: 11:30 A.M.–11:30 P.M. daily. *Kohaku-don, maguro,* and *ika* on sushi rice are their specialties. About ¥2,000 per person. [M-7]

SUSHI BAR SAI スシ・バー彩　渋谷区神南 1-7-5 ランブリング・コア・アンドス・ビル
Rambling Core Andos Bldg., 2F, 1-7-5 Jinnan, Shibuya-ku. Tel: 3496-6333. Hours: 5:30 P.M.– 1:00 A.M. daily, hol. 4:00–10:00 P.M. Western-influenced sushi bar serves *California-maki,* (rolled sushi with avocado) and *tofu-zushi* using tofu instead of rice. Courses only, from ¥1,200. [M-3]

GENROKUZUSHI 元禄寿司　渋谷区神宮前 5-8-5
5-8-5 Jingumae, Shibuya-ku. Tel: 3498-3968. Hours: 11:00 A.M.–9:00 P.M. daily. Fast-food sushi by this chain of sushi restaurants. A conveyor belt moves plates of sushi along in front of the customer. You just pick out what you want. Cost is ¥120 per plate. There is a branch of this shop in most major districts. [M-4]

Tempura

While some people claim that tempura was originally a Portuguese recipe, others will say the Portuguese stole the idea from China. Whatever the case, tempura has become one of the mainstays of Japanese cooking. Many tempura fanatics claim the secret to the tempura lies in the oil. The best Tokyo restaurants will use expensive sesame oil, that leaves no aftertaste. In Osaka a lighter vegetable oil is preferred. Most tempura restaurants also serve *sashimi*.

Menu

teishoku	A set menu that usually consists of *ebi* (shrimp), *kisu*(light, white fish), *ika*(squid), *anago* (Conger eel), *piman* (small green peppers), *kakiage* (shrimp in balls of batter), rice, pickles, and miso soup.
tendon, tenju	These two are usually prawns and vegetables served on rice, with a sauce poured over the top.

You can also order a la carte:

kaibashira	shell ligament
nori	dried seaweed
tamanegi	onion
shiitake	mushrooms
shiso	perilla
shishito	a very small green pepper
nasu	eggplant
kabocha	squash
satsumaimo	sweet potato
tentsuyu	dipping bowl of soy sauce and *dashi* fish-stock soup base to which is added grated *daikon* (white radish) and ginger, the usual accompaniment to tempura

How to Order

• You can order the set meal *teishoku* and if you want more, then order a la carte. This is the best and cheapest way.

• Tempura should be eaten while it's hot. The *tentsuyu* sauce will be in a small pitcher, pour it into the empty bowl you're given, and mix in the ginger and radish. Dip the *tempura* into the sauce. Don't let it stay there and soak or it will not only lose its taste, but will look disgusting.

TEN'ICHI　天一　中央区銀座 6-6-5

6-6-5 Ginza, Chuo-ku. Tel: 3571-1949. Hours: 11:30 A.M.–10:00 P.M. daily. One of the best and most famous *tempura* restaurants in Tokyo, Ten'ichi has more than ten branches throughout the city. Lunch is from ¥7,000, dinner from ¥8,500. *Tendon* served until 4:00 P.M. is ¥4,000. [M-8]

TSUNAHACHI　つな八　新宿区新宿 3-31-8/渋谷区宇田川町 23-3 第一勧銀共同ビル

Shinjuku: 3-31-8 Shinjuku, Shinjuku-ku. Tel: 3352-1011. Hours: 11:00 A.M.–10:00 P.M. daily. [M-7] Shibuya: Daiichi Kangin Kyodo Bldg., 6F, 2-23-3 Udagawa-cho, Shibuya-ku. Tel: 3476-6059. Hours: 11:30 A.M.–10:30 P.M. daily. [M-3] A reasonably priced *tempura* restaurant with over thirty-six branches in Tokyo, their *teishoku* set is only ¥1,050. Try a la carte if you still have room for it: *hashira no norimaki* (shellfish wrapped in seaweed), *tamago no kimi* (egg yolk), or *ice cream* (fried!) for dessert.

MIYAGAWA　みや川　港区南青山 6-1-6

6-1-6 Minami Aoyama, Minato-ku. Tel: 3400-3722. Hours: noon–2:00 P.M., 5:00–11:00 P.M., closed Sun. & hol. This small and unpretentious restaurant right in the middle of Tokyo's most fashionable district serves excellent Osaka-style tempura. Lunch from ¥1,500, dinner courses from ¥6,000. [M-5]

NAKASEI 中清　台東区浅草 1-39-13
1-39-13 Asakusa, Taito-ku. Tel: 3841-4015. Hours: noon–3:00 P.M., 4:00–8:00 P.M., closed Tue. Pleasant restaurant preserving the atmosphere of old Tokyo. Situated near Asakusa Kokaido Hall. *Teishoku* set ¥2,800. [M-12]

TENSHIGE 天茂　港区赤坂 3-6-10 第 3 セイコービル
Daisan Seiko Bldg., 2F, 3-6-10 Akasaka, Minato-ku. Tel: 3583-3230. Hours: 11:30 A.M.–2:00 P.M., 6:00–8:30 P.M., closed Sun. & hol. The master of this small and friendly restaurant will personally fry your meal of authentic Edo-style tempura. The lunch special is *tendon* or *kakiage-don* at ¥1,300 . Dinner courses from ¥7,000. [M-6]

UKIYO 宇喜代　港区麻布十番 2-1-11
2-1-1 Azabu-juban, Minato-ku. Tel: 3455-2254. Hours: 11:30 A.M.–2:00 P.M., 5:00–10:00 P.M., closed Tue. A simple neighborhood restaurant, the tempura is great and the staff very friendly. Lunch from ¥1,100, dinner course from ¥4,000. [M-1]

Yakitori

A favorite hangout for the Japanese *salariman* on his way home from work, most *yakitori* restaurants are technically not restaurants, but *nomiya*. The art refined is served in more sophisticated restaurants for those who find the under-the-tracks *yakitori* spots not quite to their taste. *Yakitori* at its best is skewered bits of chicken, charcoal broiled to the perfect crispy on the outside, succulent on the inside stage.

Menu

sei-niku	chicken dark meat
sasami	chicken breast meat
negima	chicken and leeks (other combinations of chicken and vegetables are also served, depending on the restaurant)
reba	chicken liver
tsukune	meatballs
kawa	skin
tebasaki	wings
piman	green peppers
shiitake	large mushrooms
negi	leek
ginnan	ginkgo nuts
uzura	quail eggs

Side Dishes:

oroshi	grated white radish with a raw quail's egg on top to be used mixed with soy sauce or as a dip for *yakitori*
nikomi	stew of pork, tripe, etc.
kamameshi	steamed seasoned rice with vegetables and a choice of chicken, crab, salmon, etc.

How to Order

- Order a side dish to eat while you're waiting for the grilled items.
- The grilled food is usually served meat first and vegetables last. You can usually see what's available since seats tend to be at a counter surrounding the grill.
- Some of the dishes are good with *tare* (a slightly sweet sauce), others are best with just lemon and salt. There will be a small jar of *shichimi,* a hot combination of seven spices that can be sprinkled at will.
- You can bite the food right off the skewers or slip it off with your chopsticks.

TORIGIN　鳥ぎん　港区六本木 4-12-6

4-12-6 Roppongi, Minato-ku. Tel: 3403-5829. Hours: 11:30 A.M.–2:00 P.M., 5:00–10:30 P.M., closed Sun. One of the best known *yakitori* restaurants in town, this is just one of a chain of many Torigins spread throughout the city. The restaurants are all comfortably casual, and the food is basic but good. Courses from ¥940. [M-1]
Other branches are at Shibuya: Kakugin Bldg., B1, 1-13-9 Shibuya, Shibuya-ku. Tel: 3486-9831. Hours: 11:30 A.M.–10:00 P.M. daily. (11:30 A.M.–9:00 P.M. Sun. & hol.) [M-3]
Ginza: 5-5-7 Ginza, Chuo-ku. Tel 3571-3333. Hours: 11:30 A.M.–9:30 P.M. daily. (11:30 A.M.–9:00 P.M., Sun. & hol.) [M-8]

TORICHO　鳥長　港区六本木 7-14-1

7-14-1 Roppongi, Minato-ku. Tel: 3401-1827. Hours: 5:00–11:00 P.M. daily. This rather classy *yakitori* restaurant even made it into the *Town & Country* list of recommended Tokyo restaurants a few years back. It is very good, the setting very relaxed. *Omakase* course ¥4,000. [M-1]

NANBANTEI　南蛮亭　港区六本木 4-5-6/渋谷区渋谷 2-21-12

4-5-6 Roppongi, Minato-ku. Tel: 3402-0606. Hours: 5:30–11:30 P.M. daily. [M1] Shibuya branch: Tokyu Bunka Kaikan 2nd Fl., 2-21-12 Shibuya, Shibuya-ku. Tel: 3498-0940. Hours: 11:00 A.M.–2:00 P.M., 5:00–10:45 P.M. daily. [M3]. Try their *nanban-yaki*—beef dipped in hot *miso* and grilled. The *asupara-maki* is green asparagus wrapped in thinly sliced pork. Dinner course from ¥3,500.

ISEHIRO　伊勢廣　中央区京橋 1-5-4

1-5-4 Kyobashi, Chuo-ku. Tel: 3281-5864. Hours: 11:30–2:00 P.M., 4:30–9:00 P.M., closed Sun. & hol. In this nearly sixty-year-old restaurant, you can eat an entire hen, bit-by-bit, for ¥4,500. If you can't make it through the whole bird, just say you've had enough, and you'll only pay for what you've eaten. Lunch costs around ¥1,500. [M-9]

GANCHAN　がんちゃん　港区六本木 6-8-23 岡上ビル

Okaue Bldg., 1F, 6-8-23 Roppongi, Minato-ku. Tel: 3478-0092. Hours: 6:00 P.M.–2:00 A.M. daily, until midnight on Sun. & hol. This place can best be described as pure Japanese funk. The interior is classic *yakitori-ya* style, the music is either *enka* or California surfer tunes. The crew is amicable and casual. Food is great. Course meal ¥2,500. [M-1]

Robata-yaki

Probably the noisiest restaurants in the world, *robata-yaki* restaurants are known for the lively shouting of the staff welcoming the guests and calling in orders. Though some first-time foreigners mistake the shouts for anger, it's all in good fun. *Robata-yaki* is country-style cooking, a variety of simple and hearty dishes of mostly seafood and vegetables prepared over a *robata* grill. The atmosphere is usually postcard perfect with Japanese decor and a restaurant crew in provincial costume. The food is great, very simple, and filling.

Menu—Just about anything can be ordered in a *robata-yaki* restaurant, but the specialty is the food grilled on the open *robata* in front of the counter.

Shio–yaki: a whole fish grilled with a bit of salt

nishin	herring
karei	flounder/turbot
sanma	pike
aji	horse mackerel
ika	squid
shishamo	smelt
ebi	shrimp

Vegetables:

nasu	eggplant
piman	green peppers
negi	leek
shiitake	mushrooms
ginnan	ginkgo nuts
atsu-age	deep-fried tofu
satsuma-age	deep-fried ground fish

Side dishes:

nikujaga	a stew of meat and potatoes
jagabata	grilled potatoes with butter

How to Order

- Because grilled foods take time to cook, order *sashimi* first, or a couple of side dishes along with the grilled fish. The fish will be displayed in front of you so you can just point. Finish the meal with *onigiri* and *oshinko* (pickles).

- There will usually be some special seasonal fish. To order, just ask *Kyo wa nani ga oishii desu ka?* or "What's good today?"

- Eat the grilled fish and vegetables with a bit of soy sauce. *Onigiri* are eaten plain.

INAKAYA 田舎屋　港区六本木 7-8-4/港区赤坂 3-12-7
Roppongi: 7-8-4 Roppongi, Minato-ku. Tel: 3405-9866. Hours: 5:00 P.M.–5:00 A.M. daily. [M-1] Akasaka: 3-12-7 Akasaka, Minato-ku. Tel: 3586-3054. Hours: 5:00–11:00 P.M. daily. [M-6] One of the most picturesque *robata-yaki* restaurants in town, the cooks sit on a platform right in front of the counter. Dinner will cost about ¥10,000 per person.

OKAJOKI 陸蒸気　中野区中野 5-59-3
3-59-3 Nakano, Nakano-ku. Tel: 3228-1239. Hours: 11:30 A.M.–1:00 P.M., 5:00–11:00 P.M., (4:00–10:00 P.M., Sun. & hol.). A huge hearth and kitchen, surrounded by an equally huge counter, they serve food in appropriately huge portions. A single *onigiri* is enough for two. Cost is about ¥3,000–¥4,000 per person. [M-26]

GONIN BYAKUSHO 五人百姓　港区六本木 3-10-3 六本木スクエアビル 10F
Roppongi Square Building, 4F, 3-10 Roppongi, Minato-ku. Tel: 3470-1675. Hours: 11:30 A.M.– 2:30 P.M., 5:00–10:30 P.M., closed Sun. & hol. At the entrance you'll find lockers. Just like in the public baths, put your shoes in and lock them up. The restaurant is run by a famous sushi company called *Kyotaru,* and they have the usual *robata-yaki* menu plus specialty items like *chakin-*

shumai—steamed minced meat wrapped in a thin egg casing. Courses start at ¥4,000. The name means "the five farmers," and the atmosphere is suitably rural. [M-1]

TORA 寅 渋谷区恵比寿 3-49-1

3-49-1 Ebisu, Shibuya-ku. Tel: 3440-0917. Hours: 6:00 P.M.–midnight, closed Sun. & hol. A rather fashionable, newer restaurant, with simple but good food. [M-2]

OKAJU 岡重 目黒区自由ヶ丘 1-26-3

1-26-3 Jiyugaoka, Meguro-ku. Tel: 3717-0781. Hours: 5:00–11:30 P.M. daily. This shop has some interesting additions to the usual *robata-yaki* menu: *manju*, minced chicken wrapped with mashed potato and served in a soup; *kintoki-guratan*, a sweet potato gratin, etc. About ¥5,000 per person. [M-21]

Kushi-age

Originally an Osaka specialty, *kushi* means skewer and *age* means deep fried. Fish, meat, or vegetables are skewered, dipped in batter then bread crumbs, and deep-fried. This is a delicious, but comparatively little-known Japanese meal.

Menu

Set Course	Usually consists of salad, six to ten skewers of *kushi-age*, rice or noodles, miso soup, and pickles.
ebi	prawn
kani no tsume	crab claw
tori	chicken
gyuniku	beef
shiitake	mushroom
asupara	asparagus
imo	potato
konnyaku	arrowroot gelatin

Side Dishes:

soba	Japanese buckwheat noodles
kayaku gohan	seasoned rice
ochazuke	a bowl of rice covered with hot green tea or fish broth

How to Order

• Ordering the set menu is the easiest and usually cheapest way.

• The chef will tell you if the *kushi-age* skewer needs sauce (*sosu de dozo*=please use the sauce), salt (*shio de dozo*=please use salt), or if it's best plain (*kono mama de dozo*). When you are almost through with your *kushi-age*, the chef will ask *Gohan to soba no dochira ni shimasu ka?* or "Will you have rice (*gohan*) or noodles (*soba*)?" You decide.

CHISEN 知仙 港区六本木 4-12-5/ 六本木 7-16-5

4-12-5 Roppongi, Minato-ku. Tel: 3403-7677. Hours: 5:30–11:00 P.M., closed Mon. Another branch in Roppongi is at 7-16-5 Roppongi, Minato-ku. Tel: 3478-6241, closed Sun. They have a great course for ¥4,500, then another "flexible" course where you get all of the side dishes, but pay only for as much *kushi-age* as you can eat. [M-1]

HANTEI　はん亭　文京区根津2-12-15

2-12-15 Nezu, Bunkyo-ku. Tel: 3828-1440. Hours: 5:00–10:30 P.M., closed Sun. & third Mon. This three-story wooden structure looks like an old country house. Part of the restaurant is a converted storehouse with a small tatami seating area. *Kushi-age* course menus start with twelve skewers for ¥4,000. Next door is a quiet coffee shop. [M-13]

KUSHINOBO　串の坊　港区赤坂3-10-17

3-10-17 Akasaka, Minato-ku. Tel: 3586-7390. Hours: 11:30 A.M.–2:00 P.M., 5:00–9:30 P.M. daily. One skewer from ¥150. Try their *shiitake-toriniku-hasami,* a large mushroom stuffed with minced chicken; or their *shiso-maki-ebi,* a prawn wrapped in *shiso* leaves. Lunch ¥720. Dinner about ¥2,500 per person. [M-6]

Tonkatsu

When eating meat became possible during the Meiji period, pork and beef were popularly served as *katsu,* cutlets dipped in flour, egg, and bread crumbs, then deep fried. Now, mainly pork is served this way, the best having a light and flaky crust while the meat is thick, moist, and tender. A fairly inexpensive meal, *tonkatsu* is popular both as a lunch and a family dinner. Fish and vegetables are also sometimes served this way.

Menu

hire-katsu	fillet cutlets (all lean meat)
rosu-katsu	loin cutlets (some fat meat)
kushi-katsu	meat skewered with onions
ebi-furai	fried prawns
korokke	potato croquette
tonjiru	miso soup with pork and vegetables
akadashi	red miso soup

TONKI　とんき　目黒区下目黒1-1-2

1-1-2 Shimo-meguro, Meguro-ku. Tel: 3491-9928. Hours: 4:00 P.M.–10:45 P.M., closed Tue & third Mon. One of the great Tokyo *tonkatsu* restaurants, you may have to wait a while for a seat here since it's always busy. They dip their *katsu* in the egg and flour batter three times (once is usual); this keeps the pork crunchy on the outside and moist on the inside. *Katsu teishoku* is ¥1,450. [M-19]

HONKE PONTA　本家ぽん多　台東区上野3-23-2

3-23-2 Ueno, Taito-ku. Tel: 3831-2351. Hours: 11:00 A.M.–2:00 P.M., 4:30–8:00 P.M., closed Mon. The oldest *tonkatsu* restaurant in Tokyo, their *tonkatsu* is also the thickest and most tender. Other special dishes on their menu are *ebi* cream croquettes and tongue or beef stew. *Tonkatsu* is ¥2,500. [M-13]

MAISEN　まい泉　渋谷区神宮前4-8-5

4-8-5 Jingumae, Shibuya-ku. Tel: 3470-0071. Hours: 11:00 A.M.–10:00 P.M. daily. This big and busy *tonkatsu* restaurant offers a huge selection of other items including vegetable *tonkatsu* that even vegetarians will love. [M-4]

Sukiyaki and *Shabu-shabu*

Sukiyaki has been a popular meal since eating meat lost its taboo status in the Meiji period. A fairly easy dish to prepare, it's often produced in the home. Specialized restaurants have their own "secret" broth that makes the dish particularly good and most will cook it for you at the burner on your table. The basic ingredient is the beef, sliced paper-thin and sautéed for just a few seconds in the hot pan in front of you. A broth is then added, and the beef is lightly simmered. The best beef is that from Matsuzaka, where the cattle are pampered and protected, even massaged, to ensure the most tender of meats. After the beef is cooked, a selection of vegetables will be added to the pot.

Shabu-shabu is named for the *shabu-shabu* sound of the thinly-sliced beef swishing in the boiling broth. The major difference between *sukiyaki* and *shabu-shabu* is the broth. For *sukiyaki,* the broth is soy-based, thick, and slightly sweet, while the *shabu-shabu* broth is a clear stock, only lightly seasoned. Restaurants often serve both dishes.

Menu

- Sukiyaki—A set menu will include the beef (*gyuniku*) and vegetables such as leeks (*negi*), carrots (*ninjin*), mushrooms (*shiitake* and *enok-idake*), chrysanthemum leaves (*shungiku*), tofu, etc. In addition, you'll be served rice, miso soup, and pickles.

- *Shabu-shabu*—The set menu is similar to that of *sukiyaki,* but at the end of the meal noodles will be added to the broth.

Ordering and Eating

- Sukiyaki—The waitress will do most of the cooking for you. Each person is given a bowl with a beaten raw egg in it. Use the egg as a dip for the beef.

- *Shabu-shabu*—The waitress will help, but you will cook the meat piece by piece in the boiling pot (it only takes a few seconds). Dip the cooked meat in the ground sesame, chopped green onions, the *ponzu* sauce made with soy and vinegar, or the *goma-dare*, a sauce of ground sesame and fish stock. After the meat is finished, the vegetables will be added to the broth. The waitress will probably do this for you.

ZAKURO ざくろ 港区赤坂 1-9-15 日本自転車会館 B1/赤坂 5-3-3 赤坂 TBS 会館 B1
Nihon Jitensha Kaikan, B1, 1-9-15 Akasaka, Minato-ku. Tel: 3582-2661. [M-11] Akasaka TBS Kaikan, B1, 5-3-3 Akasaka. Tel: 3582-6841. [M-6] Ginza Sanwa Bldg., B1, 4-6-1 Ginza, Chuo-ku. Tel: 3538-4421. [M-8] Hours: 11:00 A.M.–10:00 P.M. (Ginza branch until 9:00 P.M.). This top-rated *shabu-shabu* restaurant has three branches. The atmosphere is suitably Japanese and the food excellent. *Shabu-shabu* from ¥3,000, sukiyaki from ¥ 14,000.

CHIN'YA ちんや 台東区浅草 1-3-4
1-3-4 Asakusa, Taito-ku. Tel: 3841-0010. Hours: 11:30 A.M.–9:30 P.M., closed Wed. A famous restaurant since the Meiji period, the current restaurant is in a seven-story building (in the basement part, you don't have to take off your shoes). *Sukiyaki-teishoku* (B1) ¥2,400. Sukiyaki from ¥6,000. *Shabu-shabu teishoku* from ¥2,600. [M-12]

HASEJIN はせ甚 港区麻布台 3-3-15
3-3-15 Azabu-dai, Minato-ku. Tel: 3582-7811. Hours: 11:30 A.M.–10:30 P.M., closed Sun. A great beef restaurant, they have a *gyu-kaiseki* course (beef *kaiseki*) from ¥10,000. Sukiyaki courses from ¥12,000, *shabu-shabu* from ¥8,000. [M-1]

SHABUSEN しゃぶせん 中央区銀座 5-8-20 銀座コアビル
Ginza Core Bldg., B2 & 2F, 5-8-20 Ginza, Chuo-ku. Tel: 3572-3806/3571-1717. Hours: 11:00 A.M.–10:00 P.M. daily. One of the most inexpensive *shabu-shabu* restaurants in town with courses from ¥3,200. [M-8]

NARUSE なるせ　港区六本木6-8-17
6-8-17 Roppongi, Minato-ku. Tel: 3403-7666. Hours: 5:00–11:00 P.M., closed Sun. Sukiyaki and *shabu-shabu,* all-you-can-eat courses for just over ¥4,000. [M-1]
BOTAN ぼたん　千代田区神田須田町1-15
1-15 Kanda Suda-cho, Chiyoda-ku. Tel: 3251-0577. Hours: noon–8:00 P.M., closed Sun. & hol. Chicken sukiyaki served in private tatami rooms with charcoal braziers. Homey atmosphere. Sukiyaki course from ¥5,300. [M-14]

Soba

Soba is a very serious subject for many Tokyoites. The buckwheat noodles have been popular since the Edo period, when more restaurants served *soba* than any other type of food (sushi was a close second). Some *Edokko* still have to have their daily *soba* "hit."

But *soba* restaurants are a hotly debated subject, and everyone has a favorite to which they remain stubbornly loyal. **Yabu Soba** in Kanda is probably the overall winner. The best *soba* is handmade, *teuchi,* and has a slightly hard and chewy texture. Fast-food *soba tachigui* served at stand-up noodle stalls is an almost completely different species of noodle. Noodles are served either in a hot soup or cold. A bowl of good soba will cost from ¥1,000–¥2,000.

Menu

Soup Soba — All come in a hot soy- and fish-stock soup flavored with finely chopped leeks.

kake	with leek slices.
kitsune	with *abura-age* (thin fried slices of tofu).
tanuki	with pieces of fried batter floating on top.
okame	with *kamaboko* (fish cake), *fu* (wheat cakes) and vegetables.
tempura	served topped with shrimp tempura.
tsukimi	or "moon-viewing"—the raw egg on top looks like a full moon.
tamago-toji	with a cooked egg on top.
kamo-nanban	with chicken and leeks.
tororo	served with grated Japanese potato.

Cold Soba

mori or *seiro*	plain noodles.
zaru	with *nori* (strips of dried seaweed).
tenzaru	with shrimp and vegetable tempura.

How to Order

• For lunch, most people just have a bowl of noodles. For dinner, start off with *tsumami* (appetizers) such as *itawasa* (sliced fish cake) or *morokyu* (cucumber served with *miso* sauce).

- *Soba* etiquette involves slurping the noodles quickly into your mouth. The Japanese love doing this and claim that the flavor is better this way.
- For soup *soba*, you can just mix up the ingredients in the bowl (at the end, you can lift the bowl and drink the remaining soup).
- *Zaru*, cold *soba*, will be served plain, usually in a lacquered box. The sauce will be brought in a small pitcher, along with an extra bowl, and a small dish with grated horseradish (*wasabi*), thinly sliced leeks, and grated white radish (*daikon*) if you are having tempura. The sauce should be poured into the bowl and the other ingredients mixed in as you go along. You eat the *soba* by dipping the noodles into the small bowl and slurping them quickly into your mouth. When the noodles are finished, a pitcher of hot water called *soba-yu* (the stock the noodles were boiled in) will be brought to the table. Mix the water with the remaining sauce in your bowl and drink the soup.

YABU SOBA　薮蕎麦　千代田区神田淡路町 2-10
2-10 Kanda Awaji-cho, Chiyoda-ku. Tel: 3251-0287. Hours: 11:30 A.M.–7:00 P.M., closed Mon. Perhaps the most famous *soba* restaurant in Tokyo, **Yabu Soba** is in a beautiful old Japanese-style house. Their specialties are *tendane* (a round patty of fried shrimp tempura) which is best ordered with *seiro* noodles and *anago-nanban* (soup *soba* with cooked conger eel). [M-14]

NAGASAKA SARASHINA　永坂更科　港区麻布十番 1-8-7
1-8-7 Azabu-juban, Minato-ku. Tel: 3585-1676. Hours: 11:00 A.M.–8:30 P.M. daily. A favorite of the shogun during the Edo period, this is still one of the best *soba* restaurants in town. They have two different sauces: *amakuchi* (slightly sweet) and *karakuchi* (slightly hot). You can choose either. Try their *gomakiri soba* (ground sesame added to the noodles) or *chakiri soba* (green tea noodles). [M-1]

OMATSUYA　大松屋　中央区銀座 5-4-18 銀座 I.N. ビル
Ginza I.N. Bldg., 2F, 5-4-18 Ginza, Chuo-ku. Tel: 3571-7053. Hours: 5:00–10:30 P.M., closed Sun. & hol. A branch of a restaurant in Yamagata Prefecture, the interior was taken from a seventeenth-century samurai's house in northern Japan. They specialize in *teuchi*, handmade *soba*. In the evening, they serve *sumiyaki* (game meat, fish, and vegetables grilled over the charcoal burner at each table). *Sumiyaki* (evening only) from ¥5,500. [M-8]

KUROMUGI　くろ麦　港区南青山 1-1-1 青山ツインタワー B1
Aoyama Twin Towers, B1, 1-1-1 Minami Aoyama, Minato-ku. Tel: 3475-1850. Hours: 11:30 A.M.–9:00 P.M., closed Sun. Located in the basement arcade of this office complex, Kuromugi is a convenient place to find good handmade noodles. [M-5]

ISSA-AN　一茶庵　品川区上大崎 2-14-3
2-14-3 Kami-osaki, Shinagawa-ku. Tel: 3444-0875. Hours: 11:30 A.M.–4:00 P.M., until 7:00 P.M. on Sun. & hol., closed Wed. Very basic, good *soba* is served in this rather tattered, old wooden house. [M-19]

Udon

Invented in Osaka, *udon* is the name for the thick, white wheat noodles served in specialized *udon* restaurants, as well as in most *soba* shops. *Udon* is prepared exactly like *soba* and is similarly best when handmade. *Udon* prices are similar to those for *soba*.

Menu

kake-udon	with leeks.
kamo-nanban	with chicken and leeks.

kare-nanban	in a curry-flavored soup with pork.
chikara-udon	with *mochi* (rice cake).
nabeyaki-udon	with vegetables and shrimp tempura, served in a lidded casserole.

How to Order—Basically, the same rules apply as for *soba*.

MIMIU 美々卯　中央区京橋 3-6-4
3-6-4 Kyobashi, Chuo-ku. Tel: 3567-6571. Hours: 11:30 A.M.–8:30 P.M., closed Sun. This shop is originally from Osaka. *Udon-suki, udon* boiled in a light broth with a combination of vegetables and chicken, shrimp, and clams—was their invention, ¥3,200. They also serve *soba*. [M-9]

CHOTOKU 長徳　渋谷区渋谷 1-10-5
1-10-5 Shibuya, Shibuya-ku. Tel: 3407-8891. Hours: 11:30 A.M.–9:30 P.M., closed Mon. This restaurant has a great menu with more than twenty kinds of handmade *udon* dishes, all shown on an illustrated menu. Their *udon* is slightly thicker than usual and a bit more expensive. [M-3]

INANIWA いなにわ　港区西麻布 1-8-20
1-8-20 Nishi Azabu, Minato-ku. Tel: 3401-4966. Hours: 11:00 A.M.–2:30 P.M., 5:00–10:30 P.M., closed Sun. & hol. This lovely, small restaurant serving *inaniwa-udon*, a thin *udon* noodle from Akita Prefecture, offers an extensive menu and a good selection of saké from around Japan. Try the *misoniku udon* (*udon* with minced meat and *miso*). [M-1]

Unagi

Eel is a traditional health food, believed by the Japanese to restore energy and to improve eyesight and virility. *Unagi no kabayaki,* grilled eel, is a surprisingly popular dish with even the most squeamish of foreigners. The eel is first split open, steamed, then charcoal-grilled and basted with a sweet sauce. The resulting fillet is rich and tender, not at all what you would expect of an eel.

A set meal will generally cost ¥3,000–¥4,000.

Menu

kabayaki	basic grilled eel (see above).
shiroyaki	steamed eel with the sweet sauce.
kimoyaki	eel liver, grilled and basted with sweet sauce, and served with ginger.
kimosui	*suimono* is clear soup. This one is served with eel liver.

Set Meals:

unaju	*kabayaki* on rice in a lacquered box with *kimosui* and pickles.
kabayaki teishoku	*kabayaki* plus rice, *kimosui,* and pickles.
unadon	*kabayaki* on a bowl of rice with sauce poured over, plus *kimosui* and pickles.

Ordering and Eating

- *Unaju* is recommended. There are no special rules or tricks to ordering and eating. *Sansho*, Japanese pepper (spicy but not hot), tastes good sprinkled on eel.

NODAIWA　野田岩　港区東麻布 1-5-4
1-5-4 Higashi Azabu, Minato-ku. Tel: 3583-7852. Hours: 11:00 A.M.–1:30 P.M., 5:00–8:00 P.M., closed Sun. & hol. They serve natural, as opposed to bred, eel so the meat is sweeter and more tender. The restaurant is in a lovely old building with tatami rooms upstairs. [M-1]

KANDAGAWA HONTEN　神田川本店　千代田区外神田 2-5-11
2-5-11 Soto-kanda, Chiyoda-ku. Tel: 3251-5031. Hours: 11:30 A.M.–2:00 P.M., 5:00–8:00 P.M., closed Sun. & hol. Expect a rather long wait for your delicately grilled eel in this very traditional restaurant located in an old house with a garden. [M-16]

CHIKUYOTEI HONTEN　竹葉亭本店　中央区銀座 8-14-7
8-14-7 Ginza, Chuo-ku. Tel: 3542-0787. Hours: 11:30 A.M.–2:00 P.M., 4:30–8:00 P.M., closed Sun. & hol. Built right after the big earthquake of the twenties, this restaurant has a number of small huts built in the tea ceremony-style and surrounded by a garden. A delicious menu focusing on eel is served on an assortment of beautiful ceramic tableware. The main building has a larger dining area with tables and chairs, but try to reserve a tatami room. Courses from ¥12,000. [M-8]

YAMA NO CHAYA　山の茶屋　千代田区永田町 2-10-6
2-10-6 Nagatacho, Chiyoda-ku. Tel: 3581-0656. Hours: 11:30 A.M.–1:30 P.M., 6:00–9:00 P.M., closed Sun. & hol. *Kaiseki*-style cuisine centering on grilled eel. Beautiful, quietly traditional setting and service. Lunch course ¥15,000, dinner ¥17,000. [M-6]

Fugu-ryori

Fugu, poison blowfish, is considered a great delicacy in Japan. Fanatics will eat a tiny bit of the poison part, that leaves one with a pleasantly benumbed sensation. Like Russian roulette, it's a rather dangerous game, a famous actor died from the poison some years back. But most restaurants won't serve you the poison part, so there is no cause for concern. The fish itself is delicious, though so delicately flavored as to be lost on some palates. *Fugu* is only in season from October through March. The rest of the year, *fugu* restaurants serve less dangerous fish, or sometimes *kaiseki-ryori.*

Menu

fugu-sashi	blowfish, sliced and eaten raw with *ponzu* sauce.
fugu-chiri	thinly sliced blowfish served in a thick vegetable soup.

TENTAKE　天竹　中央区築地 6-16-6
6-16-6 Tsukiji, Chuo-ku. Tel: 3541-3881. Hours: noon–10:00 P.M., closed Sun. (Apr.–Sept.), the first Sat. & third Wed. (Feb.–Mar., Oct.–Nov.). One of the cheapest *fugu* restaurants in town. *Fugu-chiri* ¥2,500, *fugu-sashi* ¥3,600. [M-22]

SANTOMO　さんとも　台東区上野 6-14-1
6-14-1 Ueno, Taito-ku. Tel: 3831-3898. Hours: 11:30 A.M.–1:00 P.M., 5:00–9:30 P.M., closed Sun. (April–Sept.), and open daily Oct.–Mar. Sumo wrestlers are big *fugu* fans, and this is one of the places they frequent. *Fugu teishoku* ¥12,000. [M-13]

Tofu-ryori

Tofu, soybean curd, is a high-protein, low-calorie, vegetarian food that has long been a staple part of the Japanese diet. There are a few specialized tofu restaurants that serve a variety of tofu dishes, many similar to those served in *shojin-ryori*. Tofu restaurants are not strictly vegetarian, however.

Many tofu restaurants will serve small dishes of chicken or fish along with the tofu.

The restaurants themselves are also similar in atmosphere and service to *shojin-ryori* restaurants. Most offer their food in set courses that make ordering easy.

GOEMON　五右エ門　文京区駒込 1-1-26
1-1-26 Hon-komagome, Bunkyo-ku. Tel: 3811-2015. Hours: 5:00–10:00 P.M., closed Mon. You'll feel like you're in Kyoto in this lovely restaurant. Most of the rooms open up in the summer and overlook the garden and its trickling waterfall. Slightly out of the way, this restaurant is definitely worth the trip. Courses from ¥4,000. Try to reserve one of the rooms next to the garden. [M-32]

SASANOYUKI　笹乃雪　台東区根岸 2-15-10
2-15-10 Negishi, Taito-ku. Tel: 3873-1145. Hours: 11:00 A.M.–9:00 P.M., closed Mon. A famous tofu restaurant since the Edo period, **Sasanoyuki** prepares tofu in more ways than seem possible. Set menus cost between ¥1,000–¥3,000 and are divided by how many dishes come along with the rice, miso soup, and pickles. A nice, understated traditional interior. [M-13]

Okonomi-yaki

Often called "Japanese pizza," *okonomi-yaki* is a cheap food that originated in Osaka. (Osaka people, by the way, are considered "cheap" by most Tokyoites.) *Okonomi-yaki* is made from a pancake-like batter to which is added egg, meat or fish, shredded cabbage, and other vegetables. You can cook it yourself, or a chef will cook it in front of you. *Okonomi-yaki* is also served by street vendors.

Individual *okonomi-yaki* patties will cost from ¥600-¥1,000.

Menu

gyuniku-ten	*okonomi-yaki* with beef.
butaniku-ten	with pork.
ebi-ten	with shrimp.
ika-ten	with squid.
mikkusu	a mix of all the above.
yakisoba	Chinese-style fried noodles with vegetables and pork.

How to Order

- You should order some vegetables or a salad to go along with the meal. A combination of *okonomi-yaki* and *yakisoba* is nice.
- If you are cooking the *okonomi-yaki* yourself, here are the rules: the batter will come in a small cup, so stir up the ingredients and pour it out like pancake batter on the hot grill in front of you (be sure the grill has been oiled). When the center starts to solidify, flip the patty and pat it soundly. When cooked, move the patty to the side of the grill, spread on the sauce, add the toppings and cut it up like a pizza with the side of the spatula.

- There are two kinds of sauce: *amakuchi* (slightly sweet) and *karakuchi* (hot). There will also be seaweed flakes, shaved dried fish (both delicious), and sometimes mayonnaise—all go as toppings on the "pizza."

WAKATSUKI　若月　中央区銀座 4-13-16
4-13-16 Ginza, Chuo-ku. Tel: 3541-6730. Hours: noon–9:30 P.M., closed Sun. & hol. A do-it-yourself-style restaurant with some tatami rooms available. [M-8]

MOTOMACHI　モトマチ　目黒区自由ヶ丘 1-17-13
1-17-13 Jiyugaoka, Meguro-ku. Tel: 3723-9477. Hours: 5:00 P.M.–2:00 A.M., (3:00–11:00 P.M. Sun. & hol.), closed Mon. The cook prepares your meal here. Try their *motomachi okonomi-yaki*, *chahan* (fried rice) and *yasai-yaki* (fried vegetables). They also serve *teppan-yaki* and Kobe steak. [M-2]

SOMETARO　染太郎　台東区西浅草 2-2-2
2-2-2 Nishi Asakusa, Taito-ku. Tel: 3844-9502. Hours: noon–10:00 P.M., closed Mon. This famous restaurant serves no frill, Edo-style *okonomi-yaki*. The eccentric-old-woman owner who made it famous has now passed away, but the slightly wacky atmosphere remains. [M-12]

JONGSON　ジョンソン　港区白金 1-7-3
1-7-3 Shirogane, Minato-ku. Tel: 3444-4588. Hours: 11:30 A.M.–11 P.M., closed Sun. Try their Korean-style *okonomi-yaki*. [off Map]

Ramen

These Chinese noodles are one of the most popular kinds of fast food in Japan. *Ramen* shops are not known for their decor, but with prices that are often under ¥1,000, who cares?

Menu

ramen	noodles in chicken or pork soup with slices of leek, bamboo shoots, and other green vegetables.
chashu-men	with sliced, roasted pork.
wantan-men	with won ton (square pockets of noodle dough filled with pork and vegetables).
gomoku soba	with various ingredients (sliced pork, vegetables, etc.).
miso-ramen	with *miso* soup.
yakisoba	fried noodles.
gyoza	minced pork and vegetables in a crescent shaped Chinese pastry.
chahan	rice fried with meat and vegetables.

How to Order

- People will usually order a bowl of *ramen* and a side order of *gyoza*. As with other noodles, slurp at will.

- Pepper and chili oil are usually provided to spice up the soup if you so please.

NAOKYU　直久　中央区銀座 5-2-1 東芝ビル B2
Toshiba Bldg., B2, 5-2-1 Ginza, Chuo-ku. Tel: 3571-0957. Hours: 11:00 A.M.–9:00 P.M. daily. [M-8]

DAIHACHI　大八　港区六本木 7-12-1
7-12-1 Roppongi, Minato-ku. Tel: 3405-0721. Hours: 7:00 P.M.–3:00 A.M. daily [M-1]
SUSUKINO　薄野　港区赤坂 5-3-10
5-3-10 Akasaka, Minato-ku. Tel: 3582-2060. Hours: 11:30 A.M.–3:00 A.M. daily. Good *miso-ramen*. [M-6]
CHARLIE HOUSE　チャーリーハウス　渋谷区神南 1-15-11
1-15-11 Jinnan, Shibuya-ku. Tel: 3464-5552. Hours: 11:30 A.M.–2:30 P.M., 5:00–8:30 P.M., closed Sun. & hol. The thin, handmade soup noodles and toppings come separately here. [M-3]
DARUMAYA　だるま屋　港区南青山 5-9-5
5-9-5 Minami Aoyama, Minato-ku. Tel: 3499-6295. Hours: 11:00 A.M.–9:30 P.M., closed Sun. Famous for their *takana soba*—handmade Chinese noodles topped with an exotic Japanese vegetable. [M-5]

Katei-ryori

Basic, good food just like mom used to make, *katei-ryori* (home-cooking), is usually served in restaurants that have a functional Japanese decor and a friendly atmosphere. Many of the dishes listed on our general restaurant menu are served in these restaurants. Others are listed below. This kind of restaurant is found in every neighborhood. Individual dishes are generally between ¥500–¥800; a meal will cost between ¥3,000–¥5,000.

Menu

Yasai no nitsuke (nimono)	Cooked seasonal vegetables in a sugar and soy sauce.
natto	fermented soybeans, usually served with raw egg, sliced leek, and soy sauce. The mixture is usually poured over rice.
tori no kara-age	fried chicken.
yaki-zakana	grilled fish.
buri no teriyaki	yellowtail, broiled teriyaki-style.
ohitashi	boiled green vegetables served in a small bowl, seasoned with soy sauce and dried bonito flakes.

KAPPA　かっぱ　港区六本木 4-10-7 エルビル 2F
Eru Bldg., 2F, 4-10-7 Roppongi, Minato-ku. Tel: 3408-8696. Hours: 5:30 P.M.–1:00 A.M. daily. Try their *shumai* and *wafu* (Japanese-style) salad. [M-1]
BANSAI TEI　番菜亭　港区西麻布 2-25-19 木島ビル 2F
Kishima Bldg., 2F, 2-25-19 Nishi Azabu, Minato-ku. Tel: 3486-8955. Hours: 6:00–10:30 P.M., closed Sun. & hol. Friendly, home-style restaurant, a meal with a main course of fish will run about ¥5,000. [M-2]
ANRI　安里　港区西麻布 2-8-6
2-8-6 Nishi Azabu, Minato-ku. Tel: 3400-7389. Hours: 6:00 P.M.–midnight, closed Sun. & hol. [M-5]
ROPPONGI SHOKUDO　六本木食堂　港区六本木 3-10-11
Aoki Bldg., B1F, 3-10-11 Roppongi, Minato-ku. Tel: 3404-2714. Hours: 10:00 A.M.–2:00 P.M., 4:00–7:00 P.M. (10:00 A.M.–2:00 P.M. on Sat.), closed first and third Sat., Sun., & hol. A classic *shokudo* (cafeteria), you pick out your food at the counter and pay under ¥1,000 when you go. [M-1]

Yoshoku

Western food as cooked by the Japanese since the Meiji period. A modest meal should cost ¥3,000–¥4,000.

TSUTSUI 津つ井　港区赤坂 5-5-7

5-5-7 Akasaka, Minato-ku. Tel: 3584-1851. Hours: 11:00 A.M.–9:00 P.M., closed Sun. & hol. Their *bifuteki-don* (teriyaki beef on rice) is good. *Yoshoku-bento* (Western-style lunch box with fish, vegetables, croquettes, rice, etc.) from ¥2,000. [M-6]

HOMITEI 芳味亭　中央区日本橋人形町 2-9-4

2-9-4 Nihombashi Ningyo-cho, Chuo-ku. Tel: 3666-5687. Hours: 11:00 A.M.–2:00 P.M., 5:00–9:00 P.M., closed Sun. You can have *yoshoku* in one of several tatami rooms in this little house. Try their beef or tongue stew or the *shiba-ebi-korokke* (shrimp croquette). [M-23]

SHOEITEI 松栄亭　千代田区神田淡路町 2-8

2-8 Kanda Awaji-cho, Chiyoda-ku. Tel: 3251-5511. Hours: 11:00 A.M.–2:30 P.M., 4:30–7:30 P.M., closed Sun. & hol. Great *shitamachi* people and atmosphere, their food is good and cheap. Specialties include *yofu-kakiage* (fried pork and sliced onions with tempura batter) and *korokke* (potato croquettes). [M-14]

Other Japanese Restaurants

The following restaurants are all great, but don't fit into any of our categories.

YOTARO 与太呂　港区六本木 4-11-4

4-11-4 Roppongi, Minato-ku. Tel: 3405-5866. Hours: 5:30–9:30 P.M., closed Sun. A branch of the famous Osaka restaurant, their tempura is Osaka-style. Sleek, contemporary Japanese interior. *Taimeishi* course with tempura plus rice, cooked in a casserole with a whole *tai* (sea bream) for ¥11,000. [M-1]

KIKU きく　渋谷区神宮前 2-20-27

4-26-27 Jingumae, Shibuya-ku. Tel: 3408-4919. Hours: 11:00 A.M.–2:00 P.M., 5:00–10:30 P.M., closed Sun. This contemporary, Japanese-style building on the back streets of Harajuku offers an inexpensive taste of refined Japanese cooking. There are several Japanese-style rooms for groups of people. Lunch courses from ¥900, dinner courses from about ¥3,000. [M-4]

SHUNJU 春秋　港区赤坂 2-16-19 赤坂飯沼ビル

Akasaka Inuma Bldg., B1, 2-16-19 Akasaka, Minato-ku. Tel: 5561-0009. Hours: 6:00–11:00 P.M., closed Sun. & hol. Very elegant, restrained, contemporary Japanese decor in this restaurant where you can have your *nabe* sitting around a charcoal fire or drinks and a late meal at a long counter. Courses from ¥6,000. [M-6]

SHUNJU-HIBIKI 春秋響　港区西麻布 4-7-10

4-7-10 Nishi Azabu, Minato-ku. Tel: 5485-0020. Hours: 6:00–11:30 P.M. daily. Beautifully designed by Tadashi Sugimoto, this very contemporary restaurant serves a combination of Japanese, Western, and Korean meals. Favored by the Japanese design crowd. From about ¥7,000–8,000 per person. [M-2]

KAI 開　渋谷区猿楽町 23-6 岩本ビル

Iwamoto Bldg., 2F, 23-6 Sarugaku-cho, Shibuya-ku. Tel: 3770-5794. Hours: noon–1:30 P.M., 6:00–11:00 P.M., closed Sun. The modern interior is matched here by Japanese food prepared in a nouveau style. Fresh, light, and delicious cuisine. Courses from ¥5,500. [M-20]

SAKURA さくら　港区南青山 7-10-10

7-10-10 Minami Aoyama, Minato-ku. Tel: 3409-8683. Hours: 6:00–midnight daily. Kimono are worn with contemporary flair by the young staff of this sleek, fashionable restaurant. The food is likewise Japanese with a modern sensibility. Courses from ¥6,000. [M-5]

DAIKAN KAMADO 代官かまど　港区六本木 4-11-4 六本木ビル

Roppongi Bldg., 1F, 4-11-4 Roppongi, Minato-ku. Tel: 3403-5364. Hours: 5:00 P.M.–2:00 A.M. daily. This is a great seafood restaurant, but they also serve *shabu-shabu* and steak. Impressive selection of saké. Try a la carte: *hotate no shumai* (scallop dumpling) or *ebi-dango* (shrimp ball). A *shabu-shabu* course at ¥7,000 includes a variety of their specialty side dishes. [M-1]

HAYASHI はやし 港区赤坂2-14-1山王会館ビル
Sanno Kaikan Bldg., 4F, 2-14-1 Akasaka, Minato-ku. Tel: 3582-4078. Hours: 11:30 A.M.–2:00 P.M., 5:30–11:00 P.M., closed Sun. Most tables in this atmospheric country-style restaurant have tatami seating and a charcoal grill. The cooking style is called *sumibi-yaki* where you cook a variety of meat, fish, and vegetables over the grill at your table. Dinner courses from ¥5,000. *Oyako-donburi* is served for lunch at ¥800. [M-6]

TATSUMIYA 東南屋 台東区浅草1-33-5
1-33-5 Asakusa, Taito-ku. Tel: 3842-7373. Hours: noon–2:00 P.M., 5:00–9:30 P.M., closed Mon. Like dining in a private home during the Edo period, this cozy restaurant full of antiques is located in an old house transported from Gifu Prefecture. The food is home-style cooking and fairly inexpensive. For lunch try *gyu-rosu bento* (teriyaki beef and egg cakes on rice), ¥900. Their dinner course is ¥4,200. [M-12]

KUREMUTSU 暮六つ 台東区浅草2-2-13
2-2-13 Asakusa, Taito-ku. Tel: 3842-0906. Hours: 4:00–10:00 P.M., closed Thur. The owner of the restaurant is the brother of **Tatsumiya's** owner (listed above). This is another transplanted Gifu farmhouse, but slightly more eccentric than **Tatsumiya**. *Kaiseki* course ¥8,000, a la carte dishes as well. [M-12]

JIZAKE 地酒 渋谷区道玄坂2-19-3
2-19-3 Dogenzaka, Shibuya-ku. Tel: 3496-5295. Hours: 5:00–midnight, closed Sun. & hol. This place is best known for its huge selection of saké from all over Japan. Their *sashimi* is also particularly good. A course with different kinds of cooking styles runs from ¥3,000. [M-3]

YASUKO やす幸 中央区銀座5-4-6
5-4-6 Ginza, Chuo-ku. Tel: 3571-0621. Hours: 4:00–11:00 P.M. daily, except closed Sun. in August. This shop serves a sophisticated version of *oden*—a typical street and festival food. *Oden* is a Japanese stew of fish cakes, tofu, and vegetables simmered in a fish stock soup. From ¥1,400. [M-8]

MARUTA-GOSHI 丸太ごうし 台東区浅草2-32-11
2-32-11 Asakusa, Taito-ku. Tel: 3841-3192. Hours: 5:00–9:30 P.M., closed Sun. A more casual *oden* restaurant with a very lively *shitamachi* atmosphere. *Nabemono* (*oden* in a pot) for two, ¥1,300. [M-12]

UKAI TORIYAMA うかい鳥山 八王子市南浅川町3426
3426 Minami Asakawa-cho, Hachioji-shi. Tel: 0426-61-0739. Hours: 11:00 A.M.–9:30 P.M. (8:30 P.M. on Sun. & hol.). Take the Keio Line from Shinjuku Station to Takao Sanguchi Station (about fifty min.). A free shuttle bus will be waiting to take you to the restaurant. Like a small village surrounded by mountains, this extraordinary restaurant consists of twelve dining rooms, each a separate, traditional wooden house with a charcoal *robata* grill. The grounds are like a nature park with ponds, rivers, and trees. Course menus from ¥4,000. [off Map]

HEALTH FOOD RESTAURANTS

Because Japanese food was originally based on rice and vegetables, vegetarian restaurants were never really necessary. But with the increased use of chemical fertilizers, artificial ingredients, and pollution, the concern for health has grown. There are a number of good natural-food restaurants in town. Notable are those listed earlier in this chapter that offer *shojin-ryori*, the traditional vegetarian meal served in temples. Other restaurants serve basically home-style cooking without meat. American-style health-food restaurants are not as good as they are in America, so we haven't included them. Lunch will cost from ¥1,000, dinners from about ¥3,000.

TENMI 天味 渋谷区神南1-10-6第1岩下ビル
Daiichi Iwashita Bldg., 2F, 1-10-6 Jinnan, Shibuya-ku. Tel: 3498-9073. Hours: 11:30 A.M.–2:00 P.M., 5:00–10:00 P.M. (11:30 A.M.–6:00 P.M. on Sun. and hol.), closed 2nd and 3rd Wed. Macrobiotic vegetarian food in a Japanese-style restaurant. [M-3]

MOMINOKI HOUSE　モミノキハウス　渋谷区神宮前2-18-5
2-18-5 Jingumae, Shibuya-ku. Tel: 3405-9144. Hours: 11:00 A.M.–10:00 P.M., closed Sun. The decor of this casual restaurant is as eclectic as its menu. An extensive variety of natural foods is offered. [M-4]

BODAIJU　菩提樹　港区芝4-3-14仏教伝道センター
Bukkyo Dendo Center Bldg., 2 & 3F, 4-3-14 Shiba, Minato-ku. Tel: 3456-3257. Hours: 11:30 A.M.–2:00 P.M., 5:30–8:00 P.M., closed Sun. & hol. Chinese vegetarian cuisine, using meat substitutes that fool most people. [off Map]

INTERNATIONAL CUISINE

Korean

Korean *yakiniku* (grilled beef) restaurants are incredibly popular in Japan, perhaps more so than they are in Korea. Thin-sliced beef and vegetables are cooked on a grill at your table and eaten with a variety of spicy side dishes like hot Korean *kimuchi* pickles. These are usually great family restaurants, with an average meal costing around ¥3,000–¥4,000.

KUSA NO YA　4-6-7 Azabu-juban, Minato-ku. Tel: 3455-8356. Hours: 11:30 A.M.–2:30 P.M., 5:00–10:30 P.M. (until 10:00 P.M. on Sun. & hol.), closed the first Mon. of every month. One of the best *yakiniku* restaurants in town. A favorite with local celebrities and families. Good side dishes are *pidento* (Korean-style *okonomi-yaki*) and *namuru* salad. [M-1]

YANSANDO　6-5-3 Ueno, Taito-ku. Tel: 3831-7333. Hours: 11:00 A.M.–2:00 A.M. daily (until midnight on Sun.) The house specialty is *komutan* soup. [M-13]

JOJOEN　Morino Bldg., 2 & 3F, 7-12-2 Roppongi, Minato-ku. Tel: 3478-1446. Hours: 11:30 A.M.–6:30 A.M. daily. This restaurant has a reputation for their high quality meats. [M-1]

TOKAIEN　1-6-3 Kabukicho, Shinjuku-ku. Tel: 3200-2924. Hours: 11:00 A.M.–4:00 A.M. daily. This restaurant has nine floors: 1–4F are home-style *yakiniku*, 6F is all-you-can-eat, and 7–9F offer a traditional Korean "Royal Family" course. [M-7]

GRACE　1-7-2 Azabu-juban, Minato-ku. Tel: 3475-6972. Hours: 11:30 A.M.–2:00 P.M., 5:00 P.M.–midnight, closed third Sun. Not your typical *yakiniku*-style restaurant, **Grace** offers a variety of dishes and is best known for its *sangetan*—a boiled, stuffed chicken dish favored by the former Korean royal family. [M-1]

Chinese

TOKALIN　Hotel Okura, 6F, 2-10-4 Toranomon, Minato-ku. Tel: 3505-6068. Hours: 11:30 A.M.–2:30 P.M., 5:30–10:00 P.M. Mainly Cantonese, expensive but consistently good. Extensive wine list and excellent service. Lunch course ¥5,000, dinner ¥10,000. [M-11]

HOKKAIEN　2-12-1 Nishi Azabu, Minato-ku. Tel: 3407-8507. Hours: 11:30 A.M.–2:00 P.M., 5:00–10:00 P.M. Peking-style cooking. Lunch about ¥1,000, dinner course from ¥7,000. [M-2]

NEW HOKKAIEN　Togensha Bldg., 2F, 3-16-15 Roppongi, Minato-ku. Tel: 3505-7881. Hours: 11:30 A.M.–10:30 P.M. daily. Great dim-sum menu for lunch. [M-1]

ROGAIRO　2-12-8 Akasaka, Minato-ku. Tel: 3586-3931. Hours: 11:30 A.M.–2:30 P.M., 5–10 P.M. daily. The best Shanghai-style restaurant in Tokyo. About ¥10,000 per person. [M-6]

TOKYO DAI HANTEN　5-17-13 Shinjuku, Shinjuku-ku. Tel: 3202-0121. Hours: 11:00 A.M.–10:00 P.M. daily. The biggest Chinese restaurant in Tokyo (twelve floors) serves almost every style of Chinese cooking. For small groups, go to the 3F, where you can order lunch for about ¥1,000 and dinners for ¥5,000. Not the best Chinese restaurant in town, but one of the few places where dim sum is served all day. [M-7]

RYUNOKO　1-8-5 Jingumae, Shibuya-ku. Tel: 3402-9419. Hours: 11:30 A.M.–3:00 P.M., 5:00–9:30 P.M., closed Sun. Szechwan-style cooking. Lunches from ¥900, dinner ¥5,000. [M-4]

DAINI'S TABLE　6-3-14 Minami Aoyama, Minato-ku. Tel: 3407-0363. Hours: 5:30 P.M.–midnight daily. Chinese nouvelle cuisine served with style in this elegant, and after many years, still-fashionable restaurant. About ¥8,000–10,000 per person. [M-5]

KAEN 3-10-12 Moto-azabu, Minato-ku. Tel: 3401-1051. Hours: 6:30–10:00 P.M., closed Sun. & hol. Run by a rather hip couple, **Kaen** is in an old two-story house on the back streets. Food is an interesting Chinese-Japanese mix. There is no sign; look for a long, narrow window where a single-flower arrangement is spotlit. About ¥7,000 per person. [M-1]

TAINAN-TAMI 1-17-6 Dogenzaka, Shibuya-ku. Tel: 3464-0494. Hours: 11:00 A.M.–2:00 P.M., 5:00 P.M.–2:00 A.M. daily (11:00 A.M.–2:00 A.M. on Sat. & Sun.). A variety of dim sum-type Taiwanese specialties are served in this inexpensive restaurant. The funky Asian atmosphere is great. About ¥2,000–3,000 per person. [M-3]

Other Asian and African Cuisines

BAN THAI 1-23-14 Kabukicho, Shinjuku-ku. Tel: 3207-0068. Hours: 11:30 A.M.–midnight daily. Still one of the best Thai restaurants in town. About ¥4,000 per person. [M-7]

CAY Spiral Bldg. B1, 5-6-23 Minami Aoyama, Minato-ku. Tel: 3498-5790. Hours: 6:00–11:00 P.M., closed Sun. & hol. Large, rather fashionable restaurant theater that often features exotic and interesting music from around the world. Food is good, but not cheap, easily ¥4,000–5,000 per person. [M-5]

ANGKOR WAT 1-38-13 Yoyogi, Shibuya-ku. Tel: 3370-3019. Hours: 11:00 A.M.–2:00 P.M., 5:00–11:00 P.M. daily (no lunch time on Sun. & hol.). A sushi bar turned Cambodian restaurant and run by real Cambodians. The food is wonderful and very cheap. Hardly a surprise that it's popular with students [M-28]

DUSIT THIEN DUONG Century Tower Bldg., B1, 2-2-9 Hongo, Bunkyo-ku. Tel: 5800-0099. Hours: 11:30 A.M.–2:30 P.M. (no lunch on Sat.), 6:00–11:00 P.M., closed Sun. & hol. Thai chefs prepare refined Vietnamese cuisine in this elegant restaurant located in the Norman Foster-designed Century Tower. Lunch courses from ¥3,000, dinner from ¥10,000. [M-16]

AOZAI 5-4-14 Akasaka, Minato-ku. Tel: 3583-0234. Hours: 5:00–10:30 P.M., closed Sun. & hol. Vietnamese cuisine in moderately stylish setting. Reasonably priced, courses from ¥3,500. [M-6]

BENGAWAN SOLO 7-18-13 Roppongi, Minato-ku. Tel: 3403-3031. Hours: 11:30 A.M.–3:00 P.M., 5:00–11:00 P.M. daily. Established long before the late eighties, chic for ethnic restaurants, **Bengawan Solo** serves good, cheap Indonesian food. Suitable for large groups. About ¥4,000 per person. [M-1]

MOTI Roppongi Hama Bldg., 3F, 6-2-35 Roppongi, Minato-ku. Tel: 3479-1939. Hours: 11:30 A.M.–11:00 P.M. daily (10:00 P.M. last order), Sun. & hol. from noon. Roppongi Plaza Bldg., 3F, 3-12-6 Roppongi, Minato-ku. Tel: 5410-6871. Hours: 11:30 A.M.–2:00 A.M. (Sun. & hol. noon–11 P.M.). Popular with foreign residents, **Moti** serves inexpensive, basically good, Indian food. From about ¥2,000 per person. [M-1] Akasaka branch: Floral Plaza, 2F, 3-8-8 Akasaka, Minato-ku. Tel: 3582-3620. [M-6]

GANGA PALACE Wind Bldg., B1, 7-4-8 Roppongi, Minato-ku. Tel: 3796-4477. Hours: 11:30 A.M.–2:30 P.M., 5:00–11:00 P.M. daily. Bar open until 5:00 A.M. Perhaps Tokyo's most luxurious Indian restaurant. Upmarket prices. [M-1]

BINDI Apartment Aoyama, B1, 7-10-10 Minami Aoyama, Minato-ku. Tel: 3409-7114. Hours: noon–2:00 P.M., 6:00–10:00 P.M., closed Sun. & hol. Home-style Indian cooking in this unpretentious restaurant run by a friendly Indian couple. You can chat with Mrs. Menta as she prepares your meal behind the counter. [M-5]

ASHOKA Pearl Bldg., 2F, 7-9-18 Ginza, Chuo-ku. Tel: 3572-2377. Hours: noon–7:30 P.M. daily, Sun. from 11:30 A.M.–9:30 P.M. Another long-established Indian restaurant serving mainly northern Indian cuisine. Courses from ¥6,000. [M-8]

ARABIA 1-6-1 Jinnan, Shibuya-ku. Tel: 5489-3047. Hours: 5:00–10:30 P.M., closed Sun. & hol. The only Lebanese restaurant in Tokyo, Arabia is located in a fantastic Showa Era house. Dinners from around ¥4,000. [M-3]

QUEEN SHEBA 1-3-1 Higashiyama, Meguro-ku. Tel: 3794-1801. Hours: 5:30–11:00 P.M. daily. Ethiopian cuisine running about ¥5,000 per person. [off Map]

PIGA PIGA Nanshin Ebisu Ekimae Bldg., B2, 1-8-16 Ebisu Minami, Shibuya-ku. Tel: 3715-3431. Hours: 6:00 P.M.–1:00 A.M., closed Sun. Almost always crowded, **Piga Piga** offers light African meals, drinks and live African music. Very fun and inexpensive. [M-20]

French

TOUR D'ARGENT   New Otani Hotel Main Bldg., 2F, 4-1 Kioi-cho, Chiyoda-ku. Tel: 3239-3111. Hours: 5:30–10:30 P.M., closed Mon. Perhaps the most beautiful, theatrical place to dine in the entire city, the Tokyo branch of this famous French restaurant lives up to its reputation. Pricey, but worth it for a special occasion. Courses from ¥20,000. [M-6]

PACHON   Hillside Terrace, B1, 29-18 Sarugaku-cho, Shibuya-ku. Tel: 3476-5025. Hours: 11:30 A.M.–2:00 P.M., 6:00–10:00 P.M. daily. Chef André Pachon produces indisputably French cuisine; there are no cross-cultural compromises made with the food here. A huge fireplace doubles as a grill where meats, fish, and poultry are cooked to your specifications. The wine cellar is extensive and the staff attentive. The only thing mediocre about this restaurant is the interior. Lunch from ¥2,500, dinner from ¥6,000. [M-20]

MADAME TOKI'S   14-7 Hachiyama-cho, Shibuya-ku. Tel: 3461-2263. Hours: noon–2:30 P.M., 6:00–10:00 P.M., closed Mon. The elegant Madame Toki will greet you in this charming older home. Courses from ¥5,000. [M-20]

CRESCENT   1-8-20 Shiba-koen, Minato-ku. Tel: 3436-3211. Hours: 11:30 A.M.–2:30 P.M., 5:00–10:30 P.M., closed Sun., July & Aug. Luxurious French restaurant in a Victorian-style building with several private rooms and a chapel. Great old-fashioned cellar bar. Lunch courses from ¥6,000, dinner from ¥17,000. [M-11]

L'ORANGERIE DE PARIS   Hanae Mori Bldg., 5F, 3-6-1 Kita Aoyama, Minato-ku. Tel: 3407-7461. Hours: 11:30 A.M.–2:30 P.M., 5:30–10:00 P.M., Sun. brunch from 11:00 A.M.–2:30 P.M. daily. Sister restaurant to l'Orangerie in Paris. The interior is discreetly elegant as is the food. Lunch from ¥4,000, dinner from ¥8,000. [M-4]

L'ECRIN   Mikimoto Bldg., B1, 4-5-5 Ginza, Chuo-ku. Tel: 3561-9706. Hours: 11:30 A.M.–2:30 P.M., 5:30–10:00 P.M., closed Sun. Highly respected and favored for business entertainment. Excellent food, wine, and service. Lunch about ¥5,000, dinner from ¥12,000. [M-8]

HIRAMATSU   5-15-13 Minami Azabu, Minato-ku. Tel: 3444-3967. Hours: noon–2:00 P.M., 6:00–9:30 P.M., closed Mon. Not a personal favorite, but loved by many. Expensive and elegant. Lunch course from ¥6,000, dinner courses from ¥15,000. [M-2]

BISTROT DE LA CITE   4-2-10 Nishi Azabu, Minato-ku. Tel: 3406-5475. Hours: noon–2:00 P.M., 6:00–10:00 P.M., closed Mon. Since 1973, good, solid food has been served in this cozy bistro. Lunch courses from ¥2,500, dinner from ¥6,500. [M-2]

LES CHOUX   Rirent Azabu-juban, B1, 2-8-12 Azabu-juban, Minato-ku. Tel: 3452-5511. Hours: noon–3:00 P.M., 5:30–10:30 P.M., closed Tues. A great standby, not too casual, not too formal. Lunch courses from ¥1,500, dinner from ¥7,000. [M-1]

ILE DE FRANCE   Dai Han Bldg., 2F, 3-6-23 Kita Aoyama, Minato-ku. Tel: 5485-2931. Hours: 11:30 A.M.–2:00 P.M., 6:00–10:30 P.M. daily. Recently relocated, this restaurant has a twenty-year history in Tokyo. Casual country cuisine, fabulous fish soup, and *pomme frités*. Sister restaurant to **Pachon**. Lunches from just over ¥2,000, dinner around ¥6,000. [M-5]

BRASSERIE BERNARD   Kajimaya Bldg., 7F, 7-14-3 Roppongi, Minato-ku. Tel: 3405-7877. Hours: 11:30 A.M.–2:00 P.M., 5:30–midnight, closed Sun. A low-priced favorite with the local French crowd, homey food and atmosphere. [M-1] There is also a branch restaurant in the Franco-Japan Institute in Ichigaya. Tel: 3260-9639.

AUX BACCHANALES   Palais France, 1F, 1-6 Jingumae, Shibuya-ku. Tel: 5474-0076. Hours: Brasserie/Café 10:00 A.M.–midnight; Restaurant 5:30 P.M.–midnight daily. At last, a traditional Parisian-type big café replete with bar and tiled floor. French home cooking in a casual setting, with a quieter restaurant space downstairs. Dinner around ¥5,000. [M-4]

FLO   4-3-3 Jingumae, Shibuya-ku. Tel: 5474-0610. Hours: 11:30 A.M.–11:30 P.M. daily. Huge, stylish bistro. Not great food, but reasonably priced and nearly always full. [M-4]

LA FETE   1-4-43 Nishi Azabu, Minato-ku. Tel: 5411-3931. Hours: 11:30 A.M.–2:00 P.M., 6:00–11:30 P.M. daily. A moderately-priced restaurant run by the same people who run **Chez Hiramatsu**. Fashionable among well-bred young Japanese. About ¥8,000 per person. [M-1]

OMIYA   2-1-3 Asakusa, Taito-ku. Tel: 3844-0038. Hours: 11:30 A.M.–1:30 P.M., 5:00–8:30 P.M., closed Sun & hol. Unpretentious, marginally decorated, but good value for the money. Incredible wine selection and prices. [M-12]

HOTEL DE MIKUNI   1-18 Wakaba, Shinjuku-ku. Tel: 3351-3810. Hours: noon–1:30 P.M.,

6:00–9:30 P.M., closed Sun. Expensive, but very fine restaurant in a former home where art, often contemporary Japanese, hangs on the walls. Lunch from ¥6,000, dinner ¥14,000. [off Map]

A. LECOMTE Shimbashi Kaikan Bldg., 2F, 8-6-3 Ginza, Chuo-ku. Tel: 3575-4142. Hours: 11:30 A.M.–2:30 P.M., 5:30–9:30 P.M., closed Sun. & hol. Run by the well-known resident French chef André Lecomte. Lunches around ¥4,000, dinners around ¥8,000. [M-8]

AUX SIX ARBES 7-13-10 Roppongi, Minato-ku. Tel: 3479-2888. Hours: noon–2:00 P.M., 6:00–10:00 P.M., closed Sun. Intimate and elegant, medium-price range restaurant. [M-1]

BRASSERIE D 3-5-14 Kita Aoyama, Minato-ku. Tel 3470-0203. Hours: 6:00 P.M.–midnight, closed Sun. Basic French food. Formerly trendy, still serves a good Sunday brunch. [M-5]

PAS A PAS 5 Funamachi, Shinjuku-ku. Tel: 3357-7888. Hours: noon–1:30 P.M., 6:00–9:30 P.M., closed Sun. Tiny, cheap, and very casual. [off Map]

Italian

L'OSTERIA Piramide Bldg., 3F. 6-6-9 Roppongi, Minato-ku. Tel: 3475-1341. Hours: noon–2:00 P.M., 6:00–11:00 P.M., closed Sun. & hol. Understated interior, fine service, and excellent food. A terrace allows for pleasant outdoor dining in the spring and summer. Lunch from ¥2,500, dinner ¥8,000. [M-1]

EL TOULA From 1st Bldg., 5-3-10 Minami Aoyama, Minato-ku. Tel: 3406-8831. Hours: 11:30 A.M.–10:00 P.M. daily. In the famous film *Tampopo* by Juzo Itami there is a scene where young Japanese women are taught the proper way to eat spaghetti. That scene was shot in this excellent restaurant. Lunch from ¥2,500, dinner about ¥15,000. [M-5]

CIBREO The Wall, 4F. 4-2-4 Nishi Azabu, Minato-ku. Tel 3409-2700. Hours: 5:00–10:30 P.M. daily (also 1:00–3:00 P.M. on Sat. & Sun.). Very elegant, contemporary design, good food and service. Best to reserve on the upper level. Building by Nigel Coates. Lunch from ¥2,500, dinner ¥6,000. [M-2] Same company has a **Trattoria** in the Piramide Bldg. in Roppongi, 6-6-9 Roppongi, Minato-ku. Tel: 3746-0230. [M-2]

LA GRANATA TBS Kaikan, B1 (in the TBS Television Bldg.). 5-3-3 Akasaka, Minato-ku. Tel: 3582-3241. Hours: 11:00 A.M.–10:30 P.M. daily. A café-like atmosphere, a favorite of the local Italians. Lunch from ¥1,500, dinner from about ¥7,000. [M-6]

LA PATATA 2-9-11 Jingumae, Shibuya-ku. Tel: 3403-9665. Hours: noon–2:00 P.M., 6:00–10:30 P.M., closed Mon. Simple modern interior and regional Italian cooking. Lunch from ¥2,500, dinner from about ¥9,000. [M-5]

CUCINA HIRATA Endo Bldg., 3F. 2-13-10 Azabu-juban, Minato-ku. Tel: 3457-0094. Hours: from 6:00 P.M., closed Sun. & hol. Small and cleanly contemporary interior, fabulous food on a menu that is carefully chosen daily. Set menu is ¥12,000. [M-1]

IL BOCCALONE 1-15-9 Ebisu, Shibuya-ku. Tel: 3449-1430. Hours: 5:30–11:00 P.M., closed Sun. Very popular, moderately-priced restaurant with a relaxed, very Italian atmosphere. From ¥6,000–¥7,000 per person. [M-20]

CARMINE 1-19 Saiku-machi, Shinjuku-ku. Tel: 3260-5066. Hours: noon–2:00 P.M., 6:00–10:00 P.M., closed Sun. Very inexpensive, run by a resident Italian. Lunch course ¥2,500, dinner ¥3,500. [off Map]

SABATINI AOYAMA/PIZZERIA ROMANA SABATINI Suncrest Bldg., B1, 2-13-5 Kita Aoyama, Minato-ku. Tel: 3402-3812. Hours: 11:30 A.M.–2:30 P.M., 5:30–11:00 P.M. Pizzeria: 3402-2027. Both open daily. The main restaurant is loved or hated for its cheerful Italian atmosphere and strolling musicians. Lunches from about ¥5,000, dinners about ¥15,000. The Pizzeria next door is good and reasonably priced. [M-5]

CHIANTI 3-1-7 Iikura, Azabu-dai, Minato-ku. Tel: 3583-7546. Hours: noon–3:00 A.M. daily. A former hangout of Roppongi celebrities and bohemians, it remains a great casual standby. Averages ¥8,000–¥10,000 per person. [M-1]

CHIANTI Nishi Azabu Goyo Bldg., B1. 3-17-26 Nishi Azabu, Minato-ku. Tel: 3404-6500. Hours: noon–3:00 A.M. daily. Relaxed, yet still elegant favorite, always good food and service. Meals run around ¥8,000. [M-2]

L'ALFRESCO Hibiya Chanter Bldg., B2, 1-2-2 Yurakucho, Chiyoda-ku. Tel: 3581-7421. Hours: 11:00 A.M.–2:30 P.M., 5:30–10:30 P.M. daily. Not for a romantic dinner, but genuine Venetian cooking with no compromises. Lunches from about ¥2,500, dinner from ¥5,000. [M-10]

IL FORNO   Piramide Bldg., 3F, 6-6-9 Roppongi, Minato-ku. Tel: 3796-2641. Hours: 11:30 A.M.–3:00 P.M., 5:30–10:00 P.M. daily. A rather California-style, casual Italian restaurant running about ¥3,000 per person. [M-1]

Other European and American Cuisines

SPAGO   5-7-8 Roppongi, Minato-ku. Tel: 3423-4025. Hours: 5:00 P.M.–11:00 P.M. daily. Southern Californian cuisine and atmosphere in this branch of the famous L.A. restaurant. From about ¥6,000 per person. [M-1]

ROKKO GRILL   2-3-8 Minami Aoyama, Minato-ku. Tel: 3404-8995. Hours: 6:00 P.M.–midnight, closed Sat., Sun., & hol. Tiny, very informal counter restaurant serving a menu of home-style American ethnic cuisine. [M-5]

HARD ROCK CAFE   5-4-20 Roppongi, Minato-ku. Tel: 3408-7018. Hours: 11:30 A.M.–2:00 A.M., until 4:00 A.M. on Fri. & Sat., and 11:30 P.M. on Sun. Tokyo branch of this famous L.A. restaurant. So popular here that people often line up to get in. [M-1]

HOMEWORKS   5-1-20 Hiro-o, Shibuya-ku. Tel: 3444-4510. Hours: 11:00 A.M.–9:00 P.M., until 6:00 P.M. on Sun. Thirty different types of charcoal-grilled burgers, sandwiches, fries at this now much-copied café. From about ¥2,000 per person. [M-2]

ROCK 'N' ROLL DINER   Big Ben Bldg., B1, 2-5-2 Kitazawa, Setagaya-ku. Tel: 3411-6565. Daily from 4:00–11:30 P.M., Fri. and Sat. until 2:00 A.M., weekends from noon. A bit out of the way, but lively and enjoyable, full of young student types, U.S. style & Tex-Mex food. [off Map]

VICTORIA STATION   Haiyuza Bldg., 4-9-2 Roppongi, Minato-ku. Tel: 3479-4601. Hours: 11:00 A.M.–2:00 A.M. daily, until 11:00 P.M. on Sun. & hol. An American chain steakhouse, good for cheap beef, their salad bar, and their American atmosphere. Prime-rib dinners from ¥3,000, lunch sets from ¥2,500. [M-1]

ANDERSON'S   5-1-26 Aoyama, Minato-ku. Tel: 3407-4833. Hours: 8:00 A.M.–10:00 P.M. (9:00 P.M. on Sun.). Most famous as a bakery, Anderson's also has a café serving American breakfasts and a comforting menu of American favorites.

1066   3-9-5 Meguro, Meguro-ku. Tel: 3719-9059. Hours: 6:00–10:30 P.M., Sun. from noon–3:00 P.M., 6:00–9:00 P.M., closed Mon. Traditional British food, live folk music every second and fourth Wed. Dinners from about ¥5,000. [off Map]

LAS CHICAS   5-47-6 Jingumae, Shibuya-ku. Tel: 3407-6865. Hours: 10:30 A.M.–11:00 P.M. daily. Secluded, with a relaxed tasteful atmosphere, this restaurant features an inexpensive and modern, "borderless" menu and has been popular with the local ex-pat community for some years. [M-5]

BEWLEY'S   6-5-6 Jingumae, Shibuya-ku. Tel: 3499-3145. Hours: 8:00 A.M.–11:00 P.M., Mon.–Sat., from 11:00 A.M.–9:00 P.M. on Sun. & hol. Like an Irish pub, with Irish cuisine and Guinness beer. [M-4]

LA ESCONDIDA   Okabe Bldg., B1, 2-24-12 Nishi Azabu, Minato-ku. Tel: 3486-0330. Hours: 5:00 P.M.–midnight, Sun. from 4:00–10:00 P.M. Very Mexican atmosphere, good food, Mexican chefs. [M-2]

LA MEX   1-15-23 Minami Aoyama, Minato-ku. Tel: 3470-1712. Hours: 11:45 A.M.–2:00 P.M., 6:00–10:30 P.M., closed Sun. Tex-Mex food and jolly ambience, reasonable prices. [M-5]

EL MACAMBO   Chitose Bldg., B2, 1-4-38 Nishi Azabu, Minato-ku. Tel: 5410-0468. Hours: 6:00 P.M.–midnight daily (Fri. & Sat. until 2:00 A.M.). A variety of Latin-American cuisine is served in this exuberant restaurant. Dinners from around ¥5,000. [M-1]

BARBACOA GRILL   Evergreen Bldg., B1, 4-3-24 Jingumae, Shibuya-ku. Tel: 3407-0571. Hours: 11:30 A.M.–3:00 P.M., 5:00–11:00 P.M. daily. For ravenous carnivores, this place offers all the barbecue you can eat, with a salad bar, for ¥2,900, or just ¥1,200 at lunchtime. [M-4] Also at Hummox Pavilion Shibuya, B1, 20-15 Udagawa-cho, Shibuya-ku. Tel: 5489-1391. [M-3]

NINNIKUYA   1-26-12 Ebisu, Shibuya-ku. Tel: 5488-5540. Hours: 6:15–10:30 P.M., closed Sun. & hol. *Ninniku* is Japanese for "garlic" and this surprisingly popular restaurant serves an entire menu of garlic dishes. About ¥5,000 per person. [M-20]

Mainly for Atmosphere

Some people choose their restaurants for the food, some for the atmosphere, some for the price, and some for the other types of people who will be there. Even if your first priorities are food and price, there is something to be said for restaurants that look great and, for whatever reasons (not always the quality of the food), tend to attract a livelier-than-usual group of customers. Of course, what we are talking about is fashion in restaurants and fashionable people, categories that are inherently subject to change. The fashionable place today may well be the dive of tomorrow. Some of the restaurants offering a more fashionable and fun atmosphere have already been recommended above: **Daini's Table, Chianti, Kisso, Spago's.** Below we have listed restaurants where the interiors are interesting, the customers chic, or perhaps the experience merits a try.

MANIN 2-22-12 Jingumae, Shibuya-ku. Tel: 3478-3778. Hours: 6:00–10:00 P.M., closed Sun. Beautiful interior designed by Philippe Starck, expensive French nouvelle cuisine. From about ¥12,000 per person. [M-4]

OZAWA 4-9-23 Shirogane-dai, Minato-ku. Tel: 3442-1171. Hours: noon–2:00 P.M., 6:00–10:00 P.M., closed Mon. Another restaurant in a Starck-designed building. French nouvelle cuisine. Lunches from ¥3,500, dinners from ¥10,000. [M-19]

TABLEAUX Sunroser Daikanyama, B1, 11-6 Sarugaku-cho, Shibuya-ku. Tel: 5489-2201. Hours: 11:30 A.M.–2:00 P.M., 5:30–10:30 P.M. (until 11:00 P.M. on weekends), bar until 2:00 A.M. daily. Eclectic Southern California menu, glitzy Hollywood decor, moderately priced. [M-20]

ROY'S Soho's West, 2F, 5-25-10 Nakamachi, Setagaya-ku. Tel: 5706-6555. Hours: 11:30 A.M.–3:30 P.M., 5:30–11:00 P.M. daily. Fantastic interior in this rather out-of-the-way restaurant serving California-style cooking. About ¥6,000 per person. On the ground floor of the same eccentric building is **Seiryu-Mon West.**

SEIRYU-MON WEST Soho's West, 1F, 5-25-10 Nakamachi, Setagaya-ku. Tel: 5707-1990. Hours: 11:30 A.M.–3:00 P.M., 5:30 P.M.–4:00 A.M. daily (until 11:00 P.M. on Sun. & hol.). A solid wall of pachinko machines casts an eerie light in this futuristic Chinese restaurant. About ¥2,500 a person. [off Map]

LA FLAMME D'OR 1-23-1 Azumabashi, 1–2F, Taito-ku. Tel: 5608-5381. Hours: 11:30 A.M.–10:00 P.M. daily. One of Tokyo's more recent and amusing landmarks is the Philippe Starck Asahi Beer building in Asakusa where this upmarket beer restaurant is located. The food is not very good, but the interior and location are great. [M-12]

KIHACHI 4-18-10 Minami Aoyama, Minato-ku. Tel: 3403-7477. Hours: noon–2:30 P.M., 6:00–9:30 P.M. Mon.–Sat., noon–8:00 P.M. Sun. Fresh fish (there is a market downstairs) and Japanese-inspired Western food. Rather like a modern *brasserie*. [M-5]

HAMA RIKYU TEIEN TEAHOUSES Tel: 3541-0200. These two teahouses located in the center of the beautiful Hama Rikyu Gardens are not restaurants, but you can hire them for gatherings (no alcohol or singing allowed!). You must reserve at an office near the garden gates two months in advance on the sixteenth of every month. The larger teahouse can fit forty people and is ¥18,000 for three hours; the smaller is for twenty and costs ¥3,000. There are several other gardens (like Kiyosumi Garden) in Tokyo with similar possibilities. [M-11]

YAKATABUNE RESTAURANT BOATS

Another great idea for a celebration is to charter a rather old-fashioned *yakatabune* restaurant boat for an evening dinner floating down the Sumida or Edogawa rivers. The boats are flat-bottomed and lit with lanterns. Inside are low tables. Generally, you must organize a group of fifteen to twenty people at a rate of between ¥10,000–¥15,000 per head for a three-hour cruise, Japanese meal, and drinks. Here are some numbers: **Funasei:** 5479-2731 and **Nodaya:** 3863-6450.

店

SHOPPING

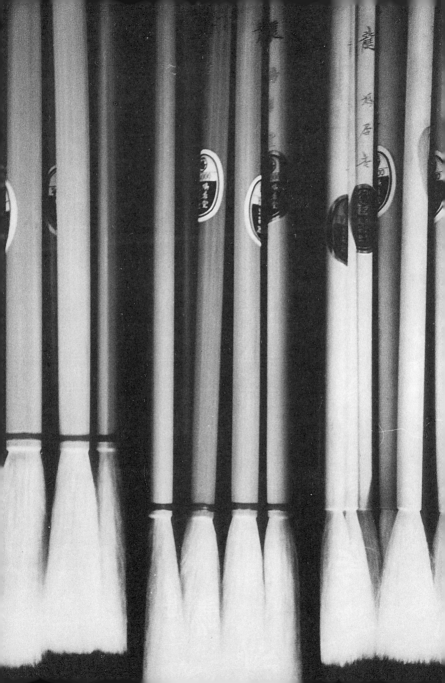

SHOPPING

Surprisingly, Japan does not survive off its export markets. Consumerism is rampant and shopping a favorite Japanese pastime.

Besides the usual arts, crafts, and antiques, Japan is setting international shopping standards in the fashion, electronics, and camera equipment fields. Don't expect to find many real bargains. Tokyo is an expensive city and even with the discounts given on electronics in the Akihabara district or at the tax-free centers, the merchandise can often be obtained for the same price back home. Still, the quality and quantity of products available in Tokyo is hard to beat.

There are a number of shopping options. Tokyo has districts specializing in certain kinds of merchandise such as Kanda for books, or Kappabashi for wholesale restaurant supplies (where you can buy the plastic food models seen in restaurant windows). The department stores are full-service institutions, from the basement food departments to the rooftop playgrounds. There are labyrinthine underground arcades in the basements of major buildings or at the larger train and subway stations and there are, of course, a multitude of small shops and boutiques scattered throughout the city.

Shopping Districts

One of the best and most entertaining ways to shop in Tokyo is to find the district that specializes in what you're looking for and just wander through the neighborhood. Though there is some overlap, and some districts have one of everything, these specialized districts generally have rows of shops that allow you to compare merchandise and prices. Here is a brief description of the major areas.

AKIHABARA Electronics paradise with dozens of discount stores.

AOYAMA Fashion in the medium to expensive range, designer boutiques and fashion buildings. Also **Kotto-dori**, a street with numerous antique shops.

ASAKUSA   Traditional Japanese products, workmen's clothing and wonderfully corny "Japanese-y" souvenirs.

GINZA   One of the most expensive areas in town, there are several major department stores: **Mitsukoshi, Matsuzakaya, Matsuya, Hankyu, Wako, Printemps, Sogo,** and **Seibu,** numerous fashion buildings, and scores of exclusive boutiques. Ginza also has some of the oldest and most prestigious shops specializing in traditional Japanese goods.

HARAJUKU   The best area for youngish fashion, the **Laforet** fashion building is a central landmark. **Takeshita-dori** is thick with cheap boutiques. For antiques there is the **Oriental Bazaar** and the basement of the **Hanae Mori** building. For toys, there's **Kiddyland.**

IKEBUKURO   The main **Seibu** and branches of **Parco, Tokyu Hands, Wave, Marui, Mitsukoshi,** and **Tobu** department stores, also the **Sunshine City** complex.

KANDA   Lots of old and new books, antique and old print shops, martial arts equipment and sporting goods.

NIHOMBASHI   Tokyo's oldest department stores are here: **Mitsukoshi** and **Takashimaya, Tokyu,** the famous book shop **Maruzen,** also numerous shops specializing in traditional crafts.

ROPPONGI   Good shopping at **Axis** for designer goods, **Wave** for music, the **Piramide** building for expensive imported goods.

SHIBUYA   More and more department stores, fashion buildings, and buildings specializing in a variety of goods for the home and office.

SHINJUKU   Good for cameras and smaller electronic goods, reasonably-priced fashions in **Takano** and the various fashion buildings. **Isetan** is great, **Marui** occupies several separate buildings, there's a **Barney's,** a **Virgin Records,** and the whole of Shinjuku Station building is one enormous arcade-like building called **My City.**

UENO   A good place to find discount merchandise is **Ameyoko,** an arcade with cheap food, clothing, cosmetics, and toys. For traditional Japanese goods, there is **Matsuzakaya** and numerous small shops.

Department Stores

Ask any Japanese where to buy a specific item and the answer will probably be "in a department store." A pivotal institution in Japanese life, in a *depato* you can buy food, fashion, furniture, fine art, a round-trip ticket to France, or a new home.

Service is a basic part of the system. Japan is probably the only country in the world where department store elevator operators have been trained by the company robot to bow at just the right angle (we suspect that the robot also teaches them to speak in that uniformly falsetto voice).

Most department stores start off with one or two floors in the basement devoted entirely to food. There will be plenty of free samples to ensure that you have the stamina to get through the rest of the building. After shopping your way through the fashion and housewares, you can stop off on the restaurant floor and choose from a variety of eating spots. Later, take in a bit of culture at one of the art galleries. Next, look for bargains on the discount floor, usually located near the top of the building. On a pleasant afternoon, finish off the day in the rooftop playground or beer garden.

Department stores are good places to shop for traditional Japanese products. The work of well-known crafts people is often on exhibition. Custom orders are generally taken for items such as kimono or *byobu,* folding screens.

Some department stores have two or three branch stores, but the main store is usually the best. Department stores are open every day except one day during the week, which is often a general day-off for the neighborhood. Many stores provide printed English directories at the ground floor information counter.

MITSUKOSHI 1-7 Nihombashi Muromachi, Chuo-ku. Tel: 3241-3311. Hours: 10:00 A.M.–6:30 P.M., closed Mon. [M-9] Ginza Branch: 4-6-16 Ginza, Chuo-ku. Tel: 3562-1111. Hours: Same as above. [M-8] Ebisu Branch: 4-20-7 Ebisu, Shibuya-ku. Tel: 5423-1111. Hours: 11:00 A.M.–7:30 P.M., closed first and third Mon. [M-20] Branches also in Shinjuku and Ikebukuro.

The classic Japanese department store, **Mitsukoshi** opened in 1673 as a kimono shop. In the later Meiji period, it was the first to add a second floor and glass display cases. In competition with the nearby **Takashimaya** from the beginning, Mitsukoshi kept its number one position until 1982 when a well-publicized scandal implicated its president. The scandal surfaced when Mitsukoshi sponsored an exhibition and sale of "Persian Art Treasures" that were later proved to be fakes. An investigation followed and the president and his mistress (dubbed the emperor and empress of Mitsukoshi by the press) were charged with embezzlement and tax evasion, among other things. The Nihombashi store still remains one of the great examples of a traditional department store. Japanese goods are probably the most interesting, including their large and excellent selection of kimono on the fourth floor.

Also a new branch in **Yebisu Garden Place,** smaller but offering a wide range of goods (clothes are mainly casual). The fresh food department is outstanding.

TAKASHIMAYA 2-4-1 Nihombashi, Chuo-ku. Tel: 3211-4111. Hours: 10:00 A.M.–6:30 P.M., closed the first and third Wed.

A few years older than its rival **Mitsukoshi, Takashimaya** has a warrant from the imperial family. During the Meiji period, Takashimaya was the first department store to hire saleswomen instead of just men, and the first to sell Western clothes. Like Mitsukoshi, Takashimaya is eminently conservative and is perhaps more interesting as a view of daily Japanese life than for its merchandise. It does, however, have a good selection of toys. [M-9]

SEIBU 1-28-1 Minami Ikebukuro, Toshima-ku. Tel: 3981-0111. Hours: 10:00 A.M.–8:00 P.M., closed Thurs. [M-18]. Shibuya branch: 23-1 Udagawa-cho, Shibuya-ku. Tel: 3462-0111. Closed Wed. [M-3] Yurakucho branch: 2-5-1 Yurakucho, Chiyoda-ku. Tel: 3286-0111. Closed Thur. [M-8]

The main Ikebukuro **Seibu** is one of the largest and best department stores in the world. In some ways it's too large for convenient shopping. All of the Seibu stores are known for their high-quality and comparatively contemporary merchandising.

For residents, the Shibuya branch is good, not too big, not too small. For visitors, the Yuraku-cho branch offers a more limited but well-selected range. Seibu has one of the best selections of Japanese designer boutiques and a range of contemporary Japanese crafts and household items.

The Shibuya Seibu also has a Foreign Customer Liaison Office to assist foreign visitors and residents.

ISETAN 3-14-1 Shinjuku, Shinjuku-ku. Tel: 3352-1111. Hours: 10:00 A.M.–7:30 P.M., closed Wed.

Along the same lines as **Seibu,** though not quite as good. Oriented to a youngish market, the merchandise is interesting and of good quality. There is a separate building for men's fashion. They also have a service for foreigners called the "I Club." [M-7]

MARUI Fashion Bldg., 3-30-16 Shinjuku, Shinjuku-ku. Tel: 3354-0101. Hours: 10:30 A.M.–7:30 P.M., closed the second or third Wed. [M-7] Shibuya: 3464-0101 [M-3] Ikebukuro: 3989-0101 [M-18]

Geared to a young market, there are several separate Marui buildings in the Shinjuku Station area. The most interesting is their **Fashion** building, with boutiques of known and unknown local designers. Other buildings include: **Young**—for more normal teenage fashion, **Mens'**—with about fifty boutiques, and **Interiors**—for furniture and housewares. We have only listed the address of the **Fashion** building, but the others are all located in the same area. In Shibuya, Marui has several buildings dedicated to fashion and **In the Room** for interiors.

MATSUZAKAYA 3-29-5 Ueno, Taito-ku. Tel: 3832-1111. Hours: 10:00 A.M.–7:30 P.M., closed Wed. [M-13] Ginza Branch: 6-10-1 Ginza, Chuo-ku. Tel: 3572-1111. Hours: Same as the Ueno branch. [M-8]

With a 370-year history, you can imagine how conservative this store is. Most interesting is its famous selection of combs and hair ornaments.

MATSUYA 3-6-1 Ginza, Chuo-ku. Tel: 3567-1211. Hours: 10:00 A.M.–7:30 P.M. (until 8:00 P.M. on Thr., Fri., Sat.), closed Tues. [M-8] Asakusa Branch: 1-4-1 Hanakawado, Taito-ku, Asakusa. Tel: 3842-1111. Hours: Same as above. [M-12]

The Asakusa store is a downtown working-class institution. Best known for its selection of reasonably priced Japanese products and exhibitions of traditional crafts. The Ginza store is more fashionable and has some interesting boutiques of well-known Japanese designers and a notable selection of design goods.

TOKYU 2-24-1 Dogenzaka, Shibuya-ku. Tel: 3477-3111. Hours: 10:00 A.M.–7:30 P.M., closed Tue.

Where your average Japanese person shops. Good, basic, and reasonably priced contemporary and traditional merchandise. Right at Shibuya Station is the Tokyu Toyoko-ten. [M-3]

DAIMARU 1-9-9 Marunouchi, Chiyoda-ku. Tel: 3212-8011. Hours: 10:00 A.M.–7:30 P.M. (until 7:00 P.M. on Sat., Sun., hol.), closed Wed.

Located above Tokyo Station's Yaesu Central Exit, Daimaru is another "basic" department store. Twice a year, they have good sales on rental kimono and formal wear (See "Bargain Sales"). [M-9]

ODAKYU 1-1-3 Nishi Shinjuku, Shinjuku-ku. Tel: 3342-1111. Hours: 10:00 A.M.–6:00 P.M. (until 7:00 P.M. on Fri., Sat., Sun.), closed Thur.

Not very interesting as a department store but their **Halc** interior division in a separate building next door has a good selection of housewares and furniture. [M-7]

SOGO 1-11-1 Yurakucho, Chiyoda-ku. Tel: 3284-6711. Hours: 10:00 A.M.–7:00 P.M., closed Wed.

A basic department store (but the Yokohama branch is one of the biggest). [M-10]

PRINTEMPS 3-2-1 Ginza, Chuo-ku. Tel: 3567-0077. Hours: 10:00 A.M.–7:00 P.M., closed Wed.

Tokyo branch of the famous French department store operated by the successful Daiei supermarket-department store chain. Merchandise is geared for young women. [M-8]

WAKO 4-5-11 Ginza, Chuo-ku. Tel: 3562-2111. Hours: 10:00 A.M.–5:30 P.M., closed Sun. & hol.

Opened by Hattori Kintaro of Seiko watch fame, the store features expensive, often imported, merchandise. For cheap thrills, you can check out their window display; it's changed every forty days at an average cost of ¥2,500,000. [M-8]

DAIEI 4-1 Himonya, Meguro-ku. Tel: 3710-1111. Hours: 10:00 A.M.–8:00 P.M., closed Wed. (Gakugei-daigaku Station, Tokyu Toyoko Line).

A big discount supermarket-department store chain offering good quality but inexpensive food, clothing, and household goods. [off Map]

Fashion Buildings

A cross between department stores and arcades, "fashion buildings" are Japan's high-rise answer to the sprawling shopping malls of America. Owned by department stores or real estate companies, boutique space is rented out for a share of the profits. There are hundreds of such buildings in Tokyo, though it's a case of "if you've seen one, you've seen them all." The best have a distinctive character and a good selection of merchandise.

PARCO   15-1 Udagawa cho, Shibuya-ku. Tel: 3464-5111. Hours: 10:00 A.M.–8:30 P.M. daily.

By far, the best of the "fashion buildings," **Parco** comes in three parts. Parts 1 and 2 specialize in fashion, Part 3 in interior merchandise. A division of **Seibu**, Parco is likewise predictably innovative. [M-3]

LAFORET   1-11-6 Jingumae, Shibuya-ku. Tel: 3475-0411. Hours: 11:00 A.M.–8:00 P.M. daily.

Quintessential Harajuku in spirit, **Laforet** is the home-away-from-home for thousands of trendy Japanese kids. There's a great selection of moderately-priced fashions and a few boutiques of the top designers. [M-4]

FROM 1ST   5-3-10 Minami Aoyama, Minato-ku. Hours and holidays vary with each shop.

Small and somewhat exclusive, **From 1st** is an interesting building designed by architect Yamashita Kazumasa. Boutiques include Issey Miyake, Jurgen Lehl, and Matsuda's Nicole. There is a great flower shop in the central plaza, **El Toula** for Italian food, and **La Poisson Rouge** for inexpensive French food. [M-5]

LA COLLEZIONE   6-1-3 Minami Aoyama, Minato-ku. Tel: 3470-9695. Hours: vary according to each shop, but basically 11:00 A.M.–8:00 P.M., closed Mon.

This startling concrete building is Osaka-based architect Ando Tadao's first major project in Tokyo. Its circular interior spaces house overseas designer boutiques and a beautiful furniture showroom for Cassina. [M-5]

BARNEY'S NEW YORK   3-18-5 Shinjuku, Shinjuku-ku. Tel: 3352-1200. Hours: 11:00 A.M.–8:00 P.M. daily.

Seven floors of fashion and accessories in this branch of the famous New York shop. [M-7]

SEED   21-1 Udagawa-cho, Shibuya-ku. Tel: 3462-0111. Hours: 11:00 A.M.–8:00 P.M., closed Wed.

Another great **Seibu** spin-off, this ten-story building is designed to attract the hippest of the hip generation. [M-3]

PIRAMIDE   6-6-9 Roppongi, Minato-ku. Tel: 3746-1205. Hours: vary with each shop, but basically 11:00 A.M.–8:00 P.M., closed Sun. & Mon.

One of the late eighties additions to the Tokyo consumer scene—full of Italian designer boutiques and Italian restaurants. [M-1]

Bargain Sales

Twice a year the department stores and "fashion buildings" have huge bargain sales to clear the store for the next season's merchandise. The large department stores have major sales in February, August, and December. **Parco** is usually the first fashion building to have a sale. Offering discounts of up to 50%, their sale on winter clothing starts the second Friday in January, on summer clothes from the second Friday in July. Both last one week. The **Laforet** sales at the end of January and July are becoming world-famous. The other fashion buildings follow.

Rental *kimono* and formal wear are put on sale at **Daimaru** department store in March and September. This sale is great for cheap wedding *kimono* and funny men's tuxedos.

Specialized and Special Interest Buildings

AXIS 5-17-1 Roppongi, Minato-ku. Tel: 3587-2781. Hours vary with each shop, generally from 11:00 A.M.–7:00 P.M., closed Sun.

Contemporary design is the main focus of this building. Of particular interest are: **Matrix** for monochrome office supplies, **Nuno** for fabulous fabrics, **Kisso** for Japanese food, and the **Kuramata Shiro-**designed Yamagiwa lighting gallery. [M-1]

WAVE 6-2-27 Roppongi, Minato-ku. Tel: 3408-1111. Hours: 11:00 A.M.–9:00 P.M., closed the first and third Wed.

Ostensibly an enormous record, video, and bookstore, **Wave** is an extravagant demonstration of the application of new technology in the search for pleasure and personal satisfaction. There is a customer-access, computerized music reference system on the ground floor, and a **Sound Bank** with hundreds of top songs on cassettes hooked up to eight sets of headphones. **Art Vivant** on the fourth floor features a good selection of art books. [M-1]

SPIRAL 5-6-23 Minami Aoyama, Minato-ku. Tel: 3498-1171. Hours: 11:00 A.M.–8:00 P.M. daily.

Designed by architect Maki Fumihiko, the façade of this building is a great play on the way streets in Tokyo are fronted with an eclectic collection of building styles. Japan's foremost undergarment manufacturer, Wacoal has erected this building in an attempt at establishing a new corporate image. There are coffee shops, restaurants, a gallery that focuses on contemporary art, and a shop selling miscellaneous goods, most notably Japanese tableware and wrapping supplies. [M-5]

TOKYU HANDS 12-18 Udagawa-cho, Shibuya-ku. Tel: 3476-5461. Hours: 10:00 A.M.–8:00 P.M., closed the second and third Wed. of the month. [M-3] Ikebukuro branch: 1-28-10 Higashi-Ikebukuro, Toshima-ku. Tel: 3980-6111. Hours: 10:00 A.M.–8:00 P.M., closed the second and third Thurs.

Eight floors of merchandise for crafts, hobbies, home improvements, etc. The store is almost always claustrophobically crowded—but it is good. [M-18]

LOFT 21-1 Udagawa-cho, Shibuya-ku. Tel: 3462-0111. Hours: 11:00 A.M.–8:00 P.M., closed Wed.

Seibu's answer to the Tokyu chain's Tokyu Hands—full of household goods and miscellany. Great selection of storage boxes, wrapping, and bits and pieces. Located just behind the Shibuya Seibu B-kan. [M-3]

SUNSHINE CITY 3-1-1 Higashi Ikebukuro, Toshima-ku. Tel: 3989-3331. Hours: Shops 10:00 A.M.–8:00 P.M. daily.

Built on the site of the former Sugamo Prison, **Sunshine City** is an enormous complex that includes a branch of **Mitsukoshi** Department Store, **Alpa** fashion building, the **Ancient Orient Museum,** the **Sunshine Theater,** exhibition halls, a culture center for art and sports classes, a **Prince Hotel,** a planetarium and aquarium, and lots of junk food restaurants. Planned as a cultural focal point for the Ikebukuro area, it has become a favorite playground for suburbanites from the North. [M-18]

Arcades

Japan has a rather long history of arcade shopping. In the Meiji period, when department stores in the developmental stages were still checking in, and occasionally losing, hundreds of pairs of shoes a day, arcades were a more convenient way to shop. At one time, there were over twenty throughout the city.

There are still a number of arcades in Tokyo, though now most of them have literally gone underground. The basements of major train stations such as Tokyo Station (the largest in Asia) and Shinjuku Station have miles of shops serving commuters on the way home. Merchandise is usually a mixed bag of fashion, food, cosmetics, books, and electronics.

Most major hotels have arcades geared to tourists who don't know any better than to buy there. The general and hotel arcades listed below do have some interesting shops:

AMEYOKO   4-7-8 Ueno, Taiko-ku. Hours vary with each shop, but most are open from 10:30 A.M.–7:00 P.M. and closed on Wed.

The last of Tokyo's post-war black markets, **Ameyoko** feels more like Hong Kong than Japan. An antiseptic new building houses the spill over from the old shops beneath the train tracks. There are hundreds of shops and it is one of the cheapest places to buy cosmetics, fresh, and bulk foods. Some shops will bargain a bit. [M-13]

INTERNATIONAL ARCADE   1-7-23 Uchisaiwai-cho, Chiyoda-ku. Tel: 3591-2764. Hours: 10:00 A.M.–7:00 P.M. daily, until 6:00 P.M. on Sun. & hol.

A tourist-oriented arcade with some good shops including Hayashi Kimono for old and new kimono. Other shops sell pearls, electronics (tax-free), etc. [M-10]

IMPERIAL HOTEL ARCADE   Not to be confused with the new **Imperial Tower** full of imported merchandise, this one is in the basement of the old wing. Good shops include **Ueda Pearls** for good quality and service, and two well-known but expensive antique shops: **Odawara Shoten** and **Maruyama & Co.** Most shops open from 9:30 A.M.–7:00 P.M. daily. [M-10]

HOTEL OKURA   Antique shops: **Mildred Warder, Ltd.,** and **Yokoyama, Inc.,** contemporary prints in **Franell Gallery.** Most of the shops are open between 10:00 A.M.–6:00 P.M., closed Sun. & hol. [M-11]

HOTEL NEW OTANI   Various good, but expensive, arts and antique shops, notably **Kandori** for ceramics. Most shops open from 10:00 A.M.–6:00 P.M. daily [M-6]

Tax-Free Stores

Most tourist publications, maps, and guide books will direct you to the big tax-free stores around the city. They do a lot of advertising, which they can well afford with the profits they make selling over-priced, shoddy goods to unsuspecting tourists. The definitive "tourist trap," tax-free stores offer only passably acceptable deals on export models of Japanese electronics. But most electronics stores in Akihabara have their own tax-free departments where the prices are usually lower. The worst buys at tax-free centers are the Japanese souvenirs. Why buy a cheap polyester kimono at one of these shops when you can get a beautiful antique silk one at **Hayashi Kimono** and **Oriental Bazaar,** or find an even cheaper bargain at one of the Sunday flea markets? We recommend that you do not shop at these tax-free emporiums.

If you are buying anything tax-free, you must present your passport and fill out a form called a "Record of Purchase of Commodities Tax-Exempt for Export," and then sign a "Covenant of Purchase of Commodities Tax-Exempt of Ultimate Export" form. The store will provide both. Attach the first form to your passport and show the form and article to customs officials when leaving Japan.

Some of the items that can be purchased tax-free are precious stones, pearls, articles made of precious metal, items plated or coated with precious metal, tortoise-shell, coral ware, amber products, rifles, cameras, projectors, television sets, and other electrical goods.

Wholesale Markets

There are a few specialized wholesale market districts in the city that will also sell retail. Since the shops are generally concentrated along a single street, once you find the area you won't need the names of specific shops. We have given the name of the nearest station and information for which map to use. Most shops open early in the morning through early afternoon and close on Sundays and holidays.

ASAKUSABASHI-KURAMAE   Between the Sobu Line and Toei Asakusa Line Asakusabashi Stations. Toys, model kits, party favors, novelties, costumes, stationery supplies, and seasonal decorations (e.g. plastic cherry-tree boughs). [M-24]

KAPPABASHI   Tawaramachi Station on the Ginza Line, in the Asakusa area about five minutes walk from Senso-ji temple. Plastic and wax restaurant food models, restaurant supplies, including sushi-chef costumes. [M-12]

NIPPORI   Nippori Station on the JR Yamanote Line. Toys and cheap, unsophisticated kid's sweets and snack foods. Also a wholesale fabrics and sewing notions market. Most shops close on the third Tue. of the month. [M-13]

TSUKIJI FISH MARKET   5-2 Tsukiji, Chuo-ku. Hours: Outer market from 5:30–2:00 P.M. (some shops close at noon), closed Sun. & hol. Tokyo's famous fish market. The general public is not supposed to enter the wholesale market area, but you probably won't be stopped. The outer retail market is open to all and on the second Sunday of the month there is a special morning market for the public with discounts of twenty to thirty percent. There are a number of cheap sushi restaurants in the area that open from 6:00 A.M.–1:00 P.M. to serve the hungry fish buyers. True sushi fans shouldn't miss the chance to breakfast on the freshest fish in town. [M-22]

OTA WHOLESALE MARKETS (Ota Shijo)   3-2-1 Tokai, Ota-ku. Tel: 3790-8311. Closed Sun. & hol. Take the monorail for Haneda and get off at Ryutsu Center. The market is about an eight minute walk from there. At the present time, there are three wholesale markets located here in separate buildings: one for flowers, one for fish, and one housing the old Kanda Fruit and Vegetable Market. Its all far more high-tech than the old ones in downtown Tokyo, but even though you are supposed to be a wholesaler to get in, you can often just wander in and buy. Auctions start early: fish at 5:30 A.M., fruit and vegetables at 6:30 A.M. [off Map]

FASHION

Since the early eighties, the Western image of a Japanese populace clad in either kimono or functional blue suits has slowly shifted to one of a neat and tidy people dressed in either obviously name-brand goods, black and gray experimental Japanese designs, or the functional blue suits. With a seemingly insatiable appetite for the most exclusive designer goods from around the world, the Japanese market proved a boon for the international fashion world. Elegant and expensive boutiques proliferated at an astonishing rate and soon any designer who had any kind of a reputation anywhere in the world could be found in Tokyo. Meanwhile, the blue (gray in summer) business suits are still the daily uniform for many.

Perhaps less noticed by all but a few fashion-conscious individuals was the growing strength of work by Japanese designers. By the early eighties, the Paris shows of designers such as **Miyake Issey, Kawakubo Rei,** and **Yamamoto Yohji** were followed by a fashion press often shocked by iconoclastic designs that were clearly the products of a non-Western sensibility.

More than a decade later, these designers have earned their place in fashion history. Their work is admired and followed by a growing public who find the clothing exciting and liberating.

Not all Japanese fashion is avant-garde, however. There are several designers of more traditional European-influenced haute couture such as **Mori Hanae, Ashida Jun,** and **Kimijima,** as well as designers such as **Koshino Junko, Hanai Yukiko,** and **Shimada Junko** whose elegant, wearable clothes show very little Asian influence. A still younger generation are perhaps equally influenced by the urban landscape of Tokyo and the work of the wildest Japanese and Western (often British) designers.

There are wonderful clothes to buy here, but prices are high and large enough sizes are difficult to find. As much of the work by the more avant-garde designers tends to be somewhat free in form, there is generally something that will fit even the largest of Western bodies. The selection and quality in the shops is usually excellent.

Japanese Designer Boutiques

Following is a selective list of Japanese designers and design labels. The list is in alphabetical order by designer's name or by the name of the designer's line, depending on which tends to be better known. Many boutiques are located in one of the stores or fashion buildings listed in the previous sections. For boutiques in other locations, we have listed addresses and opening hours.

• Women's Fashions

A.T. by Atsuro Tayama   Parco Part 1, 3F. Tel: 3477-5998.

A rather recent line by this designer who has formerly worked with both Yamamoto Yohji and Cacherel. Very popular, easy-to-wear Japanese style. [M-3]

BOUTIQUE YUYA by Nagahata Yuya   3-6-4 Nishi Azabu, Minato-ku. Tel: 5474-2097. Hours: noon–6:30 P.M., closed Sun.

Stunning kimono silk, both new and antique fabrics, are fashioned into unusual and versatile day and evening wear. Custom orders accepted. [M-1]

BIGI by Inaba Yoshie   4-13-33 Higashi, Shibuya-ku. Tel: 3797-4480. Hours: 11:00 A.M.–7:00 P.M., closed Mon.

Designs tend to be a Japanese interpretation of nostalgic American clothes. [off Map]

C'EST VRAI by Ota Norihisa   Seibu Shibuya A-kan, 3F. Tel: 3770-6018.

Often good knits from this designer of attractive, somewhat feminine clothes. [M-3]

COMMES DES GARÇONS by Kawakubo Rei   5-2-1 Minami Aoyama, Minato-ku. Tel: 3406-3951. Hours: 11:00 A.M.–8:00 P.M. daily.

Perhaps the most unconventional of the leading designers, her main shop in Tokyo sells all of her different lines. [M-1]

MORI HANAE   3-6-1 Kita Aoyama, Minato-ku Tel: 3400-3301. Hours: 10:30 A.M.–7:00 P.M. daily.

Madame Mori is best known for her pretty and classic evening wear. [M-4 & 5]

KOSHINO HIROKO   Tokyo Creator Bldg., 3-51-40 Sendagaya, Shibuya-ku. Tel: 3475-5329. Hours: 10:00 A.M.–7:00 P.M., closed Sun.

Sister to Junko, she designs sophisticated casual and evening wear. [M-4]

YOSHIDA HIROMI 3-21-22 Nishi Azabu, Minato-ku. Tel: 3403-0857. Hours: 11:00 A.M.–8:00 P.M., closed Sun.

Designs a line called **Clove-vs-Clove**, nothing extraordinary but nice, feminine clothing. Better with summer wear. [M-2]

OKAWA HITOMI 4-30-6 Jingumae, Shibuya-ku. Tel: 3403-6555. Hours: 11:30 A.M.–8:30 P.M. daily.

A favorite designer of the Harajuku young, her popular lines include the very cute **Milk**, **Milk Boys** favored by young skaters. [M-4]

MIYAKE ISSEY Main shop: 3-18 Minami Aoyama, Minato-ku. Tel: 3423-1408. Hours: 11:00 A.M.–8:00 P.M. daily.

Definitively "Japan Style," his designs are both elegant and simple, utilizing wonderful fabrics. [M-5]

KOSHINO JUNKO 6-5-36 Minami Aoyama, Minato-ku. Tel: 3406-7370. Hours: 10:00 A.M.–7:00 P.M., closed Sun. & hol.

Koshino designs clothing (and a growing line of licensed products for the home) that often has a slightly high-tech, Japanese feel to it. [M-5]

SHIMADA JUNKO 49th Ave. Aobadai Terasu, 1-1-4 Aobadai, Meguro-ku. Tel: 3463-2346. Hours: 11:00 A.M.–7:00 P.M., closed Mon.

This designer lives much of the year in France and designs clothing that tends to be a bit more sexy than the usual. Nice suits. [M-20]

WATANABE JUNYA Sold at the Aoyama **Comme des Garçons** shop.

This young designer for the Comme des Garçons Tricot line creates his own line of rather wild, avant-garde Japanese fashions. [M-5]

JÜRGEN LEHL From 1st Bldg., B1. Tel: 3498-6723. Hours: 11:00 A.M.–8:00 P.M. daily.

This long-term Tokyo resident designs simple, Asian-influenced clothing that reflects the designer's interest in textures and colors. [M-5]

YAMAMOTO KANSAI 3-28-7 Jingumae, Shibuya-ku. Tel: 3478-1958. Hours: 11:00 A.M.–8:00 P.M. daily.

Colorful and theatrical sportswear with an often forthright Japanese flavor. [M-4]

KENZO Printemps, 3F. Tel: 3535-5098. Hours: 11:00 A.M.–8:00 P.M., closed third Thur.

This designer has lived in Paris for so long he is not really considered part of the Japanese design crowd. [M-8]

MADAME HANAI by Hanai Yukiko Roi Bldg., 2F. 5-5-1 Roppongi, Minato-ku. Tel: 3404-5791. Hours: 11:00 A.M.–8:00 P.M., closed third Thur.

Pretty, sophisticated clothing. [M-1]

KOHGA MARIKO Nihombashi Mitsukoshi, 3F.

Part of the Nicole group, she designs rather elegant, somewhat sexy clothing. Often good evening wear. [M-9]

MATSUSHIMA MASAKI 3-6-26 Jingumae, Shibuya-ku. Tel: 5411-2080. Hours: 10:00 A.M.–6:00 P.M. daily.

Former assistant for the well-known (late) Kumagai Tokio, he has recently launched his own line of rather pop, youngish but avant-garde fashions. [M-4]

MATSUDA Nicole Bldg., 3-1-25 Jingumae, Shibuya-ku. Tel: 3478-0998. Hours: 11:00 A.M.–8:00 P.M. daily.

Matsuda Mitsuhiro's clothing goes by his name abroad but in Japan it is known as Madame Nicole. The designs combine a slight retro-American feeling with Japanese sensibility. [M-4 & 5]

MUSÉE DÚJI by Uji Masato 6-11-1 Minami Aoyama, Minato-ku. Tel: 3406-0816. Hours: 11:00 A.M.–7:00 P.M., closed Mon.

This line of colorful, wanna-be Lacroix and Chanel fashions is extremely popular with the more well-bred and showy Japanese young woman. [M-5]

NICOLE by Eno Hiroko and Chiba Mie Parco Part 2, 5F. Tel: 3476-2133.

Japanese avant-garde for a slightly younger crowd. [M-3]

NOVESPAZIO by Yamafuji Noboru Ginza Mitsukoshi, 3F.

Slightly showy clothing favored by well-dressed Japanese office ladies. [M-8]

MAEDA OSAMU Shibuya Seed, 6F. Tel: 3462-3761.

This younger designer, known for his "body conscious" clothing, creates well-made, rather minimal but interesting clothes. [M-3]

PINK HOUSE by Kaneko Isao Nest Daikanyama Bldg., B1. 28-11 Sarugaku-cho, Shibuya-ku. Tel: 3476-7063. Hours: noon–8:00 P.M., closed Tue.

For years now, this extremely popular designer has produced nearly identical, unbelievably *kawaii* (cute) fashions. Lots of petticoats, storybook prints, lace, and pastels. [M-20]

ROSE IS A ROSE by Higa Kiyoko 6-9 Hachiyama-cho, Shibuya-ku. Tel: 3780-0506. Hours: 10:00 A.M.–8:00 P.M., closed Sun.

Very unusual use of bright colors by this Okinawa-born designer. [off Map]

SHIMURA by Shimura Masahisa Ginza Sogo Department Store, 3F.

Follows the Yamamoto Yohji/Kawakubo Rei trends. [M-10]

ONO TAKASHI Shibuya Seed, 3F. Tel: 3462-3780.

Promising designer of avant-garde Japanese designs. [M-3]

NAGASAWA YOICHI Barney's (Shinjuku), 3F. Tel: 3352-1200.

Another former assistant to Kumagai Tokio, Nagasawa tries to create clothes that are avant-garde but that don't overwhelm the wearer. One of the new designers to watch. [M-7]

YAMAMOTO YOHJI "Y's" 5-3-6 Minami Aoyama, Minato-ku. Tel: 3486-5314. Hours: 11:00 A.M.–9:00 P.M. daily.

Another one of the big names. [M-5]

TORII YUKI 5-7-16 Ginza, Chuo-ku. Tel: 3574-8701. Hours: 11:30 A.M.–7:30 P.M. daily.

Well-mannered, attractive clothing, Fall–Winter collections tend to be best. [M-8]

ZUCCA by Onozaka Akiyoshi Yurakucho Seibu, 5F. Tel 3213-3910.

Part of the Issey group, interesting casual clothes, a sort of Japanese-natural style. [M-8]

• Men's Fashions

Unfortunately for most men, shopping for Japanese clothing in Tokyo will be a somewhat disappointing experience—the clothes are almost uniformly too small. This is particularly true for the more conservative styles. The wilder designs are often free-sized and easier to fit. Some of the best collections of men's wear can be found at **Parco, Seibu,** and **Marui.** Please check the **Department Stores** and **Fashion Buildings** listings for addresses, hours, and locations.

Below we have listed a few of the more interesting designers for men, noting when information duplicates that for women.

ARSTON VOLAJU by Sato Koshin 3-24-22 Nishi Azabu, Minato-ku. Tel: 3401-7543. Hours: 11:30 A.M.–8:30 P.M., closed Sun. & Wed.

Fun, slightly off-beat clothing, often favored by musicians (Miles Davis shopped here). [M-2]

BIGI (MEN'S) see **Women's Fashions**

COMMES DES GARÇONS HOMME see **Women's Fashions**

FICCE UOMO by Konishi Yoshiyuki Marui (Shinjuku) Men's-kan. Tel: 3356-0694.

Beautifully-colored hand-knits. [M-7]

MIYAKE ISSEY 3-18 Minami Aoyama, Minato-ku. Tel: 3423-1407. Hours: 11:00 A.M.–8:00 P.M. daily.

This top designer's main shop was designed by the brilliant Shiro Kuramata. [M-5]

KATO KAZUTAKA Marui (Shinjuku) Men's, 6F. Tel: 3354-3173.

This designer's "Tete Homme" line is known for its colorful knits and having a rather Italian flair. [M-7]

MATSUDA see **Women's Fashions**

PASHU by Hosokawa Shin 8-11-37 Akasaka, Minato-ku. Tel: 3479-0196. Hours: noon–7:30 P.M.

Modern monotone fashions. Great shop designed by Sugimoto Takashi. [M-5]

KIKUCHI TAKEO 3-17-25 Nishi Azabu, Minato-ku. Tel: 3401-7346. Hours: noon–9:00 P.M. daily.

European casual style. [off map]

BARBICHE 3-1-28 Jingumae, Shibuya-ku. Tel: 3404-8957. Hours: 11:00 A.M.–8:00 P.M. daily.

Part of the Bigi group, basically British style. [M-5]

• Designers from Abroad

More and more designers from abroad are opening boutiques in Tokyo. For most non-Japanese, these shops will be of little interest—the prices are very high and the clothes tailored to Japanese sizes and tastes. If you are interested, however, you can find boutiques in major department stores and fashion buildings. The **La Collezione** building in Aoyama and the **Piramide** building in Roppongi have a good selection of shops, and the Aoyama area is full of them.

Cheap Fashion

Exchange rates being what they are, even the less expensive clothing available in Japan seems overpriced to many visiting and resident foreigners. Bargains are to be had, however, they just take a bit longer to find.

Inexpensive clothing can be found in Shibuya, Shinjuku, and perhaps with most fun in Harajuku where there is a wide selection of wild clothes that are often knock-offs of the major designers. The back streets of Harajuku are full of tiny boutiques. Along **Takeshita-dori** [M-4] the merchandise spills out onto the sidewalks, enticing you into the shops. The basement floors of most fashion buildings are another good bargain shopping spot. Earlier, we listed the times for some of the best bargain sales at department stores and **Fashion Buildings.** If there is a designer whose clothing you particularly yearn for, try to get on their list for information on their seasonal sales (Issey Miyake's sale, for example, is fantastic).

SEIYU 6-27-25 Minami Oi, Shinagawa-ku. Tel: 3768-1211. Hours: 10:00 A.M.–7:00 P.M., closed Wed.

A large supermarket-department store that is a great place to shop for cheap food, fashion, and household goods. [off Map]

DAIEI see **Department Stores**

YOFUKU NO AOYAMA 2-8-15 Ginza, Chuo-ku. Tel: 3561-6731. Hours: 10:00 A.M.–8:00 P.M. daily.

Like a wholesale outlet, this shop has a huge selection of normal clothes, some in large sizes. [M-8]

ZENMALL 29-4 Udagawa-cho, Shibuya-ku. Tel: 3770-1641. Hours: 11:00 A.M.–8:30 P.M. daily.

Several-storied clothing outlet, with some cheap Italian imports for women. [M-3]

DESIGNER'S COLLEZIONE 6-8-10 Roppongi, Minato-ku. Tel: 3746-5768. Hours: 6:00 P.M.– 10:00 P.M. Mon.–Fri., noon–6:00 P.M. on Sat, until 5:00 P.M. on Sun. & hol.

Imports (Armani, etc.) and designer's men's, women's, and children's clothing often fifty to seventy percent off. [M-1]

DEP'T EAST Daikanyama Twin Bldg. A, 2F. 30-3 Sarugaku-cho, Shibuya-ku. Tel: 3464-6141. Hours: 11:00 A.M.–8:00 P.M. daily.

Secondhand, hip clothes, often American and European vintage clothing. [M-20]

SCANDAL BOY   1-26-15 Ebisu, Shibuya-ku. Tel: 3444-4886. Hours: 11:00 A.M.–8:00 P.M. daily.

New and used, Ladies' & Men's, often designer or major brand off-season goods. [M-20]

ULTRA QUEEN   2-6-32 Ebisu, Shibuya-ku. Tel: 3449-9531. Hours: 11:00 A.M.–8:00 P.M. daily.

Secondhand, some off-season designer clothing. [M-2]

BUNKAYA ZAKKATEN   1-9-5 Jinnan, Shibuya-ku. Tel: 3461-0985. Hours: 11:00 A.M.–8:00 P.M., closed on the twentieth of each month.

This shop sells a wide range of curios and clothing, much of it pure kitsch and quite cheap. There are a number of other shops selling similar goods on either side of **Bunkaya** (which literally means "culture shop"). [M-3]

For Children

Japanese children are perhaps the world's best dressed. The clothes here are cute (sometimes too cute) and pricey. They are, however, well-made. Children's toys here are also great. If you are looking for a gift for a child you might consider a cotton kimono (for example from Iseyoshi in the kimono section), or an antique one from a flea market. Traditional hair ornaments and ribbons are sweet on little girls and boys love the ninja-like traditional clothing items—these can be found in shops along **Nakamise** in Asakusa.

Most department stores have good children's sections. Notable is **Takashimaya's** toy department. **Shibuya Seibu** and **Parco** have good selections as well. **Daiei** offers a selection of inexpensive goods.

For more information on how to deal with children in Tokyo look at *Japan for Kids* by Diane Kanagawa and Jeanne Erickson (Kodansha, 1992).

FAMILIAR   6-10-16 Ginza, Chuo-ku. Tel: 3574-7111. Hours: Mon.–Fri. 11:00 A.M.–6:30 P.M., until 7:00 P.M. on Sat. & Sun., closed Wed.

This popular maker of children's clothing has a several-storied building with a wide selection of items for children, as well as a hair salon and café tailored for tykes. [M-8]

CRAYON HOUSE   5-7-5 Jingumae, Shibuya-ku. Tel: 3406-6492. Hours: 11:00 A.M.–7:00 P.M. daily.

Perhaps the best shop for children's books in Tokyo. English and Japanese. [M-4]

AKACHAN HONPO   There are several branches around Tokyo. Gotanda Branch: 4-13-3 Osaki, Shinagawa-ku. Tel: 3492-7530. Hours: 9:00 A.M.–5:30 P.M. daily (until 5:00 P.M. on Sun. & hol.).

This co-op costs ¥2,000 to join but offers reasonable prices for baby needs and toys. [off Map]

ELECTRONICS AND CAMERAS

Both the "Japanese Miracle" and "Japan Bashing" are to a great degree the result of this country's undisputed world leadership in the field of consumer electronics. But while Japanese products are found almost everywhere in the world, the largest percentage of all Japanese consumer electronics are sold domestically. Competition for a share of this market is relentless and a company strong enough to survive at home is almost guaranteed success abroad.

Quality control is one of the hallmarks of the Japanese electronics industry. Workers take great pride in their jobs, a hold-over from artisan traditions with a little *samurai* Confucian loyalty ethic thrown in. Domestic success is determined by quality, competitive pricing, and most importantly, innovation. The Japanese consumer is easily swayed by the attraction of new technology. New, slightly improved models will be snapped up, while last year's machine is unceremoniously trashed in perfect running order.

It's worth noting, however, that despite the competition at home, prices for Japanese products here are often higher than those of identical products abroad. If you're planning on making a major purchase while in Japan, check the prices at home first.

The distribution system is now so advanced that products are almost simultaneously introduced in both domestic and overseas markets. Some products are manufactured solely for domestic use, but since voltage in Japan is different, you should buy only export models of any sophisticated equipment. Most of the major shops in Akihabara have special export departments that also allow duty-free purchasing. If you're just interested in looking at the latest electronic toys, most manufacturers have showrooms in convenient locations where consumers can go and play.

Showrooms

SONY SHOWROOM   Sony Bldg., 1, 3, & 4F. 5-3-1 Ginza, Chuo-ku. Tel: 3573-2371. Hours: 11:00 A.M.–8:00 P.M. daily.

    Audio, video, and computers. [M-8]

TOSHIBA GINZA SEVEN   Toshiba Ginza Seven Bldg., 1–6F. 7-9-19 Ginza, Chuo-ku. Tel: 3348-2226. Hours: 11:00 A.M.–7:00 P.M., closed Wed. and the second and fourth Tues.

    Audio, video. [M-8]

NIPPER (Victor)   1-7-1 Shimbashi, Minato-ku. Tel: 3289-2811. Hours: 11:00 A.M.–7:00 P.M., closed Sat., Sun., & hol.

    Audio, video, etc. [M-8]

TOYOTA AUTO SALON AMLUX   3-3-5 Higashi Ikebukuro, Toshima-ku. Tel: 5391-5900. Hours: 11:00 A.M.–8:00 P.M. (until 7:00 P.M. on Sun. & hol.), closed Mon.

    Six floors focused on Toyota cars, displays on auto manufacturing, and hands-on computer car design facilities. [M-18]

NAIS PLAZA   Monoris Bldg., 3–5F. 2-3-1 Nishi Shinjuku, Shinjuku-ku. Tel: 5381-8211 Hours: 10:00 A.M.–6:00 P.M. daily.

    Several thousand electronic products by Matsushita. [M-7]

PIONEER SHOWROOM   1-4-1 Meguro, Meguro-ku. Tel: 3494-1111. Hours: 10:30 A.M.-6:50 P.M. daily.

    Audio and laser disc technology. [M-19]

NEC SHOWROOM   Hibiya City, Hibiya Kokusai Bldg., B1. 2-2-3 Uchisaiwai-cho, Chiyoda-ku. Tel: 3595-0511. Hours: 10:00 A.M.-6:00 P.M. daily.

    Computers. [M-10]

O.A. CENTER   NS Bldg., 5F., 2-4-1 Nishi Shinjuku, Shinjuku-ku. Tel: 3348-1128. Hours: 9:30 A.M.–5:00 P.M., closed Sat., Sun., & hol.

    Showroom for several different computer makers, both hard and software. [M-7]

TEPIA   2-8-44 Kita Aoyama, Minato-ku. Tel: 5474-6111. Hours: 10:00 A.M.–6:00 P.M. (until 5:00 P.M. on Sat. & Sun.), closed Mon.

    A government-run showcase for Japanese makers of machines—cars, electronics, etc. This Fumihiko Maki-designed building houses a gallery, an audiovisual library, and a rental space for events. [M-5]

TOTO SHOWROOM   Shinjuku L Tower, 26–27F. 1-6-1 Nishi Shinjuku, Shinjuku-ku. Tel: 3345-1010. Hours: 10:00 A.M.-6:00 P.M. daily.

    This and the showroom for **INAX** (next listing) are Japan's premiere lavatory furnishings and fixtures manufacturers. Both offer interesting insights into the aspirations of the Japanese middle class. [M-7]

INAX Shinjuku L Tower, 20–21F. Tel: 3340-1700. Hours: 10:00 A.M.–6:00 P.M. daily. [M-7]

Electronics and Computers

• Akihabara [M-14]

Akihabara is famous as the electronics discount district of Tokyo. Though by no means the only area for cheap electrical goods, the vast selection of products laid out in one place makes it the most convenient. Prices quoted by the shops are usually discounted from the manufacturer's suggested retail price. In some shops, you can talk the price down even further. If you're making a large purchase, you should insist on it.

The district has a special Electronics Fair from the middle of June through the middle of July and again from the end of November through the middle of January. Prices during the fair are even cheaper than usual.

There are over a thousand shops in Akihabara, most of which offer more or less the same range of merchandise and prices. It's impossible to miss the larger, general stores, but below is a list of some specialty shops that we thought worthy of mention. Access to Akihabara is by the JR Yamanote Line, the Sobu Line's Akihabara Station (West Exit), or the Hibiya Line's Akihabara Station (Exit 3).

RAJIO KAIKAN 1-15-16 Soto-kanda, Chiyoda-ku. Hours: 10:00 A.M.–7:00 P.M. daily.

This is a big building with about fifty shops dealing in audio, radio, video, tapes, secondhand articles, etc. Many of the shops on the following list are located here.

TOKYO RAJIO DEPATO 1-10-11 Soto-kanda, Chiyoda-ku. Tel: 3251-9173. Hours: 11:00 A.M.–6:30 P.M. (depends on the shop).

Another building full of parts shops, mostly dealing with radios.

KIMURA MUSEN Rajio Kaikan, 4F. Tel: 3251-7391. Hours: 10:30 A.M.–7:00 P.M. daily.

Everything for audio fans from cartridges to speakers. They even sell the screws to put together your own cabinets.

SATO MUSEN 1-11-11 Soto-kanda, Chiyoda-ku. Tel: 3253-5871. Hours: 10:30 A.M.–7:00 P.M. daily.

A very wide selection (over 130 types) of headphones alone, with full listening facilities.

SHOJIN SHOKAI Rajio Kaikan, 4F. Tel: 3251-0797. Hours: 10:00 A.M.–7:00 P.M. daily.

A first-rate secondhand dealer for over thirty years.

HIROSE MUSEN AUDIO CENTER 1-12-1 Soto-kanda, Chiyoda-ku. Tel: 3255-2221. Hours: 10:00 A.M.–6:50 P.M., closed Wed.

Enormous premises, wide selection.

F. SHOKAI Rajio Kaikan, 7F. Tel: 3251-2301. Hours: 10:00 A.M.–7:00 P.M. daily (until 6:30 P.M. on Sun. & hol.).

Discount videotape and audio cassettes.

ROCKET HONTEN 1-14-1 Kanda Sakuma-cho, Chiyoda-ku. Tel: 3257-0606. Hours: 10:15 A.M.–8:00 P.M.

An electronics superstore.

FUJIONKYO "MAIKON" CENTER RAM Rajio Kaikan, 7F. 1-15-16 Soto-kanda, Chiyoda-ku. Tel: 3255-7846. Hours: 10:00 A.M.–7:00 P.M. daily (until 6:30 on Sun. & hol.).

Computer store stocking both domestic brands and Apple.

LAOX COMPUTER-KAN 1-7-6 Soto-kanda, Chiyoda-ku. Tel: 5256-3111. Hours: 11:00 A.M.–9:00 P.M., Mon.–Fri., (from 10:00 A.M. on Sat. & Sun., and until 7:00 P.M. on hol.).

Six stories of all you need for computers.

• Other Areas

DYNAMIC AUDIO   Villa Bianca 206, 2-33-12 Jingumae, Shibuya-ku. Tel: 3473-5881. Hours: 11:00 A.M.–8:00 P.M., closed Tue.

Secondhand audio and video at incredibly cheap prices. Good discounts on new items as well. [off Map]

JONAN DENKI   2-19-21 Shibuya, Shibuya-ku. Tel: 3499-0550. Hours: 10:00 A.M.–6:50 P.M., closed Wed.

Claims to have the lowest prices in Japan. If you find something cheaper elsewhere, they will refund the difference. [M-3]

MAIKON BASE GINZA   1-8-21 Ginza, Chuo-ku. Tel: 5543-3055. Hours: 10:00 A.M.–6:30 P.M., closed Sun., hol., first, second & third Sat.

A nine-story computer superstore, one of the biggest in town. [M-8]

The next two shops are primarily wholesalers, but will also sell retail, if somewhat reluctantly. Nothing is on display though, so you must check the merchandise elsewhere in advance and bring a note giving the maker and the catalogue number.

MARUBOSHI DENKI   3-7-2 Ueno, Taito-ku. Tel: 3833-4541. Hours: 10:00 A.M.–6:30 P.M. (until 5:00 P.M. on Sat.), closed Sun. & hol. [M-13]

MARUYU SHOKAI   3-3-2 Taito, Taito-ku. Tel: 3835-8843. Hours: 10:00 A.M.–6:30 P.M., closed Sun. & hol. [off Map]

Cameras

• Shinjuku [M-7]

Like Akihabara for electronics, Shinjuku is known as the discount camera district. Some shops also sell smaller electrical goods.

YODOBASHI CAMERA   (Nishiguchi Honten—West Exit Main Store), 1-11-1 Nishi Shinjuku, Shinjuku-ku. Tel: 3346-1010. Hours: 9:30 A.M.–9:00 P.M. daily.

Claims to be the largest camera shop in the world, stocking nearly everything in production at twenty to fifty percent off.

CAMERA NO DOI   (Nishiguchi Nigo-ten), 1-18-27 Nishi Shinjuku, Shinjuku-ku. Tel: 3348-2241. Hours: 10:00 A.M.–8:30 P.M. daily.

Watch for seasonal special bargain sales.

CAMERA NO SAKURAYA   3-17-2 Shinjuku, Shinjuku-ku. Tel: 3354-3636. Hours: 10:00 A.M.–8:30 P.M. daily.

Six floors of camera and electrical goods at twenty to sixty percent discounts.

MIYAMA SHOKAI   3-32-8 Shinjuku, Shinjuku-ku. Tel: 3356-1841. Hours: 10:30 A.M.–8:00 P.M. daily, until 7:00 P.M. on Sun. & hol.

New and secondhand cameras, lenses, parts exchange. Popular with professional photographers and semi-pros looking for quality equipment.

• Ikebukuro [M-18]

BIC CAMERA   1-11-7 Higashi Ikebukuro, Toshima-ku. Tel: 3988-0002. Hours: 10:00 A.M.–8:00 P.M. daily.

Cheapest in Japan, will refund the difference if you find the same article cheaper elsewhere. In addition to cameras, they sell video and audio equipment, tapes, computers, even contact lenses.

CAMERA NO KIMURA   1-18-8 Nishi Ikebukuro, Toshima-ku. Tel: 3981-8437. Hours: 8:00 A.M.–8:00 P.M. daily, 10:00 A.M.–7:00 P.M. on Sun. & hol.

Great selection of secondhand cameras.

• Other Areas

SHIMIZU CAMERA   4-3-2 Ginza, Chuo-ku. Tel: 3564-1008. Hours: 9:30 A.M.–6:30 P.M. daily, 10:00 A.M.–5:00 P.M. Sun. & hol.

A professional photographer's favorite place for low prices and good selections. [M-8]

NITTO SHOJI   5-49-6 Nakano, Nakano-ku. Tel: 3387-0111. Hours: 10:00 A.M.–8:00 P.M., closed Thur.

Reputable dealer for cheap, quality, secondhand cameras, lenses, and other attachments and accessories. [M-26]

MATSUZAKAYA   1-27-34 Takanawa, Minato-ku. Tel: 3445-1311. Hours: 10:00 A.M.–7:00 P.M., (until 5:00 P.M. on Sun. & hol.).

Biggest used camera shop in Tokyo. Huge selection. [M-19]

TRADITIONAL ARTS AND CRAFTS

In a city where fashion and technology sometimes seem to be a form of new religion, it always comes as a relief to find a tiny shop that still produces by hand the same goods the shop has been famous for since the Edo period. The reputation of these shops passes down from generation to generation. A true *Edokko*, the rare born and bred Tokyoite, will know these specialty shops, where straw *zori* (sandals) are made with the toes squared off just as they were in Edo, where Kabuki actors and geisha buy their cosmetics, and where famous architects still have their lamps designed. These shops, often hundreds of years old, preserve traditions of quality and fine craftsmanship in simple utilitarian products.

Most are proud and will tell stories of fathers and grandfathers, of how things have changed, of concessions to modern technology. *Zori,* once made with rope soles, are now mass-produced in rubber, hand-bent bamboo lamps are now formed by machines that cannot reproduce the craftsman's spirit. Many of the artisans live behind their shops. Asking one about holidays, he replies that he doesn't take any. Then his wife corrects him from the back room—the next afternoon they'll close for their grandson's wedding. Another shopkeeper says that since theirs is the only such shop left, people come from all over Japan. If they close for a day, those people may have to go home empty-handed.

Though prices sometimes seem modest and sometimes exorbitant, considering the work involved, they're clearly justified. These craftsmen do not get rich from their work, but their pride prevents them from selling cheap. One craftsman tells a story of how, once, when a customer complained to his grandfather about the price of a bamboo spoon, the old man broke the spoon in two and offered half of the spoon for half of the price. It's not the money that's important—but an appreciation of the beauty of their work.

Shops like these are usually found in the *shitamachi,* old downtown districts, a traditional home of craftspeople. In the shadow of reinforced concrete buildings that have slowly surrounded them, these proud artisans maintain their old wooden shops. Some finally give up and move away. Others have no one to continue their tradition and the skill dies with the last son. A few will survive in spite of, or maybe because of, the advance of modern technology. Even now, Japanese children of the computer generation have begun to look again to their past.

In the following section, we've selected a variety of arts, crafts and traditional products, given short explanations, and listed the best shops for each category. Much of the merchandise from the more famous shops can also be found in department stores (Seibu is particularly good for contemporary crafts), but visiting the shops themselves is part of the pleasure.

General Shops
CRAFTS CENTER   Plaza 246, 2F. 3-3-3 Minami Aoyama, Minato-ku. Tel: 3403-2460. Hours: 10:00 A.M.–6:00 P.M., closed Thurs.

Arts and crafts from around Japan on display and for sale. Particularly good for lacquer, paper, ceramics, and bamboo. [M-5]

KYOTO CENTER "KYO-NOREN"   Kyoto Shimbun Ginza Bldg., 1F. 8-2-8 Ginza, Chuo-ku. Tel: 3572-6484. Hours: 11:00 A.M.–7:00 P.M., until 6:00 P.M. on Sat., closed Sun. & hol.

Arts and crafts from Kyoto. [M-8]

ORIENTAL BAZAAR   5-9-13 Jingumae, Shibuya-ku. Tel: 3400-3933. Hours: 9:30 A.M.–6:30 P.M., closed Thur.

Slightly touristy but has a good selection of merchandise including old kimonos, antiques, prints, etc. [M-4]

BLUE AND WHITE   2-9-2 Azabu-juban, Minato-ku. Tel: 3451-0537. Hours: 10:00 A.M.–6:00 P.M., closed Sun. & hol.

All of the merchandise in this small shop is in Japanese blue and white. A good place for interior decorating, they have an excellent selection of textiles, some made-up clothing, cushions, napkins, etc. Other items include pottery, paper, and baskets. [M-1]

AIKOBO   6-33-14 Okusawa, Setagaya-ku. Tel: 3703-8110. Hours: 11:00 A.M.–7:00 P.M., closed Tue.

This shop specializes in the traditional blue-dyeing method called *aizome*. Fabrics, tapestry, clothing, decorator items, etc. Quite pricey. [M-21]

Mingei—Folk crafts

Mingei, "people's arts," are enjoying something of a boom in Japan. Now more or less thought of as souvenirs, *mingei* are practical things made simply and strongly for use in everyday life. *Mingei* are deeply rooted in local customs and traditions, with a particular item usually originating in a particular region. A broad range of products falls into the folk crafts category: toys, kitchen utensils, textiles, clothing, and furniture. Good selections are to be found in many of the shops listed above. Besides the several stores that specialize in *mingei*, there is a terrific museum: the Nihon Mingei-kan, Japan Folk Art Museum (see **Museums**).

TAKUMI   たくみ　中央区銀座 8-4-2
8-4-2 Ginza, Chuo-ku. Tel: 3571-2017. Hours: 11:00 A.M.–7:00 P.M., until 5:30 P.M. on hol., closed Sun. [M-8]

BENIYA   べにや　渋谷区渋谷 2-16-8
2-16-8 Shibuya, Shibuya-ku. Tel: 3400-8084. Hours: 10:00 A.M.–7:00 P.M., closed Thurs.
Four floors of well-selected folk crafts. [M-3]

UCHIDA   うちだ　港区麻布十番 2-8-6
2-8-6 Azabu-juban, Minato-ku. Tel: 3455-4595. Hours: noon–6:00 P.M., closed Tue.
A gallery and shop specializing in contemporary crafts. [M-1]

TSUKAMOTO   つかもと   渋谷区道玄坂 1-2-2 東急プラザ 4 階
Tokyu Plaza, 4F. 1-2-2 Dogenzaka, Shibuya-ku. Tel: 3461-4410. Hours: 10:00 A.M.–8:00 P.M.
daily.
     Small, but well-stocked. [M-3]
BINGOYA   備後屋   新宿区若松町 10-6
10-6 Wakamatsu-cho, Shinjuku-ku. Tel: 3202-8778. Hours: 10:00 A.M.–7:00 P.M., closed Mon.
[off Map]

Edo Gangu—Toys

In the Edo period, *gangu* were cheap toys made of paper, wood, or clay.
Popular shapes were puppets, dolls, or animals such as tigers and dogs. In
this day of techno-toys, *Edo gangu* are primarily bought as souvenirs by
nostalgic adults. They are found in most *mingei* shops.

SUKEROKU   助六   台東区浅草 2-3-1
2-3-1 Asakusa, Taito-ku. Tel: 3844-0542. Hours: 10:30 A.M.–6:00 P.M., closed Thur.
     Specialists in miniatures of life in the Edo period. [M-12]

Tako—Kites

During the Nara period (710-794), kite making was the rage among the
court nobility and by the time the Edo period began, kites had become
popular children's toys. Adults still participated in hotly contested kite
competitions that often ended in rowdy brawls. Numerous government
attempts were made to outlaw these contests. Hand-painted kites made of
washi (handmade Japanese paper) can still be bought, and kite fanatics still
hold contests at the Tama River on New Year's Day, Children's Day (May 5),
and Health-Sports Day (October 10). The Japan Kite Association also has a
kite museum in Nihombashi.

Our favorite old kite shop is now gone, but good selections of kites can
be found at **Washikobo** paper shop and folk craft shops like **Bingoya** (see
Mingei) and **Beniya.**

Koinobori—Carp Banners

While in certain parts of America these have become popular porch
decorations, in Japan they're hung from tall poles on Boy's Day in May.
Originally used as banners by the *samurai,* they came into use for Boy's Day
during the Sino-Japanese War in the later nineteenth century. The fluttering
streamers are symbolic of the hope that all little Japanese boys will grow up
to be as strong and persistent as the carp that, fearing nothing, climbs
waterfalls up a stream. *Koinobori* can be bought at most shops selling
traditional dolls, at **Bingoya** (see **Mingei**), and on the second floor of the
Oriental Bazaar.

MUSASHIYA SHOTEN   むさしや商店   台東区蔵前 1-7-1
1-7-1 Kuramae, Taito-ku. Tel: 3851-5817. Hours: 9:00 A.M.–6:00 P.M., closed Sun. & hol.
     The *koinobori* are not usually on display, but they have them in stock. If you call ahead, they'll
have them ready to show when you arrive. [M-24]

Ningyo—Dolls

Dolls are one of the most common souvenirs given to foreigners. Some have black hair styled in traditional coiffures, and wear kimonos as Japanese are supposed to—clearly the perfect visual aid for explaining the Japanese to overseas visitors.

The earliest dolls in Japan were talismans, made of paper or straw, used to charm away illness and other misfortunes. A carry-over of this custom is seen in festivals where paper dolls are floated down a river. By the Edo period, doll making had become quite advanced. The *bunraku* puppet theater dolls were two-thirds life-size and highly mechanized. Wealthy Edo families would often order a doll modeled after a beloved child.

Dolls are still popular, though less as playthings than as souvenirs or display objects. The most common type of dolls are the *hina ningyo* representing imperial court figures and displayed during the Girl's Festival in March. *Gogatsu ningyo* are dolls dressed in samurai costumes for the Boy's Festival. Other dolls representing figures from various periods of Japanese history are also very popular. Collectively known as *nihon ningyo* (Japanese dolls), some are painted, but more are gorgeously costumed. The most famous are those from Kyoto *(kyo ningyo)* and those from Fukuoka *(hakata ningyo)*. Another popular type are *kokeshi* dolls that are painted, wooden, spindle-like dolls carved in various sizes.

In Asakusabashi, a number of wholesale and retail doll shops line a street called Edo-dori. The most famous are **Kyugetsu, Yoshitoku,** and **Kuramae Ningyo-sha** [M-24]. Flea markets are excellent places to buy old dolls at very reasonable prices.

KYUGETSU 久月 台東区柳橋 1-20-4
1-20-4 Yanagibashi, Taito-ku. Tel: 3861-5511. Hours: 9:15 A.M.–6:00 P.M. daily.
This is one of the biggest doll shops in town. [M-24]

Washi—Paper

For over twelve hundred years, the Japanese have been making the best handmade paper in the world. Used in a multitude of ways, paper has long been a basic material in Japan. Umbrellas, fans, lanterns, and toys are only a few of the common paper products. In the arts, paper is used for painting and calligraphy and many contemporary artists use it in sculptural ways. Even more exemplary are the traditional houses that, with their expanses of shoji and *fusuma,* paper-covered windows and doors, are said to be made of paper and wood.

Though machine-made paper is common now, the best papers are still handmade. Shops specializing in paper products have files of handmade and often hand-printed paper called *chiyogami*. The shops also carry a wide variety of articles made from paper such as wallets, toys, boxes, lanterns, cards, stationery, and *kaishi*—a kind of tissue paper used in the tea ceremony and by Kabuki actors.

Japanese paper products make terrific gifts.

PAPER NAO 紙舗 直 文京区千石 1-29-12 KS 千石ビル 201
1-29-12 Sengoku, KS Sengoku Bldg., 2F. Bunkyo-ku. Tel: 3944-4470. Hours: 10:00 A.M.–6:00 P.M., closed Sun.
Good selection of beautifully textured plain and dyed papers, no prints. [off Map]

ISETATSU いせ辰 台東区谷中 2-18-9
2-18-9 Yanaka, Taiko-ku. Tel: 3823-1453. Hours: 10:00 A.M.–6:00 P.M. daily.
A beautiful little shop with papers and paper craft items. [M-13]

OZU SHOTEN 小津 中央区日本橋 2-6-3
2-6-3 Nihombashi Honcho, Chuo-ku. Tel: 3663-8788. Hours: 10:00 A.M.–6:00 P.M., closed Sun.
A large selection of papers and calligraphy supplies. [M-9]

HAIBARA 榛原 中央区日本橋 2-7-6
2-7-6 Nihombashi, Chuo-ku. Tel: 3272-3801. Hours: 9:30 A.M.–5:30 P.M., until 5:00 P.M. on Sat., closed Sun. & hol. [M-9]

WASHIKOBO 和紙工房 港区西麻布 1-8-10
1-8-10 Nishi Azabu, Minato-ku. Tel: 3405-1841. Hours: 10:00 A.M.–6:00 P.M., closed Sun. & hol.
Wide selection of papers and gift items. [M-2]

KYUKYODO (see **Ko—Incense**)

KURODAYA 黒田屋 台東区浅草 1-2-11
1-2-11 Asakusa, Taito-ku. Tel: 3845-3830. Hours: 11:00 A.M.–8:00 P.M., closed Mon. [M-12]

SAKURA HORIKIRI さくらほりきり 台東区柳橋 1-25-3
1-25-3 Yanagibashi, Taito-ku. Tel: 3864-1773. Hours: 9:30 A.M.–5:30 P.M., closed Sun. & hol.
This shop offers free classes in paper crafts usually between 10:00 A.M.–4:00 P.M. Each class lasts about two hours. [M-24].

Fude—Brushes

Fude were brought to Japan from China in the sixth century with the introduction of the Chinese writing system. Used now for *sumi-e* (ink painting) and *shodo* (calligraphy), the brush must be able to produce a line that moves from a deep, intense black through a faint gray using strokes of varying force, from thick and powerful through fine and feathery. The best brushes are handmade; the hair is selected, matched, and wrapped in a time-consuming process. The type of hair used differs according to the purpose of each particular brush. Shops selling handmade brushes also sell less expensive machine-made brushes as well.

GYOKUSENDO 玉川堂 千代田区神田神保町 3-3
3-3 Kanda Jimbocho, Chiyoda-ku. Tel: 3264-3741. Hours: 9:00 A.M.–7:00 P.M., closed Sun. & hol.
A great selection of *fude* for calligraphy and *sumi-e,* calligraphy supplies, and books. [M-15]

KOUNDO 光雲堂 台東区浅草橋 1-30-11
1-30-11 Asakusabashi, Taito-ku. Tel: 3861-4943. Hours: 9:00 A.M.–5:30 P.M., closed the second Sat., Sun., & hol. [M-24]

Tsuzura—Lacquered Bamboo Trunks

Traditionally used for storing kimono, *tsuzura* are boxes made of woven bamboo that has been lacquered in bright orange, dark brown, or black. The boxes come in three sizes: the largest for kimono, medium size for undergarments and footwear, and small ones for stationery and letters. Usually custom-ordered, the boxes can be painted with a family crest (your own can be used if you have an appropriate stencil). Small boxes can be found at some stationery stores such as **Kyukyodo** in Ginza.

IWAI-SHOTEN 岩井商店　中央区日本橋人蒄町 2-10-1
2-10-1 Nihombashi Ningyocho, Chuo-ku. Tel: 3668-6058. Hours: 8:00 A.M.–8:00 P.M., closed Sun. & hol.
You can watch the craftsmen at work. [M-23]

Sudare—Bamboo Blinds

In the intense heat of the Japanese summer, the doors and windows of traditional-style homes were removed and *sudare* (bamboo blinds) were hung. Blinds were also used as room partitions. Another kind of blind, *misu*, is edged in silk binding and adorned with two heavy tassels. *Misu* are used in shrines and temples. *Nawa noren* are curtains of twisted rope hung in the entrance way of Japanese-style drinking spots and tea houses. *Yoshizu* are the large rough bamboo screens used to shade vegetable shops.

Most city dwellers no longer remove their doors and windows during the hot summer, but bamboo blinds still appear outside the windows of homes and older apartment buildings in Tokyo. For handmade blinds, young bamboo is carefully selected and matched, then tightly laced together. At smaller shops, blinds are often custom made. Blinds can be bought at most department stores and used *misu* blinds are often sold at flea markets.

TANAKA SEIRENJO 田中製簾所　台東区千束 1-18-6
1-18-6 Senzoku, Taito-ku. Tel: 3873-4653. Hours: 8:00 A.M.–7:00 P.M., closed Sun.
Indoor and outdoor *sudare* can be custom ordered. There is nothing on display, but the people are friendly and can show you samples. [M-12]

Chochin—Paper Lanterns

Though *chochin* are most frequently seen like signboards outside traditional Japanese *nomiya* (drinking spots), they were originally used for religious services. You can still see strings of lanterns at temples, shrines, and festival sites. *Chochin* can be bought ready-made in various sizes, or you can order one with your name written in Japanese characters. Prices start at about ¥3,000.

HANATO 花藤　台東区浅草 2-25-6
2-25-6 Asakusa, Taito-ku. Tel: 3841-6411. Hours: 10:00 A.M.–8:30 P.M., closed Tues. [M-12]
KASHIWAYA 柏屋　中央区新富 2-3-13
2-3-13 Shintomi, Chuo-ku. Tel: 3551-1362. Hours: 9:00 A.M.–5:00 P.M., closed Sun. [M-22]

Interior Lamps

Traditional lamps were wooden-framed floor lamps covered with white paper and lit by a candle. The design has been modified for modern use and a variety of functional and beautiful lamps and lighting fixtures are available. The most beautiful are made from bamboo or unfinished-wood frames lined with white paper that softly diffuses the light. Others are collapsible paper lanterns in contemporary designs.

LIVINA YAMAGIWA　リビナヤマギワ　千代田区外神田 1-5-10
1-5-10 Soto-kanda, Chiyoda-ku. Tel: 3253-2111. Hours: 10:00 A.M.–7:00 P.M. (until 7:30 on Sat.), closed the third Wed. of May & Nov.
　Traditional lamps on 4F. [M-14]
WASHIKOBO (see **Washi**). A good selection of interior paper lamps. [M-2]
MATSUYA DEPARTMENT STORE (Ginza) has a good selection of Isamu Noguchi's paper Akari lamps on 7F. [M-8]

Kasa—Umbrellas

The bamboo-ribbed umbrella was, for a long time, one of the inevitable accessories for the Asian girl of the Western imagination. Ironically, in Kabuki, the umbrella was often a symbol of masculine virility. Later, to share an umbrella became a mark of lovers. Even now, when school children write their name together with a sweetheart's, it's not inside a heart pierced by an arrow, but beneath an umbrella.

There are two types of traditional umbrellas, *bangasa*, a rain umbrella made of oiled paper, and *higasa*, a sunshade made originally of paper but sometimes of cotton or silk. Traditional *kasa* are rather hard to find these days. Stores dealing in traditional footwear sometimes have them. Department stores carry them occasionally. You can usually find them at **Nakamise,** the shopping street leading to Senso-ji temple in Asakusa.

IDAYA　飯田屋　台東区浅草 1-31-1
1-31-1 Asakusa, Taito-ku. Tel: 3841-3644. Hours: 9:30 A.M.–7:30 P.M. daily.
　Bangasa (available all year), fans, etc. [M-12]
HASEGAWA HAKIMONOTEN　長谷川履物店　台東区上野 2-4-4
2-4-4 Ueno, Taito-ku. Tel: 3831-3933. Hours: 10:00 A.M.–8:00 P.M., closed Sun. & hol.
　This shop sells footwear, but usually has a few umbrellas in stock. [M-13]

Ko—Incense

Incense was brought to Japan with Buddhism in the sixth century. Important in religious ritual, it later developed into a ceremonial esthetic cult called *kodo,* in a style similar to the tea ceremony. There are three main types of incense: *koboku*—smokeless wood chips from naturally scented trees, used in tea and *kodo* ceremonies; *neriko*—a smokeless cone of combined wood chips; and *senko*—smoke-producing stick incense used for religious purposes. Most shops selling incense also sell *nioibukuro*—small sachets of fragrant wood chips in tiny brocade bags.

KYUKYODO　鳩居堂　中央区銀座 5-7-4
5-7-4 Ginza, Chuo-ku. Tel: 3571-4429. Hours: 10:00 A.M.–7:30 P.M. (11:00 A.M.–7:00 P.M. on Sun. & hol.).
　The store's specialty is incense, but they also stock a wide variety of calligraphy supplies, stationery, and small, lacquer letter-boxes. [M-8]

124 SHOPPING

Cha-dogu—Tea Ceremony Utensils

For an explanation of the tea ceremony, see **Traditional Art.** There are five main categories of utensils used in the tea ceremony: vases and scrolls used to decorate the room; the bowl, tea caddies, scoops, and whisks used to prepare the tea; the trays and bowls for serving the food; the gong and straw mats placed outside the entrance; and the water jar and charcoal brazier for the washing and preparation area.

RYUZENDO　竜善堂　中央区銀座 5-8-5

5-8-5 Ginza, Chuo-ku. Tel: 3571-4321. Hours: 10:30 A.M.–7:00 P.M., closed the first and third Sun. [M-8]

Katana—Swords

Imported from China in the Heian period, by samurai times the sword had become the tool of the ruling class and its symbol of power. Swords were considered the "soul" of the samurai, and the best were produced in a semi-religious ceremony where the artisan maintained a state of ritual purity to allow the entrance of "spirit" into the blade. The process of sword-making required up to several months of tempering to produce a razor sharp edge and a flexible blade of incredible durability. The skill developed into a fine art, and swords became a major export item—in 1483 over 37,000 were sent to China.

Old swords are hard to come by these days. Highly prized by the Japanese, swords come on the market only rarely, and then at astronomical prices. Sword shops also sell *tsuba* (sword guards), *menuki* (metal sword ornaments), and complete suits of armor.

JAPAN SWORD　日本刀剣　港区虎の門 3-8-1

3-8-1 Toranomon, Minato-ku. Tel 3434-4321. Hours: 9:30 A.M.–6:00 P.M., closed Sun. & hol. New and old swords. [M-11]

Hocho and *Hasami*—Knives and Scissors

Tightly controlled by the Tokugawa government, Edo period Japan settled into over two hundred years of peace. As the samurai gradually became more of a bureaucrat and less of a soldier, the need for swords declined. With the beginning of the Meiji period, the samurai lost political control and soon the wearing of swords was outlawed. The swordsmiths turned to knife and scissors making. Produced by the same techniques used in sword making, Japanese knives and scissors are some of the best in the world. The knife capital of Japan is Seki City in Gifu Prefecture. For over seven hundred years the area has been famous for making the bulk of the nation's blades. You can also find knife shops at the Tsukiji Fish Market.

KIYA　木屋　中央区日本橋室町 1-5-6

1-5-6 Nihombashi Muromachi, Chuo-ku. Tel: 3241-0111. Hours: 10:00 A.M.–6:00 P.M. (11:15 A.M.–5:45 P.M. Sun. & hol.). [M-9]

UBUKEYA　うぶけや　中央区日本橋人形町 3-9-2
3-9-2 Nihombashi Ningyocho, Chuo-ku. Tel: 3661-4851. Hours: 9:00 A.M.–7:00 P.M., closed Sun. & hol. [M-23]
KIKUHIDE CUTLERY SHOP　菊秀　中央区銀座 5-14-2
5-14-2 Ginza, Chuo-ku. Tel: 3541-8390. Hours: 10:00 A.M.–8:00 P.M., closed Sun.
　Specializes in knives and cutlery. [M-8]

Sashimono—Furniture

The typical Japanese home was (and sometimes still is) furnished sparsely. Rooms were multi-functional: kept open for daytime living space, at night futon were pulled from the closets for sleeping. Furniture was minimal; a *hibachi* for heating, a *tansu* chest for storing clothing, another chest—*chadansu*–for dishes. Small chests for letters and other personal items were brought out when needed.

The best furniture was made of *kiri*, paulownia wood. Nails were never used, the pieces being jointed and glued. A few shops still make traditional furniture, though even small pieces are quite expensive. Perhaps more appealing to Western tastes are antique furniture or contemporary designs.

KYOYA　京屋　台東区上野 2-12-10
2-12-10 Ueno, Taito-ku. Tel: 3831-1905. Hours: 10:00 A.M.–6:00 P.M., closed Sun. & hol. [M-13]
HIRATSUKA　平つか　中央区銀座 8-7-6
8-7-6 Ginza, Chuo-ku. Tel: 3571-1684. Hours: 11:00 A.M.–7:00 P.M., closed Sun. & hol.
　This shop makes lovely small chests. [M-8]
NODAZEN　野田善　港区東麻布 1-4-2
1-4-2 Higashi Azabu, Minato-ku. Tel: 3582-5833. Hours: 11:00 A.M.–6:00 P.M., closed Sun. & hol.
　Reproductions of traditional Japanese furniture, *tansu,* tables, lamps, etc. [M-11]

Oke—Wooden Buckets

Oke are buckets made of cypress wood with copper hoops holding the hand-planed pieces of wood tightly together. Most often seen in sushi shops holding large portions of marinated rice, small *oke* called *furo-oke* are used as scoops and wash basins for the bath. *Oke* are generally custom ordered.

ITO OKE-TEN　伊東桶店　墨田区立川 2-4-6
2-4-6 Tatekawa, Sumida-ku. Tel: 3633-7108. Hours: 8:00 A.M.–5:00 P.M., closed Sun. & hol. [M-24]

Hardware

Fascinating insights to traditional everyday life can still be gleaned from the traditional tools.

NAOHEI　直平　中央区八丁堀 3-14-4
3-14-4 Hatchobori, Chuo-ku. Tel: 3552-4576. Hours: 8:00 A.M.–6:00 P.M. (until 3:30 on Sat.), closed Sun. & hol. and the first and third Sat.
　Knives, scissors, and other carpentry tools and hardware. The shop is over one hundred years old. [M-25]
OEYAMA　大江山　新宿区新宿 2-3-10
2-3-10 Shinjuku, Shinjuku-ku. Tel: 3356-7007. Hours: 7:00 A.M.–7:00 P.M. daily.
　A hardware store for professional Japanese carpenters. [M-7]

Yoji—Toothpicks

Toothpicks are not normally a terribly exciting subject, but one shop in Tokyo, **Saruya,** has turned the humble tool into as fine an art as possible. At Saruya, you can buy toothpicks individually cased in brightly printed Japanese paper with a fortune poem wrapped around inside. Also sold are *kashi-yoji,* used for eating Japanese sweets. Hand-cut from pieces of camphor wood, a strip of bark is retained for artistic effect. Saruya's toothpicks are sold throughout Japan and at most major department stores.

SARUYA　さるや　中央区日本橋人形町 3-4-9

3-4-9 Nihombashi Ningyocho, Chuo-ku. Tel: 3666-3906. Hours: 9:00 A.M.–5:00 P.M., closed Sun., hol., & third Sat. [M-9]

Shikki—Lacquerware

First imported from China as a technique for making objects of daily use more durable, in Japan lacquerware became a highly refined art form. In very simplistic terms, the process involves painting layers of tree sap called *urushi* over a base usually of wood, but sometimes of metal, paper, leather, or bamboo. Cloth is sometimes applied, then the lacquer coating is reapplied and repolished in a lengthy process that can involve over one hundred separate steps. In the final decorative stages, gold, silver, and colors are often applied. The final product is both durable and beautiful. Good lacquerware is expensive and requires a certain amount of special care when taken to a climate dryer than that of Japan. Dishes, furniture, small boxes, and trays are a few common lacquerware products.

INACHU JAPAN　稲忠漆芸堂　港区赤坂 1-5-2

1-5-2 Akasaka, Minato-ku. Tel: 3582-4451. Hours: 10:00 A.M.–7:00 P.M., closed Sun.
　Lacquerware from the city of Wajima. [M-9]

HEIANDO　平安堂　中央区日本橋 3-10-11

3-10-11 Nihombashi, Chuo-ku. Tel: 3770-3641. Hours: 10:00 A.M.–6:00 P.M., closed Sun. & hol. [M-9]

KUROEYA　黒江屋　中央区日本橋 1-2-6 黒江屋国分ビル

Kuroeya Kokubu Bldg., 2F. 1-2-6 Nihombashi, Chuo-ku. Tel: 3271-3356. Hours: 9:00 A.M.–5:00 P.M., closed Sat., Sun., & hol. [M-9]

BUSHI　ブシ　港区六本木 5-17-1 アクシスビル

Axis Bldg., B1. Hours: 11:00 A.M.–7:00 P.M., closed Sun. Tel: 3587-0317.
　Gorgeous lacquerware with a contemporary flair. Mostly furniture and accessories. [M-1]

SEIBU DEPARTMENT STORE　Generally offers a good selection of both contemporary and more traditional lacquerware, some expensive and some quite reasonably priced

Tojiki—Ceramics

The history of ceramics in Japan dates back to Neolithic times, to the Jomon period (7,000–300 B.C.) when unglazed earthenware pots with distinctive rope-pattern designs were produced. As an art form, pottery became important during the Kamakura period with the development of the tea ceremony. Later, when Japan invaded Korea during the Momoyama period, continental potters were brought back to Japan. The new Korean wares and pottery techniques greatly influenced the domestic art. By the Edo period, *daimyo* (hereditary feudal noblemen) were competing for superiority in pottery production, especially for tea ceremony utensils, and pottery centers were developed throughout Japan.

Around 1616, a Korean potter discovered clay suitable for porcelain production in the south of Japan. The Japanese have always preferred pottery over porcelain, but porcelain soon became a major export product with designs adapted to European tastes. Shapes were altered for Western table use with bright colors and fancy designs in matched sets of china, a practice never seen in Japan.

The Japanese use unmatched sets of dishes, with each piece selected for its suitability to the dish being served. Most items are sold in sets of three or five, four being considered a particularly unlucky number. For tea ceremony ware, imperfections and irregularities in simple, undecorated pottery are considered aesthetically pleasing. Passed down through history, famous tea bowls are easily worth ¥4 million–¥5 million.

Some of the most important types of pottery are *mino-yaki* (from Gifu Prefecture), *karatsu-yaki* (Kyushu), *arita-yaki* (formerly called Imari, from Kyushu), *hagi-yaki* (Yamaguchi), *raku-yaki* (famous tea master Sen no Rikyu's favorite, from Kyoto), *kyo-yaki* (Kyoto), *mashiko-yaki* (Tochigi, near Tokyo), *bizen-yaki* (Okayama), *kiyomizu-yaki* (Kyoto), *kutani-yaki* (Ishikawa), and *satsuma-yaki* (Kyushu).

A good day trip outside Tokyo is a visit to the kilns in Mashiko, a short train ride from the city. Contact TIC for details.

Galleries specializing in contemporary pottery are in the **Contemporary Art Galleries** list. Other good places to buy ceramics are department stores (**Seibu** has a good selection) and **Kandori** (New Otani Hotel Arcade). The Kappabashi wholesale market area also has a wide selection of restaurant and inexpensive sturdy dishes.

DAIMONJI　大文字　渋谷区神宮前 5-48-3
5-48-3 Jingumae, Shibuya-ku. Tel: 3406-7381. Hours: 10:00 A.M.–7:00 P.M., closed Sun.
　　A wide selection of rather elegant and daily-use ceramics. [M-5]
TACHIKICHI　たち吉　中央区銀座 5-5-8
5-5-8 Ginza, Chuo-ku. Tel: 3571-2924. Hours: 11:00 A.M.–6:30 P.M., closed Sun.
　　Kiyomizu-yaki porcelain. Across the street is a gallery where shows are often given. [M-8]
TOROKU　陶六　千代田区麹町 2-4
2-4 Kojimachi, Chiyoda-ku. Tel: 3239-0565. Hours: 11:00 A.M.–7:00 P.M. (until 5:30 on Sat.), closed Sun.
　　Contemporary daily-use ceramics. Very nice shop. [M-6]
ISERYU SHOTEN　伊勢竜商店　中央区日本橋人菰町 3-8-2
3-8-2 Nihombashi Ningyocho, Chuo-ku. Tel: 3661-4820. Hours: 10:00 A.M.–6:30 P.M., closed Sat. & Sun.
　　Everyday dishes. [M-23]

YUSEI-SHA 遊星社 渋谷区東 3-21-6
3-21-6 Higashi, Shibuya-ku. Tel: 5485-3271. Hours: noon–8:00 P.M., closed Sun. & hol.
  Very well-selected, contemporary ceramics, some folk crafts, and a tiny tea shop. [off Map]
TOKYO 桃品 港区西麻布 2-25-13
2-25-13 Nishi Azabu, Minato-ku. Tel: 3797-4494. Hours: 11:00 A.M.–7:00 P.M., closed Sun. & hol.
  Good shop for contemporary ceramics and pottery. [M-2]
UCHIDA (see **General Craft Shops**) Very contemporary, rather natural rough ceramics.
SAVOIR VIVRE Axis Bldg., 3F. Tel: 3585-7365.
  Contemporary. [M-1]

Ukiyo-e—Woodblock Prints

Not originally considered an art form, *ukiyo-e* were often advertisements, handbills, or cheap posters produced for mass consumption. The height of *ukiyo-e* printing was from the mid- to late eighteenth century when figurative prints were most popular. Famous artists were Kitagawa Utamaro (1754–1806), known for his *bijin-e,* portraits of beautiful women, and Toshusai Sharaku (active 1794–95) known for his *yakusha-e,* exaggerated actor's portraits. *Ukiyo-e* means literally "illustrations of the floating world." An originally Buddhist concept, the "floating world" referred to the evanescent and transient nature of day-to-day life. By the Edo period, it came to mean the life of the city's pleasure quarters and the courtesans and actors who occupied it. In the nineteenth century, landscape prints grew in popularity. Two important artists were Hokusai (1760–1849), known for his *Thirty-six Views of Mt. Fuji,* and Hiroshige (1797–1858), known for his series *Fifty-three Stages of the Tokaido.*

The prints were considered vulgar by the samurai aristocracy, and their low esteem even among the merchant classes was shown by their frequent use as packing materials. Original prints eventually found their way to Europe wrapped around packages of exported tea, where European artists such as Vincent van Gogh and Henri de Toulouse-Lautrec were the first to recognize the work as fine art. Even today, some of the best *ukiyo-e* collections remain outside of Japan.

Numerous shops in Tokyo deal in old prints. The best are expensive and should be bought from certified dealers who will guarantee the work. Moderately priced prints (¥5,000–¥30,000) of lesser quality are still fun and are good buys. Reproductions are also available. For contemporary prints, see the list of **Contemporary Art Galleries.**

MATSUSHITA ASSOCIATES 松下同人社 渋谷区南青山 6-3-12
6-3-12 Minami Aoyama, Shibuya-ku. Tel: 3407-4966. Hours: 10:00 A.M.–5:30 P.M., closed Sun. & Mon.
  This shop usually has a good selection of moderately priced works. [M-5]
SAKAI KOKODO GALLERY 酒井好古堂 千代田区有楽町 1-2-14
1-2-14 Yurakucho, Chiyoda-ku. Tel: 3591-4678. Hours: 10:00 A.M.–7:00 P.M. daily, from 11:00 A.M. on Sun.
  This shop has been selling prints for over one hundred years. [M-10]

OYA SHOBO   大屋書房   千代田区神田神保町 1-1
1-1 Kanda Jimbocho, Chiyoda-ku. Tel: 3291-0062. Hours: 11:30 A.M.–6:30 P.M., closed Sun.
   A good selection of *ukiyo-e* can be found on the first and second floors of this secondhand bookstore. [M-15]
ORIENTAL BAZAAR   (see **General Shops**) New and old prints. [M-4]

TRADITIONAL INSTRUMENTS

Shamisen

   One of the most versatile of Japanese instruments, the *shamisen* was brought to Japan from the Ryukyu Islands. *Shamisen* music is primarily designed to accompany narrative or lyrical vocal work, and is important in all forms of Japanese drama. The instrument has a body made from four pieces of wood (best are those of red sandalwood, mulberry, or Chinese quince) covered top and bottom with cat skin; dog is used for less expensive models. The long neck is made of three pieces that can be disjointed. The *shamisen* is played with a large plectrum called a *bachi*.

KIKUYA SHAMISEN-TEN   菊屋三味線店   文京区湯島 3-45-11
3-45-11 Yushima, Bunkyo-ku. Tel: 3831-4733. Hours: 9:30 A.M.–7:00 P.M., closed Sun. & hol.
   The least expensive costs ¥55,000. [M-13]
BACHI-EI GAKKITEN   ばち英楽器店   中央区日本橋人菰町 2-10-11
2-10-11 Nihombashi Ningyocho, Chuo-ku. Tel: 3666-7263. Hours: 9:00 A.M.–8:00 P.M., closed Sun. & hol. [M-23]

Koto

   Popular with the Heian court aristocracy, the *koto* remains an instrument, like the Western piano, considered one of the genteel accomplishments of a well-bred Japanese. The music is played solo or in ensembles. Made of two pieces of paulownia wood, the instrument has thirteen or seventeen strings, movable bridges, and is at least six feet long. Ivory picks attached to three fingers of the right hand, or sometimes bare hands, are used to pluck the *koto*.

TSURUKAWA GAKKI HONTEN   鶴川楽器本店   中央区京橋 1-12-11
1-12-11 Kyobashi, Chuo-ku. Tel: 3703-1872. Hours: 10:00 A.M.–6:00 P.M. (Sat. until 3:00 P.M.), closed Sun. & hol. [M-9]

Biwa

   Imported from China during the Nara Period, this pear-shaped lute has four strings, four frets, and is played with a small plectrum. *Biwa*-playing was an essential skill for the early Japanese courtier, and later became important as an accompaniment to the musical storytelling of itinerant blind priests in the tenth century. The body of the *biwa* is carved from a single piece of wood, a second piece covers the base.

ISHIDA BIWA-TEN   石田琵琶店   港区虎の門 3-8-4
3-8-4 Toranomon, Minato-ku. Tel: 3431-6548. Hours: 9:00 A.M.–6:00 P.M., closed Sun. & hol.
[M-11]

Shakuhachi

Probably the easiest of Japanese instruments for foreigners to understand, the *shakuhachi* flute was first introduced into Japan during the Nara period. The most important *shakuhachi* music is from the Edo period. At the time, a group of ex-samurai organized themselves as a temple sect and played on the street corners as beggar priests. They later worked as spies for the Tokugawa government, and the basket hat covering their faces became a general method of disguise for anyone wishing to travel incognito. The instrument was also redesigned in a longer and thicker form to serve as a weapon (ex-samurai were forbidden to wear swords).

The *shakuhachi* is now played solo and in concert with *shamisen* or *koto*. The standard length is fifty-four to fifty-five centimeters. Most have four holes on top and one in the back and a mouthpiece of ivory or bone.

CHIKUYUDO　竹友堂　新宿区三栄町3

3 San'ei-cho, Shinjuku-ku. Tel: 3351-1270. Hours: 10:00 A.M.–5:00 P.M., closed Sun. & hol.
This is a school with a shop attached where the flutes are made. [off Map]

Drums

There are two main types of Japanese drums, the large barrel-like *taiko*, and the smaller hour-glass shaped *tsuzumi*. Both come in a variety of sizes capable of producing a range of tones. The drums are used primarily to mark rhythm in folk dances, Kabuki, and Noh drama.

MIYAMOTO UNOSUKE SHOTEN　宮本卯之助商店　台東区浅草6-1-15

6-1-15 Asakusa, Taito-ku. Tel: 3874-4131. Hours: 8:00 A.M.–5:00 P.M., closed Sun. & hol.
The shop carries festival drums and portable shrines. [M-12]

TRADITIONAL CLOTHING AND ACCESSORIES
Kimono

Apart from a few ceremonial occasions, most young Japanese women no longer wear kimono. Most, in fact, are incapable of dressing themselves correctly in one. Special schools will teach them this, as well as the proper way of walking and appropriate forms of manners and behavior.

Beautiful and graceful though it may be, kimono is a terribly restrictive form of dress. The pace of modern life in the city makes wearing one wholly impractical. Just watch a kimono-clad woman climbing the stairs or trying to get into a taxi. Older women with established social positions still wear kimono for school functions and formal affairs, though whether or not today's young will do so in the future is hard to say.

The prohibitive cost of kimono doesn't exactly serve to encourage its use. A normal, everyday, mass-produced kimono will cost a minimum of ¥50,000. A hand-dyed silk one, kimono *haute-couture,* will cost from ¥300,000 to over ¥1,000,000. Kimono are a major investment. Parents will give a daughter several, which most of the time stay folded in her closet. When she marries, a wedding kimono is usually rented—for at least ¥100,000 a day.

In the Heian period, kimono were worn in multiple layers of subtly coordinated colors. The inner kimono were loosely tied with a low sash-like belt. Taste in kimono changed through history, with different patterns, dyes, colors, and embroidery techniques going in and out of fashion. By the Edo period, the Tokugawa government, in its efforts to control conspicuous consumption among the merchant class, passed laws restricting them to modest clothing considered more appropriate to their lowly position in the samurai social hierarchy. The merchants managed to get around the laws by wearing kimono of apparent simplicity but made from extravagantly expensive hand-dyed and woven silks and lined with sumptuous fabrics. During the Meiji-period infatuation with Western civilization, Western-style clothing was slowly adopted, first by men and very gradually by women. But women continued to wear kimono regularly until the Second World War.

The rules of taste for kimono today are extremely complicated and based on variables such as the wearer's age and the occasion. Colors and patterns considered in good taste follow a concept of coloring totally unlike Western ideas of complementary or clashing colors.

Men's kimono are less decorative than women's, being usually black, gray or shades of brown, and tied low at the waist with a narrow obi. For formal occasions a crested *haori,* the short jacket kimono, and *hakama,* culotte-like pants, are worn with a black kimono. For informal occasions, after a bath, or at a *ryokan,* blue-and-white cotton *yukata* are worn by men and women.

The cost of kimono will probably keep most non-Japanese from buying new ones. Antique silk kimono are a great alternative and stores selling them are listed later in the **Antiques** section. Cotton *yukata* are also inexpensive and useful. Children's *yukata* are adorable and make good gifts. *Yukata* can be bought at department stores, in hotel arcades, and at the **Oriental Bazaar.** Listed below are a few shops that custom-make kimono. The fabrics are beautiful in themselves, but as the bolts are measured to make exactly one kimono each, you have to buy the entire roll.

SHIMAKAME　志ま亀　中央区銀座 6-5-15
6-5-15 Ginza, Chuo-ku. Tel: 3571-4651. Hours: 10:00 A.M.–7:00 P.M., 11:00 A.M.–6:00 P.M. Sun. & hol.
　This shop is originally from Kyoto. [M-8]
MASUDAYA　増多屋　中央区銀座 2-8-15
2-8-15 Ginza, Chuo-ku. Tel: 3561-3362. Hours: 10:00 A.M.–6:30 P.M., closed Sun. & hol.
　Kimono, *haori,* and obi fabrics. [M-8]
TSUMUGIYA KICHIHEI　紬屋吉平　中央区銀座 5-9-20
5-9-20 Ginza, Chuo-ku. Tel: 5401-3450. Hours: 10:00 A.M.–7:00 P.M., closed Sun. & hol.
　Famous for their *tsumugi,* hand-spun silks. [M-8]

BUSHOAN　撫松庵

The ready-made kimono and accessories sold here are so beautiful it is hard to believe that the fabrics are all synthetic. This shop is popular with younger Japanese. Boutiques are in **Seibu** and **Matsuya**.

ISEYOSHI　伊勢由　中央区銀座 8-8-19

8-8-19 Ginza, Chuo-ku. Tel: 3571-5388. Hours: 11:00 A.M.–8:00 P.M. (until 6:00 P.M. on Sat.), closed Sun. & hol.

This is a serious kimono shop but they also have beautiful *ubugi* (cotton gauze-lined kimonos) for newborns. [M-8]

Obi

Obi are the wide belts worn with kimono. Intended as the main attraction of traditional dress, the obi is chosen to go with a particular kimono and is usually more expensive than the kimono itself. The obi is wrapped around twice and tied in a bow at the back. There are countless ways to tie it, and for women unable to do it on their own, hairdressers provide the service for a nominal fee. Obi can be bought at most shops dealing in kimono.

Kimono Accessories

Worn with the kimono are various belts and sashes. *Obiage* are wide sashes of soft fabric, often of silk, and dyed in tie-dye like patterns. Colors are usually pastels. The *obiage* is tucked into the top of the obi.

Obijime are woven cords tied around the center of the obi and knotted in front.

DOMYO　道明　台東区上野 2-11-1

2-11-1 Ueno, Taito-ku. Tel: 3831-3773. Hours: 10:30 A.M.–6:30 P.M. daily.

This shop makes *obijime* and decorative cords for other purposes. [M-13]

KUNOYA　くのや　中央区銀座 6-9-8

6-9-8 Ginza, Chuo-ku. Tel: 3571-2546. Hours: 11:00 A.M.–8:00 P.M. daily.

Famous for their kimono accessories. [M-8]

Geta and Zori

Though for a time during the Meiji period, Western shoes were popularly worn with kimono, now only Japanese-style footwear is acceptable. The two main types of footwear are *zori,* leather or straw sandals, and geta, wooden clogs. Both are worn with the *tabi* split-toed sock. With formal kimono, *zori* must be worn, and *tabi* are required of all but geisha. With daily kimono, both *zori* and geta are acceptable, but *tabi* must be worn. With *yukata,* geta without *tabi* are worn.

HASETOKU　長谷徳　台東区浅草 1-18-10

1-18-10 Asakusa, Taito-ku. Tel: 3841-2153. Hours: 7:00 A.M.–7:30 P.M. daily.

One of the only places you can find one-hundred-percent straw *zori*. [M-12]

YOITAYA　与板屋　中央区銀座 5-4-5

5-4-5 Ginza, Chuo-ku. Tel: 3571-9069. Hours: 11:00 A.M.–7:00 P.M., closed Sun.

Zori and geta. [M-8]

HASEGAWA HAKIMONOTEN　(see **Kasa**)

Tabi—Socks

Tabi are Japanese socks with one toe sewn separately to fit into the geta or *zori*. *Tabi* evolved from a leather shoe worn by farmers. Its popularity as a sock rose when it became part of the required outfit for tea-ceremony participants. The socks are commonly made of cotton, with metal clasps at the ankle. *Jikatabi* are cotton boots worn by workmen and they fasten above the ankle, like high-top tennis shoes. The split-toed sock tradition is so strong in Japan that even fishermen's waders come with one toe separated.

KIKUYA　喜久屋　墨田区緑 1-9-3
1-9-3 Midori, Sumida-ku. Tel: 3631-0092. Hours: 9:00 A.M.–6:00 P.M., closed Sun. & hol.
　Tabi for dancers, sumo wrestlers, and tea-ceremony wear. [M-24]

ONOYA SHOTEN　大野屋総本店　中央区新富 2-2
2-2 Shintomi, Chuo-ku. Tel: 3551-0896. Hours: 9:00 A.M.–5:00 P.M., closed Sun. & hol. [M-22]

Sensu—Fans

One of the few wholly Japanese inventions and originally a symbol of power and authority, fans were used by the emperor and his court, and later as part of samurai battle dress. Early fans were often painted by famous masters and were considered very elegant gifts. Lovers often exchanged fans as a sign of intimacy.

There are two types of fans. The *ogi*, ornamental folding fan is still an essential accessory for formal occasions. *Ogi* are also used in traditional dance to symbolize travel, landscapes, etc. *Uchiwa* are flat, round fans used to fan fires and to create a small breeze in the summertime.

HOSENDO KYUAMI　宝扇堂久阿弥　台東区浅草 1-19-6
1-19-6 Asakusa, Taito-ku. Tel: 3845-5021. Hours: 10:30 A.M.–8:00 P.M., closed Sun. & hol. [M-12]

KYOSENDO　京扇堂　中央区日本橋人蔵町 2-5-3
2-5-3 Nihombashi Ningyocho, Chuo-ku. Tel: 3666-7255. Hours: 10:00 A.M.–8:00 P.M., closed Sun. & hol. [M-23]

WAN'YA SHOTEN　わんや書店　千代田区神田神保町 3-9
3-9 Kanda Jimbocho, Chiyoda-ku. Tel: 3263-6771. Hours: 9:30 A.M.–5:30 P.M., closed the second and fourth Sat., Sun. & hol. [M-15] Ginza branch: 8-7-5 Ginza, Chuo-ku. Tel: 3571-0514. Hours: 10:00 A.M.–6:00 P.M., closed the first and third Sat., Sun. & hol. [M-8]
　This shop specializes in articles for Noh drama including scripts (in Japanese), small mask copies, and fans. They even sell tickets.

Kushi and *Kanzashi*—Combs and Hair Ornaments

A comb is one thing you should never give a Japanese until the final *sayonara;* it means you'll probably never see them again. If you break a comb, it means bad luck. When breaking up with a lover, one throws away the comb he or she gave as a present.

In the Heian period, long hair—preferably trailing a foot or so behind when one walked—was considered a sign of beauty. From the end of the Momoyama period through the Edo period, hair was knotted up in a variety of elaborate styles that went in and out of fashion with ever increasing frequency. Hair ornaments, used to hold the hair in place, ranged from simple box wood combs to lacquered gold and silver. Geisha, *maiko* (apprentice geisha), and *oiran* (prostitutes) favored extravagant styles where the ornaments covered the head like pins in a pin cushion.

Hair ornaments are now worn on festive occasions. Combs and hair ornaments can be found in various shops along the Nakamise shopping street leading to Senso-ji temple in Asakusa. **Matsuzakaya** department store is well-known for its selection.

YONOYA　よのや　台東区浅草 1-37-10

1-37-10 Asakusa, Taito-ku. Tel: 3844-1755. Hours: 10:00 A.M.–7:00 P.M., closed Wed.
　The best shop for natural-wood combs, the shop itself is a jewel. [M-12]

JUSANYA　十三や　台東区上野 2-12-21

2-12-21 Ueno, Taito-ku. Tel: 3831-3238. Hours: 10:00 A.M.–7:00 P.M., closed first and third Sun.
　Beautiful boxwood combs and hair ornaments are sold in this shop that is nearly 250 years old. [M-13]

Keshohin—Cosmetics

There is one shop where almost all the Kabuki actors, traditional dancers, and geisha go for their make-up—Hyakusuke in Asakusa. Besides cosmetics, the shop carries skin-care products including *uguisu no fun*—politely translated as "nightingale droppings"—a traditional facial mask. They also have a good selection of brushes and hair ornaments.

HYAKUSUKE　百助　台東区浅草 2-2-14

2-2-14 Asakusa, Taito-ku. Tel: 3841-7058. Hours: 11:00 A.M.–5:00 P.M., closed Tues. [M-12]

Festival Clothing

This list is for those who want to dress right for their next neighborhood festival. *Momohiki* are the tight-fitting pants that wrap around at the top, often of dark blue cotton. *Shita-shatsu* are tight-fitting, long-sleeved cotton shirts. *Haragake* are a type of apron is worn over the two garments listed above. *Shirushi-banten* or *hanten* are short, cotton kimono-like jackets printed in bright colors with the name of the owner's neighborhood, association, etc. *Sanjaku* is a narrow, cotton, obi-like belt. *Tabi* are split-toed socks, and *waraji* are a type of straw sandal. The final touch is a *tenugui* wrapped around your head, or draped casually around your neck.

KIRIYA GOFUKUTEN　桐屋呉服店　台東区浅草 2-22-10

2-22-10 Asakusa, Taito-ku. Tel: 3844-4233. Hours: 11:00 A.M.–8:30 P.M., closed Tues. [M-12]

ADACHIYA　あだちや　台東区浅草 2-22-12

2-22-12 Asakusa, Taito-ku. Tel: 3841-4915. Hours: 10:00 A.M.–8:00 P.M., closed Thurs. [M-12]

ISOGAI TETSUZO SHOTEN (see **Workmen's Clothing** below)

Workmen's Clothing

A terrific form of alternative fashion, workmen's clothing is well-made and reasonably priced. A few of the more useful items are *shichibu-zubon*, wool or cotton pants similar to jodhpurs; *shita-shatsu,* like those worn for festivals; *dabo-shatsu,* a loose-fitting shirt worn as a jacket; and *jika-tabi,* cotton and occasionally leather split-toed boots.

ISOGAI TETSUZO SHOTEN　磯貝鉄蔵商店　墨田区業平 1-10-2

1-10-2 Narihira, Sumida-ku. Tel: 3622-2665. Hours: 7:30 A.M.–9:00 P.M. daily, until 5:00 P.M. on Sun.

Workmen from all over Tokyo and the surrounding area order their gear from this great shop. [M-44]

Traditional Dance Accessories

Dance kimono and costumes, straw hats, umbrellas, fans, wigs, *tenugui,* masks, artificial flowers, dancer's footwear, etc., can all be found at:

HOSENDO KYUAMI (see *Sensu*)

Tenugui—Towels

Tenugui are small cotton towels used in traditional forms of dance and theater, as well as in other towel-like ways. The fashionable *Edokko* had countless ways of tying and wrapping towels around the head. The Japanese buy them now as souvenirs, and at the Kabuki-za you can buy them printed with your favorite actor's crest. The towels are usually white, printed with a blue pattern.

Isogai Tetsuo is the fourth generation to run Isogai Tetsuzo Shoten, the family *tabi* and workmen's clothing shop. © 1984 Tobias Pfeil

FUJIYA TENUGUITEN ふじ屋手拭店　台東区浅草 2-2-15
2-2-15 Asakusa, Taito-ku. Tel: 3841-2283. Hours: 10:00 A.M.–8:00 P.M., closed Thurs. [M-12]
KAMAWANU かまわぬ　渋谷区猿楽町 23-1
23-1 Sarugaku-cho, Shibuya-ku. Tel: 3780-0182. Hours: 11:00 A.M.–7:00 P.M., closed Mon.
　Traditional and modern *tenugui*. [M–20]

Men—Masks

Masks are used in most forms of Japanese dance and drama, except Kabuki. They range in size from the large and exaggerated *gigaku* dance masks, to the subtly expressive masks of Noh. Many of the masks are independently considered art objects and fetch astronomical prices if and when they're offered for sale. Folk dance and festival masks are more affordable. Made of paper or wood, the masks are usually caricatures of typical country bumpkins or animals. Festival masks can be found at most *mingei* shops. Bingoya (see **Mingei**) and Washikobo (see **Washi**) usually have a good selection.

Martial Arts Clothing and Equipment

There are a number of shops in the Kanda area that specialize in martial arts gear. The following shop is one of the better-known.
YOMEIDO BUDOGUTEN 陽明堂武道具店　千代田区神田神保町 3-1
3-1 Kanda Jimbocho, Chiyoda-ku. Tel: 3261-4668. Hours: 10:00 A.M.–7:00 P.M., until 5:00 P.M. on Sun., closed Mon. & hol. [M-15]

ANTIQUES
Antique Shops

The following list of shops covers only a fraction of the antique stores in Tokyo. We have concentrated on shops for the average buyer. There are two streets famous for antique shops: Kotto-dori in Aoyama [M-5] and the street leading from Iikura Crossing [M-11] toward Kamiya-cho Station. We haven't listed all the shops in these areas, but finding them as you walk along should be no problem. A number of serious collector's shops are in Nihombashi.
MORITA ANTIQUES　5-12-2 Minami Aoyama, Minato-ku. Tel: 3407-4466. Hours: 10:00 A.M.–7:00 P.M. daily (from noon on Sun. & hol.).
　A good assortment of *mingei*, textiles, ceramics, etc. [M-5]
KUROFUNE　7-7-4 Roppongi, Minato-ku. Tel: 3479-1552. Hours: 10:00 A.M.–6:00 P.M., closed Sun. & hol.
　A good selection of Japanese furniture. Not cheap. [M-1]
KATHRYN MILAN　3-1-14 Nishi Azabu, Minato-ku. Tel: 3408-1532. 11:00 A.M.–6:00 P.M., closed Sun.
　Good selection of furniture and decorative accessories in a Taisho period home. [M-2]
HARUMI ANTIQUES　9-6-14 Akasaka, Minato-ku. Tel: 3403-1043. Hours: 10:00 A.M.–6:00 P.M., closed Sun.
　Wide range of moderately-priced items. [M-1]
ART PLAZA MAGATANI　5-10-13 Toranomon, Minato-ku. Tel: 3433-6321. Hours: 10:00 A.M.–6:00 P.M., closed Sun. & hol.
　A wide variety of antiques are packed into this shop. [M-11]

OKURA ORIENTAL ART   3-3-14 Azabudai, Minato-ku. Tel: 3585-5309. Hours: 10:00 A.M.–6:00 P.M., closed Mon.

A good selection of decorative objects, porcelains, and furniture. [M-1]

ANTIQUE GALLERY MEGURO   Stork Mansion, 2F. 2-24-18 Kami-osaki, Shinagawa-ku. Tel: 3493-1971. Hours: 11:00 A.M.–7:30 P.M., closed Mon.

Various dealers have set up shop on one floor of this building. A wide selection, reasonably priced. [M-19]

ANTIQUE MARKET   Hanae Mori Bldg., B1. 3-6-1 Kita Aoyama, Minato-ku. Tel: 3406-1021. Hours: 10:00 A.M.–7:00 P.M. daily.

Numerous dealers of Japanese and Western antiques have set up shop here. [M-4]

ORIENTAL BAZAAR (see **ARTS & CRAFTS, General Shops**)

ANTIQUES NISHIKAWA   2-20-14 Azabu-juban, Minato-ku. Tel: 3456-1023. Hours: 11:00 A.M.–7:00 P.M., closed Tue.

Specializes in old ceramics and porcelain. [M-1]

KARAKUSA   5-13-1 Minami Aoyama, Minato-ku. Tel: 3499-5858. Hours: 11:00 A.M.–6:00 P.M., closed Sat., Sun., & hol.

Specializes in antique blue and white plates. [M-5]

MAYUYAMA & CO., LTD.   2-5-9 Kyobashi, Chuo-ku. Tel: 3561-5146. Hours: 9:30 A.M.–6:00 P.M., closed Sun. & hol.

A good shop for serious collectors. [M-9]

SETSU GATODO   3-7-9 Nihombashi, Chuo-ku. Tel: 3271-7571. Hours: 10:00 A.M.–6:00 P.M., closed Sat. & Sun.

Well-known for its high-quality and pricey merchandise. [M-9]

Flea Markets

Flea markets in Tokyo are like sidewalk antique sales. Often held at shrines and temples on designated Sundays, they're a great way to spend a quiet morning or afternoon. Serious antique hunters show up while the dealers are still unpacking at 5:00–6:00 A.M., so the best merchandise goes early. The outdoor markets are held weather permitting, and usually last until 4:00–4:30 P.M.

Some of the merchandise is overpriced, or at least not significantly less expensive than if you went directly to an antique shop. As foreigners make up a large part of the crowd, dealers often figure they can charge tourist prices. Most will bargain somewhat, especially if the crowd hasn't been good that day. The best deals are to be had on not-so-old, but still interesting ceramics, used kimono, obi, and Japanese kitsch. If you're looking for high quality merchandise you should stick to antique shops. In any case, the markets are great fun and shouldn't be missed.

A few markets are held indoors in underground arcades like the **Sunshine City** Building, though somehow it's not quite as much fun. Also twice a year (usually in the summer and end of December) the flea market association sponsors huge indoor markets with dealers from all over Japan. Dealers at the weekly markets will usually have information and flyers printed in English with the dates and location. A monthly schedule for the main flea markets in the Tokyo area is as follows.

First Saturday: **Iidabashi** (RAMLA center, JR Iidabashi Station)

First Sunday:	**Togo Shrine** (Harajuku) [M-4]
	Arai Yakushi Temple (Not in the book, but is located a short distance on foot from Araiyakushi-mae Station on the Seibu Shinjuku Line)
Second Sunday:	**Nogi Shrine** (near Roppongi) [M-1]
	Hanazono Shrine (behind Isetan Department Store in Shinjuku) [M-7]
Third Sunday:	**Hanazono Shrine**
Fourth Sunday:	**Togo Shrine**
Last Thur. & Fri.:	On the steps of the Roi Building in Roppongi [M-1]

Antique Kimono

The real thing is probably too expensive, but secondhand and antique kimono are one of the truly great bargains to be had in Tokyo. A number of shops carry kimono and obi ranging from twenty to fifty years old and from ¥1,000 up in price. Genuine antiques are harder to find and much more expensive. Flea markets are another good place to find used kimono. Takashimaya and Daimaru Department Stores have bargain sales on used, rental kimono and formal wear about twice a year.

HAYASHI KIMONO   International Arcade, 1-7-21 Uchisaiwai-cho, Chiyoda-ku. Tel: 3591-9826. Hours: 10:00 A.M.–7:00 P.M. daily, until 6:00 P.M. on Sun. [M-10]

KONJAKU NISHIMURA   Hanae Mori Bldg., B1. 3-6-1 Kita Aoyama, Minato-ku. Tel: 3498-1759. Hours: 11:00 A.M.–7:30 P.M., closed Thur. & Sun.

This shop is originally from Kyoto. [M-4]

ORIENTAL BAZAAR   B1 and 2F (see **ARTS & CRAFTS, General Shops**) [M-4]

IKEDA   5-22-11 Shiroganedai, Minato-ku. Tel: 3445-1269. Hours: 10:00 A.M.–6:30 P.M. (until 5:30 on Sat.), closed Sun. & hol.

A large selection of kimono and fabrics. [M-19]

AYAHATA   2-21-2 Akasaka, Minato-ku. Tel: 3582-9969. Hours: 11:00 A.M.–8:00 P.M., closed Sun. & hol.

Antique kimono, obi, blue and white textiles, *furoshiki* (wrapping cloths), *hanten* (thick, short, winter kimono), etc. [M-6]

Other Secondhand Clothes

There are a few places in town selling a variety of rather junky, but interesting used clothes including kimono, old military uniforms and accessories, and *moningu* (men's black formal suits). One of the best places is along Dempo-in Dori in Asakusa, just off Nakamise to the left as you approach the temple. The stall-like junk shops offer a wide variety of curious merchandise. A few stores also dealing with secondhand clothing are listed in **Cheap Fashion.**

NAKATA SHOTEN   In the middle of the old, under-the-tracks part of Ueno's Ameyoko arcade, the shop is famous for military uniforms and paraphernalia. Tel: 3832-8577. [M-13]

IWATAYA   3-39-7 Ebisu, Shibuya-ku. Tel: 3441-7588. Hours. 10:00 A.M.–7:00 P.M., closed on all dates that include 3's or 8's.

Secondhand and dead stock, from kimono to formal suits, fur coats, and jeans. [off Map]

FOOD AND DRINK
Traditional Sweets

While most Westerners have grown accustomed to the idea of eating raw fish Japanese-style, few have managed to surmount the conceptual barrier of eating sweet bean and sticky rice cakes for dessert.

Actually, the Japanese don't generally have dessert per se; after meals a small dish of fruit is considered sufficient. But there is a broad range of between-meal snack sweets that taste better with a cup of green tea, just as a piece of chocolate cake seems to call for a cup of coffee.

It's not particularly surprising considering that originally the sweets developed as an accompaniment to the tea ceremony in the Azuchi-Momoyama period. The extreme sweetness of the cakes complimented the strong and slightly bitter tea. By the Edo period, the taste had filtered down to at least the urban masses and dozens of specialty shops began developing variations on the basic sweet-bean theme.

Many of the Edo-period shops are still in business. Often in slightly inconvenient locations, the famous shops sell out most days by noon. Many have small tea rooms where you can order a cup of green tea and a plate of the house specialty.

• *Namagashi*—highly "artistic," these sweet bean paste cakes are exquisitely molded and decorated somewhat like fancy marzipan. The shapes and colors change with the season.

KIKUYA HONTEN 5-13-2 Minami Aoyama, Minato-ku. Tel: 3400-3856. Hours: 9:30 A.M.–6:00 P.M., closed Sun. & hol.

This beautiful little shop makes twenty different kinds of handmade *namagashi* daily, ¥160–¥330. [M-5]

KOTOBUKIDO KYOGASHI-TSUKASA 2-1-4 Nihombashi Ningyocho, Chuo-ku. Tel: (0120) 480-400. Hours: 9:00 A.M.–9:00 P.M., closed Sun.

Established in 1883, the shop is famous for its *kogane-imo*—cakes made of white beans coated in cinnamon. [M-23]

• *Dango* are dumplings made of steamed or boiled rice. Served usually skewered in threes called *kushi-dango*, *dango* are either broiled and served with a soy or a sweet red bean sauce.

HABUTAE DANGO 5-54-3 Higashi Nippori, Arakawa-ku. Tel: 3891-2924. Hours: 9:00 A.M.–5:30 P.M., closed Tue.

When this shop opened in 1819, their famous *kushi-dango* was praised for being as fine as *habutae*, a type of silk fabric. The name was adopted for the shop and its *kushi-dango*. A lovely tea room overlooks a small garden where you can sample their *habutae-dango* and tea for ¥400. [M-13]

KOTOTOI DANGO 5-5-22 Mukojima, Sumida-ku. Tel: 3622-0081. Hours: 9:15 A.M.–6:30 P.M., closed Thur.

This shop was so famous that the government named a nearby bridge after it. [M-12]

SHIBAMATAYA 7-7-5 Shibamata, Katsushika-ku. Tel: 3659-8111. Hours: 9:00 A.M.–6:00 P.M., daily.

Located in the hometown of the beloved movie character Tora-san, the shop is full of old posters from his more than thirty movies. The restaurant is a rather funky place, with over one hundred kinds of Japanese food on the menu. In front of the shop they make *kusa-dango*, a type of skewered *dango* flavored with the leaves of the *yomogi* plant, a mountain vegetable. [off Map, see **Shibamata Taishakuten Temple**]

• *Mochi*—the ingredients and method preparation are similar to that of *dango,* but *mochi* comes in a much wider variety.

CHOMEIJI SAKURA-MOCHI   5-1-14 Mukojima, Sumida-ku. Tel: 3622-3266. Hours: 9:00 A.M.–6:00 P.M., closed Mon.

Hanging in the shop are *ukiyo-e* prints that were early advertisements for this famous shop. Named after the nearby Chomei-ji temple, this shop has been famous since the Edo period for its *sakura-mochi*—cherry *mochi*. The thin, crepe-like rounds of *mochi* are folded over a sweet bean paste filling then wrapped in three specially-prepared, edible, fragrant cherry leaves. Tea and two *sakura-mochi* cost ¥300. A wonderful spot for viewing the spring blossoms of the grove of nearby cherry trees, the shop is located on the far side of the Sumida River. [M-12]

• *Manju* is a white or brown unsweetened sponge cake filled with sweet bean paste.

TAKEMURA   1-19 Kanda Suda-cho, Chiyoda-ku. Tel: 3251-2328. Hours: 11:00 A.M.–8:00 P.M., closed Sun. & hol.

In a lovely old house, they serve various kinds of desserts such as *oshiruko* (a thick, sweet bean soup with mochi). Try their *age-manju* (fried *manju*). [M-14]

• *Kasutera*—A Portuguese import popularized in the early Meiji period, *kasutera* is a sponge cake that, along with its spin-offs, *dora-yaki* and *ningyo-yaki,* revolutionized the world of Japanese sweets.

USAGIYA   1-10-10 Ueno, Taito-ku. Tel: 3831-6195. Hours: 9:00 A.M.–6:00 P.M., closed Wed.

Known for its *dora-yaki,* sponge pancakes, and *kisaku-monaka,* crisp wafers, both filled with sweet bean paste. [M-13]

SHIGEMORI EISHINDO   2-1-1 Nihombashi Ningyocho, Chuo-ku. Tel: 3666-5885. Hours: 9:00 A.M.–8:00 P.M., closed Sun, except on the fifth of every month, when they open for the local fairs.

Their specialty, *ningyo-yaki,* is hot bean-paste-filled, spongecake cookies baked in various shapes. [M-23]

YANAGIYA   2-11-3 Nihombashi Ningyocho, Chuo-ku. Tel: 3666-1822. Hours: 10:30 A.M.–7:00 P.M., closed Sun.

A long queue of people wait in front of this shop to get some of the best *taiyaki* in town while it's still hot. *Taiyaki* are sea bream-shaped cakes of unsweetened dough filled with sweet bean paste. The test for quality is whether the bean paste fills even the *taiyaki* tail. [M-23]

Sembei—Crackers

Sembei, Japanese crackers, are the most common snack food in Japan. Most are salty crackers made from rice flour with soy or salt flavoring often spiced-up with a bit of seaweed (even potato chips in Japan are frequently flavored with seaweed). Sweet *sembei* are made from wheat flour, sugar, and eggs. Usually found in the downtown districts, *sembei* shops are worth visiting as much for the shop as for the crackers.

IRIYAMA SEMBEI   1-13-4 Asakusa, Taito-ku. Tel: 3844-1376. Hours: 10:00 A.M.–6:00 P.M., closed Thur.

You can watch the shop people facing each other in front of a grill, earnestly turning over dozens of roasting crackers. They close shop early when they sell out. [M-12]

HINODE SEMBEI   1-26-4 Asakusa, Taito-ku. Tel: 3844-4110. Hours: 10:00 A.M.–7:00 P.M., closed Tue. [M-12]

KIKUMI SEMBEI   3-37-16 Sendagi, Bunkyo-ku. Tel: 3821-1215. Hours: 10:00 A.M.–7:00 P.M., closed Mon. [M-13]

MIDORIYA   1-4-5 Kanda Suda-cho, Chiyoda-ku. Tel: 5256-0688. Hours: 10:00 A.M.–7:00 P.M., closed Sun. & hol.

Isono-ishi, literally "beach pebbles," are the hit cracker of this adorable shop where the shopkeeper sits on a raised tatami floor next to rows of round glass pots filled with a variety of *sembei.* [M-14]

MAMEGEN   1-8-12 Azabu-juban, Minato-ku. Tel: 3583-0962. Hours: 9:00 A.M.–8:00 P.M., closed Tue.

Their specialty is *mame-gashi,* a small cracker wrapped around various kinds of roasted nuts and beans. Their freshly made *age-sembei,* fried *sembei,* are also delicious. [M-1]

Saké

Saké is the general Japanese word for any kind of alcohol. What most foreigners call saké is more properly referred to as *nihonshu.* Made from fermented rice, there are two main types of *nihonshu. Seishu* became popular after World War II when a shortage of rice led to the production of saké by adding alcohol and sometimes sugar to the brew. Most of the less expensive, commercial brands are made this way. *Junmaishu,* pure rice wine, is by far the best. Recommended brands are Tamano-hikari, Taruhei, and Uragasumi.

Shochu is a distilled liquor made from rice or sweet potatoes. A Japanese version of vodka or tequila, it's a cheap, formerly low-class drink that became popular with young Japanese in the mid-eighties. *Goma-jochu, shochu* flavored with sesame, and *kuri-jochu,* flavored with chestnut, are also good. **Umeshu** is a plum wine made, often at home, by adding *ume,* Japanese plums, and sugar to *shochu,* then aging the mixture for at least one year.

The easiest place to buy saké is in the liquor corner of department store food sections where you will often find a selection of saké from all over Japan.

Amazake, literally "sweet saké," is traditionally made from a mixture of boiled rice and rice malt that has fermented for a few weeks. The resulting drink is a thick, naturally sweet, non-alcoholic beverage. Commonly served at festivals, the *amazake* syrup is mixed with hot water before drinking. The process is often speeded up these days by using a combination of rice kernels left over from making other kinds of saké, and sugar instead of malt.

NIHONSHU CENTER   5-9-1 Ginza, Chuo-ku. Tel: 3575-0656. Hours: 10:30 A.M.–6:30 P.M., closed Thurs. & hol.

A sort of saké trade center providing information on over six thousand brands of Japanese saké. Besides the displays and information provided, there is also a sampling corner where you can have a taste of various brews. [M-8]

SAKAGURA   Yurakucho Seibu Department Store Bldg., B–B1. Tel: 3286-0111. Hours: 10:00 A.M.–7:00 P.M., closed Wed.

This shop carries two to three hundred types of saké. [M-8]

AMANOYA   2-18-15 Soto-kanda, Chiyoda-ku. Tel: 3251-7911. Hours: 9:00 A.M.–6:00 P.M., 10:00 A.M.–5:00 P.M. on hol., closed Sun.

Possibly the only place you can drink the traditional form of *amazake* in Tokyo, this shop has been in business since 1597. They serve it hot in winter, cold in summer, and accompanied by a small serving of *hisakata-miso,* another house specialty, made from thick soy bean paste and rice grains. [M-14, 16]

Ocha—Tea

There are six main kinds of *ocha,* Japanese tea. The most popular is *bancha,* an inexpensive, everyday tea made from the tougher tea leaves and stems. *Hojicha* is a roasted version of *bancha* with a subtle smoky flavor. *Genmai-cha* is roasted *bancha* mixed with kernels of popped brown rice. *Matcha* is a powdered green tea used for the tea ceremony. *Gyokuro,* the most expensive tea, has a mild, slightly sweet taste. *Sencha* is another better tea, usually served to guests. In the summer, *mugi-cha,* chilled wheat tea, is also popular. Japanese tea is never served with sugar or milk. There are tea shops in most neighborhoods, while department stores also offer a good selection.

YAMAMOTO-YAMA   2-5-2 Nihombashi, Chuo-ku. Tel: 3271-3361. Hours: 9:30 A.M.–6:30 P.M. daily.

Established in 1690, this is the most famous tea shop in all of Tokyo. [M-9]

Oshinko

An essential part of most Japanese meals, *oshinko* (pickles) are considered primarily a condiment for the rice. There are thousands of variations, the most common being *daikon* (white radish), *nasu* (eggplant), and *kyuri* (cucumber). In the good old days, people made their pickles at home; now, that's mostly seen in the countryside.

SHUETSU   2-7-11 Ueno, Taito-ku. Tel: 5688-5052. Hours: 9:00 A.M.–6:30 P.M., daily.

This shop has been doing business since 1675. Their specialties are *fukujinzuke* (a purplish-colored cucumber pickle), *kukiwakame* (seaweed stalks), *nori no tsukudani* (sweetened seaweed), and *honboshi kakoi takuwan* (a kind of *daikon* pickle). [M-13]

Tsukudani

Invented by a fisherman who lived on Tsukuda Island to the southeast of Tokyo, *tsukudani* is a rice condiment made from small fish or seaweed boiled in a soy and sugar sauce.

TEN-YASU   1-3-14 Tsukuda, Chuo-ku. Tel: 3531-3457. Hours: 9:00 A.M.–6:00 P.M., closed Mon. Since 1837. [M-25]

TANAKAYA   1-3-13 Tsukuda, Chuo-ku. Tel: 3531-2649. Hours: 9:30 A.M.–5:30 P.M., 10:00 A.M.–5:00 P.M. on hol., closed Mon. [M-25]

Grocery Stores

Most Japanese still do their daily shopping on the neighborhood shopping street; at the fruit and vegetable stand, the fishmonger, the butcher, etc. Strict zoning regulations have prevented the infiltration of big supermarkets into most areas. For convenience or for Western goods, you can shop at one of the big three Western-style supermarkets listed below. They charge top prices for their stock, but sometimes it's worth it. Department store food departments are also a great place to shop for semi-prepared foods.

Recently, several home delivery services have emerged that offer reasonably priced foods, the system works like mail order. **Chikyu-jin Club** provides natural and organic foods (Tel: 045-942-3288), and **Foreign Buyers' Club** offers inexpensive foods in bulk (Tel: 078-221-2591).

KINOKUNIYA INTERNATIONAL 3-11-7 Kita Aoyama, Minato-ku. Tel: 3409-1231. Hours: 9:30 A.M.–8:00 P.M. daily. [M-5] Todoroki Branch: 7-18-1 Todoroki, Setagaya-ku. Tel: 3704-7515. Hours: 10:00 A.M.–7:00 P.M., daily. [M-21]

The most up-market supermarket in town.

NATIONAL AZABU SUPERMARKET 4-5-2 Minami Azabu, Minato-ku. Tel: 3442-3181. Hours: 9:30 A.M.–6:30 P.M. daily (until 7:00 P.M.. on Sun.). [M-2] In Setagaya, it is called Den-en: 2-6-21 Tamagawa-denenchofu, Setagaya-ku. Tel: 3721-4161. Hours: 10:00 A.M.–8:00 P.M. daily. [M-21]

Catering to the foreign community, this is a full-service supermarket offering phone- and fax-ordering and delivery service.

MEIDIYA Roppongi Store: 7-15-14 Roppongi, Minato-ku. Tel: 3401-8511. Hours: 10:00 A.M.–10:00 P.M. daily. [M-1] Hiro-o Store: Hiro-o Plaza, 5-6-6 Hiro-o, Shibuya-ku. Tel: 3444-6221. Hours: 10:00 A.M.–9:00 P.M. daily.

Upscale supermarket catering primarily to the Japanese, with a great new store located in Hiro-o. [M-2]

NATURAL HOUSE 3-6-18 Kita Aoyama, Minato-ku. Tel: 3498-2277. Hours: 10:00 A.M.–10:00 P.M. daily. [M-5] Jiyugaoka Branch: 1-13-14 Jiyugaoka, Meguro-ku. Tel: 3718-1738. Hours: 10:00 A.M.–9:00 P.M. daily. [M-21]

A large, health and natural foods supermarket.

MUSIC

Perhaps because of the Japanese predilection for collecting things, Tokyo is a fascinating place to go shopping for music. While in the early nineties there has been some talk of abolishing the practice of fixing the retail price of domestically manufactured CDs, records, and tapes, until that becomes law, Japan is one of the few countries where imported recordings are cheaper than the local variety.

A cursory look at the local music scene may be in order here. Although Japan has the second largest recording market in the world, the bulk of it comprises locally produced pop music, much of which is of little interest to the average English-speaking music fan. The so-called "idol stars"–generally mid-to-late teen practitioners of the worst kind of prepackaged pap who made the running in the popularity stakes for many years–have given way somewhat to a new generation of Japanese musicians influenced by rock and black music, albeit still in a very derivative stage. New trends in music attain popularity here simultaneously with the West, but they are often not mimicked long enough to be fully assimilated. There is also a type of romantic singer-songwriter style, going back perhaps beyond the mid-1970s debut of the phenomenally popular **Matsutoya Yumi** (universally known as "Yumin"), that, while appropriating the decorative trappings of the more modern fads, remains basically unchanged. The new generation of this style is embodied by another phenomenally popular group, **Dreams Come True,** a female vocalist with two male accompanists, whose CDs sell into the millions, particularly to the young women to whose emotions the lyrics appeal.

On the more traditional side, there is *enka,* which, in many ways, is to Japan what traditional country music is to rural white America; conservative values expressed with melancholy, in a fixed musical form from which only rarely is any deviation made. The death of **Misora Hibari,** for decades the Queen of Enka, left a hole hard to fill even for **Miyako Harumi,** a fine intuitive singer who recently made a comeback after a temporary retirement. As the line between country music and soul music can be very thin, so in *enka* too the best singers can be extremely moving, although in many cases the emoting tends to look manufactured for TV. In recent years, there has been a vogue for Korean *enka* singers (the style derives from Korea originally), whose more natural predisposition for emotional interpretation is immediately evident. Particularly popular is **Kei Unsuku.**

The *karaoke* phenomenon that grew out of, and was fueled by, *enka,* has now become so powerful that it in turn has begun to influence new trends in *enka:* singability is now mandatory. And the advent of *karaoke* rooms rented by the hour during the daytime has changed what began as a primarily male entertainment, invariably associated with drinking and late hours, into a pastime for women too. This in turn has brought about a demand for young female *enka* singers with whom their audience can empathize, as opposed to the traditional image of women being fans of male singers and vice versa. The staid quality of *enka* is gradually falling out of step with the changes in Japanese society, but its hold on the Japanese psyche remains strong.

Jazz has always been popular in Japan, and there are many musicians playing in all the different styles. The best known are trumpeter **Hino Terumasa,** saxophonist **Watanabe Sadao,** pianist **Yamashita Yosuke,** guitarist **Watanabe Kazumi,** and another trumpeter **KondoToshinori,** whose experiments with free music have begun to take in angular punk funk too.

During the early eighties, the **Yellow Magic Orchestra (YMO)** revolutionized Japanese contemporary pop music by taking a typically Western image of what Japanese music sounds like and setting it to a computerized beat. Despite (or perhaps because of) anticipating the global trend toward drum machines and sampling, the group suffered the fate of so many others who were "ahead of their time," and disbanded in 1983. In the wake of their demise, the "alternative" scene that was brought into existence largely through YMO's influence, lost most of its spirit. The solo records by each of the group's ex-members also failed to live up to the promise of some of their collective work, and, in fact, YMO reformed in 1993, ostensibly for just one comeback album.

The group's keyboard player **Sakamoto Ryuichi** has become, on his own, Japan's single most prestigious musical export, winning an Academy Award for his part in composing the soundtrack for Bernardo Bertolucci's film *The Last Emperor.* Sakamoto, who now lives in New York, is a musical magpie, mixing sounds and melodies from around the globe, including Japan and Okinawa, into his own version of World Music. In fact, if you walk into the larger record shops in Tokyo these days, you will sometimes find a section within the World Music part of the store featuring Japanese traditional music beside Okinawan music, a sign of changing times since the Japanese have hitherto been loath to lend an ear to their indigenous heritage.

Lastly, we would like to make mention of a few musicians whose work, although outside the mainstream, is consistently of interest: **Ito Takio** has taken the traditional ethnic singing style of Aomori and embellished it with rock instrumentation, making a unique and potent hybrid; master of the Japanese *taiko* drums, **Hayashi Eitetsu** continues to experiment with new forms of performance, mixing Eastern and Western influences in a manner purely his own; another percussionist, **Takada Midori,** whose marimba playing in particular stands out, has been involved in some intriguing collaborations with jazz pianist/composer **Sato Masahiko. Yano Akiko,** who is married to **Sakamoto Ryuichi,** is an outstanding piano player and a distinctive, high-voiced singer and songwriter in her own right; and look out for a traditional singer from Aomori called **Kishi Chieko,** whose abandoned delivery is pure soul music!

Classical Japanese Music

Recordings by classical musicians can be found in most record shops, but the largest selections are at the Ikebukuro Seibu Department Store, the Roppongi Wave Building and at Ishimaru Denki Honten in Soto-kanda (all are included in the list of record shops that follows). The best label is CBS-Sony, which releases multi-disc sets of excellent quality at exorbitant prices. When buying a CD, it's best to ask for a recording by one of the artists or groups listed below. Titles go in and out of print but most of these artists continue to produce new recordings.

Shamisen   The basic repertoire consists of narrative works called *kata-rimono* and lyrical works called *utaimono.* There are three main genres of *shamisen* music that are better known than the particular artists: *kiyomoto, tokiwazu,* and *shinnai.*

Gagaku   The Imperial Court Orchestra is most representative.

Koto   Most koto players also perform on the *shamisen.* The following two artists are designated "National Living Treasures" by the Japanese government: **Nakanoshima Kin'ichi** of the Yamada-Ryu School, and **Yonekawa Fumiko** of the Ikuta-Ryu School.

Biwa Most famous player is **Tsuruta Kinshi.**

Shakuhachi **Yokoyama Katsuya** performs classical and contemporary works. **Yamaguchi Goro** performs solo and in *san-kyoku*, a trio of *koto*, *shamisen*, and *shakuhachi*. **Aoki Reibo** is the most classical of the three and has recorded the entire classical repertoire.

Record Shops

The following list includes a number of large general shops, plus a selection of specialist places that often deal in just one genre of music. The list is only a small selection, and if you are interested in secondhand rare deletions, or bootlegs, for example, you may care to wander around Shimokitazawa or Nishi Shinjuku respectively, where dealers in such commodities tend to be concentrated.

Also, if you have a friend who'll translate Japanese for you, it's worth getting hold of a book called *Record Map*, which is published by Gakuyo Shobo and updated yearly. This book lists hundreds of record shops not only in Tokyo (area by area), but nationwide, and in considerable detail; so however recherché your taste, fear not, someone is there for you.

It should be noted that all of the major foreign chains constantly poach each other's buyers, with the result that stocking policies can vary from time to time. The recorded music market in Tokyo is volatile, so please remember that listings which were accurate as of going to press are subject to change.

• General

TOWER RECORDS Shibuya: 1-22-14 Jinnan, Shibuya-ku. Tel: 3496-3661. Hours: 10:00 A.M.– 10:00 P.M. daily. [M-3] Shinjuku: LUMINE, 6F. Hours: 11:00 A.M.–10:00 P.M. daily. [M-7] Ikebukuro: Satomi Bldg., 1F. 3-9-5 Minami Ikebukuro, Toshima-ku. Tel: 3983-2010. Hours: 10:00 A.M.–10:00 P.M. daily. [off Map]

A branch of the California chain, it's usually the first place you can find new U.S. releases and one of the cheapest places to buy them. Tower's flagship Shibuya store, opened in March 1995, is currently the largest music retail store in the world, with seven floors above ground and a basement café. In addition to individual floors of over 7,000 square feet allotted to jazz and classical music, and books (possibly the most impressive feature of the whole store—see separate entry under **Bookstores**), the store also features sections devoted to videos, CD ROM, computer software, and games.

VIRGIN MEGASTORE Shinjuku Marui Fashion-kan, B1. 3-30-16 Shinjuku, Shinjuku-ku. Tel: 3354-0101. Hours: 11:00 A.M.–8:00 P.M., closed two Weds. per month.

Over 100,000 music titles in this branch of the famous Virgin Store in London. [M-7]

HMV Nishi Ginza department store INZ2, Tel: 5250-2451. Hours: 10:00 A.M.–9:00 P.M. daily. [M-8] Also in Shibuya ONE OH NINE, B–2F. 28-6, Udagawa-cho, Shibuya-ku. Tel: 3477-6880. Hours: 10:00 A.M.–9:00 P.M. daily. [M-3]

WAVE In Shibuya, the **Quattro** store is very well stocked, good location. 13-32 Udagawa-cho, Shibuya-ku. Tel: 3477-8800. Hours: 10:00 A.M.–9:00 P.M. daily. [M-3] Also in Shibuya LOFT. Tel: 3462-3118 (see **Special Buildings**). Roppongi **WAVE** is the original flagship store, recently refurbished. Particularly good selection of jazz LP's. 6-2-27, Roppongi, Minato-ku. Tel: 3408-0111. Hours: 11:00 A.M.–9:00 P.M. daily. [M-1]

ISHIMARU DENKI NO. 3 SHOP   1-2-13 Soto-kanda, Chiyoda-ku. Tel: 3257-1300. Hours: 10:00 A.M.–7:30 P.M. daily (until 8:00 P.M. on Fri. & Sat.).

Especially good for domestic releases, and with its remarkable depth of inventory can sometimes be useful for tracking down the items that none of the others have. [M-14]

• Specialist Shops

DISC UNION   3-31-4, Shinjuku, Shinjuku-ku. Tel: 3352-2691. Hours: 11:00 A.M.–8:00 P.M. daily, until 7:00 P.M. on Sun. & hol.

In various locations, but check the basement of the Shinjuku branch for jazz selections, in particular. [M-7]

WINNERS   Rokuei Bldg., 2F. 7-14-11, Roppongi, Minato-ku. Tel: 3405-8190. Hours: noon–6:00 A.M. daily.

Caters to club DJ's, selling European bootlegs of rare, deleted soul. [M-1]

CISCO   Ryuko Bldg., 2F. 11-1 Udagawa-cho, Shibuya-ku. Tel: 3462-0366. Hours: 11:00 A.M.–9:00 P.M. daily. [M-3]

Good for rock imports, often cheaper than the big stores.

FRISCO   Studio Parco, 2F. 4-7, Udagawa-cho, Shibuya-ku. Tel: 3770-8451. Hours: 11:00–9:00 P.M. daily. Classical music only, sister shop to **Cisco**. [M-3]

SUMIYA   Toho Seimei Bldg., 2F. 2-15-1 Shibuya, Shibuya-ku. Tel: 3409-6091. Hours: 11:00 A.M.–7:30 P.M., closed the third Wed. of the month.

For soundtracks, and oldies. [M-3]

BUNKADO   5-14-1, Ginza, Chuo-ku. Tel: 3541-8325. Hours: 10:00 A.M.–8:00 P.M., closed Sun. & hol.

Japanese traditional. [M-8]

RECOFAN   Shibuya Beam Bldg., 4F. 31-2 Udagawa-cho, Shibuya-ku. Tel: 5454-0161. Hours: 11:00 A.M.–8:00 P.M. daily.

Particularly good for secondhand. [M-3]

BOOKS

There are plenty of bookstores in Tokyo, but only a few that carry English books. All the shops in the following list have a good selection. Some hotels also have well-stocked shops with good selections of books on Japan. The best hotel bookstores are in the Okura, the Imperial and the New Otani.

Bookstores

KINOKUNIYA   3-17-7 Shinjuku, Shinjuku-ku. Tel: 3354-0131. Hours: 10:00 A.M.–7:00 P.M., closed the third Wed. of the month.

Foreign books on 6F. [M-7]

MARUZEN   2-3-10 Nihombashi, Chuo-ku. Tel: 3272-7211. Hours: 10:00 A.M.–6:30 P.M., closed Sun.

Foreign books on 2F & 4F. A good selection of traditional crafts also on 4F. [M-9]

JENA (pronounced "Yena")   5-6-1 Ginza, Chuo-ku. Tel: 3571-2980. Hours: 10:30 A.M.–7:50 P.M., 12:00–6:00 P.M. on Sun., closed hol.

Foreign books on 3F. [M-8]

SANSEIDO   1-1 Kanda Jimbocho, Chiyoda-ku. Tel: 3233-3312. Hours: 10:00 A.M.–6:30 P.M., March–April open daily, May–Feb. closed on Tue.

Foreign books on 5F, maps on 1F. [M-15]

KITAZAWA SHOTEN   2-5 Kanda Jimbocho, Chiyoda-ku. Tel: 3263-0011. Hours: 10:00 A.M.–6:00 P.M., closed Sun. & hol.

2F: secondhand books, 1F: English literature & philosophy. [M-15]

BIBLOS F. I. Bldg., 4F. 1-26-5 Takadanobaba, Shinjuku-ku. Tel: 3200-4531. Hours: 10:30 A.M.–8:00 P.M., 11:00 A.M.–6:30 P.M. on Sun. & hol., closed third Sun.

Over 6,000 Penguin Book titles are carried by this shop. [off Map: just in front of the JR Takadanobaba Station main exit.]

NATIONAL BOOKSTORE National Azabu Supermarket, 2F. Tel: 3442-3181.

This shop offers a good selection of books on Japan, English-language cookbooks, magazines, and novelties. [M-2]

LA RIVIERE Bell Commons, B1. 2-14-6 Kita Aoyama, Minato-ku. Tel: 3475-6541. Hours: 11:00 A.M.–8:00 P.M.

English books. [M-5]

AOYAMA BOOK CENTER 6-1-20 Roppongi, Minato-ku. Tel: 3442-1651. Hours: 10:00 A.M.–5:00 A.M. daily (until 10:00 P.M. on Sun. & hol.).

Not such a large selection of English books, but many books on contemporary architecture and design. [M-1]

GOOD DAY BOOKS Asahi Bldg., 3F. 1-11-2 Ebisu, Shibuya-ku. Tel: 5421-0957. Hours: 11:00 A.M.–8:00 P.M. daily (until 6:00 P.M. on Sun. & hol.).

New and used books on a wide range of subjects, at very competitive prices. Helpful staff will also take individual orders, either personally or by phone or fax. Bulk orders are sent out about twice monthly, with delivery approximately ten days after that. [M-20]

PAPERWEIGHT BOOKS Chatelet Shibuya #401, 2-20-13 Higashi, Shibuya-ku. Tel: 3498-5260. Fax: 3498-5404. Hours: 12:30–7:00 P.M., closed Sun. & hol.

This smallish shop, on Meiji-dori between Shibuya and Ebisu, specializes mainly in psychology, self-help, women's issues, and the like, but also has a great selection of unusual children's books. Ten to twenty percent below regular bookstore prices, they also do mail order. Individual orders are possible, but require five weeks minimum. [off Map]

TOWER BOOKS Tower Records, 7F. 1-22-14 Jinnan, Shibuya-ku. Tel: 3496-3661. Hours: 10:00 A.M.–10:00 P.M. daily.

Probably the largest selection of English language books in Tokyo. Predictably, a heavy emphasis on music and other aspects of popular culture, but also good sections on social issues, art, etc. Numerous magazines, and a range of newspapers too (weekend editions only). [M-3]

ON SUNDAYS 3-7-6 Jingumae, Shibuya-ku. Tel: 3470-1424. 11:00 A.M.–8:00 P.M., closed Mon.

Art books, mostly foreign, great cards. [M-5]

GA GALLERY (see **Contemporary Art Galleries**)

Best selection of books on architecture in Tokyo.

ART VIVANT Sezon Museum, B1. [M-18]; Roppongi Wave Bldg., 4F. [M-1]

Japanese and foreign art books and magazines. Tel: 3408-0111.

BONJINSHA Ryoshin Kirakawa-cho Bldg., 1F. 1-3-13 Hirakawa-cho, Chiyoda-ku. Tel: 3472-2240. Hours: 10:00 A.M.–7:00 P.M., closed Sun. & hol.

Textbooks on Japan and Japanese language. [M-31]

YAESU BOOK CENTER 2-5-1 Yaesu, Chuo-ku. Tel: 3281-1811. Hours: 10:00 A.M.–7:00 P.M., closed Sun.

Foreign-language books on 4F. [M-9]

A branch is also located in the **Yebisu Garden Place Mitsukoshi,** 2F. Tel: 5423-1158.

CRAYON HOUSE A great children's bookstore (see **For Children**).

HOSHIO BOOKSHELF Located in Gunma, but a good source for rare and out-of-print books on Japan. Fax: 0274-87-3128. 1290 Hoshio, Nanmokumura, Kanragun, Gunma-ken. [off Map]

Jimbocho Book District

Jimbocho in Kanda is the Tokyo "secondhand book district." Shops here only occasionally carry books in English, but often have a wide stock of items such as *ukiyo-e* prints, old magazines, maps, stamps, movie posters, etc. The list below notes only a few of the more interesting shops. Because most shops are concentrated along one street clearly marked on the Jimbocho/Kanda map [M-15], we have only included the phone numbers here. Shops are open from 10:00 A.M.–6:00 P.M., and closed the first and third Sunday of the month.

SANCHA SHOBO   Tel: 3291-0453

OYA SHOBO   Tel: 3291-0062. Edo-period literature, maps, and *ukiyo-e*.

CHARLES E. TUTTLE   Tel: 3291-7072. Books on Japan and the Far East. Most in English.

MATSUMURA SHOTEN   Tel: 3291-2410. Art books.

KANDA KOSHO CENTER   This building has seven floors and eleven shops, most of which specialize in one area such as old movie memorabilia, maps and old prints, old magazines, old comic books, etc. You could spend hours here.

HARA SHOBO   Tel: 3261-7444. *Ukiyo-e*, books on astrology.

TOKYO TAIBUNSHA   Tel: 3261-1273.

TOYODA SHOBO   Tel: 3261-1589. Books on Japanese theater.

HAGA SHOTEN   Tel: 3263-1956. Pornography and adult video.

OTHER SHOPS
Art and Office Supplies

ITOYA   2-7-15 Ginza, Chuo-ku. Tel: 3561-8311. Hours: 10:00 A.M.–7:00 P.M. daily, 10:30 A.M.–6:00 P.M. on Sun. & hol.

Established since 1904, this is one of the best supply shops in town, with eight floors of merchandise. On 5F is a good stock of Japanese paper. [M-8]

LAPIS   Axis Bldg., 3F. 5-17-1 Roppongi, Minato-ku. Tel: 3583-0861. Hours: 10:00 A.M.–7:00 P.M., closed Sun. & hol. Also Roppongi (next to Wave Bldg.) Tonichi Bldg., 1F. 6-2-31 Roppongi, Minato-ku. Tel: 3405-2821. Hours: 10:00 A.M.–8:00 P.M. daily, 11:00 A.M.–7:00 P.M. on Sun. & hol.

A well-stocked office and art supply store, they offer a sophisticated copy service. [M-1]

UEMATSU   2-20-8 Shibuya, Shibuya-ku. Tel: 3400-5558. Hours: 10:00 A.M.–7:00 P.M., closed the first and third Sun.

Wide selection of art supplies. [M-3]

MATRIX   Axis Bldg., 2F. Tel: 3587-2463. Hours: 11:00 A.M.–7:00 P.M., closed Sun.

Everything for the contemporary office and all in designer's black, white or gray. This is a terrific place to buy contemporary souvenirs. [M-1]

LEMON   2-6 Kanda Suruga-dai, Chiyoda-ku. Tel: 3295-4681. Hours: 10:00 A.M.–8:00 P.M. daily, 11:00 A.M.–7:00 P.M. Sat. & Sun.

This shop is best known for its good selection of art supplies. [M-15]

KIYA   3-44-8 Yushima, Bunkyo-ku. Tel: 3831-8688. Hours: 9:00 A.M.–6:30 P.M., closed Mon.

Japanese art supplies; paper, ink, and brushes for *sumi-e*, etc. [M-13]

Cosmetics

SHU UEMURA BEAUTY BOUTIQUE   5-1-3 Jingumae, Shibuya-ku. Tel: 3486-0048. Hours: 10:00 A.M.–8:00 P.M. daily.

The largest Tokyo shop for this now internationally-known cosmetics firm. [M-4]

ORIENTAL   4-9-9 Roppongi, Minato-ku. Tel: 3401-8882. Hours: 11:00 A.M.–9:00 P.M. (noon–8:00 P.M. on hol.), closed Sun.

A favorite of Tokyo fashion models, this shop offers a good selection of domestic and imported cosmetic lines, brushes, pencils, make-up boxes, some lingerie. [M-1]

THE BODY SHOP   6-3-9 Jingumae, Shibuya-ku. Tel: 3499-6396. Hours: 11:00 A.M.–8:00 P.M., closed the third Tues.

Tokyo branch of the famous British skincare product shop. [M-4]

Discount Shops

The following shops carry a variety of merchandise at discount prices.

KOBUTSU NO DAIMARU   19-17 Maruyama-cho, Shibuya-ku. Tel: 3462-0781. Hours: 9:00 A.M.–7:00 P.M. (until 5:00 P.M. on Sun.), closed Wed.

Secondhand furniture, appliances, just about everything in this huge shop that's literally overflowing with bargains. [off Map]

KIMURAYA   2-1 Kanda Suruga-dai, Chiyoda-ku. Tel: 3294-0800. Hours: 10:00 A.M.–8:00 P.M. daily, until 7:30 on Sun.

Twenty- to thirty-percent discounts on electronics, watches, cameras, toys, shoes and socks, bags, etc. This is one of Tokyo's most famous discount shops. [M-15]

SAMPEI STORE   3-22-12 Shinjuku, Shinjuku-ku. Tel: 3352-1634. Hours: 10:30 A.M.–9:00 P.M. daily.

Clothing, food, electronics, etc., at about twenty percent off. [M-7]

TOKYO HYAKKA FUNABASHIYA   1-17-8 Midori, Sumida-ku. Tel: 3634-5555. Hours: 10:30 A.M.–8:00 P.M., closed Wed.

Furniture, interior goods, food, clothing, sporting goods, etc. [M-24]

Fabrics

Besides the shops listed below, fabrics can be found in Nippori, a wholesale fabric district, in department stores, and at **Tokyu Hands.**

NUNO "FUNCTIONAL TEXTILE SHOP"   Axis Bldg., 5-17-1 Roppongi, Minato-ku, B1. Tel: 3582-7997. Hours: 11:00 A.M.–7:00 P.M., closed Sun.

This shop sells fabrics that Issey Miyake and Rei Kawakubo of Commes des Garçons would love. The fabrics are in natural or neutral tones, a few prints, and amazing weaves. [M-1]

KAWAMURA   8-9-17 Ginza, Chuo-ku. Tel: 3572-0181. Hours: 10:00 A.M.–7:30 P.M., closed Sun.

A huge selection of silk fabrics is carried by this shop. [M-8]

TOA FABRICS   1-19-3 Jinnan, Shibuya-ku. Tel: 3463-3351. Hours: 10 A.M.–8:00 P.M. daily.

Fabrics, notions, and some Western-sized patterns. A good shop for Tokyo residents. [M-3]

FABRIC FIRM   2-24-1 Dogenzaka, Shibuya-ku. Tel: 3477-9700. Hours: 10:00 A.M.–7:00 P.M., closed Tue.

Three floors of fabrics, custom curtains, and upholstery services. [M-3]

AIKOBO   (see **General Craft Shops**) For very serious, traditional blue and white fabrics.

Interiors

Furniture and housewares are available at all department stores. A good selection is found in **Seibu** (Shibuya's is perhaps best), and **Isetan.** Furniture here is expensive, and not generally sized to large Western bodies.

AXIS BUILDING   5-17-1 Roppongi, Minato-ku. Tel: 3587-2781.

Most shops close on Sun. Several shops here specialize in contemporary designs for interiors. [M-1]

TOKYO DESIGN CENTER   5-25-19 Higashi Gotanda, Shinagawa-ku. Tel: 3445-1121. Hours: 10:00 A.M.–6:00 P.M., closed Sun.

A fantastic building designed by Mario Bellini that houses the showrooms of around twenty design firms, many that produce furniture. Also has a nice little restaurant with outdoor terrace. [off Map]

ODAKYU HALC   1-1-3 Nishi Shinjuku, Shinjuku-ku. Tel: 3342-1111. Hours: 10:00 A.M.–7:00 P.M., closed Tues.

Halc (Happy Living Center) is Odakyu Department Store's interior section and is in a building next to the main store. [M-7]

INNOVATOR SHOP   1-4-7 Kita Aoyama, Minato-ku. Tel: 3403-7544. Hours: 10:00 A.M.–6:00 P.M. daily.

Furniture, some imported, some made in Japan from Swedish designs. Has a good selection of furniture for smaller apartments. [M-5]

PARCO PART 3 Shibuya Parco, 15-1 Udagawa-cho, Shibuya-ku. (see **Fashion Buildings**)
Furniture and housewares. [M-3]
TOKYU HANDS (see **Specialized & Special Interest Buildings**)
Good for do-it-yourself interiors and home improvements [M-3]
LOFT (see **Specialized & Special Interest Buildings**)
Furniture, housewares, storage goods, etc. [M-3]
IN THE ROOM 1-12-13 Jinnan, Shibuya-ku. Tel: 3464-0101. Hours: 11:00 A.M.–8:00 P.M.,
daily.
Marui's interiors division in Shibuya. [M-3]
ACTUS Shinjuku: 2-19-1 Shinjuku, Shinjuku-ku. Tel: 3350-6011. Hours: 10:00 A.M.–6:30 P.M.,
closed Wed.
Furniture in a variety of styles, also a counter that can make up cushions, covers, and curtains.
[M-7]
AMBIENTE 4-11-1 Minami Aoyama, Minato-ku. Tel: 3405-6720. Hours: 10:30 A.M.–6:30 P.M.,
closed Sun.
Beautiful but expensive imported, mostly Italian furniture and accessories. Fantastic building
by Aldo Rossi. [M-5]

Luggage

Cheap soft bags can be found in buildings like Shibuya **Parco Part 1, Loft
B1** and the Harajuku **Laforet.** Department stores have bags as well as
luggage. Cheaper suitcases can be found at places like the **Ameyoko Arcade**
in Ueno.

Sembei displayed in the traditional way (near Shibamata Taishakuten
Temple). © 1984 M. Yoshida

Pearls

MIKIMOTO 4-5-5 Ginza, Chuo-ku. Tel: 3535-4611. Hours: 10:30 A.M.–6:00 P.M., closed Wed.

The most famous of Tokyo pearl shops, Mikimoto's merchandise is of high quality with comparably high prices. The main Ginza store has displays of their original designs. [M-8]

MORI SILVER Oriental Bazaar, (see **General Shops**), 2F. Tel: 3407-7010.

A reputable local manufacturer and wholesaler of silver and pearls, the prices at their retail shop are some of the most reasonable in town. The shop also accepts custom orders for jewelry. [M-4]

UEDA PEARLS Imperial Hotel, Arcade B1.

Another famous shop. [M-10]

Shoes

The Japanese make terrific, inexpensive, fashionable shoes—most of which are sized for tiny Japanese feet. A few shops do specialize in large- and small-sized shoes, or will have a few in stock. Charles Jourdan will often have a few larger sizes or will special order (shops are in major department stores).

DIANA Ginza: Kyodo Bldg., 6-9-6 Ginza, Chuo-ku. Tel: 3573-4001. Hours: 11:00 A.M.–8:00 P.M. daily (large and small sizes on 4F). [M-8] Harajuku: 1-8-6 Jingumae, Shibuya-ku. Tel: 3478-4001. Hours: 10:30 A.M.–8:30 P.M. daily (large and small sizes on 2F). [M-4]

A good selection of women's shoes up to size 26 cm. The Harajuku shop is geared to a younger clientele.

WASHINGTON 5-7-7 Ginza, Chuo-ku. Tel: 3572-5911. Hours: 10:30 A.M.–8:00 P.M., closed the third Wed of Feb. & Aug.

Large- and small-sized men's and women's shoes on 5F. [M-8]

CALZERIA HOSONO Aoyama Elle Bldg., 2F. 5-1-2 Minami Aoyama, Minato-ku. Tel: 3409-9425. Hours: 11:00 A.M.–8:00 P.M. daily, noon–7:00 P.M. on Sun. & hol.

This shop doesn't carry large shoes, but accepts custom orders. Sandals from ¥40,000, pumps from ¥50,000. [M-5]

Toys

Toys are widely available in Tokyo. Good selections are found in department stores, particularly **Seibu, Takashimaya, Parco Part 1** in the basement. Also in our "On Children" section, several shops described have a floor or area for toys.

KIDDYLAND 6-1-9 Jingumae, Shibuya-ku. Tel: 3409-3431. Hours: 10:00 A.M.–8:00 P.M., closed the third Tues. of the month.

A favorite hang-out for Harajuku "kids," Kiddyland has a huge selection of toys, party favors, jokes, etc. [M-4]

TOY PARK Hakuhinkan 1–4F. 8-8-11 Ginza, Chuo-ku. Tel: 3571-8008. Hours: 11:00 A.M.–8:00 P.M. daily.

The largest toy shop in Japan [M-8]

BORNELUND 6-10-9 Jingumae, Shibuya-ku. Tel: 5485-3430. Hours: 11:00 A.M.–7:30 P.M., closed Tues.

European educational aids, toys, books, furniture, etc. [M-4]

SANRIO GALLERY 2-7-17 Ginza, Chuo-ku. Tel: 3563-2731. Hours: 11:00 A.M.–8:00 P.M., closed Tues.

A fantasy land of Sanrio character toys (Hello Kitty, etc.) that kids love. [M-8]

Miscellaneous Shops

MUJIRUSHI RYOHIN "No Brand Goods Shop"   2-12-28 Kita Aoyama, Minato-ku. Tel: 3478-5800. Hours: 10:00 A.M.–8:00 P.M. daily.

Known abroad as "Muji," this "hip" shop sells generic non-brand goods often made from neutral, not always natural, materials. Their relatively cheap merchandise includes food, clothing, housewares, accessories, even bicycles. [M-5] Branch in the Shibuya Seibu B-kan, 5F. [M-3]

DAICHU   Shibuya: 16-13 Udagawa-cho, Shibuya-ku. Tel: 3463-8756. Hours: 11:00 A.M.–9:00 P.M. daily. [M-3] Roppongi: 3-16-26 Roppongi, Minato-ku. Tel: 3584-0725. Hours: 11:00 A.M.–11:00 P.M. daily. [M-1]

A Chinese import store with clothing, baskets, bamboo blinds, and other amusing items. Not as cheap as Hong Kong.

PINK DRAGON   1-23-23 Shibuya, Shibuya-ku. Tel: 3498-2577. Hours: 10:00 A.M.–8:00 P.M. daily.

This shop stocks clothing, housewares and accessories—all copies of fifties antiques. The building itself is a huge monument to nostalgia. Great Thai restaurant in the basement. [M-3]

演

ENTERTAINMENT

ENTERTAINMENT

TRADITIONAL THEATER

The beginnings of Japanese theater are recorded in the oldest history of Japan, the *Kojiki*. There is a legend that tells how the Sun Goddess, angry with her brother, blocks herself in a cave for revenge. The world is left in darkness, while the other gods and goddesses try, in vain, to coax her out. When one of the goddesses begins performing a comical, erotic dance, the rest break out in laughter. Not wanting to be left out of the fun, the Sun Goddess peeks out and stays to watch the performance. By the end of the dance, she has forgotten her anger and returns to the heavens. The religious aspects, the dance, the eroticism of this legendary performance are all important elements of later theater.

The various forms of Japanese theater developed in different periods, under the patronage of different social classes. All became formalized at a certain stage of development and for hundreds of years performance has rigidly preserved the traditions. Japanese theater audiences tend to be older; most young people will confess to having viewed Kabuki, perhaps once or twice, on television.

The major forms of Japanese traditional theater are covered in the next section. Music and dance, both integral parts of all Japanese theater, have not been covered independently. They are performed separately throughout the year at various small concert halls and theaters (most often at the National Theater), and can occasionally be seen at festivals. Following the description of the theater forms is information on theater locations and tickets.

Gagaku and *Bugaku*

The *gagaku* orchestra and the *bugaku* dance performed to *gagaku* music were among the arts imported from the Asian continent during the seventh century. A favorite entertainment of the Heian court, by the eleventh century the nobility was rewriting the music in a more Japanese style. The decline of the court in the thirteenth century likewise resulted in a period of decline in these arts that lasted until the Meiji Restoration. Possibly the oldest form of orchestral music in the world, *gagaku* music heard today is almost identical to the music performed over one thousand years ago.

The composition of the *gagaku* orchestra will vary according to the origins of the piece (i.e. from what part of Asia) and whether it is performed as a concert or for the dance. The major instruments are *hichiriki,* a small oboe that plays the main melody; flutes of various kinds that play a variation of the *hichiriki* melody; *sho,* a bamboo mouth organ with seventeen pipes that provides a harmonic background; *kakko,* a small drum that rests on the floor and is usually played by a senior member of the orchestra who acts as a conductor; *taiko,* a large drum; *shoko,* a small gong; *dadaiko,* a large drum used to mark rhythm in dance pieces; *koto,* a thirteen-stringed instrument that rests on the floor (not used for dance pieces); *biwa,* a lute used in dance pieces; and voice, used only with music of Japanese origin. The Imperial Court Orchestra is the most famous *gagaku* performing group.'

Noh

When the warrior class entered Kyoto in the Muromachi period (1336–1575), they brought along their taste for the popular *dengaku* field dances and *sarugaku* "monkey music" comic mimes. Under the patronage of the third Ashikaga shogun, Yoshimitsu, the *sarugaku* performer and writer Kan'ami (1333–84) polished and perfected these early dramatic forms. The resultant theater was called Noh.

The form of Noh seen today follows the aesthetic principles laid down by Kan'ami. His son Zeami (1363–1443) is credited with writing most of the extant 250 Noh plays. Unlike Western theater, where plot and intellectual experience are important, Noh is an almost purely aesthetic experience—the dance, music, chanting, and costuming—are painstakingly calculated to achieve this. Action proceeds at a slow and deliberate pace, with movements and gestures carefully measured and stylized. Gorgeous costuming furthers the impact by adding color and pattern to the dance.

The subject matter of Noh is concerned with the transient nature of this world, the sins of lust and killing, the power of Buddha, and the truth of an afterlife. These were problems raised by the political realities of the time. Warfare was endemic and Noh served as a spiritual release for the warrior class.

All roles in Noh are performed by men. Make-up is not used, but masks are worm by the principle actor for certain roles. Often created by master craftsmen, the masks themselves are valuable works of art.

An orchestra and chorus of five to eight persons is on stage throughout. The principle role of the chorus is to comment on the action and to provide vocal accompaniment to the dance. The orchestra is composed of three kinds of drums and a flute.

Noh was originally performed out of doors on a roofed wooden stage, with a narrow bed of sand or stone separating the audience from the stage while providing the proper visual perspective. Actors enter and exit by a passageway, extending off the back of the stage to the left, that symbolically separates the real from the spirit world. The stage is bare except for a painting of a twisted pine tree on the back wall. Though the scene may change a number of times within the play, concrete expression through backdrops and scenery changes is not given. Rather, a symbolic and spiritual atmosphere is sought; the occasional stage prop will be little more than a suggestion—a pine branch will represent an entire forest.

The language used in Noh is archaic. Even most Japanese need a script to follow the dialogue since it is ridden with ambiguous phrases and allusions to ancient verse. For both Japanese and foreigners alike, Noh is a profoundly difficult form of art. When Zeami first began to write the plays, he wanted them to be accessible to even the peasants. In the end, however, he admitted that he alone could grasp their meaning.

Kyogen

Kyogen are short comical "relief" plays performed between Noh plays. *Ai-kyogen* are Kyogen performed between the acts of a Noh play. There are usually two or three actors and no musical or vocal accompaniment. Where Noh is stately, stylized, and symbolic, Kyogen is plebeian, realistic, and satirical. Nearly one-third of the remaining Kyogen plays center on the relationship between a feudal lord and his servant Tarokaja. The daimyo is made ridiculous by the servant, but in the end is always proven right (the daimyo were, after all, the rulers and patrons of the arts). Buddhism, the often corrupt religion of the upper class, was also a major subject of satire.

Bunraku

Bunraku is the common name for a form of classical drama using puppets. The proper name is *ningyo joruri,* meaning puppet drama with voice and *shamisen* accompaniment. Though it developed into a sophisticated form of theater, its origins were in a form of amusement for children performed by street puppeteers who manipulated the puppets on top of a box while singing and providing dialogue. Later, the puppeteers combined their skills with those of the *joruri,* musical storytellers popular in the fourteenth century.

While early developments in Bunraku theater were made in Kyoto and Osaka, the next stage of development was in Edo. In response to the rather "martial" temperament of the Edo population, a puppeteer named Satsuma Joun introduced a more "heroic" style in the theater. Violent and bombastic action and recitation soon dominated the puppet theater, even affecting the acting styles of humans in the less popular Kabuki. After the great Edo fire of 1657, the theater moved back to Osaka and Kyoto.

With the establishment of the Osaka Takemoto-za Bunraku Theater in 1685, two major artists from different fields combined their talents and perfected the art. Takemoto Gidayu (1651–1714) refined the singing and chanting styles. Chikamatsu Monzaemon (1653–1724) wrote some of the greatest masterpieces of Japanese theater. Bunraku became immensely popular and flourished through the middle of the eighteenth century when it was surpassed by Kabuki.

Bunraku puppets are about one-third human size. Only the head is completely modeled, but the bodies and facial features are fully jointed (even the eyeballs roll). The main puppets are manipulated by three men. The master puppeteer, dressed in formal kimono, controls the head and the right arm. The remaining two are dressed in black with their faces covered with hoods. One controls the left arm, the other controls the legs. The Bunraku stage allows the puppeteers to work in a semi-concealed standing position.

On a platform to the right of the stage sits the *gidayu* singer, accompanied by a *shamisen* player who supplies the dialogue for all roles. As much actor as singer, the *gidayu,* through an intense range of vocal and facial expression, brings life to the puppets.

Osaka continues to be the home of Bunraku, but it can be seen on occasion at the National Theater in Tokyo.

Kabuki

In the pleasure quarters of the great Edo-period cities, Kabuki became the definitive theatrical form of the masses. Considered vulgar by the military aristocracy, Kabuki grew through the generous patronage of the wealthy merchant class. After the Meiji Restoration, Kabuki became a respectable art form, with the final seal of approval given by an imperial viewing in 1887. Until twenty or thirty years ago, the Kabuki Theater was a favorite place to have the first meeting between the potential partners of an arranged marriage.

Kabuki originated in erotic dance-dramas performed by a woman named Okuni in the mid-sixteenth century. As her dances grew in popularity, troupes of men and women performers began to tour the country. These early performances served mainly as a cover for prostitution, and eventually women were prohibited from appearing on stage. The performances were continued, but with beautiful young men performing as erotically as had the women. These too were eventually outlawed and Kabuki was forced to develop a dramatic style that no longer depended solely on erotic appeal. Though men continued to play women's roles, plots became increasingly sophisticated, and acting skills developed into a master art.

While Kabuki is now considered a serious, "elevated," form of traditional theater, the Edo-period audiences were a predominantly drunk and rowdy crowd. Desperately attempting to gain their attention, the actors used to shout their lines. They eventually found that by suddenly falling silent and striking a dramatic, often cross-eyed, pose, they could effectively shut the audience up for a few moments. The pose has become one of the "trademarks" of Kabuki.

The Kabuki repertoire consists of around 350 plays, the last major works written in the later nineteenth century. Popular plays from the Noh and Bunraku repertoire were also adapted for the kabuki stage. Drama in Kabuki often revolves around the struggle between social obligation, *giri,* and personal feelings and emotion, *ninjo.* Evidence of the intensity of social pressures during samurai rule, this *giri/ninjo* conflict usually ends in tragedy. Revenge is another common theme. Harm done to one's lord or loved ones must be repaid and often results in death for the avenger.

Music is an essential element in Kabuki. The combination of instruments and singers will vary according to the kind of play. The major instrumental components are flute, hand drums, and *shamisen.* Occasionally used are a big Chinese drum and cymbals. In plays derived from Bunraku, a *gidayu* singer and a *shamisen* player are visible on a raised platform to the right of the stage.

In both the Edo and Meiji periods, Kabuki actors had tremendous followings and were fashion trendsetters, starting fads for a certain kind of hair style or kimono. Families of actors, such as the Danjiro family, have been established since the early Edo period. Kabuki skills continue to be passed from father to son. As an actor's level of artistic achievement rises, he inherits increasingly prestigious family-related stage names. If a son proves untalented, names are passed to a talented apprentice or left unused until an appropriate candidate appears. Certain families specialize in particular types of roles; some families are known for the *aragoto* style of the strong hero figures (derived originally from the puppet theater), while others are known for *onnagata,* women's roles. Recently a few actors have begun appearing in other forms of theater. Tamasaburo Bando, probably the most famous player of women's roles in Kabuki, has performed, as a woman, in various Western stage and movie productions. Other young actors are regulars in television dramas.

Kabuki has changed little in the past hundred years. Repertoire, acting styles, costumes, and staging follow precedents established long ago. There are few real surprises for the audience, but actors continue to be a source of freshness. Within the strict conventions of the theater, the actor is still able to interpret a part in a new way. An extreme example is the well-known actor Ennosuke Ichikawa who once pulled out a pair of dark glasses and a microphone and began performing a rock and roll song in the middle of a traditional play. During high points of the performance, true fans in the audience will shout their approval, calling out the actor's family name, or the name of a famous actor of the past for comparison.

Kabuki is perhaps the most accessible form of classical Japanese theater for contemporary audiences. In Tokyo, the main theater is the **Kabuki-za** where performances are given every month except in July and August. There are matinees and evening programs. Each program consists of three or four separate works, usually ending with a dance piece. Any one of them can be missed if the whole program is too long for your attention span. There are short intermissions between each play, sometimes between acts, and one longer break for lunch or dinner. Bring your own food, or eat in one of the theater restaurants (you can reserve your meal when you arrive at the theater). English programs are available as are small radio receivers that give translations and explanations on the background, symbolism, and action in the play.

The dance element in Kabuki developed into a traditional art in its own right called **nihon buyo.** Practiced more by women than by men, its 14 original Edo period schools have grown to over 170.

There are more than five hundred performances of *nihon buyo* held every year, but the events are rarely advertised. The best way to get information is to call the main theaters directly and ask when the next performance will be held. Theaters where *nihon buyo* is often performed are the **National Theater, Iino Hall, Asahi Seimei Hall,** and **Yasuda Seimei Hall.**

Rakugo

There is even a traditional form of comic monologue in Japan, called *rakugo.* This "art of talking" has a history of over four hundred years. It is still performed today in small variety halls called *yose,* but its biggest audiences are on television and radio.

The *rakugo* storyteller wears a kimono and sits in front of the audience on a tatami-matted stage. For props, he carries a fan and a small *tenugui* towel.

In his hands, these two props become anything from chopsticks to calculators.

The predecessors of *rakugo* were street entertainers, popular even before the Edo period. But the fashionable Edo public loved the fast talking and sophisticated jokes of these storytellers. Many of the jokes they told hundreds of years ago have become part of the language, almost like proverbs, although most people are unaware of their *rakugo* origins.

While there is a standard repertoire of old jokes and dialogues, young *rakugo* artists cover contemporary events such as the Recruit scandal, former U.S. President Bush's illness at an official banquet, or humorous incidents from daily life. As in Kabuki and Noh, the storytellers belong to traditional *rakugo* families and spend long years in training. The art of the Japanese comedian is not to be taken lightly.

Geisha

The geisha remains a misunderstood symbol of the more exotic aspects of Japan and Japanese history. The question most often asked by foreigners is an unimaginative "does she, or doesn't she?" Basically she doesn't, at least that isn't her main role. Prostitution was rather the work of the *oiran,* who was last in line after the client was entertained in the teahouses by the accomplished geisha.

The geisha was first and foremost an entertainer, the highest class being so accomplished in a variety of arts, so perfectly mannered and attired, that she came as close to a human work of art as is possible.

In the licensed pleasure quarters of the Edo period, the geisha kept company with some of the wealthiest and most influential men of the time. Now, aside from powerful businessmen and politicians who can afford the costs, few people ever see a geisha in action. While the steepness of the price has cut down on the clientele, the rigors of the training, in an art with rules as fixed as those of all forms of traditional theater, has diminished the numbers of women willing to undertake it. In their place, the hostesses in hundreds of bars, nightclubs, and cabarets entertain businessmen by chatting, mixing endless glasses of *mizuwari* (whiskey and water), and occasionally dancing with them to nostalgic music played by the club's live band. Now people always want to know "do the hostesses, or don't they?" The answer is some do, but some, in fact most, don't.

Unless you're willing to pay the nearly $500 a head it will cost to be entertained by a geisha during a *ryotei* meal, your opportunities to see one are rather limited. The geisha do make an appearance at two local festivals, where they parade down the street in all their finery. The two are the Sanja Matsuri in Asakusa on the third Saturday and Sunday of May, and the Oiran

Parade that happens annually at an unfixed date in the fall. They also perform traditional dances twice a year. At the end of April, geisha perform the *Asakusa Odori* at the Kabuki-za in Ginza, and at the end of May they perform the *Azuma Odori* at the Shimbashi Enbujo. Both performances are given for about three days only.

You can see an "*oiran* and folk dance" performance at Matsubaya in the old Yoshiwara pleasure quarters. Formerly a famous *oiran* house, they now cater to tourists and provide a show (with a slightly goofy English commentary) that is by no means authentic, but about as close as you'll get to the real thing.

MATSUBAYA 4-33-1 Senzoku, Taito-ku. Tel: 3874-9401. Geisha show plus one bottle of beer or saké for ¥2,500. From 6:00 P.M. daily (for a forty-minute show with English guide). You can also have a sukiyaki or tempura dinner before the show for ¥8,500. Reservations required. [off Map]

Tickets, Theaters, and Information

While both Kabuki and Noh are regularly performed at specialized theaters, other traditional theater arts are performed on occasion at any number of halls around the city. Tickets can generally be purchased at **Playguides** or at the theater (in advance or sometimes on the day of the performance). Tickets, or at least the best seats, sell out early.

Information on current events can be found in the tourist publications, at TIC, and from the TIC teletourist service.

• General Theaters
KOKURITSU GEKIJO 4-1 Hayabusa-cho, Chiyoda-ku. Tel: 3265-7411. [M-6]
SHIMBASHI ENBUJO 6-18-2 Ginza, Chuo-ku. Tel: 3541-2211. [M-8]

• Noh The best way to purchase tickets for Noh is to go directly to the theater. Noh tickets are also sold at **Wan'ya Shoten,** but they tend to sell out quickly. Tickets cost between ¥2,000–¥10,000.

KANZE NOGAKUDO 1-16-4 Shoto, Shibuya-ku. Tel: 3469-5241. The Kanze school of Noh is the oldest, and closest to the original form. [M-3]
HOSHO NOGAKUDO 1-5-9- Hongo, Bunkyo-ku. Tel: 3811-4843. Hosho School. [M-30]
YARAI NOGAKUDO 60 Yarai-cho, Shinjuku-ku. Tel: 3268-7311. Yarai School. [off Map]
KITA ROKUHEITA KINEN NOGAKUDO 4-6-9 Kami-osaki, Shinagawa-ku. Tel: 3491-7773. Kita school. [off Map]
KOKURITSU NOGAKUDO (National Theater Noh Hall) 4-18-1 Sendagaya, Shibuya-ku. Tel: 3423-1331. [M-29]
GINZA NOGAKUDO Ginza Nogakudo Bldg., 8F. 6-5-15 Ginza, Chuo-ku. Tel: 3571-0197. [M-8]
UMEWAKA NOGAKU GAKUIN KAIKAN (Noh School) 2-6-14 Higashi Nakano, Nakano-ku. Tel: 3363-7748. [off Map]
TESSENKAI NOGAKU KENSHUJO 4-21-29 Minami Aoyama, Minato-ku. Tel: 3401-2285. [M-5]

• Kabuki
KABUKI-ZA 4-12 Ginza, Chuo-ku. Tel: 3541-3131. This is the main Kabuki theater. Tickets are sold at the theater, in advance, or on the day of the show. Prices range from ¥2,000–14,000 for ground floor seats, tatami-matted box seats cost ¥1,400–1,600. Balcony seats are ¥3,000 (try to

get seats near the front) and ¥1,500. You can see just one of the plays for ¥700–1,200. If you decide you want to stay and watch more, there is a ticket booth on the fourth floor. [M-8]

• *Gagaku and Bugaku*   *Gagaku* music is performed more regularly than is *bugaku* dance. Concerts are held two or three times a year at the **National Theater,** and occasionally at the local shrine festivals. You can try to watch *gagaku* practice at **Onoterusaki Shrine** (2-13-14 Shitaya, Taito-ku. Tel: 3872-5514) every day except Saturday from 6:30 P.M.–8:30 P.M. Call beforehand to arrange permission for your visit.

A group called the **Junionkai,** young musicians from the Imperial Court Orchestra, hold performances twice a year at the **Tokyo Bunka Kaikan** (see pg. 169), usually in June and sometime in the autumn. Call the theater for the next date.

• *Rakugo*   *Rakugo* is performed at a number of variety halls called *yose.* Tickets can be bought in advance or on the day of the show.
SUEHIROTEI   3-6 Shinjuku, Shinjuku-ku. Tel: 3351-2974. [M-7]
SUZUMOTO ENGEIJO   2-7-12 Ueno, Taito-ku. Tel: 3834-5906. [M-13]
ASAKUSA ENGEI HALL   1-43-12 Asakusa, Taito-ku. Tel: 3841-8126. [M-12]
ASAKUSA MOKUBATEI   2-7 Asakusa, Taito-ku. Tel: 3844-6293. [M-12]

CONTEMPORARY THEATER
General Theater
Contemporary theater in Japan can be basically divided into mainstream s*hingeki* and underground theater. *Shingeki,* or the "new drama movement," started early in the century and was initially an attempt to create a modern theater for Japan. European classics were favored and companies using non-traditional methods of training actors were formed. The best known *shingeki* troupes are the **Haiyu-za** and **Bungaku-za.** Both perform Western and Japanese drama, though the Haiyu-za's performances are generally of Western works. The third major *shingeki* troupe is **Gekidan Shiki,** best known for their productions of musicals such as *Cats* and *West Side Story.*

The huge, five-hundred-strong **Takarazuka Kagekidan** is another troupe that is enormously popular with teenage girls and middle-aged housewives. The performances are extravagantly staged and costumed, often musical revues with song, dance, and a classic chorus line. Most interesting is that, in Takarazuka, women play all the male roles, just as in traditional theater men play the women's.

Avant-garde Theater
There are also a number of underground, or avant-garde, theater troupes in Tokyo. Most perform in short runs, two or three times a year. The plays are usually original and, unlike the *shingeki* troupes which generally perform

well-known plays, the stories will be totally unfamiliar and the dialogue will be, naturally, in Japanese. This is not, however, a major problem. Like Kabuki and Noh, avant-garde theater tends to be very visual, with less concern for plot and story line. Here are some of the more important troupes. Information on performances can be had by calling the telephone numbers listed.

KUROTENTO   Directors: Sato Makoto and Kato Tadashi. Tel: 3926-4021. This troupe's name means "black tent," which may refer to their avant-garde performances that often focus on urban themes.

SCOT/ACM   Director: Suzuki Tadashi. Tel: 3205-7664. Suzuki lives in Ibaraki Prefecture and is responsible for the annual Toga International Arts Festival.

DAISAN BUTAI   Director: Kogami Naofumi. Tel: 3367-0292. One of most popular younger groups.

CONTEMPORARY DANCE AND PERFORMANCE ART

No other form of contemporary performance art in Japan has received as much international attention as has *buto*. And, as is generally the case, when the outside world notices, so then do the Japanese.

In the early fifties *buto* emerged as a Japanese reaction to the modern and expressionistic dance styles of the West. The late Hijikata Tasumi is credited with the first performances of this new dance form. Hijikata attempted to develop a form of dance that was suited to the Japanese physique as well as being more expressive of Japanese concerns. His contemporary, Ono Kazuo, developed an improvisational and expressionistic style based on Hijikata's theories.

Early supporters of the developing genre were Mishima Yukio and Terayama Shuji, but its general underground nature kept *buto* from gaining mass appeal. When Ono Kazuo, Tanaka Min, Sankaijuku, and others appeared at the 1980 Nancy Theater Festival in France and at the Munich Festival in 1983, the news of favorable reviews reached home and kindled Japanese interest in the hitherto neglected art. In 1985 the first large-scale *buto* festival was held in Tokyo.

In the late eighties performances of *buto* increased in Japan. Still performing are **Ono Kazuo,** his son **Yoshito,** the **Dairakudakan** group, and troupes that splintered off from it such as **Sankaijuku** and **Byakkosha. Kisanuki Kuniko** is another interesting dancer whose work combines influences from *buto* and modern Western dance. Another well-known artist is **Tanaka Min.**

The late eighties also saw the growth of other performance artists and troupes. Difficult to categorize or neatly describe, some of the best-known are **Teshigawara Saburo** and his troupe **Karas,** and **Papa Tarahumara** (led by Koike Hiroshi).

OTHER PERFORMANCES

Aside from performances of traditional or avant-garde Japanese art forms, there are vast numbers of musicals, concerts, ballets, operas, and so on, by both domestic and overseas artists. There is even a theater—the Panasonic Globe—that is a copy of the original Shakespearean Globe Theater. Everyone who is anyone (and many who aren't) comes to Japan these days. The audiences are appreciative and, in spite of all the overtime everyone seems to put in at the office, performances are nearly always sold out. In fact, one of the main complaints made by resident foreigners is that tickets are often sold out months before any public notice is ever made. If you are interested in getting tickets, you need to be quite persistent in checking early notices at ticket outlets and perhaps subscribe to one of the local ticket clubs.

Concert Halls and Theaters

Here we have listed concert halls and theaters that are primarily venues for performances of music, theater, and dance. Movie theaters are listed

Maro Akaji, leader of the Dairakudakan *buto* group. © 1996 Nakafuji Takehiko

later in this chapter. Sometimes you will find performances given at gallery spaces or movies shown at general theaters. If you can't find a particular venue, please check in the index—perhaps it is listed elsewhere in the book.

ABC KAIKAN HALL ABC Kaikan, 5F. 2-6-3 Shiba-koen, Minato-ku. Tel: 3436-0430. [M-11]

AOYAMA GEKIJO/AOYAMA ENKEI GEKIJO National Children's Castle, 5-53-1 Jingumae, Shibuya-ku. Tel: 3797-5678. [M-5]

ASAHI SEIMEI HALL 1-7-3 Nishi Shinjuku, Shinjuku-ku. Tel: 3342-3164. [M-7]

ASAKUSA KOKAIDO 1-38-6 Asakusa, Taito-ku. Tel: 3844-7491. [M-12]

BUNKAMURA THEATER COCOON/ORCHARD HALL 2-24-1 Dogenzaka, Shibuya-ku. Tel: 3477-9111. [M-3]

CASALS HALL 1-6 Kanda Suruga-dai, Chiyoda-ku. Tel 3294-1229. Building designed by Maki Fumihiko. [M-15]

FM TOKYO HALL Toho Honsha Bldg., 4F. 1-7 Kojimachi, Chiyoda-ku. Tel: 3221-0080 (Ext. 2211). [M-6]

GEIJUTSU-ZA 1-2-1 Yurakucho, Chiyoda-ku. Tel: 3591-2333. [M-10]

GINZA GAS HALL Gas Hall Bldg., 6F. 7-9-15 Ginza, Chuo-ku. Tel: 3573-1871. [M-8]

HAIYUZA GEKIJO 4-9-2 Roppongi, Minato-ku. Tel: 3470-2880. [M-1]

HAKUHINKAN GEKIJO Hakuhinkan Bldg., 8F. 8-8-11 Ginza, Chuo-ku. Tel: 3571-1003. [M-8]

HIBIYA KOKAIDO 1-3 Hibiya-koen, Chiyoda-ku. Tel: 3591-6388. [M-10]

HIBIYA YAGAI ONGAKUDO 1-5 Hibiya-koen, Chiyoda-ku. Tel: 3591-6388. [M-10]

HITOMI KINEN KODO Showa Women's University, 1-7 Taishido, Setagaya-ku. Tel: 3411-5111. [off Map]

HONDA GEKIJO 2-10-15 Kitazawa, Setagaya-ku. Tel: 3468-0030. [M-33]

INO HALL 2-1-1 Uchisaiwai-cho, Chiyoda-ku. Tel: 3506-3251. [M-10]

JEAN JEAN Yamate Church, B1. 19-5 Udagawa-cho, Shibuya-ku. Tel: 3462-0641. [M-3]

KINOKUNIYA HALL Kinokuniya Bldg., 4F. 3-17-7 Shinjuku, Shinjuku-ku. Tel: 3354-0141. [M-7]

KOKURITSU GEKIJO (NATIONAL THEATER) 4-1 Hayabusa-cho, Chiyoda-ku. Tel: 3265-7411. [M-6]

KUDAN KAIKAN DAI HALL 1-6-5 Kudan Minami, Chiyoda-ku. Tel: 3261-5521. [M-17]

LAFORET MUSEUM Harajuku Laforet, 6F. Tel: 3796-2585. [M-4]

IIKURA LA FORET 800/500 Mori 39 Bldg., 1F. 2-4-5 Azabu-dai, Minato-ku. Tel: 3433-6801. [M-11]

AKASAKA LA FORET Akasaka Twin Tower, 1F. 2-17-22 Akasaka, Minato-ku. Tel: 3582-9255. [M-6]

MEIJI-ZA 2-36-2 Nihombashi Hama-cho, Chuo-ku. Tel: 3660-3939. [M-23]

MERUPARUKU HALL 2-5-20 Shiba-koen, Minato-ku. Tel: 3459-5501. [M-11]

MITSUKOSHI GEKIJO 1-4-1 Nihombashi Muromachi, Chiyoda-ku. Tel: 3274-8675. [M-9]

NAKANO SUN PLAZA HALL 4-1-1 Nakano, Nakano-ku. Tel: 3388-1151. [M-26]

NHK HALL 2-2-1 Jinnan, Shibuya-ku. Tel: 3465-1751. [M-3]

NIHON BUDOKAN 2-3 Kitanomaru-koen, Chiyoda-ku. Tel: 3216-5100. [M-17]

NIHON SEINENKAN HALL 15 Kasumigaoka-cho, Shinjuku-ku. Tel: 3475-2455. [M-5]

NISSEI GEKIJO 1-1-1 Yurakucho, Chiyoda-ku. Tel: 3503-3111. [M-10]

OAG HAUS 7-5-56 Akasaka, Minato-ku. Tel: 3582-7743. [M-5]

PANASONIC GLOBE-ZA 3-1-2 Hyakunin-cho, Shinjuku-ku. Tel: 3360-1121. [M-27]

PARCO GEKIJO Shibuya Parco Part 1, 9F (see **Fashion Buildings**).Tel: 3477-5858. [M-3]

PLAN B 4-26-20 Yayoi-cho, Nakano-ku. Tel: 3384-2051. [off Map]

QUEST HALL 1-13-14 Jingumae, Shibuya-ku. Tel: 3470-6331. [M-4]

SANBYAKUNIN GEKIJO 2-29-10 Hon-komagome, Bunkyo-ku. Tel: 3944-5451. [M-41]

SEED HALL Shibuya Seed, 10F. Tel: 3462-3795. [M-3]

SHIBUYA KOKAIDO 1-1 Udagawa-cho, Shibuya-ku. Tel: 3463-1211. [M-3]

SHIMBASHI ENBUJO 6-18-2 Ginza, Chuo-ku. Tel: 3541-2211. [M-8]

SHINJUKU BUNKA CENTER 6-14-1 Shinjuku, Shinjuku-ku. Tel: 3350-1141. [M-7]

SHINJUKU KOMA GEKIJO 1-19-1 Kabukicho, Shinjuku-ku. Tel: 3202-8111. [M-7]

SOGETSU HALL Sogetsu Kaikan, B1. 7-2-21 Akasaka, Minato-ku. Tel: 3408-1126. [M-5]

SPACE PART 3 Shibuya Parco Part 3, 8F (see **Fashion Buildings**). Tel: 3477-5905. [M-3]

SPIRAL HALL   Spiral Bldg., 3F (see **Special Buildings**). Tel: 3498-5793. [M-5]
SUNSHINE GEKIJO   Sunshine City Bunka Kaikan, 4F (see **Special Buildings**). Tel: 3987-5281. [M-18]
SUNTORY HALL   Ark Hills, 1-13-1 Akasaka, Minato-ku. Tel: 3584-9999. [M-6]
TEIKOKU GEKIJO (IMPERIAL THEATER)   3-1-1 Marunouchi, Chiyoda-ku. Tel: 3213-7221. [M-10]
THEATER APPLE   1-19-1 Kabukicho, Shinjuku-ku. Tel: 3209-0222. [M-7]
THE SPACE   Hanae Mori Bldg., 5F. 3-6-1 Kita Aoyama, Minato-ku. Tel: 3407-5171. [M-5]
TOHO SEIMEI HALL   2-15-1 Shibuya, Shibuya-ku. Tel: 3499-2887. [M-3]
TOKYO BAY N.K. HALL   1-8 Maihama, Urayasu-shi, Chiba. Tel: 0473-55-7000. [off Map]
TOKYO BUNKA KAIKAN   5-45 Ueno-koen, Taito-ku. Tel: 3828-2111. [M-13]
TOKYO GEIJUTSU GEKIJO   1-8-1 Nishi Ikebukuro, Toshima-ku. Tel: 5391-2111. [M-18]
TOKYO KOSEINENKIN KAIKAN   5-3-1 Shinjuku, Shinjuku-ku. Tel: 3356-1111. [M-7]
TOKYO TAKARAZUKA GEKIJO   1-1-3 Yurakucho, Chiyoda-ku. Tel: 3591-1711. [M-10]
TORANOMON HALL   3-2-3 Kasumigaseki, Chiyoda-ku. Tel: 3580-1251. [M-11]
TSUDA HALL   1-18-24 Sendagaya, Shibuya-ku. Tel: 3402-1851. [M-29]
U-PORT KANI-HOKEN HALL   8-4-13 Nishi Gotanda, Shinagawa-ku. Tel: 3490-5111. [off Map]
VARIO HALL   1-28-4 Hongo, Bunkyo-ku. Tel: 3818-4151. [M-30]
YAKULT HALL   1-1-19 Higashi Shimbashi, Minato-ku. Tel: 3574-7255. [M-11]
YAMAHA HALL   7-9-14 Ginza, Chuo-ku. Tel: 3572-3139. [M-8]
YASUDA SEIMEI HALL   1-9 Nishi Shinjuku, Shinjuku-ku. Tel: 3342-6705. [M-7]
YOMIURI HALL   Sogo Department Store, 7F. 1-11-1 Yurakucho, Chiyoda-ku. Tel: 3231-0551. [M-10]
YURAKUCHO ASAHI HALL   Yurakucho Mullion, 11F. 2-5-1 Yurakucho, Chiyoda-ku. Tel: 3284-0131. [M-8]

Ticket Outlets
Here is a list of a few of the more convenient places to buy tickets for various performances and events.
GINZA: KYUKYODO TICKET SERVICE   Kyukyodo Bldg., 1F. Tel: 3571-0401. Hours: 10:00 A.M.–7:30 P.M., Mon.–Sat. (11:00 A.M.–7:00 P.M. Sun. & hol.). [M-8]
SHINJUKU: ISETAN PLAYGUIDE   Isetan Department Store, 7F. Tel: 3352-4080. Hours: 10:00 A.M.–7:00 P.M., closed Wed. [M-7]

SPORTS
Sumo
Officially speaking, sumo is not a sport, but Japan's *kokugi,* or national skill. Dating back at least 2,000 years, many of the colorful sumo rituals derive from Shinto religious beliefs. Before a sumo match, salt is sprinkled by the wrestlers in a purification ceremony; the *chikaramizu* (literally "strength water"), given to the pair of wrestlers about to compete, was originally a farewell symbol to warriors setting out to risk their lives for lord and country.

The rules of sumo are fairly simple: the loser is the first wrestler to touch the ground with any part of his body except the soles of his feet or to be propelled outside the *dohyo,* or ring. Touching of an opponent's hair or "private parts" and punching are prohibited, though slapping is acceptable. A slap in the face from a sumo wrestler would break the average person's neck. Despite their superficially flabby appearance, these men are probably the hardest in the world. Standard training for sumo wrestlers includes throwing their not inconsiderable body weight hands first into wooden pillars and a lot of feet stamping (*shiko*), an activity that develops incredible strength in the back and legs.

Sumo wrestlers tend to be tall, in general over six feet. Weight varies from about 220 pounds up to double that in a few exceptional cases. There are no weight classes, so obviously the heavier wrestlers have an advantage, but there are always a few clever, small *sumotori* (wrestlers) who avoid close combat and specialize in leg trips or other tricks taken from the rich *sumo* vocabulary.

There are six tournaments yearly, each lasting fifteen days. They take place in odd numbered months, usually beginning on the second Sunday of each month. The January, May, and September tournaments are held in Tokyo at the Ryogoku **Kokugikan** near Asakusa. Opened in January 1985, the new Kokugikan (National Skill Hall) has an enormous solar-paneled roof designed to supply the hot water for the wrestler's baths.

Sumo is tremendously popular in Japan, and unfortunately the best seats at the tournaments are bought per season by large corporations or friends and patrons of the wrestlers themselves. Balcony seats are usually available on the day of the match. Try to get *shomen* (north side) or *muko-jomen* (south side) seats for a good overall view of the wrestlers exiting and entering from the east and west sides.

The wrestlers are divided into classes, starting from the bottom with *jonokuchi, jonidan, sandanme, makushita,* and *juryo*. The top *makunouchi* class has five ranks: *maegashira, komusubi, sekiwake, ozeki,* and *yokozuna*. At any one time, there are usually between two and four *yokozuna,* or grand champions, at the top. Once attained, the *yokozuna* title is held until retirement, though wrestlers below *ozeki* rise and fall in rank and class depending on how many bouts they won in the previous tournament.

Sumo is well worth a visit for the pageantry alone. If you want to know more there is also the English-language *Sumo World* magazine, available at most bookshops, that provides helpful commentary and information.

Each day's bouts start at noon with the bottom ranked *jonokuchi* wrestlers and proceeds through the lower classes up to the *makunouchi*. The top two classes, *juryo* and *makunouchi,* are where the color and ritual start, usually from about 3:00 P.M. Until then, the house lights are dim, the wrestlers wear only murky gray loincloths, and the *gyoji* (referees) are dressed in unexciting kimonos. But because the bulk of the spectators don't arrive until later in the afternoon (*makunouchi* starts at about 4:00 P.M. and finishes at 6:00 P.M.), if you go around lunch time, you can take your pick of vacant ringside seats, at least until some ex-sumo wrestler heaves you out.

There is a restaurant in the stadium where you can eat surrounded by the wrestlers, and an arcade of *chaya* (teahouses) where snacks and drinks are sold.

Sumo is televised daily during tournaments on NHK (Channel 1) from about 3:30 or 4:00 P.M. until the close of the day's events. From 11:15 P.M. TV Asahi (Channel 10) broadcasts a digest of the *makunouchi* bouts. Though you miss the atmosphere of the real thing, television provides slow-motion replay of the fast and furious action (most bouts average under a minute, some only ten to fifteen seconds).

KOKUGIKAN 1-3-28 Yokoami, Sumida-ku. Tel: 3623-5111.

Tickets are sold from around one month before the tournament, but can also be bought on the day at the stadium. Some ticket outlets sell sumo tickets, or you can contact the box office of the stadium. Types of seat available are *sajiki* or *masu,* a four-person box that runs from ¥7,500–¥9,500 per person and is almost impossible to get, and *isu,* single balcony seats at ¥2,300–¥6,000. [M-24]

If you're interested in seeing a sumo practice session, you can visit one of the local sumo stables on the following list. The best time to visit is just before the Tokyo tournaments are held, and from around 8:00 A.M., so you can get a good place in the visitor's section. If you call ahead, you can find out who is practicing when.

KASUGANO-BEYA 1-7-11 Ryogoku, Sumida-ku. Tel: 3631-1871. [M-24]
KOKONOE-BEYA 1-16-1 Kamezawa, Sumida-ku. Tel: 3621-0404. [M-24]
TAKASAGO-BEYA 1-22-5 Yanagibashi, Taito-ku. Tel: 3861-4600. [M-24]
FUTAGOYAMA-BEYA 3-25-10 Narita Higashi, Suginami-ku. Tel: 3316-5939. [off Map]

Martial Arts

Martial arts, *bujutsu,* developed with the rise of the samurai military class in the Kamakura period (1185–1333). Early arts such as *kenjutsu*—sword art, *iaijutsu*—sword drawing, *kyujutsu*—archery, and *jujutsu*—unarmed combat, were gradually formalized and by the Edo period (1600–1868) had been organized into a number of schools. After World War II, the arts were banned by the Occupation authorities because of their military implications. In 1950, however, the ban was revoked and the "arts" were revived as "sports."

Most of these "sports" remain a form of spiritual education. With the exception of karate, all of the currently practiced arts end with the "do"— the way of—suffix attached to many Zen-related arts. Aikido, kendo, judo, and *kyudo* are all, in Zen terminology, considered a path to enlightenment. The arts, like meditation, develop powers of concentration and build physical, mental, and spiritual discipline. Training involves a total mastery of technique, through endless practice and repetition, until the body, without conscious effort, is capable of performing with absolute accuracy. But even more important than learning technique is to learn the "spirit" or "truth" and thereby reach a state of identity and harmony with the universe.

Classes are given at numerous schools, but some knowledge of Japanese is often required, and short-term students are rarely accepted. For information, contact the appropriate general organization for each.

• **Aikido**

"The way of the harmonious spirit," aikido is a nonviolent self-defense technique. It was originated by Minamoto Yoshimitsu, a member of the Minamoto family that founded the Kamakura shogunate. From 1922 to 1942 Ueshiba Morihei reorganized the skill as aikido, combining techniques from other martial arts. The emphasis is on blocking and neutralizing an attack by using "pain" holds to pin or throw an opponent.

INTERNATIONAL AIKIDO FEDERATION   17-18 Wakamatsu-cho, Shinjuku-ku. Tel: 3203-9236.

• **Judo**

Judo was organized as a school in 1882 by Kano Jigoro, who selected techniques from various schools of *jujutsu*—a traditional method of unarmed combat that had developed from sumo wrestling skills. Basic judo training teaches a student to use the opponent's strength to one's own advantage. Techniques include falling and throwing methods, strangles, and pin holds.

ALL-JAPAN JUDO FEDERATION   c/o Kodokan, 1-16-30 Kasuga, Bunkyo-ku. Tel: 3812-9580.
The **Kodokan** itself (Tel: 3818-4172) is a judo hall, offering lessons and a spectators' gallery open to the public. [M-30]
BUDO GAKUEN   Nihon Budokan, 2-3 Kitanomaru-koen, Chiyoda-ku. Tel: 3216-5143.

• **Karate**

Originally developed centuries ago in China, in the 1920s karate was introduced to Japan from Okinawa where it had been refined as a form of unarmed combat during the Japanese occupation of the islands. Techniques of jabbing, hitting, and kicking are practiced with a partner or alone in exercises called *kata* based on the motions of actual combat.

WORLD UNION OF KARATE-DO ORGANIZATIONS   Sempaku Shinko Bldg., 4F. 1-15-16 Toranomon, Minato-ku. Tel: 3503-6637.

• *Kyudo*

Of all the martial arts, *kyudo*—the way of archery—was the most closely related to Zen. Now, archery is almost invariably associated with Shinto shrines and involves an initial prayer and highly ritualized behavior. *Hakama,* a part of traditional formal dress, is worn for practice. The bow, measuring over two meters in length, is made of bamboo and mulberry wood; the arrows are made of bamboo. *Yabusame,* archery on horseback, is occasionally performed at shrines during festivals.

AMATEUR ARCHERY FEDERATION OF JAPAN   Kishi Memorial Hall, 4F. 1-1-1 Jinnan, Shibuya-ku. Tel: 3481-2387.

• **Kendo**

A Japanese form of fencing, kendo—the way of the sword—is practiced these days with bamboo staves and protective clothing. Kendo developed from *kenjutsu*—the art of swordsmanship—that was a crucial part of samurai basic training.

BUDO GAKUEN   Nihon Budokan, 2-3 Kitanomaru-koen, Chiyoda-ku. Tel: 3216-5143.

Baseball

If a contest were held to decide who was the more rabid fan of baseball, Japan and the United States would be fighting it out bitterly to the end. First introduced from the United States in 1873, baseball is the only western team sport that has captured the Japanese popular imagination.

The system is similar to that of the United States. There are two professional leagues, the Central and the Pacific, playing from April through October, then the top teams from each league meet in the play-offs. The teams are not necessarily associated with cities, but with major corporations, such as the Nippon Ham Fighters, the Chiba Lotte (a confectionery company) Marines, or the Kintetsu (railway) Buffalos.

Besides the pro games, the annual high school baseball tournament is closely and emotionally watched by the entire country—even the Tokyo stock market slows down while the games are on. Less a sport than a display of youthful purity, the ideology of high school baseball has grown curiously close to that of the traditional martial arts. The high school baseball tournaments are held in Osaka at Koshien Stadium.

At the Tokyo Dome, you can watch a *naita*—a night game, where there's lots of beer and saké drinking in the clean, astro-turfed seating area surrounding the field.

JINGU KYUJO   (Meiji Jingu Outer Gardens) 13 Kasumigaoka, Shinjuku-ku. Tel: 3404-8999. [M-5]

TOKYO DOME: BIG EGG   (near Korakuen Amusement Park) 1-3 Koraku, Bunkyo-ku. Tel: 3811-2111. [M-30]

SEIBU LIONS KYUJO   2135 Kami-yamaguchi, Tokorozawa-shi, Saitama-ken. Tel: 0429/25-1151 (Seibu Kyujo-mae Station on the Seibu Ikebukuro Line). [off Map]

YOKOHAMA STADIUM   Yokohama-koen, Naka-ku, Yokohama-shi, Kanagawa-ken. Tel: 045/661-1251. [off Map]

KAWASAKI KYUJO   2-1-9 Fujimi, Kawasaki-ku, Kanagawa-ken. Tel: 044/244-1171. [off Map]

CHIBA MARINE STADIUM   1 Mihama, Chiba-shi, Chiba-ken. Tel: (043) 296-0789. [off Map]

Soccer

Japan finally acquired its very own soccer association, the "J-League," in 1993. The league comprises sixteen teams, each of which plays the other fifteen twice per season, with games played every Wednesday and Saturday. The season begins in May, running through to winter.

A quota of five foreign players per team is being allowed, and fat checkbooks are ensuring that goal-hungry fans get their money's worth of European and South American stars. A headcount at the onset of the first season showed forty-six foreign players throughout ten teams, compared with twenty-seven on pro-baseball teams. Soccer games can be seen at the **National Stadium** as well as at the **Todoroki Rikujo Kyogijo**, **Yokohama Mitsuzawa Koen Kyugijo,** and **Kenritsu Kashima Soccer Stadium**.

J-LEAGUE OFFICE 3-19-8 Uchi Kanda, Chiyoda-ku. Tel: 3257-4871. [off Map]
NATIONAL KASUMIGAOKA STADIUM Kokuritsu Kasumigaoka Kyogijo, 10 Kasumigaoka-cho, Shinjuku-ku. Tel: 3403-1151. [M-5]

MOVIES

For fans of Japanese movies, a visit to Japan won't necessarily prove to be rewarding, at least in terms of movie viewing. Foreign language subtitles are not supplied here. And even if they were, aside from the classics, the percentage of interesting films produced by the domestic industry is negligible. Annually a huge percentage of all movies produced are soft porn. The films produced by internationally known directors such as Kurosawa, Oshima, Mizoguchi, and Itami are the handful of exceptions to the rule.

We have listed a few of the major theaters (as well as some of the smaller ones) showing films that don't make it into the big-time theater circuit. Movies are occasionally shown at theaters listed along with concert halls earlier in this chapter. Movie schedules are given in the English-language daily papers and the *Tokyo Journal*. Tickets can be bought in advance. "Reserved" seats are usually available. These are the best seats and are generally supplied with clean white covers. They cost around ¥2,500. Normal seats are generally ¥1,800. On weekends the theaters are often unbelievably crowded (think about buying reserved seats), and when all seats are sold out tickets are sold for standing room only. Be sure to check that you're actually getting a seat. There are some late-night shows to be found, but the last show at most theaters starts around 7:00–7:30 P.M.

Major Movie Theaters
• Yurakucho—Hibiya—Ginza
SCALA-ZA Takarazuka Theater, 4F. 1-1-3 Yurakucho, Chiyoda-ku. Tel: 3591-5355. [M-10]
MARUNOUCHI PICCADILLY 1 & 2 Tel: 3201-2881.
MARUNOUCHI RUBURU Tel: 3214-7761
MARUNOUCHI SHOCHIKU Tel: 3214-3366.
NICHIGEKI PLAZA Tel: 3574-1131.
NIHON GEKIJO Tel: 3574-1131.
All in the Yurakucho Marrion Bldg., 5F–11F. 2-5-1 Yurakucho, Chiyoda-ku. [M-8]
NEW TOHO CINEMA 1 & 2 New Tokyo Bldg., 3F & B1. 2-2-3 Yurakucho, Chiyoda-ku. Tel: 3571-1946/7. [M-8]
MIYUKI-ZA 1-2-1 Yurakucho, Chiyoda-ku. Tel: 3591-5357. [M-10]
SUBARU-ZA Yurakucho Bldg., 1-5 Yurakucho, Chiyoda-ku. Tel: 3212-2826. [M-10]
SHOCHIKU CENTRAL 1 Tel: 3541-2714.
SHOCHIKU CENTRAL 2 Tel: 3541-1786.
SHOCHIKU CENTRAL 3 Tel: 3541-2716.
All in the Shochiku Kaikan, 1-13-5 Tsukiji, Chuo-ku. Across from the Ginza Tokyu Hotel. [off Map]

TOGEKI   4-1-1 Tsukiji, Chuo-ku. Tel: 3541-2711. Across from the Ginza Tokyu Hotel. [off Map]
GINZA CINE PATHOS 1   Tel: 3561-4660.
PATHOS 2 & 3   Tel: 3561-4058.
All in the basement of the Miharabashi Bldg., 4-8-7 Ginza, Chuo-ku. [M-8]
HIBIYA CHANTER CINE 1 & 2   Hibiya Chanter Bldg., 2F & 4F. 1-2-2 Yurakucho, Chiyoda-ku.
Tel: 3591-1511. [M-10]
NAMIKIZA   2-3-5 Ginza, Chuo-ku. Tel: 3561-3034. [M-8]
CINE SWITCH GINZA   4-4-5 Ginza, Chuo-ku. Tel: 3561-0707. [M-8]
GINZA BUNKA GEKIJO   (same building as above) Tel: 3561-0707
GINZA TEATORU SEIYU   1-11-2 Ginza, Chuo-ku. Tel: 3535-6000 [M-8]

• Shibuya [M-3]

CINEMA RISE   13-17 Udagawa-cho, Shibuya-ku. Tel: 3464-0052.
CINE SAISON   Tel: 3770-1721.
SHIBUYA SHOCHIKU CENTRAL   Tel: 3770-1990.
Both in **The Prime Bldg.,** 6F. 2-29-5 Dogenzaka, Shibuya-ku.
EURO SPACE   Higashi Takefuji Bldg. 2F. 24-4 Sakuragaoka, Shibuya-ku. Tel: 3461-0211.
LE CINEMA 1 & 2   Bunkamura 6F. 2-24-1 Dogenzaka, Shibuya-ku. Tel: 3477-9264.
SHIBUTOH CINETOWER 1, 2, 3 & 4   2-6-17 Dogenzaka, Shibuya-ku. Tel: 5489-4210
SHIBUYA PANTHEON   Tel: 3407-7219.
SHIBUYA TOKYU   Tel: 3407-7029.
SHIBUYA TOKYU 2   Tel: 3407-7229.
SHIBUYA TOKYU 3   Tel: 3407-7019.
All in the Tokyu Bunka Kaikan, B1–6F. 2-21-12 Shibuya, Shibuya-ku.

• Shinjuku [M-7]

MILANO-ZA   Tel: 3202-1189.
SHINJUKU TOKYU   Tel: 3200-1981.
CINEMA SQUARE TOKYU   Tel: 3232-9274.
CINEMA MILANO   Tel: 3200-0888.
All at the Tokyu Bunka Kaikan, B1–4F. 1-29-1 Kabukicho, Shinjuku-ku.
SHINJKU ACADEMY   Tel: 3202-0141.
SHINJUKU ODEONZA   Tel, 3202-5657.
SHINJUKU OSCAR   Tel: 3202-5657.
All at the Grand Odeon, B1–5F. 1-20-2 Kabukicho, Shinjuku-ku.
KABUKI-CHO TOA 1 & 2   1-21-1 Kabukicho, Shinjuku-ku. Tel: 3209-3040.
SHINJUKU BUNKA CINEMA 1 & 2   3-13-3 Shinjuku, Shinjuku-ku. Tel: 3354-2097/8.
MUSASHINO-KAN   3-27-10 Shinjuku, Shinjuku-ku. Tel: 3354-5670.
SHINJUKU JOY CINEMA 1, 2 & 3   Chikyu Kaikan, 1-21-7 Kabuki-cho, Shinjuku-ku. Tel: 3209-
4338/3209-5032/3209-4974.
SHINJUKU PICCADILLY 1   Tel: 3352-1771.
PICCADILLY 2   Tel: 3352-4043.
PICCADILLY3   Tel: 3356-3614.
All at 3-15-15 Shinjuku, Shinjuku-ku.
SHINJUKU SHOCHIKU   3-15-15 Shinjuku, Shinjuku-ku. Tel: 3354-2414
SHINJUKU VILLAGE 1 & 2   3-5-4 Shinjuku, Shinjuku-ku. Tel: 3351-3128/9.
SHINJUKU TOEI PALACE   Tel: 3351-3061.
TOEI PALACE 2   Tel: 3351-3022.
TOEI PALACE 3   Tel: 3351-3022.
All at: 3-1-26 Shinjuku, Shinjuku-ku.
SHINJUKU SCALA-ZA   3-5-4 Shinjuku, Shinjuku-ku. Tel: 3351-3127.
SHINJUKU PLAZA   1-19-2 Kabukicho, Shinjuku-ku. Tel: 3200-9141.
SHINJUKU KOMA TOHO   1-19-1 Kabukicho, Shinjuku-ku. Tel: 3202-8100.
TEATORU SHINJUKU   3-14-20 Shinjuku, Shinjuku-ku. Tel: 3352-1846.

遊

NIGHT LIFE

NIGHT LIFE

Theater, cinema, and concerts end early in Tokyo—most by 9:00 P.M.—about the same time as many traditional restaurants close for the night. After that, night life is basically centered in a few districts: Roppongi, Akasaka, Shibuya, Shinjuku, and Ikebukuro. Even so, since the late eighties, hip bars and clubs have spread out around the city into the waterfront areas and in many of the less central neighborhoods.

The evening scene tends to be casual. When the working day is done, the millions of Tokyo workers disperse into thousands of tiny bars and *nomiya* where, as "regulars," they have the comfort of being known. Discos are also popular with the after-office crowd and are packed between 6:00 and 8:00 P.M. with students and office workers. After a few drinks, and possibly a few songs at a karaoke bar, the crowds hurry off to the suburbs, making sure to catch the midnight train. But enough people miss the trains, intentionally or not, to keep plenty of places packed until sunrise.

DISTRICTS

Roppongi—just as for restaurants, this is the most international night-life district. Though Shinjuku and Ginza outstrip Roppongi in numbers of night spots, the high density of bars and discos in the relatively small area makes the activity seem that much more intense.

Nishi Azabu—a Roppongi spillover area with lots of small, hip bars and restaurants.

Ginza–Shimbashi—specializing in hostess bars and Japanese restaurants for Japanese executives and their hefty expense accounts, most places in this area close before midnight. Near Shimbashi, the refined air of Ginza gives way to a more "average salaryman" clientele.

Yurakucho—best known for its rows of cheap *nomiya* beneath the railroad tracks.

Akasaka—somewhere between Ginza and Roppongi on the scale of night life activity, Akasaka claims hundreds of hostess bars.

Harajuku–Aoyama—strict zoning regulations keep this fashionable daytime area from becoming a full-fledged night life district, but interesting bars and clubs are scattered throughout the neighborhood.

Shibuya—a favorite area for the young, including students and office workers, the area has a wealth of cheap bars and *nomiya.*

Shinjuku—the latest of late night districts, this is where people go when they're ready to leave the sophistication of Roppongi, Akasaka, and Ginza behind. Much of the night life here borders on sleaze, which can admittedly be rather refreshing at times. The area near 2-chome is known for its concentration of gay clubs. The Goruden-gai area near Kabukicho has hundreds of tiny *nomiya.* Kabukicho itself forms the center of the sleaze.

Ikebukuro—similar to Shinjuku but not as interesting.

BARS

Bars open and close in Tokyo about as fast as you can say "dry vodka martini with a twist"—not surprising in a city that cherishes the new. Throughout the city ever more elegant and expensive nightspots have appeared—the hippest place invariably waning in hipness as they rise in popularity, while the best often mellow into a comfortable maturity.

Traditional drinking places are the *nomiya.* There are thousands of these places still serving drinkers on a budget. In Yurakucho you will find them under the train tracks, while in Shinjuku there is a great stretch near the west exit of the station called s*homben yokocho* or "Piss Alley." Hostess bars are the executive's favorite form of night life. Though conceptually intriguing, they are of little real interest for most foreigners (we have listed them below). Other bars cater to foreigners and this, depending on your personal point of view, can be either an attraction or a reason to avoid the place at all costs.

Most newer places often add a cover charge to your drink bill that runs from ¥800–¥1,500. Since few Japanese drink enough to pay for the expensive interiors of such places, the charge helps to make up the difference.

General Bars

RIVERSIDE LOUNGE   2-1-5 Higashiyama, Meguro-ku. Tel: 3715-6911. Hours: 8:00 P.M.–4:00 A.M. daily. This former garage sits alongside the Meguro River. The top two floors are a bar, the ground floor is a Thai restaurant. The space is huge and loft-like. Rather difficult to find, but close to Nakameguro Station. [off Map]

YAKOCHU   The House Bldg., B3. 1-34-17 Ebisu Nishi, Shibuya-ku. Tel: 5489-5403. Hours: 7:00 P.M.–4:00 A.M. daily. The late eighties rage for aquariums spawned bars such as this one where over-stressed young Japanese can mellow out. Banks of aquariums cast a soothing glow throughout the cavern-like interior. [M-20]

SOUL BAR STANDARD   Bis Bldg., 2F & 3F. 1-32-14 Ebisu Nishi, Shibuya-ku. Tel: 3477-7217.

Hours: 6:00 P.M.–5:00 A.M. daily. Bar and dance club with sixties and seventies music and decor. [M-20]

DJ BAR INK STICK Campari Bldg., 4F. 1-6-8 Jinnan, Shibuya-ku. Tel: 3496-0782. Hours: 6:00 P.M.–5:00 A.M. daily. Another club by the Ink Stick people. No dancing, but they play good DJ'd music. [M-3]

DRUG STORE The Wall Bldg., 4-2-2 Nishi Azabu, Minato-ku. Tel: 3409-8222. Open twenty-four hours a day, every day. Located in Nigel Coates' eccentric building "The Wall," this is a copy of old American drugstore cafes—but the crowd is far less than wholesome. Weekend evenings it can be packed with a rather rowdy, fairly white crowd. [M-2]

RED SHOES Azabu Palace Bldg., B1. 2-25-18 Nishi Azabu, Minato-ku. Tel: 3499-4319. Hours: 7:00 P.M.–7:00 A.M. daily. This was one of the truly hip clubs when it opened in 1981; now, more than a decade later, it is still a respectable cafe-bar and a good late-night spot for Chinese food. [M-2]

K'S BAR 2-6-8 Shibuya, Shibuya-ku. Tel: 3400-8885. Hours: 7:00 A.M.–2:00 P.M., 9:00 P.M.–midnight. Another quiet, fashionable bar of the eighties that has survived over time. [M-3]

RADIO BAR Villa Gloria, B1. 2-31-7 Jingumae, Shibuya-ku. Tel: 3405-5490. Hours: 7:00 P.M.–2:00 A.M., closed Sun. & hol. This place is professional from its wide selection of liquors to its battalion of black-tuxedoed bartenders to its great, but expensive, cocktails. The interior, by the well-known Tadashi Sugimoto, is beautiful with natural wood and rusting iron inlaid walls and tiny Tiffany lamps on the bar that seats about a dozen serious drinkers. [M-4]

FUJI 2-12-16, B1, Shinjuku, Shinjuku-ku. Tel: 3354-2707. Hours: 7:30 P.M.–2:30 A.M. daily. Long-established and popular gay bar. [M-7]

KAMIYA BAR 1-1-1 Asakusa, Taito-ku. Tel: 3841-5400. Hours: 11:30 A.M.–9:30 P.M., closed Tue. The oldest Western-style bar in Tokyo, the Kamiya Bar was established in 1880 by Kamiya Denbei, the man who also started the first brandy distillery in Japan. [M-12]

Expat Hangouts

DEJAVU 3-15-24 Roppongi, Minato-ku. Tel: 3403-8777. Hours: 7:00 P.M.–5:00 A.M. (until 6:00 A.M. on Fri. & Sat.) daily. Crowds spill out onto the street through the open front of this small but very popular bar. [M-1]

GAS PANIC 3-14-8 Roppongi, Minato-ku. Tel: 3405-0633. Hours: 7:00 P.M.–5:00 A.M. daily. Sin city. [M-1]

MOTOWN Com Roppongi Bldg., 2F. 3-11-5 Roppongi, Minato-ku. Tel: 5474-4605. Hours: 6:00 P.M.–5:00 A.M. daily. Known as "Telerate" for its telerate machine that is avidly followed by the young, international finance crowd. Soul music, white folk. [M-1]

HENRY AFRICA'S Hanatsubaki Bldg., 2F. 3-15-23 Roppongi, Minato-ku. Tel: 3403-9751. Hours: 6:00 P.M.–2:00 A.M. daily (until 4:00 A.M. on Fri. & Sat., Sun. 6:00–11:30 P.M.). Quasi-tropical motif, pinball machines, popcorn hors d'oeuvres, and tropical drinks. [M-1]

MAGGIE'S REVENGE Takano Bldg., 3-8-12 Roppongi, Minato-ku. Tel: 3479-1096. Hours: 6:30 P.M.–5:00 A.M. daily. Run by an Australian woman, this pub has reasonably priced food, live music, and lots of honestly friendly patrons. This is one of the better places for single women who don't want to be hassled but don't mind a friendly chat. [M-1]

EX 7-7-6 Roppongi, Minato-ku. Tel: 3408-5487. Hours: 5:00 P.M.–2:00 A.M., closed Sun. & hol. A German-style pub with a good selection of beer and German food that even Germans like. The place is small, friendly, and predictably jolly. [M-1]

CHARLESTON 3-8-11 Roppongi, Minato-ku. Tel: 3402-0372. Hours: 5:00 P.M.–5:00 A.M. daily. Popular with some resident foreigners, the place can be fun, but late nights tend to border on the degenerate. [M-1]

MR. STAMPS 4-4-2 Roppongi, Minato-ku. Tel: 3479-1390. Hours: 5:00–11:00 P.M., closed Sun. & hol. Wine bar and restaurant run by Mr. Al Stamp, a resident American. The food is good with reasonably priced steaks and fondues. [M-1]

DISCOS

Disco activity, which tends to be casual, is concentrated in the Roppongi, Shibuya, and Shinjuku areas. There are no real admission problems, except occasionally for men alone or in large groups. Cover charges are between ¥3,000–¥5,000, with charges for women being slightly lower than those for men. The charge usually includes a few free drinks and food.

VELFARRE 7-14-22 Roppongi, Minato-ku. Tel: 3402-8000. Hours: 6:00 P.M.–midnight daily. Opened in late 1994 in the heart of Roppongi, this is the largest disco in Japan. Three floors above ground hold a bar, restaurant, and reception area, while the disco itself occupies a full three basement floors. The clientele includes young women and middle-aged *sarariman*. Entry free for women on Sundays until 8:00 P.M. [M-1]

YELLOW Sesoras Nishi Azabu, B1 & 2. 1-10-11 Nishi Azabu, Minato-ku.Tel: 3479-0690. Hours: 8:00 P.M.–midnight, closed Sun. & Tue. Initially known as being a rather underground favorite of hip Tokyo youth, it's now far better known. Jazz nights are held every second and fourth Fri. They also schedule gay nights. [M-2]

GOLD 3-1-6 Kaigan, Minato-ku. Tel: 3769-0023. Hours: 6:00 P.M.–midnight daily. One of the hottest clubs in town when it first opened, its star has waned since management changed. A huge and minimally decorated former warehouse, each floor features a different environment, including a disco, a cavelike club, and a traditional Japanese home. [off Map]

CLUB MIX 3-6-19 Kita Aoyama, Minato-ku. Tel: 3797-1313. Hours: 8:00 P.M.–5:00 A.M., closed Sun. Minimal basement space with smallish dance floor, mixed music, reggae, etc. [M-2]

CAVE H & I Bldg., B1 & 2. 34-6 Udagawacho, Shibuya-ku. Tel: 3780-0715. Hours: 7:00 P.M.–midnight daily. An elegant cavelike interior, with world music on one floor and acid jazz on the other. Rather inexpensive as discos go. [M-3]

JAVA JIVE Square Bldg., B1. 3-10-3 Roppongi, Minato-ku. Tel: 3478-0087. Hours: 6:00 P.M.–early morning daily. Moderately expensive. Live reggae bands provide most of the music here, with a music mix between sets that is heavy on Latin music. [M-1]

TWIN STAR Kagurazaka Hills Dai-ni Bldg., 2F. 2-11 Kagurazaka, Shinjuku-ku. Tel: 3269-0005. Hours: 6:00 P.M.–midnight daily. Huge wall paintings reproduce works by Klimt and Dali in this expensive disco that insists male customers wear proper suits and ties. [off Map]

J TRIP BAR DANCE FACTORY Kokusai Bldg., B2. 13-16 Udagawa-cho, Shibuya-ku. Tel: 3780-0639. Hours: 7:00 P.M.–1:00 A.M. daily. Nineties psychedelic chic. [M-3]

NU (EROTIC NEUROTIC) Roppongi Plaza Bldg., 6F. 3-12-6 Roppongi, Minato-ku. Tel: 3479-1511. Hours: 6:00 P.M.–5:00 A.M. Rather stylish disco for upscale young Japanese. [M-1]

LEXINGTON QUEEN Daisan Goto Bldg., B1. 3-13-14 Roppongi, Minato-ku. Tel: 3401-1661. Hours: 6:00 P.M.–midnight daily. Since opening in 1980, the Lexington Queen has probably seen more celebrities (visiting rock stars, actors, sumo wrestlers, you name it) than any other club in town. The man responsible for seeing the stars through the door is Bill Hersey, a celebrity himself who writes the *Tokyo Weekender*'s social column. [M-1]

HOT CO-ROCKET (see **Live Music**)

BEER HALLS AND BEER GARDENS

The first Japanese beer hall opened on the Fourth of July in 1899 in celebration of the end of the unequal treaties with western powers. Since then, beer has become as much a part of Japanese life as green tea. Rivalry between Japanese beer makers is intense. Every summer the major brands introduce a new variation in hopes of increasing, or at least maintaining, their market share.

Serious beer drinkers frequent any one of the many beer halls found throughout the city. The beer is cheap, but the atmosphere is usually not as interesting as you might hope it would be. In the summer, beer gardens sprout up on the rooftops of department stores, hotels, and office buildings.

Easily recognized by the rows of red lanterns and Christmas tree lights strung around the edges of the roofs, beer gardens are open from about mid-June through late August.

PILSEN 6-8-7 Ginza, Chuo-ku. Tel: 3571-2236. Hours: noon–10:00 P.M. daily (until 9:00 P.M. on Sun.). Located on the first floor of the 1929 Kojunsha building, Pilsen at least tries to maintain a faintly German atmosphere. [M-8]

KUDAN BEER GARDEN Top floor of the Kudan Kaikan Hotel. Tel: 3261-5521. Open mid-May through late August, from 5:30–9:30 P.M., closed on rainy days. Rather elegant as beer gardens go, this one also has a great view. [M-17]

LION SAPPORO BEER HALL 7-9-20 Ginza, Chuo-ku. Tel: 3571-2590. Hours: 11:30 A.M.–11:00 P.M. daily. Within this cavernous, classic beer hall opened in 1934, Germany meets Japanese art nouveau. [M-8]

HANEZAWA GARDENS 3-2-15 Hiro-o, Shibuya-ku. Tel: 3400-2013. Hours: 5:00–9:00 P.M. daily from April 1 until early autumn. One of the most pleasant beer gardens in Tokyo, located a bit out of the center of things in a Japanese garden. [M-2]

YEBISU BEER STATION 4-20 Ebisu, Shibuya-ku. Tel: 3442-5111. Hours: 11:30 A.M.–11:00 P.M. (until 10:00 P.M. on Sun. & hol.). Right inside the entrance to Yebisu Garden Place, this complex includes 6 restaurants seating over 1,500. [M-20]

LIVE MUSIC

Live clubs featuring all sorts of music can be found in Tokyo: jazz, country & western, samba, African, contemporary, heavy metal. There is even a club where a group of Japanese musicians almost convincingly pretend to be a fifties sock-hop band. Cover charges tend to run between ¥2,000–¥5,000.

CLUB QUATTRO Quattro Bldg., 5F. 32-13 Udagawa-cho, Shibuya-ku. Tel: 3477-8750. Hours: Generally opens around 7:00 P.M., but depends on the show. Mainly rock music, about equally split between domestic and international acts. Probably the best live house in Tokyo. [M-3]

ON AIR WEST 2-3 Maruyama-cho, Shibuya-ku. Tel: 5458-4646. Hours vary depending on the program. Mainly rock music, about equally split between domestic and international acts. Probably the best live house in Tokyo. [M-3]

LIQUID ROOM 1-20-1 Kabukicho, Shinjuku-ku. Tel: 3200-6831. Hours vary depending on program. Newly built basic box-type club in the heart of Shinjuku's Kabukicho, which has been featuring many contemporary/alternative visiting acts. [M-7]

LOFT Daini Mizota Bldg., B1. 7-5-10 Nishi Shinjuku, Shinjuku-ku. Tel: 3365-0698. Hours: 4:30 P.M.–1:00 A.M. daily. Shows from 7:00 P.M. Loft has been an institution of rock music for about as long as anyone can remember. Still one of the best places in town to see new rock bands, the club serves its music heavy on the rock and light on interior decor. [M-7]

CROCODILE New Sekiguchi Bldg., B1. 6-18-8 Jingumae, Shibuya-ku. Tel: 3499-5205. Hours: 6:00–11:30 P.M., live from 8:00 P.M. daily. Featuring live samba, soul, reggae, blues, and rock bands, Crocodile's music programming is as eclectic as its fairly bohemian interior. [M-3]

CAY Spiral Bldg., B1. 5-6-23 Minami Aoyama, Minato-ku. Tel: 3498-5790. Hours: 6:00–11:00 P.M., closed Sun. & hol. Live music of all sorts is performed in this large restaurant and bar. Music is often of an ethnic strain, the food is Thai. [M-5]

PIGA PIGA (see **Restaurants: Other Asian & African Cuisines.**) Live African music. Six shows nightly starting from 6:40 P.M. [M-20]

HOT CO-ROCKET Daini Omasa Bldg., B1. 5-18-2 Roppongi, Minato-ku. Tel: 3583-9409. Four shows nightly, reggae music, samba, etc. Great dancing. [M-1]

EL PATIO Hinode Bldg., B1. 7-1-8 Nishi Shinjuku, Shinjuku-ku. Tel: 3363-6931. Hours: 6:00–11:30 P.M., closed Sun. & hol. Shows from 8:00 P.M. Live Latin bands and Spanish food. [M-7]

ASPEN GLOW GM Bldg., 6F. 2-28-2 Dogenzaka, Shibuya-ku. Tel: 3496-9709. Hours: 6:30 P.M.–midnight, closed Sun. Live shows from 8:00 P.M. This club has done just about everything possible to recreate a West Coast country & western bar in the center of Tokyo. They've done a pretty good job. [M-3]

NASHVILLE　Fuji-konishi Bldg., 4F. 5-5-18 Ginza, Chuo-ku. Tel: 3289-1780. Hours: 5:00–11:00 P.M., live from 7:00 P.M., closed Sun. & hol. Country & Western, but also Dixieland music. [M-8]

KENTOS　Dai 2 Renu Bldg., B1. 5-3-1 Roppongi, Minato-ku. Tel: 3401-5755. Hours: 6:00 P.M.–2:30 A.M. (until 12:30 A.M. on Sun.). Almost live comedy, the house band here plays nostalgic fifties and sixties rock and roll. [M-1]

Jazz

BLUE NOTE TOKYO　FIK Minami Aoyama Bldg., B1. 5-13-3 Minami Aoyama, Minato-ku. Tel: 3407-5781. Hours: 6:00 P.M.–2:00 A.M., shows at 7:50 and 9:30 P.M., closed Sun. & hol. Cover charge from ¥6,000. Tokyo's best venue for live jazz, presenting well-known musicians from overseas on a weekly basis. [M-5]

SHINJUKU PIT INN　Accord Shinjuku Bldg., B1. 2-12-4 Shinjuku, Shinjuku-ku. Tel: 3354-2024. Hours: noon–11:00 P.M., shows from 2:00 P.M. and 7:30 P.M. daily. Charge: Daytime ¥1,300, evening from ¥3,000. The most famous, long-standing, serious jazz club in Tokyo featuring both Japanese and some overseas acts. [M-7]

ROPPONGI PIT INN　Shimei Bldg., B1. 3-17-7 Roppongi, Minato-ku. Tel: 3585-1063. Hours: 5:00–11:00 P.M., live shows from 7:30 P.M. daily. Charge: ¥2,500. Well-known live house connected to the Shinjuku Pit Inn, but featuring more fusion and occasionally rock groups. [M-1]

J　Royal Mansion, B1. 5-1-1 Shinjuku, Shinjuku-ku. Tel: 3354-0335. Hours: 6:30–midnight (until 2:00 A.M. on Fri. & Sat.), closed Sun. & hol. Showtime from 7:15 P.M. [M-7]

BODY AND SOUL　ANIS Minami Aoyama Bldg., B1. 6-13-9 Minami Aoyama, Minato-ku. Tel: 5466-3348. Hours: 6:30 P.M.–midnight daily. Shows from 8:30 P.M. A small but respected local jazz club. [M-5]

Karaoke

Karaoke has long been a popular form of entertainment in Japan. Karaoke machines are popular items for the home, and karaoke-style pubs are a favorite place for co-workers (mostly white-collar and middle-aged) to gather after work. Everyone seems to have a terribly jolly time singing rather badly in front of friends and strangers.

While it seems a bit incongruous with the otherwise rising sophistication of the city and its inhabitants, karaoke has enjoyed an astonishing increase in popularity over the past few years. The style, however, has changed a bit. Bars with karaoke rooms where a group of friends can gather in private to indulge in atypical individualistic behavior are in favor now. Karaoke is most popular among those in their teens and twenties; female fans outnumber the males. For those wishing to improve their karaoke skills, lessons can be had for a price and are currently popularly attended by housewives.

THE ODEUM　Musashinokan Bldg., B2. 3-27-10 Shinjuku, Shinjuku-ku. Tel: 3225-3311. Hours: noon–5:00 A.M. daily. Luxuriously designed (à la Phillipe Stark) with a central lounge and individual karaoke rooms [M-7]

SMASH HITS　5-2-26 Hiro-o, Shibuya-ku. Tel: 3444-0432. Hours: 7:00 P.M.–4:00 A.M. daily. Rock music karaoke. [M-2]

HOLLYWOOD STAR　Roppongi Plaza Bldg., 8 & 9F. 3-12-6 Roppongi, Minato-ku. Tel: 3479-0700. Known for its theme rooms based on Hollywood movies including rooms designed around Dick Tracy, Tarzan, Cleopatra, and Carmen. Also has a normal karaoke pub with a deejay. [M-1]

Night life in Shinjuku's Kabukicho. © 1984 Tobias Pfeil

KEETS Dai-ju Togensha Bldg., 4F. 2-4-9 Roppongi, Minato-ku. Tel: 3584-3262. Hours: 6:00 P.M.–5:00 A.M. daily. This karaoke bar boasts over 3,000 songs in English. ¥2,000 for food and drink tickets. [M-1]

HOSTESS BARS AND CABARETS

Hostess bars are a Japanese invention, where the modern geisha pours drinks, makes conversation, and strokes the Japanese businessman's ego. Most are shockingly expensive. Charges include a cover averaging ¥10,000, plus a fee per hostess, plus expensive drinks for the two or three of you. The majority are also very straight (i.e., only the ego gets stroked) and generally not particularly thrilling for foreign visitors.

Cabarets here are like those anywhere in the world Extravagant, often featuring topless dancers, some are professional clubs while others are technically "pink." The fabulous and grand hostess bar-cabaret combination clubs of the past have, unfortunately, all closed.

CORDON BLEU 6-6-4 Akasaka, Minato-ku. Tel: 3582-7800. Showtimes: 7:30, 9:30, 11:00 P.M. A restaurant theater with French cuisine and topless dancers. Show charge: ¥3,000. [M-6]

SHOWBOAT Hilton Hotel, B1. Shinjuku. Tel: 3344-0510. Showtimes: 7:30, 9:15, 10:45 P.M. Like a Las Vegas casino show. Show charge: ¥3,000. [M-7]

KOKUCHO NO MIZUUMI (BLACK SWAN LAKE) Arao Bldg., B2. 2-25-2 Kabukicho, Shinjuku-ku. Tel: 3205-0128. Showtimes: 7:30, 9:30, 11:30 P.M. A rather whimsical gay cabaret. Show charge: ¥2,500. [M-7]

THE CRYSTAL ROOM New Otani Hotel, 1F. Tel: 3265-8000. Showtimes: 7:30, 9:30 P.M. Gorgeous, showy atmosphere. Show charge: ¥4,000. [M-6]

THE CRYSTAL SALON (next to the New Otani Hotel, above). Tel: 3234-2600. Hours: 7:00 P.M.–2:00 A.M. daily. About ¥15,000 per person. A rather safe hostess bar. [M-6]

Love Hotels

Love hotels are a Japanese invention that reflects the constraints and mores of Japanese society and lifestyle. For those with two-hour commutes home, for young adults living with their parents, for office workers in the company dorm, and privacy-seeking couples living with two children in tiny apartments, love hotels have been almost a necessity. Located in night life areas or along the suburban highways, many love hotels are readily spotted by their fantasy architecture that often ironically resembles the Disneyland castle.

In the past lavish and elegant rooms with round beds, velvet couches, and chandeliers were popular as were theme decors with a wide range of imaginary beds. Now the trend is for well-appointed rooms that Japanese women long to have in their own home.

Rooms are rented by the hour (with a two-hour minimum). Only couples are allowed to check in. The clerk remains hidden throughout the check-in procedure.

MEGURO CLUB   2-1 Shimo-meguro, Meguro-ku. Formerly known as the *Meguro Emperor* this was long the king of local love hotels with its castle-like architecture. The interior has recently been renovated. Rooms from ¥8,000. [M-19]

HOTEL PERRIER   2-7-12 Kabukicho, Shinjuku-ku. Tel: 3207-5921. They have rooms with saunas, videos, jukeboxes, etc. Their special room called *Galaxy* has an illuminated ceiling that turns off and on with the sound of your voice. Rooms from ¥7,000. [M-7]

HOTEL ROPPONGI   7-19-4 Roppongi, Minato-ku. Tel: 3403-1571. This hotel looks like a residential apartment building from the outside. Typical love-hotel rooms, some are Japanese-style with gardens. Rooms from ¥7,000. [M-1]

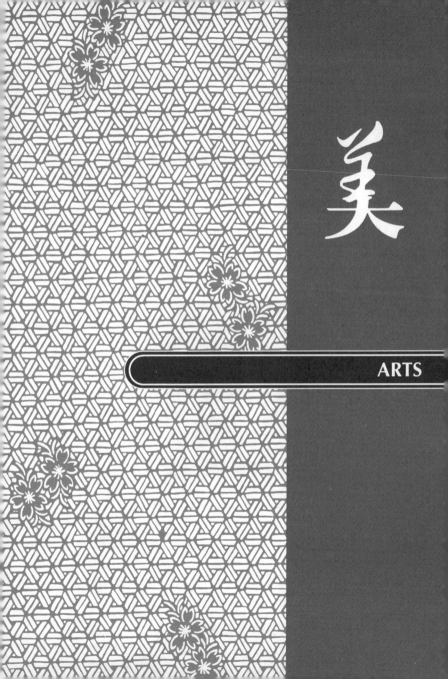

美

ARTS

ARTS

Like all aspects of Japanese culture, the arts have progressed through cycles where foreign models have been dominated, gradually assimilated, and finally reshaped by Japanese sensibilities. Most early influences on Japanese arts were from China, either directly or indirectly via Korea. Early art was usually religious in character, much of it associated with the great temples. From the introduction of Buddhism in A.D. 538, the religion continued to play a major role in the development of the arts until the present century. Changes in aesthetic sensibilities were often tied to the rise and fall in popularity of the various Buddhist sects.

Fluctuations in the political system and relations with the mainland dynasties were often a measure of Chinese influence and domestic artistic confidence. By the Edo period, all contact with the outside world was broken and the first people's art, *ukiyo-e* (woodblock prints) emerged. When the country was reopened in the nineteenth century, Western art styles became the ultimate models and have continued to be highly influential up to this day. For a further discussion of the contemporary arts see **CONTEMPORARY ART GALLERIES.**

The subject of Japanese art is so vast and involved that we could never do it justice on these pages. A brief chronological table of the major historical and artistic periods is given in the appendix.

MUSEUMS

Since the early 1980s Japan has experienced an extraordinary museum boom. There are museums now for everyone and everything. Some are devoted to special fields of interest, others are little more than rental spaces for a mixed bag of shows organized by advertising agencies or newspapers, yet others still are essentially public relations and advertising mediums for the department stores or corporations who build and back them.

While commercialism plays an often detrimental, key role in many of the newer museums and quasi-museums, there is also a genuine growth in public, private, and corporate support for the arts. The city has several important museums in the works. While this museum craze has some problems, the new interest, support, and funding for the arts is welcome, if long overdue.

With so many new museums in town, there is always something worth seeing. Information on current exhibitions is given in the local English press, in the *Tokyo Journal,* in the *Japan Times* on Saturdays, in the *Mainichi Daily News* on Mondays, and in the *Asahi Evening News* every second Friday.

Art works listed as belonging to a particular museum's collection are not always on view. It is also worth noting that the word "museum" is often used quite freely in Japan by all sorts of organizations. We have included in our list of museums only those art spaces that have permanent collections, part of which are generally on view at all times and that carry on public programs and activities in a way conventionally associated with museums internationally. All other "museums" are listed in the **CONTEMPORARY ART GALLERIES & EXHIBIT SPACES** section.

As museums in Japan tend to be crowded, it's advisable to visit early in the morning or late in the afternoon. In most cases you must enter the museum thirty minutes before the listed closing time. Most museums are closed on Mondays, the day after a public holiday, and during exhibition changes. Many close for the New Year's holiday from around December 29 through January 3.

Japanese Traditional Arts

TOKYO NATIONAL MUSEUM (Tokyo Kokuritsu Hakubutsukan)

東京国立博物館　台東区上野公園 13-9

13-9 Ueno-koen (Ueno Park), Taito-ku. Tel: 3822-1111/7. Hours: 9:00 A.M.–4:30 P.M., closed Mon.

Known before the war as the Imperial Household Museum, it is the largest museum in Japan and houses the best collection of Japanese art and archeology in the world. There are three buildings: in the center is the main building for Japanese art; on the right is the Toyokan, a gallery containing an excellent collection of art and archeology primarily from China and Korea; on the left is the Hyokeikan that houses Japanese archeological collections and early Buddhist objects. [M-13]

HORYUJI TREASURE HOUSE (Horyuji Homotsuden)　法隆寺宝物殿

To the left of the National Museum's Hyokeikan in Ueno Park. Tel: 3822-1111. Hours: Open only on Thurs. (hours same as above), closed when it rains, or when humidity within the building exceeds seventy percent.

An important collection of early Japanese art from the Horyu-ji temple in Nara that was presented to the Imperial Household in 1876. Most of the work is from the Asuka and Nara periods, including Buddhist sculpture, masks, textiles, metalwork, and some paintings. [M-13]

NEZU ART MUSEUM (Nezu Bijutsukan)　根津美術館　港区南青山 6-5-36

6-5-36 Minami Aoyama, Minato-ku. Tel: 3400-2536. Hours: 9:30 A.M.–4:30 P.M., closed Mon., the day after national holidays, and during exhibition changes.

A beautiful and well-known collection of Japanese paintings including work by Buncho, Goshun, Kenzan, and Korin. Featuring Korin's famous screen painting of irises. Also some

Chinese paintings, Japanese calligraphy, ceramics, lacquer, metalwork, and sculpture. In the museum's garden are a few teahouses where tea ceremony and instruction are held. [M-5]

GOTO ART MUSEUM (Goto Bijutsukan)　五島美術館　世田谷区上野毛 3-9-25

3-9-25 Kaminoge, Setagaya-ku. Tel: 3703-0661. Hours: 9:30 A.M.–4:30 P.M., closed Mon. and while changing exhibitions.

An excellent collection of Japanese and Chinese paintings and calligraphy. Also ceramics, sutras, lacquer, and archeological objects. Most famous are the *Genji Monogatari* scroll paintings from the Heian period. The museum is in a large garden with a teahouse. [M-21]

HATAKEYAMA MUSEUM (Hatakeyama Kinenkan)　畠山記念館　港区白金台 2-20-12

2-20-12 Shirogane-dai, Minato-ku (behind the garden of the Hannya-en Restaurant). Tel: 3447-5787. Hours: Apr. 1–Sept. 15, 10:00 A.M.–5:00 P.M.; Oct. 1–Mar. 15, 10:00 A.M.–4:30 P.M., closed Mon.

One of the most pleasant museums in Tokyo, the collection includes paintings, calligraphy, sculpture, lacquer, tea-ceremony objects, ceramics, costumes, and some Chinese and Korean works. Notable are masterpieces by Sesshu, Korin, and Kenzan, tea-ceremony objects by Koetsu, Chojiro, and pieces connected with the tea-ceremony master Sen no Rikyu. [M-19]

EISEI BUNKO FOUNDATION (Eisei Bunko)　永青文庫　文京区目白台 1-1-1

1-1-1 Mejiro-dai, Bunkyo-ku. Tel: 3941-0850. Hours: 10:00 A.M.–4:00 P.M., closed Sat., Sun., hol., and during exhibition changes.

A large and unusual collection of paintings, scrolls, masks, ceramics, and costumes housed in a warehouse behind an old Western-style building. The collection originally belonged to the Hosokawa family from Kyushu, who were important vassals of the Ashikaga shogun. The collection includes paintings by Sesshu, Takuan, Niten, Tessai, and Yokoyama Taikan. Family swords and suits of armor are also shown. [off Map]

IDEMITSU ART GALLERY (Idemitsu Bijutsukan)
出光美術館　千代田区丸ノ内 3-1-1 国際ビル 9 階

International Bldg., 9F. 3-1-1 Marunouchi, Chiyoda-ku. Tel: 3213-3111. Hours: 10:00 A.M.–5:00 P.M., closed Mon. and during exhibition changes.

An excellent collection of paintings, *ukiyo-e*, and calligraphy including the largest collection in the world of work by the Zen monk Sengai. Also ceramics, bronzes, and lacquer. Some Chinese, Korean, and Middle Eastern work. [M-10]

SEIKADO BUNKO TENJIKAN　静嘉堂文庫展示館　世田谷区岡本 2-23-1

2-23-1 Okamoto, Setagaya-ku. Tel: 3700-2250. Hours: 10:00 A.M.–4:00 P.M., Mar.–Nov., closed Mon. and during exhibition changes (call ahead).

Open to the public since 1977, the collection was made by the Iwasaki Mitsubishi family. Chinese and Japanese calligraphy and painting, *ukiyo-e*, ceramics, swords, and sculpture. [off Map]

OKURA MUSEUM (Okura Shukokan)　大蔵集古館　港区虎の門 2-10-3

2-10-3 Toranomon, Minato-ku. Tel: 3583-0781. Hours: 10:00 A.M.–4:00 P.M., closed Mon. and during exhibition changes. In front of the Hotel Okura.

Originally the collection of Baron Okura, the museum contains important works of painting, sculpture, ceramics, calligraphy, costumes, books, and Noh masks. Some Chinese, Tibetan, and Indian pieces as well. [M-11]

SUNTORY ART GALLERY (Suntory Bijutsukan)
サントリー美術館　港区元赤坂 1-2-3 東京サントリービル 11 階

Tokyo Suntory Bldg., 11F. 1-2-3 Moto-akasaka, Minato-ku. Tel: 3470-1073. Hours: 10:00 A.M.–5:00 P.M. (10:00 A.M.–7:00 P.M. on Fri.), closed Mon. and during exhibition changes.

A good collection of Japanese lacquer, ceramics, glass, costumes, masks, paintings, and prints. The gallery regularly holds loan exhibitions using the permanent collection as a base. There is also a small reading room, a library, and a tea-ceremony room. [M-6]

TOKYO NATIONAL UNIVERSITY OF FINE ART AND MUSIC, ART MUSEUM (Tokyo Geijutsu Daigaku, Geijutsu Shiryo-Kan)　東京芸術大学芸術資料館　台東区上野 12-8

12-8 Ueno, Taito-ku. Tel: 3828-6111. Hours: 9:00 A.M.–5:00 P.M., closed Sun. & hol., August, and mid-December through March.

A collection of Japanese arts, some national treasures. Former students occasionally exhibit their work. [M-13]

Modern Japanese and Western Art

TOKYO NATIONAL MUSEUM OF MODERN ART (Tokyo Kokuritsu Kindai Bijutsukan)
東京国立近代美術館　千代田区北ノ丸公園3

3 Kitanomaru-koen, Chiyoda-ku. Tel: 3214-2561. Hours: 10:00 A.M.–5:00 P.M., closed Mon.

Japanese art since the Meiji period is shown in a rotating collection on the three upper floors of the building. On the first floor are temporary exhibitions. [M-17]

CRAFTS GALLERY OF THE MUSEUM OF MODERN ART (Tokyo Kokuritsu Kindai Bijutsukan Kogeikan)　東京国立近代美術館工芸館　千代田区北ノ丸公園1-1

1-1 Kitanomaru-koen, Chiyoda-ku. Tel: 3211-7781. Hours: 10:00 A.M.–5:00 P.M., closed Mon.

Formerly the nineteenth-century home of the palace guards, the museum has a good collection of contemporary crafts. Special exhibitions are usually very well selected and installed. [M-17]

TOKYO METROPOLITAN ART MUSEUM (Tokyo To Bijutsukan)
東京都美術館　台東区上野公園8-36

8-36 Ueno-koen, Taito-ku. Tel: 3823-6921. Hours: 9:00 A.M.–5:00 P.M., closed Mon. and during exhibition changes.

Shows mainly Japanese art from the last fifty years, but also some Western works. The collection includes prints, calligraphy, sculpture, and handicrafts. [M-13]

NATIONAL MUSEUM OF WESTERN ART (Kokuritsu Seiyo Bijutsukan)
国立西洋美術館　台東区上野公園7-7

7-7 Ueno-koen, Taito-ku. Tel: 3828-5131. Hours: 9:30–5:00 P.M., closed Mon. and during exhibition changes.

An impressive collection of Western art housed in a building designed by Le Corbusier. The collection includes work from the Renaissance through the twentieth century with an especially large number of nineteenth-century works by French artists. [M-13]

SETAGAYA ART MUSEUM (Setagaya Bijutsukan)　世田谷美術館　世田谷区砧公園1-2

1-2 Kinuta-koen, Setagaya-ku. Tel: 3415-6011. Hours: 10:00 A.M.–6:00 P.M. (until 8:00 P.M. on Sat.), closed the second & fourth Mon.

One of Tokyo's major museums, best known for its special exhibitions usually of important international artists. Also shows Japanese art. [Off Map. See directions for **Tokyo Koseneinenkin Sports Center,** p. 242]

HARA MUSEUM OF CONTEMPORARY ART (Hara Bijutsukan)
原美術館　品川区北品川4-7-25

4-7-25 Kita Shinagawa, Shinagawa-ku. Tel: 3445-0651. Hours: 11:00 A.M.–4:30 P.M. (Wed. 11:00 A.M.–8:00 P.M.), closed Mon. and the day after national holidays.

The first contemporary art museum in Japan, the Hara Museum focuses on post-fifties' international & Japanese art. The building is the former home of the Hara family and an example of Bauhaus architecture from 1938. A sculpture garden and café are additional attractions. [M-37]

TOKYO METROPOLITAN TEIEN MUSEUM OF ART (Tokyo-to Teien Bijutsukan)
東京都庭園美術館　港区白金台5-21-9

5-21-9 Shirogane-dai, Minato-ku. Tel: 3443-0201. Hours: 10:00 A.M.–6:00 P.M., closed the second and fourth Wed. of the month. If these days fall on a national holiday, it is closed the following day.

The former home of Prince Asaka, this fifty-one-year-old art deco building was opened as a museum in the fall of 1983. Presently without a collection of its own, the museum is holding various exhibitions on loan. The building and garden alone are worth the visit. [M-19]

TOKYO METROPOLITAN MUSEUM OF PHOTOGRAPHY (Tokyo-to Shashin Bijutsukan)
東京都写真美術館　渋谷区恵比寿4-19-24

1-13-3 Mita, Meguro-ku. Tel: 3280-0031. Hours: 10:00 A.M.–6:00 P.M. (until 8:00 P.M. on Thu & Fri.), closed Mon.

Opened by the city in 1990, and subsequently restored in Yebisu Garden Place, this museum shows and collects international and Japanese photography. [M-20]

YAMATANE MUSEUM OF ART (Yamatane Bijutsukan)
山種美術館　中央区日本橋兜町7-12山種ビル8階

Yamatane Bldg., 8F. 7-12 Nihombashi Kabuto-cho, Chuo-ku. Tel: 3669-7643. Hours: 10:30 A.M.–5:00 P.M., closed Mon. and during exhibition changes.

A collection of contemporary Japanese-style paintings from the Meiji period to the present. There is also a library and tea room that can be used by appointment. [M-9]

BRIDGESTONE MUSEUM OF ART (Burijisuton Bijutsukan)
ブリヂストン美術館　中央区京橋 1-10-1 ブリヂストンビル 2 階
Bridgestone Bldg., 2F. 1-10-1 Kyobashi, Chuo-ku. Tel: 3563-0241. Hours: 10:00 A.M.–5:30 P.M., closed Mon.

Japanese paintings in a Western manner and European, mostly French, art. [M-9]

ASAKURA SCULPTURE GALLERY (Asakura Chosokan)　朝倉彫塑館　台東区谷中 7-18-10
7-18-10 Yanaka, Taito-ku. Tel: 3821-4549. Hours: 10:00 A.M.–4:30 P.M., Sat., Sun., Mon.

The collection consists of about twenty pieces of sculpture by Asakura Fumio (1883–1964). [M-13]

SEZON MUSEUM OF ART (Sezon Bijutsukan)　セゾン美術館　豊島区南池袋 1-28-1
1-28-1 Minami Ikebukuro, Toshima-ku. Tel: 5992-0155. Hours: 10:00 A.M.–8:00 P.M., closed Tues., and during exhibition changes.

Changing exhibitions of contemporary Japanese and Western art shown in a museum operated by the Seibu department store. [M-18]

MUSEUM OF CONTEMPORARY ART TOKYO (Tokyo-to Gendai Bijutsukan)
東京都現代美術館　江東区三好 4-1-1
4-1-1 Miyoshi, Koto-ku. Tel: 5245-4111. Hours: 10:00 A.M.–6:00 P.M. (until 9:00 P.M. Fridays), closed Mon. A fifteen-minute walk from Kiba (Tozai Line) or Kikugawa (Toei Shinjuku Line).

This big new museum, opened in 1995, has been the object of some criticism, both for its design and for its inconvenience of access. Nevertheless, it should turn out to be Tokyo's preeminent museum of contemporary art. [off Map]

Specialist Museums

RICCAR ART MUSEUM (Rikka Bijutsukan)
リッカー美術館　中央区銀座 2-3-6 リッカービル 7 階
Riccar Bldg., 7F. 2-3-6 Ginza, Chuo-ku. Tel: 3571-3254. Hours: 11:00 A.M.–6:00 P.M., closed Mon.

"Return to Self," a ceramic and log sculpture by Takamasa Kuniyasu at the Hara Museum ARC. © 1996 Yamamoto Tadasu

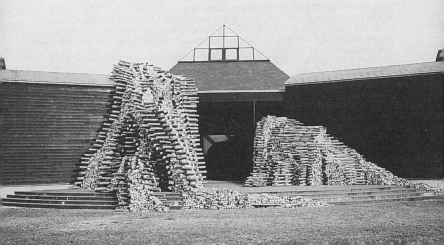

One of the best known collections of *ukiyo-e* prints in Japan. Contains around six thousand prints. There is a room with displays of printmaking techniques and a library for *ukiyo-e* studies. [M-8]

OTA MEMORIAL MUSEUM OF ART (Ota Kinen Bijutsukan)
太田記念美術館　渋谷区神宮前 1-10-10

1-10-10 Jingumae, Shibuya-ku. Tel: 3403-0880. Hours: 10:30 A.M.–5:30 P.M., closed Mon., and from the twenty-fifth until the end of each month.

A collection of over twelve thousand *ukiyo-e* prints in a lovely, small Japanese-style building. [M-4]

KURITA MUSEUM (Kurita Bijutsukan)　栗田美術館　中央区日本橋浜町 2-17-9

2-17-9 Nihombash Hama-cho, Chuo-ku. Tel: 3666-6246. Hours: 10:00 A.M.–5:00 P.M. daily.

The museum specializes in ceramics, particularly Imari ware produced during the Edo period and Nabeshima ware. [M-23] This museum is a branch of the larger **Kurita Museum** in Tochigi Prefecture (Tel: 0284-91-1026).

YOKOYAMA TAIKAN MEMORIAL GALLERY (Yokoyama Taikan Kinenkan)
横山大観記念館　台東区池之端 1-4-24

1-4-24 Ikenohata, Taito-ku. Tel: 3821-1017. Hours: 10:00 A.M.–4:00 P.M., closed Mon., Tue., & Wed.

Formerly the home of the painter Yokoyama, who died in 1958. Only a few paintings and ceramics are shown at a time, but it's worth a visit to see the house and garden. [M-13]

YAYOI ART MUSEUM (Yayoi Bijutsukan)　弥生美術館　文京区弥生 2-4-3

2-4-3 Yayoi, Bunkyo-ku. Tel: 3812-0012. Hours: 10:00 A.M.–5:00 P.M. (enter by 4:00 P.M.), closed Mon.

Paintings from the Taisho period through the beginning of Showa. Some important works. [M-13]

JAPAN CALLIGRAPHY MUSEUM (Nihon Shodo Bijutsukan)
日本書道美術館　板橋区常盤台 1-3-1

1-3-1 Tokiwa-dai, Itabashi-ku. Tel: 3965-2611. Hours: 11:00 A.M.–5:00 P.M., closed Mon., Tue., the day after national holidays, and during exhibition changes.

A collection of over two thousand works of twentieth-century calligraphy. A small garden on the grounds is a calligraphy-brush burial ground. [off Map]

MUSEUM OF CALLIGRAPHY (Shoko Hakubutsukan)　書道美術館　台東区根岸 2-10-4

2-10-4 Negishi, Taito-ku. Tel: 3872-2645. Hours: 10:00 A.M.–4:00 P.M., closed Mon., and mid-June to mid-July.

The history of calligraphy illustrated through inscribed objects such as pottery, stone, etc. Chinese pieces dominate but there are some Japanese. [M-13]

JAPAN FOLK CRAFTS MUSEUM (Nippon Mingeikan)　日本民芸館　目黒区駒場 4-3-33

4-3-33 Komaba, Meguro-ku. Tel: 3467-4527. Hours: 10:00 A.M.–5:00 P.M., closed Mon.

In the former home of folk-art enthusiast Yanagi Soetsu, the collection includes furniture, textiles, pottery, and ceramics by unknown craftsmen. In November the museum holds a sale of crafts from around the country. [M-34]

SHITAMACHI MUSEUM (Shitamachi Fuzoku Shiryokan)
下町風俗資料館　台東区上野公園 2-1

2-1 Ueno-koen, Taito-ku. Tel: 3823-7451. Hours: 9:30 A.M.–4:30 P.M., closed Mon. & hol.

In a new building at the southern end of Ueno Park's Shinobazu Pond, the museum recreates a street of merchant's shops and homes as they were before the 1923 earthquake. [M-13]

EDO-TOKYO MUSEUM (Edo-Tokyo Hakubutsukan)　江戸東京博物館　墨田区横網 1-20-26

1-20-26 Yoko-ami, Sumida-ku. Tel: 3626-9915. Hours: 10:00 A.M.–6:00 P.M., until 9:00 P.M. on Fri., closed Mon.

This new museum takes a theme park-like approach to the study of Edo-Tokyo history. A branch open-air museum in Koganei reconstructs the street life of Tokyo through buildings that have been relocated and preserved. [M-24]

MEIJI UNIVERSITY ARCHAEOLOGICAL COLLECTION (Meiji Daigaku Kokogaku Chinretsu-kan)　明治大学考古学陳列館　千代田区神田駿河台 1-1 明治大学

Meiji Daigaku, 1-1 Kanda Suruga-dai, Chiyoda-ku. Tel: 3296-4432. Hours: 10:00 A.M.–4:30 P.M. (Sat. 10:00 A.M.–1:00 P.M.), closed Sun., national & university holidays.

Chinese archaeological objects from prehistoric periods to the Tang dynasty, Japanese objects from pre-Jomon to the Kofun period. [M-15]

KOKUGAKUIN UNIVERSITY ARCHEOLOGICAL COLLECTION (Kokogakuin Daigaku Kokugaku Shiryokan) 国学院大学考古学資料館 渋谷区東 4-10-28

4-10-28 Higashi, Shibuya-ku. Tel: 3409-0111. Hours: 9:00 A.M.–5:00 P.M., closed Sun., national & university holidays.

Archaeological materials from preceramic to early historical periods. [off Map]

THE ANCIENT ORIENT MUSEUM (Kodai Oriento Hakubutsukan)

古代オリエント博物館 豊島区池袋 3-1-4 サンシャインシティ 7 階

Sunshine City, 7F. 3-1-4 Higashi Ikebukuro, Toshima-ku. Tel: 3989-3491. Hours: 10:00 A.M.–5:00 P.M., closed Mon.

Specializes in West Asian archaeology. Staff has been excavating in Syria for ten years. [M-18]

PAPER MUSEUM (Kami No Hakubutsukan) 紙の博物館 北区堀船 1-1-8

1-1-8 Horifune, Kita-ku. Tel: 3911-3545. Hours: 9:30 A.M.–4:30 P.M., closed Mon. & hol.

The largest museum of paper in the world, the museum has displays showing techniques and utensils for *washi* (Japanese paper) production. [M-45]

MEIJI SHRINE TREASURE HOUSE (Meiji Jingu Homotsuden)

明治神宮宝物殿 渋谷区代々木神園町 1-1 代々木公園内

Yoyogi Park, 1-1 Yoyogi Kamizono-cho, Shibuya-ku. Tel: 3379-5511. Hours: Mar.–Oct., 9:00 A.M.-4:30 P.M.; Nov.–Feb., 9:00 A.M.–4:00 P.M., closed the third Friday of every month.

A collection of sacred objects and articles related to the Meiji emperor. [M-4]

TREASURE HOUSE OF THE YASUKUNI SHRINE (Yasukuni Jinja Homotsu-ihinkan)

靖国神社宝物遺品館 千代田区九段北 3-1-1

3-1-1 Kudan-kita, Chiyoda-ku. Tel: 3261-8326. Hours: 9:00 A.M.–5:00 P.M.

Dedicated to the memory of Japanese war dead, the collection includes swords, helmets, and other arms, a kamikaze plane, a flag painted with blood, and other thought-provoking items. [M-17]

WASEDA UNIVERSITY TSUBOUCHI MEMORIAL MUSEUM (Waseda Daigaku Tsubouchi-hakase Kinen Engeki Hakubutsukan)

早稲田大学坪内博士記念演劇博物館 新宿区西早稲田 1-6-1 早稲田大学内

Waseda Daigaku, 1-6-1 Nishi Waseda, Shinjuku-ku. Tel: 3203-4141. Hours: 9:00 A.M.–4:00 P.M. (until 2:00 P.M. on Sat.), closed Sun., national & university holidays.

The collection covers Eastern and Western theater. Includes *bugaku* and Noh masks and puppets, Noh and Kabuki costumes, as well as instruments and stage models. The building was modeled after London's Fortune Theater. [off Map]

COSTUME MUSEUM (Bunka-Gakuen Fukushioku Hakubutsukan)

文化学園服飾博物館 渋谷区代々木 3-22-1

3-22-1 Yoyogi, Shibuya-ku. Tel: 3370-3111. Hours: 10:00 A.M.–4:30 P.M. (Sat. 10:00 A.M.–3:00 P.M.), closed Sun, hol., and June 23.

Over fifty thousand costumes from Asia, and eighteenth–nineteenth-century Europe and America. [off Map]

SWORD MUSEUM (Token Hakubutsukan) 刀剣博物館 渋谷区代々木 4-25-10

4-25-10 Yoyogi, Shibuya-ku. Tel: 3379-1386. Hours: 9:00 A.M.–4:00 P.M., closed Mon.

A collection of over six thousand swords, thirty of which are listed as National Treasures. [off Map]

KITE MUSEUM (Tako no Hakubutsukan)

凧の博物館 中央区日本橋 1-12-10 たいめい軒ビル 5 階

Taimeiken Bldg., 5F. 1-12-10 Nihombashi, Chuo-ku. Tel: 3275-2704. Hours: 11:00 A.M.–5:00 P.M., closed Sun., & hol.

Run by the Japan Kite Association, the museum has kites from Japan and other parts of the world. [M-9]

DAIMYO CLOCK MUSEUM (Daimyo Tokei Hakubutsukan)

大名時計博物館 台東区谷中 2-1-27

2-1-27 Yanaka, Taito-ku. Tel: 3821-6913. Hours: 10:00 A.M.–4:00 P.M., closed Mon. and July 1–Sept. 30.

Eighty-eight clocks from the Edo period in an interesting older building. [M-13]

MEIJI UNIVERSITY CRIMINAL MUSEUM (Meiji Daigaku Keiji Hakubutsukan)
明治大学刑事博物館　千代田区神田駿河台 1-1 明治大学内
Meiji Daigaku, 1-1 Kanda Suruga-dai, Chiyoda-ku. Tel: 3296-4431. Hours: 10:00 A.M.–4:30 P.M. (Sat. 10:00 A.M.–12:30 P.M.), closed Sun., national & university holidays.

A guillotine, many other implements of punishment, and tools used in arresting Edo-period criminals. Also documents of criminal cases and legislation. [M-15]

FURNITURE MUSEUM (Kagu no Hakubutsukan)
家具の博物館　中央区晴海 3-10JFC ビル 2 階
JFC Bldg., 2F. 3-10 Harumi, Chuo-ku. Tel: 3533-0098. Hours: 10:00 A.M.–4:30 P.M., closed Wed. and July 11–17.

Established with the intention of preserving and exhibiting traditional furniture to the public. [M-22]

TOBACCO AND SALT MUSEUM (Tabako to Shio no Hakubutsukan)
たばこと塩の博物館　渋谷区神南 1-16-8
1-16-8 Jinnan, Shibuya-ku. Tel: 3476-2041. Hours: 10:00 A.M.–6:00 P.M., closed Mon. and the second Tue. of June.

Covers the history of tobacco since Mayan culture. All exhibits are somehow connected with salt and tobacco. [M-3]

SUMO MUSEUM (Sumo Hakubutsukan)　相撲博物館　墨田区横網 1-3-28
1-3-28 Yoko-ami, Sumida-ku. Tel: 3522-0366. Hours: 9:30 A.M.–4:30 P.M., closed Sat., Sun., & hol.

Sumo history and memorabilia. [M-24]

BASEBALL HALL OF FAME AND MUSEUM (Yakyu Taiiku Hakubutsukan)
野球体育博物館　文京区後楽 1-3-61
1-3-61 Koraku, Bunkyo-ku. Tel: 3811-3600. Hours: 10:00 A.M.–5:00 P.M. daily.

The history of baseball, plus more than 23,000 volumes of Japanese and foreign publications on sports and physical education. [M-30]

NHK MUSEUM OF BROADCASTING (NHK Hoso Hakubutsukan)
NHK 放送博物館　港区愛宕 2-1-1
2-1-1 Atago, Minato-ku. Tel: 433-5211. Hours: 9:30 A.M.–4:30 P.M., closed Mon.
Displays cover historical developments in radio and television broadcasting. [M-11]

TRANSPORTATION MUSEUM (Kotsu Hakubutsukan)
交通博物館　千代田区神田須田町 1-25
1-25 Kanda Suda-cho, Chiyoda-ku. Tel: 3251-8481. Hours: 9:30 A.M.–5:00 P.M., closed Mon.
Miniatures of the JR system and other train displays. Good fun. [M-14]

SCIENCE MUSEUM (Kagaku Gijutsukan)　科学技術館　千代田区北ノ丸公園 2-1
2-1 Kitanomaru-koen, Chiyoda-ku. Tel: 3212-8471. Hours: 9:30 A.M.–4:50 P.M. daily.

The newest machines, models, and experimental apparatus displayed, with free access and operation for visitors. [M-17]

NATIONAL SCIENCE MUSEUM (Kokuritsu Kagaku Hakubutsukan)
国立科学博物館　台東区上野公園 7-20
7-20 Ueno-koen, Taito-ku. Tel: 3822-0111. Hours: 9:00 A.M.–4:30 P.M., closed Mon.
A typical science museum. [M-13]

Outside Tokyo

JAPANESE OPEN AIR MUSEUM OF TRADITIONAL HOUSES (Nihon Minka-en)
日本民家苑　神奈川県川崎市多摩区枡形 7-1-1
7-1-1 Masugata, Tama-ku, Kawasaki-shi, Kanagawa-ken. Tel: 044-922-2181. Hours: 9:30 A.M.– 4:00 P.M., closed Mon.

Nineteen traditional homes and buildings preserved in a parklike setting.

SANKEI-EN　三渓園　神奈川県横浜市中区本牧三之谷 293
293 Honmoku-sannotani, Naka-ku, Yokohama-shi, Kanagawa-ken. Tel: 045-621-0634. Hours: 9:00 A.M.–5:00 P.M. daily.

A beautiful Japanese-style garden with numerous traditional houses. [From Yokohama Station's Toyoko Line East Exit take the No. 2 Bus to Sankei-en Mae (about thirty min.)]

NATIONAL MUSEUM OF JAPANESE HISTORY (Kokuritsu Reikishi Minzoku Hakubutsukan)
国立歴史民族博物館　千葉県佐倉市城内町117
117 Jonai-cho, Sakura-shi, Chiba-ken. Tel: 043-486-0123. Hours: 9:30 A.M.–4:30 P.M., closed Mon.

This extensive museum tries to cover the full spectrum of Japanese history and culture through replicas, scale models, and artifacts. [Take the JR Sobu Line from Tokyo Station to Sakura Station, then a bus to the museum.]

ART TOWER MITO (Mito Geijitsukan)　水戸芸術館　茨城県水戸市五軒町1-6-8
1-6-8 Goken-cho, Mito-shi, Ibaraki-ken. Tel: 0292-27-8111. Hours: 9:30 A.M.–6:30 P.M., closed Mon.

Arata Isozaki-designed museum opened in 1990. Often featuring excellent exhibitions of contemporary art. [Take the Super Hitachi from Ueno Station to Mito. The museum is about a fifteen-minute walk from the Station.]

YOKOHAMA MUSEUM OF ART (Yokohama Bijutsukan)
横浜美術館　神奈川県横浜市西区みなとみらい3-4-1
3-4-1 Minato Mirai, Nishi-ku, Yokohama-shi, Kanagawa-ken. Tel: 045-221-0300. Hours: 10:00 A.M.–6:00 P.M., closed Thur.

Fumihiko Maki-designed building, often good contemporary shows. [The museum is a ten-minute walk from Sakuragi-cho Station on the JR or Toyoko Lines.Take the bus terminal exit.]

KAWASAKI SHIMIN MUSEUM (Kawasaki Shimin Bijutsukan)
川崎市民美術館　神奈川県川崎市中原区等々力3049
3049 Todoroki, Nakahara-ku, Kawasaki-shi, Kanagawa-ken. Tel: 044-754-4500. Hours: 9:30 A.M.–5:00.P.M., closed Mon.

Another recent museum that has good contemporary shows and a good collection of contemporary photography. [Take the JR Nambu Line to Musashi-kosugi station. The museum is ten minutes by bus from there.]

SAITAMA PREFECTURAL MUSEUM (Saitama Kenritsu Kindai Bijutsukan)
埼玉県立近代美術館　埼玉県浦和市常磐9-30-1
9-30-1 Tokiwa, Urawa-shi, Saitama-ken. Tel: 048/824-0111. Hours: 9:00 A.M.–4:30 P.M., closed Mon.

Good collection and exhibitions of contemporary Japanese art, buildings by Kisho Kurokawa. [Take the Keihin Tohoku Line to Kita Urawa Station. Take the West Exit and walk four minutes to Kita Urawa Park.]

THE MUSEUM OF MODERN ART, KAMAKURA (Kanagawa Kenritsu Kindai Bijutsukan)
神奈川県立近代美術館　神奈川県鎌倉市雪ノ下2-1-53
2-1-53 Yukinoshita, Kamakura, Kanagawa-ken. Tel: 0467-22-5000. Hours: 10:00 A.M.–5:00 P.M., closed Tues.

The first museum of modern art in Japan. [Take the JR Yokosuka Line from Shinagawa Station to Kamakura Station. The museum is a ten-minute walk from the station.]

MACHIDA CITY MUSEUM OF GRAPHIC ARTS (Machida Shiritsu Kokusai Hanga Bijutsukan)
町田市立国際版画美術館　東京都町田市原町田4-28-1
4-28-1 Hara-machida, Machida-shi, Tokyo-to. Tel: 0427-26-2771. Hours: 9:00 A.M.–4:30 P.M., closed Mon.

Excellent museum specializing in prints ancient through contemporary. [Take the Odakyu Line to Machida Station, walk for fifteen minutes.]

MOA MUSEUM OF ART (Moa Bijutsukan)　MOA美術館　静岡県熱海市桃山町26-2
26-2, Momoyama-cho, Atami-shi, Shizuoka-ken. Tel: 0557-81-5785. Hours: 9:30 A.M.–4:00 P.M., closed Thurs.

An extravagant, modern building located halfway up a mountain in Atami, the initials MOA stand for Mokichi Okada Association, a group connected with the Japanese Church of World Messianity. The museum houses a collection of Japanese and Chinese art, a replica of Toyotomi Hideyoshi's golden tea room, and a Noh theater. [Take the bullet train or Tokaido Line to Atami Station. Then take the bus at the No. 4 bus stop to the MOA Museum. The bus takes about eight minutes, it takes around twenty-five minutes on foot.]

HAKONE OPEN AIR MUSEUM (Chokoku no Mori Bijutsukan)
彫刻の森美術館　神奈川県足柄下郡箱根町二の平1121

1121 Ninotaira, Hakone-machi, Ashigara-shimo-gun, Kanagawa-ken. Tel: 0460-2-1161. Hours: 9:00 A.M.–5:00 P.M., Mar.–Oct.; 9:00 A.M.–4:00 P.M., Nov.–Feb. daily.

This popular open-air museum features nineteenth- and twentieth-century sculpture by Japanese and Western artists. [From Shinjuku Station take the Odakyu Line's Romance Car to Odawara Station, change to the Hakone Tozan Tetsudo Railway, and go to Chokoku no Mori Station. The museum is about a two minute walk from there.]

CONTEMPORARY ART GALLERIES AND EXHIBIT SPACES

Incredible changes occurred in Japan in the late eighties. In Tokyo speculation in the stock market and in real estate created a new sense of wealth and a new desire for luxury and leisure. While much of the new wealth went into imported cars and clothing, Japanese money began to flow into the art market. But as Japanese buyers of name-brand works by foreign artists broke auction records, a more discreet trend began as young and emerging Japanese artists began to be taken seriously at home and abroad.

When speaking of contemporary Japanese art, it is important to remember that there are really two very different kinds of contemporary art in this country. What has been long recognized by the Japanese establishment is art created by living artists who belong to either the *Nihon-ga* school (ink and watercolor painting done in the traditional manner) or the *Yoga* school (work in Western styles, often of a French impressionistic vein). The astonishing prices fetched by such works is matched only by its overall mediocrity. This art is created and sold within a self-supporting system of powerful artists' groups. It has virtually no recognition outside of Japan and it is difficult to imagine that it ever will.

The other type of contemporary art is that created by artists who do not belong to such groups, but whose work would be recognized as contemporary anywhere in the world. Many exhibit and are collected abroad.

Surprisingly, even in the early 1990s as the contemporary art scene in Japan began to blossom, few resident foreigners seem to have noticed. Most foreigners never get beyond the picturesque prints of Japanese scenes and the few shops and galleries that cater to such tastes. But there is so much more to discover and we would like to encourage our readers to do so. It is also worth remembering that while a print in an edition of 100 may only cost ¥60,000, you can also buy an original work by a young artist for about the same price. The young artists whose prices rise after sell-out shows in New York and London are the same artists who for years exhibited here at often a fraction of the price.

Still, for many newcomers, even for long-term residents, the art world can be difficult to master.

Our gallery list is divided by district. The list includes some spaces that use the word museum in their name but that are more exhibition spaces than full-fledged museums with permanent collections and a full range of programs. Most department stores and fashion buildings have galleries or museums of one kind or another. We have listed only a few here, but if you are in or near a department store it is always worth checking to see what they have on display.

While we have listed a selection of what are currently the best contemporary galleries and exhibit spaces in Tokyo, even at a particular space the quality of exhibitions may vary greatly. Few galleries are able to support their artists in the manner Western galleries are known for. Indeed, many of the galleries are strictly or primarily rental spaces where anyone can show for a price. The youngest artists tend to show at such rental galleries so these galleries are often where one can see new, albeit often unpolished, talent. Most exhibitions run for a week, typically opening on a Monday and running through Saturday. Galleries are generally closed on Sundays.

Although we can give you a list of the places to see art, we unfortunately cannot give you a history of contemporary Japanese art or a list of artists to look for. Since there are few books on the subject and only limited coverage in the local press the best strategy is to go at it alone.

We recommend that you read the English-press art listings and reviews, perhaps become a member at a local museum (the Hara Museum has a bilingual program as does the Sagacho Exhibit Space), and most importantly get out and see what is on around town. A great way to spend an afternoon

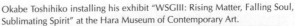
Okabe Toshihiko installing his exhibit "WSGIII: Rising Matter, Falling Soul, Sublimating Spirit" at the Hara Museum of Contemporary Art.

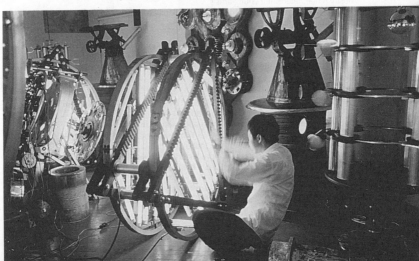

is to do a gallery tour through the Ginza area where there are hundreds of tiny galleries on the back streets. If you live in Tokyo, sign your name and address in the guest book and some galleries will send you announcements. Often exhibition openings are held on Monday evenings from 5:00–7:00 P.M., why not just stop by and meet the artists? As Tokyo gradually loses its old neighborhoods and traditional charm, it is the vibrancy of its contemporary culture that will increasingly make the city interesting. Especially for resident foreigners, the contemporary art world offers an opportunity for involvement and excitement that is not easily found elsewhere.

Galleries

• Kanda—Nihombashi—Marunouchi

AKIYAMA GALLERY 4-1-12 Nihombashi Honcho, Chuo-ku. Tel: 3241-1616. Hours: noon–7:00 P.M., closed Sun. [M-9]
 Mostly rental, young and emerging Japanese artists.

MAKI GALLERY Hongin Dai-ni Bldg., 1F. 4-4-15 Nihombashi Honcho, Chuo-ku. Tel: 3241-1310. Hours: 11:00 A.M.–7:00 P.M. daily. [M-9]
 Mostly rental, young artists.

TOKIWA GALLERY Kyoeiseimei Bldg., 1F. 4-9 Nihombashi Hongoku-cho, Chuo-ku. Tel: 3270-4643. Hours: 11:00 A.M.–7:00 P.M., closed Sun. [M-9]
 Rental only, shows primarily contemporary Japanese sculpture.

ZEIT PHOTO SALON Yagi-cho Bldg., 5F. 1-7-2 Nihombashi, Chuo-ku. Tel: 3246-1370. Hours: 10:30 A.M.–4:30 P.M., closed Sun. [M-9]
 Photography.

INFOMUSU 1-36-7 Nihombashi Kakigara-cho, Chuo-ku. Tel: 3665-1834. Hours: noon–7:00 P.M., closed Sat., Sun, & hol. [M-23]
 Some rental, mostly Japanese artists.

GALLERY SURGE Watanabe Bldg., 2F. 2-7-13 Iwamoto-cho, Chiyoda-ku. Tel: 3861-2581. Hours: 11:30 A.M.–7:30 P.M., closed Sun. [off Map]
 Mostly rental, interesting young artists.

HINO GALLERY Yaesu Bldg., 2-10-8 Yaesu, Chiyoda-ku. Tel: 3275-9099. Hours: 11:00 A.M.–7:00 P.M., closed Sun. & hol. [M-9]
 Young artists.

TOKYO STATION GALLERY 1-9-1 Marunouchi, Chuo-ku, Chiyoda-ku. Tel: 3212-2485. Hours: 10:00 A.M.–8:00 P.M., closed Mon. [M-10]
 Gallery space inside the Tokyo Station building. Shows a wide variety of art, sometimes contemporary.

• Kyobashi—Ginza (1–4 chome)

AKIRA IKEDA GALLERY Showa Bldg., B1. 2-8-18 Kyobashi, Chuo-ku. Tel: 3567-5090. Hours: 11:00 A.M.–6:00 P.M., closed Sun., Mon., & hol. [M-9]
 One of the best galleries for recent international and Japanese contemporary art.

INAX GALLERY Inax Showroom, 2F. 3-6-18 Kyobashi, Chuo-ku. Tel: 3562-1998. Hours: 10:00 A.M.–6:00 P.M., closed the first Tue. of the month. [M-9]
 Two spaces, one concentrating on more historical shows, the other more contemporary art.

NANTENSHI GALLERY Kimura Bldg., 3-6-5 Kyobashi, Chuo-ku. Tel: 3563-3511. Hours: 10:30 A.M.–6:30 P.M., closed Sun. & hol. [M-9]
 Shows well-established contemporary artists both international and Japanese.

KANEKO ART GALLERY 3-7-13 Kyobashi, Chuo-ku. Tel: 3564-0455. Hours: 11:00 A.M.–6:30 P.M., closed Sun & hol. [M-9]
 Mostly rental.

KANEKO ART G2   Takekawara Bldg., 3-5-3 Kyobashi, Chuo-ku. Tel: 3564-6895. Hours: 11:00
A.M.–6:30 P.M., closed Sun. [M-9]
    Younger and more established Japanese artists.
GALLERY TSUBAKI   Daihyaku Seimei Bldg., B1. 3-2-11 Kyobashi, Chuo-ku. Tel: 3281-7808.
Hours: 11:00 A.M.–6:30 P.M., closed Sun. & hol. [M-9]
    Young Japanese artists.
KANRANSHA   3-10-1 Kyobashi, Chuo-ku. Tel: 3567-9674. Hours: noon–7:00 P.M., closed Sun.
& hol. [M-9]
    Mainly established overseas artists, very good place to see European conceptual artists.
AI GALLERY   Shin-kyobashi Bldg., 3-3-8 Kyobashi, Chuo-ku. Tel: 3274-4729. Hours: 11:30
A.M.–7:00 P.M., closed Sun. [M-8]
    Mostly rental, young artists.
GALLERY K   Dai Ni Ginryoku Bldg., 3F. 1-9-6 Ginza, Chuo-ku. Tel: 3563-4578. Hours: 11:00
A.M.–7:00 P.M., closed Sun. [M-8]
    One of the better rental galleries, young artists.
G ART GALLERY   Ginza 18 Bldg., B1. 2-5-18 Ginza, Chuo-ku. Tel: 3562-5858. Hours: 11:00
A.M.–6:30 P.M., closed Sun. & hol. [M-8]
    Mostly rental, young artists.
GALLERY TOKORO   Ginza A Bldg., B1. 1-6-2 Ginza, Chuo-ku. Tel: 3563-3696. Hours: 10:00
A.M.–6:00 P.M., closed Sun. & hol. [M-8]
    Established and emerging Japanese and international artists.
KOYANAGI GALLERY   Koyanagi Bldg., 9F. 1-7-5 Ginza, Chuo-ku. Tel: 3561-1896. Hours:
11:00 A.M.–6:00 P.M., closed Sun, Mon., & hol. [M-8]
    Specializes in very contemporary ceramics.
NABIS GALLERY   Ginza First Bldg., 3F. 1-5-2 Ginza, Chuo-ku. Tel: 3561-3544. Hours: 10:00
A.M.–7:00 P.M., closed Sun. [M-8]
    Mostly rental, established, and emerging Japanese artists.
GALLERY HUMANITE TOKYO   Ginza Premiere Bldg., 4F. 1-8-2 Ginza, Chuo-ku. Tel: 3564-
4350. Hours: 11:30 A.M.–7:00 P.M., closed Sun. & hol. [M-8]
    Full range of contemporary Japanese artists.
GALLERY GEN   Ginza Daichi Bldg., 3F. 1-10-19 Ginza, Chuo-ku. Tel: 3561-6869. Hours:
11:30 A.M.–7:00 P.M., closed Sun. & hol. [M-8]
    High-quality rental gallery, young artists.
LUNAMI GALLERY   Zenrin Bldg., B1. 4-8-11 Ginza, Chuo-ku. Tel: 3535-3065. Hours: 11:30
A.M.–7:00 P.M. (until 5:00 P.M. on Sat.), closed Sun. & hol. [M-8]
    Rental, young artists.
GALLERY WHITE ART   Taihokosan Bldg., 3F. 2-5-4 Ginza, Chuo-ku. Tel: 3567-0089. Hours:
11:30 A.M.–7:00 P.M., closed Sun. & hol. [M-8]
    Young and emerging Japanese artists.
GALLERY YAMAGUCHI   Yamato Bldg., 3F. 3-8-12 Ginza, Chuo-ku. Tel: 3561-3075. Hours:
11:00 A.M.–7:00 P.M., closed Sun. & hol. [M-8]
    Mostly rental but interesting young artists.
GALLERY KOBAYASHI   Yamato Bldg., B1. 3-8-12 Ginza, Chuo-ku. Tel: 3561-0515. Hours:
11:30 A.M.–7:00 P.M., closed Sun. & hol. [M-8]
    Shows a good selection of contemporary Japanese artists.
GALLERY HINOKI   Takagi Bldg., 1F. 3-11-2 Ginza, Chuo-ku. Tel: 3545-3240. Hours: 11:30
A.M.–7:00 P.M., closed Sun. [M-8]
    Mostly rental.
SATANI GALLERY   Asahi Bldg., B1. 4-2-6 Ginza, Chuo-ku. Tel: 3564-6733. Hours: 11:00 A.M.–
6:00 P.M. (5:30 P.M. on Sat.), closed Sun. & hol. [M-8]
    Emerging and established Japanese, known international artists, consistently good shows.
GENDAI CHOKOKU CENTER (Contemporary Sculpture Center)   3-10-19 Ginza, Chuo-ku.
Tel: 3542-0138. Hours: 10:00 A.M.–6:00 P.M., closed Sun. & hol. [M-8]
    Specializes in contemporary sculpture.

NISHIMURA GALLERY   2-8-4 Ginza, Chuo-ku. Tel: 3567-3906. Hours: 10:00 A.M.–6:00 P.M., closed Sun., Mon., & hol. [M-8]

Established Japanese and international artists.

• Ginza (5–8 chome)

GALLERY MUKAI   Tsukumoto Bldg., 6F. 5-5-11 Ginza, Chuo-ku. Tel: 3571-3291. Hours: 10:00 A.M.–7:00 P.M., closed Sun. & hol. [M-8]

A range of Japanese and some international artists.

YOSEIDO GALLERY   5-5-15 Ginza, Chuo-ku. Tel: 3571-1312. Hours: 10:00 A.M.–6:30 P.M., closed Sun. & hol. [M-8]

Contemporary prints, mostly Japanese.

GALLERY NATSUKA   Ginza Plaza 58, 8F. 5-8-17 Ginza, Chuo-ku. Tel: 3571-0130. Hours: 11:30 A.M.–6:30 P.M., closed Sun. [M-8]

Rental, young, and emerging Japanese artists.

GINZA GRAPHIC GALLERY "GGG"   7-7-2 Ginza, Chuo-ku. Tel: 3571-5206. Hours: 11:00 A.M.–7:00 P.M. (Sat. until 6:00 P.M.), closed Sun. [M-8]

Specializes in graphic and design work.

GALLERY UEDA   Asahi Bldg., B1. 6-6-7 Ginza, Chuo-ku. Tel: 3574-7553. Hours: 10:30 A.M.–6:30 P.M., closed Sun. & hol. [M-8]

Established, some emerging Japanese and international artists.

SHISEIDO GALLERY   Shiseido Parlor Bldg., 9F. 8-8-3 Ginza, Chuo-ku. Tel: 3572-2121. Hours: 11:00 A.M.–6:30 P.M., closed Sun. & hol. [M-8]

Usually contemporary art and design exhibitions by both Japanese and international artists.

FUJI GALLERY MODERN   6-5-10 Ginza, Chuo-ku. Tel: 3571-0095. Hours: 10:00 A.M.–7:00 P.M., closed first & third Sat. & Sun. [M-8]

Some rental.

GALLERIA GRAPHICA   Ginza S2, 6-13-4 Ginza, Chuo-ku. Tel: 5550-1335. Hours: 11:00 A.M.–7:00 P.M., closed Sun. & hol. [M-8]

Some rental, mainly graphic works, prints.

GALLERY TOKYO   Dai-go Shuwa Bldg., 2F. 8-6-18 Ginza, Chuo-ku. Tel: 3571-1808. Hours: 10:00 A.M.–7:00 P.M., closed Sun. & hol. [M-8]

Established Japanese and Asian artists.

SHIROTA GALLERY   7-10-8 Ginza, Chuo-ku. Tel: 3572-7971. Hours: 11:00 A.M.–7:00 P.M., closed Sun. & hol. [M-8]

Young and emerging Japanese artists.

GALLERY MURAMATSU   Hirakata Bldg., 2F. 7-10-8 Ginza, Chuo-ku. Tel: 3571-9095. Hours: 11:00 A.M.–7:00 P.M., closed Sun. [M-8]

Some rental, young and established artists.

GALLERY TE   Tosei Bldg., 4F. 8-10-7 Ginza, Chuo-ku. Tel: 3574-6730. Hours: 11:00 A.M.–7:00 P.M., closed Sun. [M-8]

A wide range of Japanese artists.

GALLERY Q/PLUS 1   Tosei Bldg., B2. 8-10-7 Ginza, Chuo-ku. Tel: 3573-2808. Hours: 11:00 A.M.–7:00 P.M., closed Sun. & hol. [M-8]

Young Japanese artists.

• Roppongi—Azabu

PHOTO GALLERY INTERNATIONAL (PGI)   2-5-18 Toranomon, Minato-ku. Tel: 3438-8821. Hours: 11:00 A.M.–5:30 P.M., closed Sun. & hol. [M-11]

Contemporary, often Japanese photographers.

POLAROID GALLERY   30 Mori Bldg., 3-2-2 Toranomon, Minato-ku. Tel: 3438-8821. Hours: 9:00 A.M.–5:00 P.M., closed Sat., Sun., & hol. [M-11]

Contemporary photography.

UNAC SALON   Azabu Unihouse #112, 1-1-2 Azabu-dai, Minato-ku. Tel: 3585-7069. Hours: 10:00 A.M.–6:00 P.M., closed Sun. & hol. [M-1]

Contemporary Japanese and international artists.

TOKYO DESIGNERS SPACE   Axis Bldg., 4F. 5-17-1 Roppongi, Minato-ku. Tel: 3587-2007. Hours: noon–7:00 P.M., closed Sun. & hol. [M-1]

A variety of shows, often design oriented.

STRIPE HOUSE MUSEUM 5-10-33 Roppongi, Minato-ku. Tel: 3405-8108. Hours: 11:00 A.M.–6:30 P.M., closed Sun. & hol. [M-1]

Some rental, contemporary Japanese and international artists.

GALLERY HOSOMI Toshikane Bldg., 3F. 6-5-7 Roppongi, Minato-ku. Tel: 3497-1328. Hours: 11:00 A.M.–7:00 P.M., closed Sun. & hol. [M-5]

Interesting shows, young to emerging, usually Japanese artists.

GALLERY ARCHE Tokyo Bed Bldg., 302. 4-1-16 Roppongi, Minato-ku. Tel: 3583-0819. Hours: 10:00 A.M.–6:00 P.M., closed Sat., Sun., & hol. [M-1]

Specializes in prints.

• Akasaka—Aoyama—Harajuku

WATARIUM 3-7-6 Jingumae, Shibuya-ku. Tel: 3402-3001. Hours: 11:00 A.M.–7:00 P.M., closed Mon. Same building has a great book and art gift shop. [M-5]

Former Watari Gallery became an art space/museum in 1991 showing mainly cutting-edge Western artists. Building by Mario Botta.

MARS GALLERY 2-24-4 Jingumae, Shibuya-ku. Tel: 3470-7783. Hours: 11:00 A.M.–7:00 P.M., closed Sun. [off Map]

New artists, mostly Japanese.

SPIRAL GARDEN Spiral Bldg., 5-6-23 Minami Aoyama, Minato-ku. Tel: 3498-1171. Hours: 11:00 A.M.–8:00 P.M., daily. [M-5]

The open gallery spaces in the building designed by Maki Fumihiko often feature young and emerging Japanese artists.

GALLERY MA Toto Nogizaka Bldg., 3F. 1-24-3 Minami Aoyama. Tel: 3402-1010. Hours: 11:00 A.M.–7:00 P.M., closed Sun. & hol. [M-5]

Specializes in architecture.

SOGETSU HALL 7-2-21 Akasaka, Minato-ku. Tel: 3408-1126. Hours: 11:00 A.M.–5:00 P.M., closed Sun. [M-5 & 6]

This famous school of flower arranging also houses a museum, a gallery, and a beautiful plaza designed by Isamu Noguchi where contemporary art is often shown. Building by Tange Kenzo.

• Shibuya—Daikanyama—Ebisu

GA GALLERY 3-12-14 Sendagaya, Shibuya-ku. Tel: 3403-1581. Hours: noon–6:00 P.M., closed Mon. [off Map]

Specializes in architecture, good bookshop.

PARCO GALLERY Shibuya Parco I, 15-1 Udagawa-cho, Shibuya-ku. Tel: 3477-5964. Hours: 10:00 A.M.–8:30 P.M. daily. [M-3]

Several small galleries are on various floors of this three-part fashion building.

SEED HALL Seed, 10F. 21-1 Udagawa-cho, Shibuya-ku. Tel: 3462-3795. Hours: 10:00 A.M.–8:00 P.M., closed Wed. [M -3]

Part of the Seibu group.

THE MUSEUM/BUNKAMURA Bunkamura, B1. 2-24-1 Dogenzaka, Shibuya-ku. Tel: 3477-9552. Hours: 10:00 A.M.–7:00 P.M. (until 9:00 P.M. on Fri. & Sat.). [M-3]

Various exhibitions, some of high quality.

HILLSIDE GALLERY Hillside Terrace Bldg., 29-18-A1 Sarugaku-cho, Shibuya-ku. Tel: 3476-4683. Hours. 11:00 A.M.–7:00 P.M., closed Mon. [M-20]

Consistently interesting, young and emerging Japanese and some foreign artists. Their associated gallery ART FRONT is located across the street.

STUDIO EBISU PHOTO GALLERY Studio Ebisu, 2F. 1-9-2 Ebisu, Shibuya-ku. Tel: 3444-5522. Hours: 10:00 A.M.–7:00 P.M., closed during exhibition changes. [M-20]

Primarily work by Japanese photographers.

• Shinjuku and Vicinity

PENTAX FORUM Shinjuku Mitsui Bldg., 1F. 2-1-1 Nishi Shinjuku, Shinjuku-ku. Tel: 3348-2941. Hours: 10:30 A.M.–6:30 P.M. daily [M-7]

Contemporary photography.

FUJI TELEVISION GALLERY Fuji Television, 3-1 Kawada-cho, Shinjuku-ku. Tel: 3357-0660. Hours: 10:00 A.M.–6:00 P.M., closed Sun. [off Map]

One of the more established galleries, dealing in a selection of often interesting Japanese and international artists.

GALLERY NW HOUSE 1-3-7 Waseda, Shinjuku-ku. Tel: 3204-0246. Hours: 1:00 P.M.–8:00 P.M., closed Tues. [off Map]

Tiny gallery showing younger Japanese artists.

P3 ART & ENVIRONMENT Tocho-ji temple, B1. 4-34 Yotsuya, Shinjuku-ku. Tel: 3353-6866. Hours vary. [off Map]

Alternative space concentrating on exhibitions and artists' workshops. Located in the basement of a Zen temple.

• Waterfront and Warehouse Districts

SAGACHO EXHIBIT SPACE Shokuryo Bldg., 3F. 1-8-3 Saga, Koto-ku. Tel: 3630-3243. Hours: 11:00 A.M.–6:00 P.M., closed Sun. & hol. [M-25]

One of Tokyo's premiere gallery/alternative spaces, Sagacho has shown some of the best younger artists in Japan. Beautiful, art deco, former rice warehouse.

GALLERY YAMAGUCHI SOKO 1-17-4 Shin-kiba, Koto-ku. Tel: 3521-6417. Hours: 11:00 A.M.–6:00 P.M., closed Sun. [off Map]

Ginza Yamaguchi's warehouse space, contemporary art.

NANTENSHI GALLERY SHIN-KIBA 1-17-4 Shin-kiba, Koto-ku. Tel: 5569-6762. Hours: 11:00 A.M.–6:00 P.M., closed Sun. [off Map]

Like the above, Nantenshi's warehouse venue.

SHOKO NAGAI SOKO 1-17-4 Shin-kiba, Koto-ku. Tel: 5560-676. Hours: 11:00 A.M.–6:00 P.M., closed Sun. [off Map]

Japanese contemporary art.

GATODO GALLERY TAKEBASHI Suzue Warehouse #3, 4F. 1-14-24 Kaigan, Minato-ku. Tel: 3433-4479. Hours: 11:00 A.M.–6:00 P.M., closed Sun. & hol. [M-11]

Warehouse space specializing in top Western and Japanese artists.

SHIGERU YOKOTO GALLERY Suzue Soko #3, 4F. 1-14-24 Kaigan, Minato-ku. Tel: 3379-1386. Hours: 11:00 A.M.–6:00 P.M., closed Sun. [M-11]

Japanese contemporary art.

TOLMAN COLLECTION 2-2-18 Shiba-daimon, Minato-ku. Tel: 3434-1300. Hours: 11:00 A.M.–7:00 P.M., closed Tue. [M-11]

Conventional Japanese contemporary prints in a traditional Japanese house.

• Other Areas

RONTGEN KUNST INSTITUT 4-17-3 Omori-higashi, Ota-ku. Tel: 3766-8667. Hours: 1:00 P.M.–8:00 P.M., closed Thurs. [off Map]

Hip, young Japanese artists.

SCAI THE BATHHOUSE Kashiwayu Ato, 6-1-23 Yanaka, Taito-ku. Tel: 3821-1144. Hours: noon–7:00 P.M., closed Sun. Mon., & hol. [M-13]

Located in a former bathhouse, shows a range of international and Japanese contemporary art.

TRADITIONAL ARTS

In the West, they would be called hobbies: ikebana or *kado* (flower arranging), *shodo* (calligraphy), and *sado* (tea ceremony). For the Japanese, these are considered both artistic and spiritual pursuits.

The history of each is long and varied. Only *ikebana* is a Japanese invention, the others being originally Chinese imports. Calligraphy is the oldest; in the Heian period the ability to write in a beautiful hand was a sign of aristocratic taste and breeding.

All three arts were given an added philosophical dimension when Zen Buddhism became the dominant religious sect after the Kamakura period. The aim of Zen was to purge the mind of egoistic intellectualism and thus attain a sense of calm, tranquillity, and identity with the universe. *Sado, shodo, kado,* all with the suffix "do," meaning "the way of," were a means of establishing harmony between man and nature, and achieving a state of enlightenment.

Sado, the tea ceremony, was the most important of the three. Tea was first used by Zen monks to help keep themselves awake during long meditation sessions. The tea ceremony developed slowly and, as an art, was formalized by the famous tea master Sen no Rikyu (1522–91). The simple, almost rustic, tea room, sparsely decorated with a flower arrangement or an ink painting, was intended as a miniature of the world in harmony. By the Momoyama period, the art began to lose its simplicity and slowly became a ritual devoid of spiritual content, an ostentatious pursuit of the wealthy daimyo lords who competed frantically for the most extravagant, famous, and expensive tea bowls and caddies.

The arts are taught today by a number of schools that have become huge and profitable organizations. The schools teach the rules, rituals, and techniques, but this is where most stop. Only a few teachers are capable of taking the training to the next, and most important, step. Using Zen terminology, the fundamental purpose is to achieve spiritual harmony with nature through a circular process of creation and self-expression. As in the martial arts, the Zen foundations of these arts are not always consciously acknowledged.

The arts are taught by a number of schools, each of which holds to a variety of methods and theories. The difference is most extreme in *ikebana* where over twenty different schools teach the two main styles known as *rikka* or formal style, and *nage-ire* or natural style. The most traditional school is the Ikenobo, the most contemporary is the Sogetsu.

For people not interested in the Zen aspects of these arts, they all make relaxing, somewhat exotic hobbies. Demonstrations of the tea ceremony and *ikebana* are given at various locations, and some schools offer instruction for short periods of time. Calligraphy schools generally accept only long-term students.

Ikebana

IKEBANA INTERNATIONAL Shufunotomo Bldg., 2F. 1-6 Kanda Suruga-dai, Chiyoda-ku. Tel: 3293-8188.

Well-known international organization promoting ikebana. [M-15]

SOGETSU Sogetsu Kaikan Bldg. 4F. 7-2-21 Akasaka, Minato-ku. Tel: 3408-1120. Classes given in English every Mon. from 10:00 A.M.–noon. Fee: ¥3,460 per lesson, including flower cost.

You need to make an appointment by the preceding Mon. [M-5]

OHARA Ohara Kaikan, 2F. 5-7-17 Minami Aoyama, Minato-ku. Tel: 3499-1200. English lessons Mon.–Fri. from 10:00 A.M.–noon.

You can join the classes anytime, but must give 2–3 days notice. Fee: ¥1,500 per lesson, plus a flower fee of about ¥2,000. [M-5]

Tea Ceremony

TOKO-AN   Imperial Hotel, 4F. Mon.–Sat., 10:00 A.M.–4:00 P.M.

Two or three times a week they are booked by groups, so call ahead to be sure you can observe and have a cup of tea. Fee: ¥1,100. [M-10]

CHOSHO-AN   Hotel Okura, 7F. Tea demonstrations given daily from 11:00 A.M.–noon and 1:00 P.M.–5:00 P.M.

Groups also book, so call ahead. Fee: ¥1,000 for observation and tea with sweets. [M-11]

SEISEI-AN   Hotel New Otani, 7F. Thur., Fri., & Sat., 11:00 A.M.–noon and 1:00 P.M.–4:00 P.M. Fee ¥1,000. [M-6]

Contemporary Architecture

Like most of the other contemporary arts, architecture flourished in the eighties in Tokyo. The face of the city changed as both traditional structures and shoddy modern buildings were leveled for new development projects that included work by talented architects from both Japan and abroad.

Ambitious new development projects throughout the city, and particularly in the waterfront areas, were undertaken with the hope of upgrading and rationalizing the city. But the monumental scale of these projects seems at odds with the spirit of Tokyo, with the intimate scale of traditional architecture and the characteristically disjunctive face of the city's streets.

The best new architecture is often found in the quirky buildings wedged between totally incongruous structures, making the best of a bad situation and even, on occasion, being rather witty along the way. A good example being Pritzker Prize-winner Maki Fumihiko's Spiral Building in Aoyama. The façade of this building is a play on the incongruity of architectural façades through the city, and the interior reflects the spiral-like way neighborhoods progress gradually from public to intimately private spaces.

While architecture of interest is scattered throughout the city, a concentration of such buildings can be found in the Aoyama area. By following the architecture listings on maps for the Aoyama and Akasaka areas you can see a great deal in half a day. The **GA Gallery** in Harajuku specializes in exhibitions of architectural work and has an excellent selection of publications. Following is a list of buildings by top architects. We have concentrated on work by Japanese but have also included some of the more interesting buildings by architects from abroad.

MAKI FUMIHIKO
Hillside Terrace (1969, 1973, 1977), 29-9 Sarugaku-cho, Shibuya-ku [M-20]
Spiral (1983), 5-6-23 Minami Aoyama, Minato-ku [M-5]
Tokyo Metropolitan Gymnasium (1990), 1-17-1 Sendagaya, Shibuya-ku [M-29]
Tepia (1989), 2-8-44 Kita Aoyama, Minato-ku [M-5]
ISOZAKI ARATA
Ochanomizu Square (1987), 1-6 Kanda Suruga-dai, Chiyoda-ku [M-15]
Art Tower Mito (1990), Hara Museum ARC (1988) See **Museums**
Casals Hall (1989), 1-6 Kanda Suruga-dai, Chiyoda-ku [M-15]
ANDO TADAO
Collecione (1989), 6-1-3 Minami Aoyama, Minato-ku [M-5]

Aoyama To Bldg. (1985), 2-12 Kita Aoyama, Minato-ku [M-5]
Melrose (1984), 2-18-1 Aoba-dai, Meguro-ku [off Map]
TK Bldg. (1986), 3-17-25 Nishi Azabu, Minato-ku [M-2]
TANGE KENZO
National Gymnasium (1964), 2-1 Jinnan, Shibuya-ku [M-4]
Sogetsu Kaikan (1977), 2-33-6 Jingumae, Shibuya-ku [M-5]
Hanae Mori Bldg. (1978), 3-6-1 Kita Aoyama, Minato-ku [M-5]
Akasaka Prince Hotel (1983), 1-2 Kioi-cho, Chiyoda-ku [M-6]
Tokyo City Hall (1991), 2-8-1 Nishi Shinjuku, Shinjuku-ku [M-7]
KUROKAWA KISHO
Nakagin Capsule Tower Bldg. (1972), 8-16-10 Ginza, Chuo-ku [M-8, 11]
Wacoal Kojimachi Bldg. (1984), 1-1-2 Kojimachi, Chiyoda-ku [M-6]
Roppongi Prince Hotel (1984), 3-2-7 Roppongi, Minato-ku [M-1]
TANIGUCHI YOSHIHIRO
Josenji Temple (1965), 10-15 Uguisudani-cho, Shibuya-ku [off Map]
Imperial Theater (1966), 3-1-1 Marunouchi, Chiyoda-ku [M-10]
National Museum of Modern Art (1969), 3 Kitanomaru-koen, Chiyoda-ku [M-17]
Tokyo National Museum, Gallery of Eastern Antiquities (1968), Ueno Park, Taito-ku [M-13]
TANIGUCHI YOSHIO
Tokyo Sea Life Park/Kasai Rinkai Aquarium (1989), 6-2-2 Rinkai-cho, Edogawa-ku [off Map]
ITO TOYO
T Building at Nakameguro (1991), 1-17-16 Higashiyama, Meguro-ku [off Map]
Kanda M Bldg. (1987), 1-19 Kanda Suda-cho, Chiyoda-ku [M-14]
KITAGAWARA ATSUSHI
Miaon-Kaku (1984), 4-9-19 Akasaka, Minato-ku [M-6]
Rise (1986), 13-17 Udagawa-cho, Shibuya-ku [M-3]
395/Kitagawara Studio (1986), 3-9-5 Minami Aoyama, Minato-ku [M-5]
Cieux Building (1989) 3-14-17 Minami Aoyama, Minato-ku [M-5]
Metroca (1989), 5-40-10 Jingumae, Shibuya-ku [M-5]
Metrotour /Edoken Tokyo Honsha (1989), 1-1-1 Kanda Awaji-cho, Chiyoda-ku. [off Map]
EDWARD SUZUKI
Joule-A (1990), 1-10 Azabu Juban, Minato-ku [M-1]
Plaza Mikado (1990), 2-14-5 Akasaka, Minato-ku [M-6]
KURAMATA SHIRO
Livina Yamagiwa 7F. (interior), 1-5 Soto Kanda, Chiyoda-ku. [M-14]
Livina Yamagiwa, 2F. Axis Bldg. Roppongi [M-1]
PHILIPPE STARCK
Flamme d'Or (1990), 1-23-1 Azumabashi, Sumida-ku.[M-12]
Nani-Nani (1990), 4-9-23 Shiroganedai, Mianto-ku. [M-19]
NIGEL COATES
The Wall (1990), 4-2 Nishi Azabu, Minato-ku [M-2]
PETER EISENMAN & KITAYAMA KOJIRO
Koizumi Lighting Theater/IZM (1990), 3-12 Kanda Sakuma-cho, Chiyoda-ku. [M-14]
ALDO ROSSI
Ambiente International (1991), 4-11-1 Minami Aoyama, Minato-ku [M-5]
MARIO BOTTA
Watarium (1990), 3-7-6 Jingumae, Shibuya-ku [M-4]
NORMAN FOSTER
Century Tower (1991), 2-13-9 Hongo, Bunkyo-ku [off Map]

The following list is by building name:

ICHIBANKAN (1969), Takeyama Minoru, Arch. & United Actions. Kabukicho, Shinjuku-ku. [M-7]
SUPREME COURT (1974), Okada Shin'ichi. 4-2 Hayabusa-cho, Chiyoda-ku. [M-6]
NOA BLDG. (1974), Shiraii Seiichi. 2-3-5 Azabu-dai, Minato-ku. [M-11]
REIYUKAI-SHAKADEN (1975), Iwasaki Kenichi. 1-7-8 Azabu-dai, Minato-ku. [M-11]
NATIONAL THEATER (1966), Takanaka Komuten Co. 4-1 Hayabusa-cho, Chiyoda-ku. [M-6]

観光

SIGHTSEEING

SIGHTSEEING

TEMPLES AND SHRINES

Before a Japanese child is born, chances are that the mother will visit a Shinto shrine associated with childbirth to pray for a safe delivery. There, she will probably buy a special *hara-maki* (a "belly-wrap" normally worn to warm the stomach) to wear as a protective amulet. After birth, the child will be taken to the shrine and presented to the god.

Shrines are later visited during the various rites of passage. On *Shichi-go-san,* a festival for children three, five, and seven years old, and on Adult's Day, when they turn twenty, the visits are made to insure continued good health and fortune.

Throughout these years the child will attend a school where Confucian-based social ethics are taught: the hierarchy of respect, loyalty, and social obligations important to Japanese society since the feudal period. The Confucian respect for learning has become so deeply instilled that success in the Japanese sense hinges on academic success. From pre-kindergarten through university graduation, the goal is attendance at a series of increasingly elite schools that will virtually guarantee employment by a top Japanese company and entrance into *sarariman* heaven.

When it's time for marriage, a calendar will be consulted to find a propitious day (this is also common for other personal and business decisions) and the ceremony will be held in a Shinto shrine (although Western-style church weddings have become a recent vogue).

Shinto, the ancient native religion, focuses on the worship of divine spirits of mythical ancestors or natural phenomena. With no set of moral or ethical principles and a strict worldly orientation, Shinto stresses a sense of continuity between man, nature, and the gods.

Imported from China about 1500 years ago, Buddhism has had a powerful influence on the Japanese world view. With a rich history of scholarship and scripture, the religion is "otherworldly" and teaches the transitory nature of life. For the Japanese this has become the basis of a complex aesthetic system where beauty is more beautiful if it's here today and gone tomorrow. The festivities surrounding the short-lived cherry blossoms of spring is but one instance of this aesthetic.

When the child's parents die, Buddhist practices will be used at the funeral. A priest is summoned to read sutras and to pray for the safe passage of the deceased to the spirit world. A small altar will be built in the house and the child will continue to show respect for the parents, praying, burning incense, and demonstrating to the deceased that they have not been forgotten. Classical literature is full of tales of unhappy or neglected spirits returning to earth to haunt the living.

If a Japanese person is asked whether he or she is religious, the answer would probably be no. There is no regular worship as in Western religions, and very little conscious thought about it. For most Japanese, being Shintoist, Buddhist, or Confucianist is less a question of belief than of simply being Japanese. What puzzles most foreigners is the casual mixture of religious systems. People are not either Shintoists or Buddhists, but both. Confucianism is not even considered a religion, rather a system of thought and ethics.

The postwar Japanese are, for the most part, extremely casual about religion. Shrines connected with Shinto and temples connected with Buddhism are visited for specific purposes. During the summer Bon season, the family temple is visited in honor of one's ancestors. At New Year's, a shrine is visited to pray for good fortune in the coming year. Most temples and shrines are visited otherwise only for specific "requests," and then an appropriate place is chosen, e.g., students will visit the shrine of a famous scholar to pray for a passing exam score.

Throughout history, religions have been harnessed by Japanese rulers for blatantly political purposes. The early adoption of Buddhism had as much to do with undermining the Shinto-based legitimacy of a ruling family as it had with a strong belief in a foreign religion. Buddhism, associated with the well-organized Chinese political system, was seen as a powerful tool for social control. For the feudal samurai lords the Zen sect of Buddhism with its stress on austerity and action over intellectual process was a perfect form of training for samurai warriors. Later, Confucianism provided a solid theory for the feudal political system based on bonds of loyalty and obedience. When samurai rule was overthrown during the Meiji Restoration (January 3, 1868), Shintoism was revived to promote emperor worship (and the new regime) and to develop the nationalistic sentiments that carried the country, burning with religious zeal, straight into World War II. Since the war a number of new religions, mostly spin-off Buddhist sects, have become powerful organizations. Soka Gakkai, the largest, has a membership of over twenty million and its own political party, the *Komei-to*.

For both Japanese and foreigners, sightseeing is a major reason for visiting the more famous shrines and temples. Shinto shrines are easily recognized by the *torii* gate usually made of wood with two tall posts topped by one or two cross beams. The architecture is usually rather restrained. There are no images, but the resident god will be represented by an object such as a mirror or sword. Prayer at a shrine starts by waking up the god by clapping twice. You then bow your head and pray, and clap once more. A large bell or gong is also used as another way of attracting the god's attention. The wooden votive plaques, *ema,* seen at many shrines are offered by petitioners seeking anything from a healthy baby to a successful business deal. At both temples and shrines one can purchase *omikuji* and *omamori. Omikuji* are poetic fortunes written on a piece of paper. After being read, the piece of paper is knotted and tied onto the branch of a tree in hopes that a good fortune will come true and a bad one will improve. *Omamori* are amulets, usually contained in a small brocade case, that are for general or specified protective purposes.

Temples are recognized by their Chinese-style architecture that is generally more extravagant than that of Shinto shrines. Although traditionally there are a number of gates, a main hall, various outer buildings, and a pagoda, in Tokyo many of the temples' outer buildings have been destroyed. Near the entrance to the temple or shrine grounds is a small fountain, where attendees wash their hands in a symbolic purification ceremony. At the incense burner usually located nearby, people will "wash" themselves with the smoke in hopes of curing or preventing illness. The style of prayer differs according to which sect of Buddhism one adheres to, but a simple silent bow in front of the main image of the temple with hands held at chest level in the common attitude of prayer is typical.

Most temples and shrines in Tokyo have been destroyed numerous times throughout the course of history. Some are simply rebuilt on a regular basis (the most famous Shinto shrine, Ise Jingu, is rebuilt every 20 years). The rebuilding usually follows the traditional architecture, but is often of concrete. Few temples in Tokyo remain in their original condition, but for the Japanese it doesn't seem to matter much—it is the site itself, not the structure, that is sacred.

In the following list of temples and shrines, important works of art belonging to the institution have been noted. Many, however, have been placed in museums or are not shown to the general public except on rare occasions. Festivals and *ennichi* (small monthly fairs) are also listed, some as part of the calendar of events.

214 SIGHTSEEING

Temples

KAN'EI-JI 1-14-11 Ueno Sakuragi, Taito-ku. Tel: 3821-1259. [M-13]

Associated with the Tendai sect of Buddhism, this is one of the most important of the Edo-period temples. Built to protect Edo castle from the dangerous northeast direction (people are still superstitious of this direction), the temple became the family mausoleum of the Tokugawa clan and six of their fifteen shoguns were buried there. The original temple, built in 1625, was destroyed during the battle between Tokugawa loyalists and the soldiers of the Meiji Restoration in 1868. The present structure was moved in 1875 from Saitama Prefecture where it was the main hall of Kita-in temple.

SENSO-JI: Asakusa Kannon 2-3-1 Asakusa, Taito-ku. Tel: 3842-0181. [M-12]

During the Edo (1600–1868) and Meiji (1868–1912) periods the grounds of Senso-ji temple were one of the liveliest areas in the city. Ships, theaters, amusement grounds, and performers of various kinds (often freaks or monkeys) gave the area a carnival-like atmosphere. To the north was Yoshiwara, the famous pleasure quarter.

The origins of the temple are legendary. One day in 628 local fishermen found in their nets a small golden image of Kannon, the Buddhist goddess of mercy. Senso-ji was built to enshrine the statue in the seventh century. A larger temple built in 1692 was destroyed during World War II and the present building is a replica dating from 1958.

The other religious buildings in this area are covered later in a walking tour of Asakusa (see **Walking Tours**).

Festivals: Mar. 18, Apr. 8, July 9–10, Oct. 18–20, Dec. 17–18.

ZOJO-JI 4-7-35 Shiba-koen, Minato-ku. Tel: 3432-1431. [M-11]

Like Kan'ei-ji in the northeastern quarter of the city, Zojo-ji was a family temple for the Tokugawa clan built to protect the castle from the south, also considered a dangerous direction. Founded in 1393 by the priest Shoso of the Jodo sect, the main temple was destroyed in 1873 by arsonists in protest against the temple's mixture of "foreign" Buddhism and "pure" Shinto. It was rebuilt and again destroyed on April 1, 1909, in a fire set by a cold itinerant. The temple was again destroyed in World War II, and the present building dates from 1974. The imposing main gate, *Sanmon*, built in 1605 remains and is designated an Important Cultural Property.

Festival: Apr. 8 (Hana-matsuri)

ZENPUKU-JI 1-6-21 Moto-azabu, Minato-ku. Tel: 3451-7402. [M-1]

This temple was founded in 832 by Kukai (Kobo Daishi, 774–835), a Buddhist priest who brought the Shingon doctrine of Buddhism to Japan from China. Since 1232 it has been associated with the Jodo sect. Destroyed repeatedly by fire, the temple was last rebuilt after World War II. The temple is perhaps most famous as the site of the first American legation under Townsend Harris from 1859–75. A monument to the first American minister in Japan was erected here in 1936.

Fukuzawa Yukichi, a famous Meiji-period liberal and founder of Keio University, is buried on the temple grounds. His grave is a popular spot with Keio students, who believe that visiting the grave will ensure success in university exams. Another attraction is an enormous ginkgo tree that shades the temple. The oldest such tree in Tokyo, it has been designated a Natural Monument.

NISHI-ARAI-DAISHI: Soji-ji 1-15-1 Nishi Arai, Adachi-ku (Daishi-mae Station/Tobu Isezaki Line from Asakusa). Tel: 3890-2345. [M-43]

Built by Kukai in 826, by the Kamakura period (1185–1333) its popularity had grown, and in the Edo period (1600–1868) it was frequented by the third shogun, Tokugawa Iemitsu. The temple's reputation and popularity center on the wooden statue of an eleven-faced Kannon attributed to Kukai. Miraculously escaping the numerous fires that destroyed the main hall, the statue of Kannon is believed to protect supplicants from fires and other forms of evil. A painted-wood statue of Kukai dating from the Kamakura period is designated an Important Cultural Property. The current temple is a 1971 reconstruction; its peony garden is well known.

Festivals: Feb. 3–4

Ennichi: every month on the twenty-first

SHIBAMATA TAISHAKUTEN: Daikyo-ji 7-10-3 Shibamata, Katsushika-ku. [Take the Toei Asakusa Line to Oshiage Station. Change to the Keisei Dentetsu and go five stops to Aoto Station. Change there to the Keisei Kanamachi Line and take it two stops to Shibamata Station.] [off Map]

Founded in 1631 by the priest Nitchu of Hokekyo-ji temple in Chiba Prefecture, this temple of the Nichiren sect is noted for its wooden statue of Taishaku-ten (a guardian diety) attributed to the sect's founder Nichiren (1222–82). The current building dates from 1934, the *Niten-mon* gate from 1901. The street approaching the temple is lined with a number of *senbei* (rice cracker) and sweet shops including Shibamataya, a restaurant that was the model for the shop owned by the family of the famous movie character Tora-san.

JINDAI-JI 5-15-1 Jindai-ji Motomachi, Chofu-shi. [Take the #21 bus from Tsutsujigaoka Station/ Keio Line from Shinjuku.] Tel: 0424-86-5511. [off Map]

The second oldest temple in the Tokyo area, Jindai-ji was founded in 733. The legend of the temple's origins is recorded in a book kept with the other temple treasures. When the daughter of a rich family fell in love with a man of low origin, the parents sent the girl to a faraway island. The young man prayed to the Buddhist god of water, Jinjadaio. The god heard his prayers and sent a giant turtle to carry the boy to the island to save his sweetheart. The two lived happily ever after. The couple's son later built Jindai-ji to honor the god that helped his parents. Since that time the temple has been associated with the god of marriage.

The main hall of the temple, reconstructed in 1914, holds a bronze statue of Shaka Nyorai (the main Buddha) that dates from the Nara period (710–94) and is designated an Important Cultural Property. Behind the temple is the Jindai-ji Botanical Garden. On the way to the temple are several *soba* restaurants serving *Jindai-ji soba,* famous since the Edo period.

Festivals: Daruma (Buddhist good luck doll) Fair, March 3–4

SENGAKU-JI 2-11-1 Takanawa, Minato-ku. Tel: 3441-2208. [M-36]

While the temple itself is not very interesting, Sengaku-ji is famous as the burial place of the Forty-seven Ronin (masterless samurai). The graves are found in a small court to the left of the front gate. The grave of their leader Oishi Kuranosuke (1659–1703) and that of their avenged lord, Asano Naganori (1665–1701), is found in the corner of the courtyard covered by a small roof. The head of their victim, Kita Yoshinaka, was washed in the temple well-water before being placed in front of their master's tomb on the night of December 14, 1702.

Festivals: Apr. 1–7, Dec. 14.

Shrines

MEIJI JINGU 1-1 Yoyogi Kamizono-cho, Shibuya-ku. Tel: 3379-5511. [M-4]

Dedicated to the emperor and empress Meiji, the shrine is a beautiful example of restrained Shinto architecture. The shrine was opened in 1920 with an extravagant ceremony, and it remains one of the most frequently visited shrines in the city. The two large *torii* at the entrances to the shrine precincts were built of Japanese cypress trees that were over 1,700 years old. The shrine is enclosed by the extensive Meiji Jingu Gyoen gardens and Meiji Park.

Festivals: Jan. 15, Oct. 30–Nov. 3.

HIE JINJA: Sanno-sama 2-10-15 Nagatacho, Chiyoda-ku. Tel: 3581-2471. [M-6]

In the late fifteenth century Ota Dokan (a military commander) built this shrine, dedicated to Oyamakuni no Kami, a tutelary deity of Edo, on the grounds of the early Edo Castle. Later patronized by the Tokugawas, it was the most popular Edo-period shrine and held the best festivals in town. The current building dates from 1959, the main gate from 1962.

YASUKUNI JINJA 3-1-1 Kudan-kita, Chiyoda-ku. Tel: 3261-8326. [M-17]

Built in 1869, Yasukuni Shrine is dedicated to the Japanese war dead and major figures in the Meiji Restoration (January 3, 1868). The shrine architecture is classic Shinto style. The fifteen-meter-high bronze main gate was built in 1887. While classic in shape, the gate has an unusually modern monumental feeling. Since the Meiji period the shrine has been a famous spot for winter snow scenes and for its cherry blossoms in the spring. There is a small memorial museum on the grounds.

Festivals: July 13–16, traditional dance and Noh performances; Aug. 15, anniversary of the end of World War II, government ministers and politicians visit the shrine.

KANDA MYOJIN 2-16-2 Soto-kanda, Chiyoda-ku. Tel: 3254-0753. [M-14 & 16]

This shrine, dating back as far as the eighth century, was originally in Suruga-dai. Tokugawa Ieyasu needed the land and had the shrine moved to its present location, but only after diplomatically naming it the guardian shrine of Edo. The shrine was formerly dedicated to an orthodox Shinto deity, but became associated with the rebel general Taira no Masakando who led a revolt against the emperor Suzaku in 935. According to legend, when captured and decapitated,

One of the gates in the Senso-ji temple complex in Asakusa. © 1996 M. Yoshida

his head flew off and landed at the site of the Edo Shrine. The current building is a 1934 replica of the earlier structure.

Festivals: May 15 (every other year)

YUSHIMA TENJIN   3-30-1 Yushima, Bunkyo-ku. Tel: 3836-0753. [M-13, 16]

Sugawara Michizane (845–903), a famous Heian-period (794–1185) scholar, is enshrined in Yushima Tenjin. Originally built in the fourteenth century, it was later restored by Ota Dokan. Because of Sugawara's literary reputation, the shrine is popular with students studying for school entrance exams. Before the yearly testing period, hundreds of *ema* (wooden votive plaques) are hung at the temple by hopeful (or hopeless) students. The shrine has a small but lovely garden of plum trees and a dramatic bridge to the main building.

Festivals: Plum viewing, mid-Feb.–mid-Mar.

SUITEN-GU   2-4-1 Nihombashi Kakigara-cho, Chuo-ku. [M-23]

Built in 1818, Suiten-gu in Tokyo is a branch of the Kyushu Suiten-gu shrine. The original shrine was built to pray for the souls of the six-year-old emperor Antoku and his mother who jumped into the sea to escape capture during a battle between the Taira and Minamoto clans in 1185. The shrine has since been associated with childbirth. Expectant mothers come to pray for safe delivery and newborn babies are brought to be blessed. Suiten-gu was rebuilt in 1967.

Festivals: May 5

Ennichi: The fifth of each month

ASAKUSA JINJA: Sanjasama   2-3-1 Asakusa, Taito-ku. Tel: 3844-1575. [M-12]

One of the few buildings in the area to escape undamaged after World War II, the shrine building dates from the thirteenth century when it was built in honor of the three fishermen who found the Kannon image now enshrined in the nearby Senso-ji temple.

Festivals: May 17-19

TOSHO-GU 9-88 Ueno-koen, Taito-ku. Tel: 3821-8494. [M-13]

Dedicated to the first Tokugawa shogun Ieyasu, this shrine was erected in 1651 and is the only shrine in Tokyo designated as a National Treasure. The shrine was built in the elaborate and very Chinese *gongen* style popular in the Momoyama (1568–1600) and early Edo (1600–1868) periods, and is second only to the Tosho-gu shrine in Nikko (Tochigi Prefecture) as an example of this type of architecture. The path to the shrine is lined with two hundred stone lanterns donated by various daimyo when the shrine was built and a number of bronze lanterns donated when the shrine was renovated in 1651. Inside the shrine are four paintings of animals by the well-known Kano Tan'yu of the Kano school of art that was active during the Momoyama period (1568–1600).

The Chinese-style gate to the temple is attributed to Hidari Jingoro, a famous artist of the Edo period, as is the stone *torii* at the entrance of the shrine. Both are listed as National Treasures. Festivals: Apr. 17

KAMEIDO TENJIN Kamei-do, Koto-ku. Tel: 3681-0010. [M-41]

Another shrine dedicated to the Heian-period scholar Sugawara Michizane, this one, founded in 1662, was a favorite of the Tokugawa shogun. The present building dates from 1961. The shrine is famous for its wisteria vines that bloom in late April.

Festivals: The twenty-fifth of every month from June–Aug., chrysanthemum viewing from end of Oct.–mid-Nov., wisteria viewing from mid-Apr.–early May.

NEZU JINJA 1-28-9 Nezu, Bunkyo-ku. Tel: 3822-0753. [off map]

This shrine, dedicated to four Shinto deities and to the popular Sugawara Michizane, is thought to have been founded nearly two thousand years ago. The present building was rebuilt by the fifth Tokugawa shogun Tsunayoshi in 1706. The shrine's main hall (*honden*), the two story main gate (*romon*), the Chinese gate (*kara-mon*); the oratory hall (*haiden*), and a wooden fence located nearby are all designated Important Cultural Properties. The shrine is also famous for its over three thousand azalea bushes that bloom in late April. On the grounds of the shrine is a small Otome Inari Shrine famous for its rows of red *torii*. [off Map, see **Walking Tours: Ueno**] Festivals: Sept.20–21, Apr.14–May 5, azalea viewing

PARKS AND GARDENS

The best expression of the Japanese self-acclaimed love of nature is the garden. Traditionally planned before the home, the garden was an integral part of the living environment. The Japanese do love nature, but a nature discreetly tamed and controlled in an orderly, balanced miniature of reality. Grand landscapes are reproduced in a garden, mountains, lakes, and rivers but all on a smaller, more human scale. In an abstract Zen garden, the meaning of the cosmos is believed to be contained within a few symbolic rocks strategically placed in a bed of raked sand or gravel. A tea-ceremony garden is designed with the intention of creating a poetic mood of solitary detachment from the world.

Where space permits, small gardens are meticulously cultivated and cared for. Where a garden is not possible within the limited confines of the city, potted plants and trees line the pavement. Even in the most industrialized parts of the city, a night watchman will nurse a lush oasis into bloom on the back steps of a warehouse.

Parks

UENO KOEN 5-20 Ueno-koen, Taito-ku. [M-13]

A major cultural center for the city, Ueno Park has the Tokyo National Museum, the Tokyo Metropolitan Art Museum, the National Museum of Western Art, and the National Science

Museum (all in the museum section). There are numerous shrines, temples, a zoo, the Tokyo University of Fine Arts and Music, and the large Shinobazu Pond. The park is one of the wildest places for cherry-blossom viewing found in Tokyo. (see **Walking Tours: Ueno**).

HIBIYA KOEN   1-6 Hibiya-koen, Chiyoda-ku. [M-10]

Close to the Imperial Palace, the Hibiya Park area was the site of important daimyo mansions during the Edo period. After the Meiji Restoration, the daimyo packed up and left for the provinces and the land became a parade ground for the new Western-style army. Plans to build a bureaucratic center here were dropped when the ground proved too marshy to support the weight of major construction, and the land was opened in 1903 as the first Western-style park in Japan. Fairly basic as parks go, it's noted for its azaleas in April and chrysanthemums in November. There are over two hundred species of trees planted on forty-one acres, including dogwoods sent from Washington D.C. in exchange for a Japanese gift of cherry trees.

KITANOMARU KOEN   1-1 Kitanomaru-koen, Chiyoda-ku. [M-17]

On the north side of the Imperial Palace is Kitanomaru Park, the former home of the Imperial Palace guards. The park was opened to the public in 1969 in honor of the present emperor's sixtieth birthday. One small area along the moat, Chidorigafuchi Park, is famous for its cherry trees. Other attractions include the Tokyo Museum of Modern Art, the Crafts Gallery, and the Science and Technology Museum.

MEIJI JINGU GAIEN (Meiji Shrine Outer Garden)   9 Kasumigaoka, Shinjuku-ku. [M-5]

Also known as the Meiji Olympic Park, the funeral for the emperor Meiji was held here in 1912. The park opened in 1925 after ten years of work, and is used primarily as an athletic and recreational area. During the 1964 Olympics it was a major site for sports events, and now contains a baseball stadium, rugby field, the National Stadium, tennis courts, a swimming pool, and the Nihon Seinen-kan concert hall. The Shotoku Kinen Kaigakan is a small museum on the grounds and exhibits eighty paintings of events in the life of the Emperor Meiji (open 9:00 A.M.–5:00 P.M. daily).

YOYOGI KOEN   2 Jinnan, Shibuya-ku. [M-4]

Located to the left of the Meiji Shrine grounds, Yoyogi Park is dominated by the National Indoor Stadium designed by Tange Kenzo for the 1964 Olympics. The headquarters of the NHK broadcasting station are found here, as well as the NHK concert hall. After the war the area was called Washington Heights and held the U.S. Army barracks. Now it's a favorite spot for exhibitionistic Japanese kids on Sunday afternoons.

ARISUGAWA KOEN   5-7-29 Minami Azabu, Minato-ku. [M-2]

Built around a hill in the Azabu residential area near Roppongi, the park has a decidedly local feeling about it. There are lots of trees, paths, bridges, streams, a lotus pond, a plum orchard, wisteria trellises, and a flat area on top of a hill with a library. A statue in the middle of the park depicts Arisugawa no Miya Taruhito Shinno (1835–95), a member of the Arisugawa branch of the imperial family.

Gardens

KOISHIKAWA KORAKUEN   1-6-6 Koraku, Bunkyo-ku. Hours: 9:00 A.M.–4:30 P.M. Tel: 3811-3015. [M-30]

Begun in 1629 by a member of the Tokugawa clan and completed thirty years later, the garden replicates famous scenic spots in Japan and China and combines design elements from both countries. There are numerous bridges, ponds and rivers full of carp, stones, lanterns, and monuments. Most famous are the stone Full Moon Bridge and a small temple to Benten, the goddess of good luck. The garden is laid out as a strolling garden and has an area of nearly eighteen acres. Designated an Outstanding Scenic Place of Historical Importance.

RIKUGIEN   6-16-3 Hon-komagome, Bunkyo-ku. Hours: 9:00 A.M.–4:30 P.M., closed Mon. Tel: 3941-2222. [M-38]

A favorite strolling garden for the Edo-period elite, Rikugien was landscaped in the late seventeenth century by Yanagisawa Yoshiyasu, a high-ranking feudal lord. The garden recreates eighty-eight well-known scenic spots in Chinese and Japanese literature, with rivers, ponds, forests, a small mountain, and a teahouse. The land was bought by the Iwasaki family (founders of the Mitsubishi empire) in the early Meiji period (1868–1912), and donated to the city in 1934.

KIYOSUMI TEIEN   3-3-9 Kiyosumi, Koto-ku. Hours: 9:00 A.M.–4:30 P.M. Tel: 3641-5892. [M-25]

Kiyosumi Garden, built by the baron Iwasaki in 1878 on the former site of a daimyo estate, is best known for its collection of huge rocks brought from all over Japan (by Mitsubishi ships). Beautifully landscaped, the garden surrounds a small pond that holds nearly ten thousand carp, the largest being over one meter in length. Other features include an island, bridges, a teahouse, and a small play area for children. The twelve-acre garden was donated to the city in 1924.

HAMA RIKYU TEIEN (Hama Detached Palace Garden)   1-1 Hama Rikyu Teien, Chuo-ku. Hours: 9:00 A.M.–4:00 P.M., closed Mon. Tel: 3541-0200. [M-22]

A visit to this former site of a Tokugawa shogun's villa will give you a good view of what life for the upper class was like during the Edo period. The garden centers around a tidal pond and three bridges covered by wisteria-vine trellises. There are other ponds, an island, a stretch of pine-shaded beach, moon-viewing pavilions, and teahouses that can be rented out. The garden was opened to the public after World War II.

KOKYO HIGASHI GYOEN (Imperial Palace East Garden)   1 Chiyoda, Chiyoda-ku. Hours: 9:00 A.M.–3:00 P.M., closed Mon. & Fri. Tel: 3213-2050. [M-10]

Once the main part of Edo castle, the fifty-three acre park was opened to the public in 1968. The old castle moat surrounds the garden, which contains the Kyu-ninomaru garden, landscaped in 1630 by the third shogun Iemitsu. The main garden has the Imperial Music Hall (built in 1966 and designed by architect Imai Kenji) for performances of *bugaku* and *gagaku* (court music) and a few remains of old castle buildings including the base of the main castle tower. You can enter the garden through three gates: the *Ote-mon*, the *Hiradawa-mon*, or the *Kita-hanebashi-mon*.

SHINJUKU GYOEN   11 Naito, Shinjuku-ku. Hours: 9:00 A.M.–4:00 P.M., closed Mon. Tel: 3350-0151. [M-7]

One of the largest gardens in the city (nearly 150 acres), the land was formerly the estate of the family of the Edo-period Naito daimyo. The gardens became the property of the imperial family and were opened to the public after World War II. A terrific strolling garden, it contains both a traditional Japanese-style garden, a formal French garden, and a greenhouse for tropical and sub-tropical plants (open year round). The garden is noted for its cherry blossoms in the spring and its chrysanthemum exhibitions in the fall.

MEIJI JINGU GYOEN (Meiji Shrine Inner Garden)   1-1 Yoyogi Kamizono-cho, Shibuya-ku. Hours: 9:00 A.M.–4:30 P.M. daily. [M-4]

Encircling the important Meiji Shrine, this garden contains more than 126,000 trees donated from all parts of Japan when the shrine was constructed in 1920. An iris garden is located near the south entrance (near Harajuku Station), a favorite garden of the Meiji emperor and empress. In early summer more than one hundred varieties of irises are in bloom. Nearby is the South Pond, noted for its midsummer waterlilies.

Botanical Gardens

KOISHIKAWA SHOKUBUTSUEN   3-7-1 Hakusan, Bunkyo-ku. Hours: 9:00 A.M.–4:00 P.M., closed Mon. Tel: 3814-0138. [off Map]

Part of Tokyo University, the garden claims six thousand different plants including trees dating from the late seventeenth century. The garden was originally the grounds of the second shogun's detached palace, and was used by later shoguns for the cultivation of medicinal herbs. The early buildings are gone, but part of the landscaped garden remains.

JINDAI SHOKUBUTSU KOEN (Jindai-ji Temple Botanical Gardens)   5-31-10 Jindai-ji Moto-machi, Chofu-shi. Hours: 9:30 A.M.–4:00 P.M., closed Mon. Tel: 0424-83-2300. [off Map, see **Temples and Shrines**]

This rather parklike botanical garden was formerly a wild forest area next to the grounds of Jindai-ji temple. A rose garden, an azalea garden, and a special hall for plant exhibitions have been open to the public since 1961.

MUKOJIMA HYAKKAEN   3-18-3 Higashi Mukojima, Sumida-ku. Hours: 9:00 A.M.–4:30 P.M., closed Mon. Tel: 3611-8705. [M-39]

Located in the Mukojima area east of Tokyo proper, the name Hyakkaen means "garden of one hundred flowers." The garden dates back to 1804 when Sahara Kikuu, a member of the Edo-period literary crowd, planted 360 plum trees given to him by his friends. The friends later helped lay out the rest of the garden using seasonal flowers from all over Japan. The garden became a favorite meeting spot for the Edo intelligentsia, but by the Meiji period had fallen into disrepair. After changing hands several times the garden was given to the city in 1938. Small, but full of flowers, the garden is at its best in springtime when the plum and cherry trees are in bloom. Located near the Sumida River, the garden makes a good addition to the walking course leading to the temple of the Seven Gods of Good Fortune.

HORIKIRI SHOBUEN   2-19-1 Horikiri, Katsushika-ku. Hours: 9:00 A.M.–4:30 P.M. daily. Tel: 3697-5237. [M-42]

This iris garden is famous as one of the *Forty-eight Views of Edo* depicted by the well-known *ukiyo-e* artist Hiroshige in the late Edo period. Opened in 1800, the garden was planted by a farmer who had collected seeds from all over Japan. There are over thirty different species of irises represented.

SHIZEN KYOIKUEN (National Park for Nature Study)   5-21-5 Shiroganedai, Minato-ku. Tel: 3441-7176. Hours: 9:30 A.M.–4:00 P.M., closed Mon. [M-19]

Part of the National Science Museum, contains outdoor exhibitions of wild plants and animals, and some fragments of natural vegetation from *Musashino,* pre-Edo Tokyo, that have been designated "National Monuments." Admission restricted to three hundred persons at a time.

ZOOS

UENO DOBUTSUEN   9 Ueno-koen, Taito-ku. Tel: 3828-5171. Hours: 9:30 A.M.–4:00 P.M., closed Mon. [M-13]

Ueno Zoo's major claim to fame is its pair of pandas, but for true animal lovers, the zoo is likely to be a traumatic experience. Not only are the animals kept in tiny depressing cages, but on weekends people outnumber them at least two to one.

TAMA DOBUTSU KOEN   7-1-1 Hodokubo, Hino-shi. Tel: 0425-91-1611. Hours: 9:30 A.M.–5:00 P.M. (enter by 4:00 P.M.), closed Mon. [off Map]

Opened in 1958 as a branch of the Ueno Zoo, the animals run free in the Tama Zoo's parklike setting. Moats separate man from beast. There is a lion park that you ride through in a bus. [From Shinjuku take the Keio Line express train. At Takahata Fudo Station change to the Keio Line going to Dobutsu Koen Station, the last stop on the line. On Sundays and holidays there is a direct line from Shinjuku to the zoo, leaving every twenty minutes.]

NOGEYAMA DOBUTSUEN   63-10 Oimatsu-cho, Nishi-ku, Yokohama-shi, Kanagawa-ken. Hours: 9:30 A.M.–4:30 P.M., closed Mon. [off Map]

Located in one corner of Yokohama's Nogeyama Park. Despite the feel of a neighborhood facility, this relaxed and enjoyable zoo does in fact contain some 224 species, ranging from elephants and lions to free-roaming peacocks. There is also an area where toddlers can play with ducks, goats, hamsters, etc. A fifteen-minute walk from Sakuragi-cho Station on the JR Keihin Tohoku, or Tokyu Toyoko Line.

AMUSEMENT/THEME PARKS

Amusement parks first became popular in the 1920s, as the big private railroad companies started diversifying from their commuter line and department store bases. The American version of Disneyland was the model for most although since its arrival in Tokyo in 1983 the competition has intensified, bringing a much greater variety to the genre. We've listed only a few of the many amusement parks located in the Tokyo area. Besides these, some parks have small amusement centers, as do department store rooftops.

TOKYO DISNEYLAND   1-1 Maihama, Urayasu-shi, Chiba-ken. Tel: 0473-54-0001. [off Map]

Just like in America. Hours vary from 8:30 A.M.–10:00 P.M. in mid-summer to 10:00 A.M.–6:00 P.M. in winter with extended hours on weekends. Open daily, but be sure to call to check (they occasionally schedule private events). Prices vary according to the type of ticket and are subject to change.

From Nihombashi or Otemachi Station take the Tozai subway line to Urayasu Station (15 min.). From the station it's a 5-minute walk to the Disneyland shuttle bus. The bus ride takes 20 minutes. Another route is from Tokyo Station, where direct shuttle buses are operated from a stop behind the Tekko Building on the Yaesu exit side of the station. The bus takes 35 min. (50 min. for the return trip).

SESAME PLACE   600 Kamiyotsugi Shiroiwa, Akiruno-shi. Tel: 0425-96-5811. Hours: 9:00 A.M.–5:00 P.M. (Hours vary with the season.) Closed on Wed. JR Musashi Itsukaichi Line, Akikawa Station. [off Map]

A theme park based on the *Sesame Street* TV show. The attractions are designed to encourage participation and to foster creativity, with no mechanical rides.

KORAKUEN   1-3 Koraku, Bunkyo-ku. Hours: 10:00 A.M.–6:00 P.M. daily. [M-30]

Close to Korakuen garden. These pleasure grounds are famous as the site of the Japan Baseball Series. The amusement center itself is medium sized; the major attractions are its huge roller coaster and the Circus Train that follows a circular track.

HANAYASHIKI YUENCHI   2-28-1 Asakusa, Taito-ku. Tel: 3842-4646. Hours: 10:00 A.M.–5:30 P.M. (until 6:00 P.M. on Sun. & hols.), closed Tues. [M-12]

Located next to Senso-ji temple in Asakusa, this is an old-style pleasure-ground that dates back to the Edo period when the temple was visited as much for the amusements it offered as for religious purposes. At the time it featured jugglers, wrestlers, freak shows, puppet shows, performing monkeys, etc. Now it's more like a small-time fair, with game booths, goldfish-catching games, vendors, and a modest roller coaster.

WILD BLUE YOKOHAMA   2-28-2 Heian-cho, Tsurumi-ku, Yokohama-shi, Kanagawa-ken. Tel: 045-511-2323. Hours: 10:00 A.M.–9:00 P.M. (varies with the season), daily from Apr. to Sept., closed Tue. Oct.–Mar., excluding Christmas, New Year's, and spring holidays. Closed approximately three weeks from mid-January. [off Map]

An indoor theme park with several pools of water and a "big bay" complete with regularly scheduled waves for bodysurfing. Swimsuits can be worn in all restaurants.

AQUARIUMS

KASAI RINKAI AQUARIUM (Kasai Rinkai Suizoku-kan)   6-2-3 Rinkai-cho, Edogawa-ku, Tokyo. Tel: 3869-5151. Hours: 9:30 P.M.–5:00 P.M., closed Mon., Kasai Rinkai-koen Station, JR Keiyo Line. [off Map]

The special attraction is a donut-shaped giant aquarium replete with numerous tuna. Building designed by Yoshio Taniguchi.

SHINAGAWA AQUARIUM (Shinagawa Suizoku-kan)   3-2-1 Katsushima, Shinagawa-ku. Tel: 3762-3431. Hours: 10:00 A.M.–5:00 P.M., closed Tues. [off Map]

Daily performances by dolphins and sea lions. Also a *fureai suiso* (communication tank) where the adventurous visitor can touch starfish and sea urchins.

HAKKEIJIMA SEA PARADISE   Hakkeijima, Kanazawa-ku, Yokohama-shi, Kanagawa-ken. Tel: 045-788-8888. Hours: 10:00 A.M.–8:00 P.M. daily. Keihin Kyuko Line to Kanazawa Hakkei Station, then Kanazawa Seaside Line to Hakkeijima. [off Map]

A man-made island halfway between Yokohama and Yokosuka has been given over in its entirety to a leisure complex including some traditional amusement park attractions, such as a roller coaster, set in unmistakably marine surroundings. The star attraction is a twenty-meter escalator tunnel of glass that carves its way through an enormous aquarium.

HISTORICAL SITES AND BUILDINGS

IMPERIAL PALACE (Kokyo)   Chiyoda, Chiyoda-ku. [M-10]

Located in the heart of the city, the Imperial Palace stands on the former site of Edo Castle. The largest castle in the land, Edo Castle was the administrative center for the Tokugawa shogunate. While the city of Edo was planned to serve the needs of the castle, for the city of Tokyo the palace is mostly an obstruction to traffic flow in the downtown areas. The castle grounds were taken over by the imperial family after the Meiji Restoration, and the Emperor has lived there since.

Most of the original buildings were destroyed during the 1945 air raids. A Japanese-style ferroconcrete palace was built in 1968, and in 1993 a new one was completed. You can enter the inner palace grounds and see the building only twice a year, on New Year's Day and on the emperor's birthday.

Surrounding the palace are the remains of the Edo Castle moats and three gardens, Higashi Gyoen (East Garden), Kitanomaru-koen park, and the outer garden.

NIJUBASHI BRIDGE Kokyo Gaien, Chiyoda, Chiyoda-ku. [M-10]

This is the main bridge into the inner palace. There are two spans in this copy of the bridge at Kyoto's Fushimi Castle. The first is constructed of stones saved from the old walls of the castle; the second is made of iron. The bridge is a classic spot for tour-group photo sessions.

NATIONAL DIET BUILDING (Kokkaigijido) 1-7-1 Nagatacho, Chiyoda-ku. [M-6]

Large and very official-looking, the building houses the Japanese parliament. Completed in 1936 after eighteen years of work, the building has a 215-foot-tall tower and has a total floor area of about thirteen acres. Entrance is almost impossible these days owing to unbelievably strict security precautions.

YUSHIMA SEIDO 1-4-25 Yushima, Bunkyo-ku. [M-16]

A Confucian shrine, Yushima Seido was connected with a school of Confucian learning for the Tokugawa elite. The shrine, first built in the seventeenth century, was destroyed during the 1923 Kanto earthquake. The present building of traditional temple architecture dates from 1965 and contains a statue of Confucius. You can enter the main building on Sat., Sun., & hol. from 10:00 A.M.–5:00 P.M.

AKAMON (Red Gate) 7-3-1 Hongo, Bunkyo-ku. [off Map]

Was originally the gate to the home of the Maeda, an important daimyo family during the Edo period. The gate was built to celebrate the marriage in 1827 of one of the Maeda sons to the daughter of the eleventh shogun. Now classified as an Important Cultural Property, the gate stands on the grounds of Tokyo University.

NIKOLAI CATHEDRAL (Nikorai-do) 4-1 Kanda Suruga-dai, Chiyoda-ku. [M-15]

Another Important Cultural Property, Nikolai Cathedral was founded by and is named after Archbishop Nikolai, the Russian priest who first introduced the Russian Orthodox Church to Japan. The Byzantine-style cathedral was completed in 1891 after seven years of work and, extensively damaged in the 1923 Kanto earthquake, was reconstructed in 1929. Several icons in the church date from the eighteenth century.

TOKYO TOWER 4-2-8 Shiba-koen, Minato-ku. Tel: 3433-5111. Hours: 9:00 A.M.–8:00 P.M. daily. [M-11]

One of the more whimsical aspects of Tokyo's skyline, the Tokyo Tower is a model of the Eiffel Tower in Paris, with 100 extra feet of height. Built in 1958, the 1,093-foot-tall tower was a huge hit and attracted over 10,000 people a day. It still pulls in daily crowds of nearly 10,000 sightseers. There is a broadcasting studio for TV Tokyo on the fifth floor, and a science museum and a wax museum downstairs. In front of the tower is a statue of Ando Takeshi, a sculptor most famous for his statue of Hachiko at Shibuya Station. Next to him is a statue of two more famous dogs, Taro and Jiro, who went to the south pole. Like the Leaning Tower of Pisa, Tokyo Tower is slowly, but surely, tilting to the side.

NIHOMBASHI BRIDGE 1-1 Nihombashi, Chuo-ku. [M-9]

In the Edo period, all roads led to this bridge, and all distances throughout the country were measured from a spot now marked by an iron post. The bridge was first built in 1603, the year Tokugawa Ieyasu assumed the title of Shogun. Twelve men were buried alive in the foundations to give it added strength. The current bridge, built in 1911, is one of the few constructions in the city that survives from the Meiji period. Once a favorite subject of *ukiyo-e* printmakers, the bridge is now hidden in the shadows of an elevated expressway.

BANK OF JAPAN (Nihon Ginko) 2-1-1 Nihombashi Hongoku-cho, Chuo-ku. [M-9]

This institution stands on a site formerly occupied by the Tokugawa gold mint. The new bank, completed in 1896, was the first Western-style building to be designed and built entirely by Japanese people. The building, designed by architect Tatsuno Kingo (he also designed Tokyo Station), is vaguely Renaissance style. As one of the few remaining Meiji-period buildings, the bank is classified as an Important Cultural Property.

GEIHIN-KAN 2-1-1 Moto-akasaka, Minato-ku. [M-6]

Also known as the Former Akasaka Detached Palace, the building is a copy of Buckingham

Palace on the outside and Versailles on the inside. The Geihin-kan now serves as a lodging for state guests, but was formerly the home of the crown prince who was later to become the Taisho emperor (1912–26). Katayama Toyu (1854–1917), a leading architect of the time, designed the building, which was completed in 1908.

KYU IKEDA YASHIKI OTEMON   13 Ueno-koen, Taito-ku. [M-13]

The former main entrance to the home of the Ikeda family, the gate was built during the late Edo period in a grand style allowed to only the most important daimyo. The gate was originally located in Marunouchi, then moved to Takanawa-dai and used as the main east entrance to the Imperial Palace. In 1954 it was moved to its present site in Ueno and designated an Important Cultural Property.

NOGI TEI (General Nogi's House)   8-11 Akasaka, Minato-ku. [M-1]

General Nogi Maresuke was an important Meiji-period military leader famous for his role in the Japanese victory during the Russo-Japanese War. When the emperor Meiji died in September 1912, the general and his wife committed ritual suicide out of loyalty. The general cut his stomach, then his wife slit her throat with her knife before falling on it and dying herself. You can visit the room where this happened in their former home near Nogizaka (literally "Nogi Hill"). Next door is the Nogi Shrine, a Shinto shrine built in honor of the loyal general.

KODOKAN   1-16-30 Kasuga, Bunkyo-ku. [M-30]

The oldest and largest judo institute in Japan, the present building was completed in 1958.

NIHON BUDOKAN   2-3 Kitanomaru-koen, Chiyoda-ku. [M-17]

Originally built for the 1964 Olympics martial arts competitions, the Budokan is perhaps most famous as a stadium for huge rock concerts, many of which are recorded and made into records titled *Live at the Budokan*. The building itself is a modern interpretation of the architectural design of Horyu-ji temple in Nara. Seating capacity is 14,000.

CEMETERIES

AOYAMA BOCHI   2-33 Minami Aoyama, Minato-ku. [M-5]

Formerly the estate of the Aoyama daimyo family, the area became a municipal graveyard in 1872. One of the famous local spots for contemplating cherry blossoms, the cemetery has over 100,000 graves. The most famous of the interred are General Nogi (1912); Hamaguchi Osachi, a former prime minister assassinated by a young nationalist (1930); Inukai Tsuyoshi, another assassinated prime minister (1932); and Ichikawa Danjuro, one of the most famous Kabuki actors of all time (1903).

YANAKA BOCHI   7 Yanaka, Taito-ku. [M-13]

Next to Kan'ei-ji temple, Yanaka graveyard occupies the former grounds of Tenno-ji temple that was burned during the battle of the Meiji Restoration in Ueno. The area became a municipal cemetery in 1874 and is famous for its cherry blossoms and ginkgo trees. A few of the more illustrious "residents" are Tokugawa Yoshinobu, the last shogun (1913); Yokoyama Taikan, a famous painter (1958); and Father Nikolai, founder of Nikolai Cathedral (1912).

WALKING TOURS

Tokyo is full of great walking districts. Just about any neighborhood has back streets full of old houses and shops that are interesting for even longtime residents. We've written up four walks through particularly old historical areas. Shops, restaurants, and museums introduced solely in the walk section have been explained and opening hours given, all other places have been described elsewhere in the text.

Shitamachi Tour

• **Asakusa–Sumida–Kappabashi** [M-12]

There are two ways to get to Asakusa. Most fun is to take the Suijo Bus (a small ferry) from Hama Rikyu Garden. You can start off with a walk through the garden, then catch the boat that leaves from a dock on the east side. The boat normally leaves every forty minutes (from 10:00 A.M. until sunset), but departs more frequently on Sundays, holidays, and during the busy season in spring and summer. The ride to Asakusa takes thirty-five minutes. The other way is to take the Ginza subway line to Asakusa Station, the end of the line. Exit by the middle staircase on the platform, and after passing through the ticket booth, turn left and go up the staircase to street level. Cross over towards the ferry dock where Sumida Park begins.

Sumida Park has been a famous spot for viewing the cherry blossoms since the Edo period. The park follows the banks of the **Sumida River** on both the east and west banks (you're on the west). Stroll through the park until you reach the **Kototoi Bridge,** then cross the east side of the river. A ten minute walk to the left will bring you to **Chomei-ji temple,** a famous Edo period spot for snow viewing. The history of the temple is rather obscure, but its reputation rests on the story of how, when the third shogun Tokugawa Iemitsu stopped off at the temple with a stomachache after a hard day of hunting, the priest gave him a tonic using water from the temple well. The shogun's stomachache disappeared and the temple was thereafter called Chomei-ji, meaning "Long Life."

Near the temple are two Japanese sweet shops, **Kototoi Dango** and **Chomei-ji Sakuramochi** both established since the Edo period. Stop for tea and cherry mochi at Chomei-ji Sakuramochi. If the cherry trees are in bloom, you can sit beneath the pink petals in the park across the street. There is a newly built, beautiful pedestrian-only bridge called "Sakura-bashi" nearby. After finishing the fragrant cherry mochi follow the riverside Sumida Park south to the **Azuma Bridge** just before which you will see a monolithic black building with a large yellow abstract sculpture on the roof. This building belongs to Asahi beer and there is a beer hall inside (see pg. 97). When you cross the bridge you'll find yourself back where you started.

Walk down the right side of the main street that leads from the bridge. The street, called Kaminarimon-dori, is lined with shops and restaurants and will take you to the front gate of **Senso-ji temple.** Right across the street from **Kaminarimon,** on the corner, is an information center called the **Asakusa Bunka Kanko Center** (Tel: 3842-5566), where English-speaking staff are available daily (9:30 A.M.–5:00 P.M.) to answer questions about the Asakusa area. The large gate Kaminarimon with its giant lantern is named for the god of thunder, a Buddhist guardian deity whose statue is in the left side of the gate. On the right is the god of lightning. The original gate was lost in the 1867 Edo fire and wasn't rebuilt until 1960.

Pass through the gate and you're on **Nakamise-dori,** a street with over one hundred shops catering to temple visitors. The arcade-like shops were first built by the city in the mid-Meiji period. The buildings were destroyed during the great earthquake (1923), but the rebuilt shops look much the same as the earlier ones. At the end of the shopping arcade is the **Hozomon** "Treasure Storing" gate. The upper rooms of the gate store the temple's sacred library of sutras and Buddhist scriptures that date from the fourteenth century. The two statues on each side of the gate are Nio, or Deva Kings, another type of guardian deity. This gate was destroyed in the 1867 fire and rebuilt in 1964. To the left is a five story red-and-gold pagoda **"Goju-no-to"** modeled after the tenth century pagoda of Daigo-ji temple in Kyoto. The **Senso-ji pagoda** was first built in 1639, and rebuilt in 1970. Inside are four wooden statues of Buddha.

After visiting the main hall of Senso-ji, stop by the **Asakusa Jinja** shrine to the right. Both the shrine and its gate remain in their original Edo-period form and are designated "Important Cultural Properties." As you leave the shrine, walk straight up the street in front of you, which will lead you to **Hyakusuke** (see pg. 134), a traditional cosmetics shop, **Kuremutsu** (see pg. 91), a restaurant in a lovely old house, **Fujiya** (see pg. 136), specializing in *tenugui* printed hand-towels, and further down on the left **Tatsumiya** (see pg. 91), a restaurant in an old house full of antiques. Stop here for a quiet lunch. When you've finished lunch you can wander around the shopping area, being sure not to miss **Kurodaya,** for paper crafts, **Hasetoku** (see pg. 132) for traditional shoes, and **Hosendo Kyuami** (see pg. 133) for fans.

For a restful interlude in the afternoon visit the **Demboin Garden** (open until 3:00 P.M., closed Sun. & hol.) to the left as you approach the main temple hall. Permission to enter the garden can be obtained at the five-story pagoda near the temple, in an office called the *shomuka* located in the left hand side of the tower (third door on the left). Ask to see the garden, sign your name and address in the register, and you'll be given a free entry ticket. The garden dates from at least the early seventeenth century and has a double pond, a tea house, and a large bronze bell cast in 1387. On the way to the garden, there are a number of rummage-sale-like stalls set up (weather permitting). The stalls sell a mixture of old *kimono,* old military gear, used suits, etc.

Further to the left you'll reach the theater district where the first movie theater in Japan was built in 1903. Theater had been in the area since Kabuki was moved from the Ginza in 1842, when the government tried to "clean up" the central downtown neighborhoods and reform the pleasure-seeking merchant class. In the Taisho and early Showa periods, Asakusa was the city's theater center with numerous music halls, cabarets, and movie houses. There are still movie theaters, but the district is best known for its rather seamy side. The famous **Furansu-za,** an old-time strip joint, still remains. Traditional variety shows are also presented in a number of theaters including the **Mokubakan,** whose major attraction is the *"Shitamachi* (downtown)*-no Tamasaburo"*—a minor actor who has taken the name of a famous Kabuki star.

To the north, the shopping area continues. Here you'll find **Kiriya,** a shop selling festival clothing, and **Hanato** selling paper lanterns. Back towards the temple is the **Hanayashiki** pleasure grounds, a slightly corny amusement park with a small-town fair atmosphere.

Return back though the theater district and the arcade to the main street Kaminarimon-dori. Turn right and across the street on top of a building you'll see the Jintan tower, a blue building that looks rather like a light house. An advertisement for Jintan breath freshener, the tower is modeled after the Ryounkaku, a twelve-story "cloud scraper" that was the modern wonder of mid-Meiji period Asakusa. Cross the street towards the tower to **Miyamoto Unosuke Shoten** (see pg. 130) selling portable shrines and Japanese drums. On the fourth floor, there is a drum museum "Taiko-kan" (Tel: 3842-5622. Hours: 10:00 A.M.–5:00 P.M., closed Mon. & Tue. during the summer), where six hundred different kinds of drums from all over the world are on display and may be played by visitors. Take the street between the shop and the police box, turn right at the first crossing, keep going straight until the road dead-ends at Kappabashi-dori. Turn left and walk through the arcade until you reach the large street called Kappabashi-dogu-gai. Here you'll find the **Kappabashi wholesale market,** an entire district of shops specializing in restaurant supplies (wax food models, sushi chef costumes, tableware, etc.).

• **Ueno–Yanaka–Nezu** [M-13]

Take the Ginza Line to Ueno Station—climb the stairs in the middle of the platform, pass the ticket booth, turn right, then on the right you'll see the sign for exit #7. Now turn left and go out to ground level. Or take the Hibiya Line to Ueno Station (ride the last car going toward Kita Senju)—follow the signs to the Ginza Line and look for exit #7 near the Ginza Line ticket booth. If you use the JR Yamanote Line, then exit at Ueno and take the steps at the end of the platform toward Okachimachi, and use the Shinobazu exit.

Facing the crossing, you'll see a wide stone staircase diagonally to your left on the opposite side. Climb the staircase, then take the stairs on the right. On the right hand side at the top is a bronze statue of **Saigo Takamori** by Takamura Koen. The statue was erected in 1892 in honor of this Meiji Restoration Army general who negotiated for the bloodless surrender of the Tokugawa Shogunate's capitol—Edo. The surrender, however, was not quite bloodless. After the city was turned over in April 1868, Tokugawa loyalists retreated to the hills of Ueno and continued to resist. The Restoration Army led an attack a month later that broke the resistance and destroyed most of the buildings on the hill. The **Shogitai Kinenhi,** a monument to the loyal Tokugawa samurai who died in the battle, was erected close to Saigo Takamori's statue.

Nearby on the left is the **Kiyomizu Kannon Temple,** built in 1698 as a small scale copy of the Kiyomizu Temple in Kyoto. Dedicated to Kannon, the Buddhist goddess of mercy, the temple is frequented by childless parents (the temple festival is Sept. 15, see the calendar). The temple is an "Important Cultural Asset." Down the stairs behind the temple is a black gate, the *Kuromon.* This *Kuromon* is a copy of the Edo-period front gate to Kan'ei-ji temple, the main temple of Ueno hill. Pass through the gate, turn right, and keep straight on the main path until you see a large totem pole. Turn left and continue walking. On your left you will see the gate to **Toshogu Shrine,** dedicated to Tokugawa Ieyasu.

After visiting the Toshogu shrine, stop for Japanese sweets and green tea at **Shin Uguisu-dango** just to the left of the shrine's main gate (Hours: 10:00 A.M.–5:00 P.M., closed Mon.). Order a small dish of *dango.* Continue down the main path and you will come to **Ueno Zoo,** famous for its pandas. The park's four museums are also concentrated in this area: the **Metropolitan Art Museum,** the **Science Museum,** the **Museum of Western Arts,** and the **National Museum** (all discussed in the Museum section). The main path ends as it hits the street bordering the north side of the park. Directly in front is the *Kyu-Ikeda Omote-mon.* To the right of the gate is the entrance to the National Museum, housing the largest collection of Japanese art in the world. When you exit from the museum, turn right and follow the main road back past the *Omote-mon.* Turn right at the first street, then take the second left, where you'll find **Kan'ei-ji temple** on the right hand side.

Stop by the temple, then continue down the road until it meets another road in a T (there is a police box on the right), turn left, then right at the next medium-sized street (where there is the Shitamachi Culture Museum Annex on the corner). On the right you will soon pass the **Yanaka Cemetery.** The street will then curve around to the left and lead to a local shopping area where several Meiji-period buildings remain. If you have time, take a short side trip to visit the **Asakura Chosokan,** a small memorial museum in the former home of the famous sculptor Asakura Fumio (1883–1964). To reach the museum, turn right at the corner when you come to Yamasaki Store on the right, and walk for about five minutes. The museum will be on your right.

When you've returned from the museum, continue down the street lined with small temples. As the road slopes downwards, on the left you'll pass **Isetatsu** (see pg. 121), a Japanese paper shop established in 1858. Further down on the right is **Kikumi Sembei,** a cracker shop established in the Edo period. Soon after the *sembei* shop is a main intersection. Turn left and follow the main road. After the fourth traffic light is another large intersection, Sendagi Ni-chome. Turn right and follow the road as it slopes upward. Walking on the left hand side of the street you'll pass one *torii* gate, a few buildings, then reach the entrance to **Nezu Shrine.** Three to four minutes up the hill from the shrine is a noodle shop, **Mukyoan,** in an older traditional home (Tel: 3815-4337. Hours: 11:00 A.M.–8:00 P.M., closed Sun. and third Sat.). Their *mukyo soba* is highly recommended for lunch.

Go back down the hill towards the main street, turn right, and walk toward Nezu station (Chiyoda line). On the way you could take a detour and visit the **Daimyo Clock Museum** (see pg. 195). At Nezu Station, take the subway to the next stop, Yushima (you can walk the distance in about ten minutes by just continuing down the same road). Get on the last car of the train and at Yushima, take the nearest exit on the left (#3) as you pass through the ticket booth, which will let you out at a large intersection. From there, walk straight in the direction of **Shinobazu Pond,** a traditional spot for viewing water lilies in the summer. Turn right at the second small street (just before you hit the main road). This the beginning of a shopping street called Nakamachi-dori, lined with eating and drinking places and small shops. On the right is **Kiya,** a shop for Japanese art supplies. On the left is **Hotan Yakkyoku,** one of the first pharmacies in the city, in an amusing early twentieth-century building. Next on the left is **Kyoya,** a shop specializing in traditional furniture, and then **Domyo,** a shop whose skill in making silk cords has been designated an "Intangible National Property."

You'll then come to a large street called Chuo-dori. Turn to the left, cross the street and turn left again. There will be a small entrance to Ueno Park. Enter the gate and on the right is the **Shitamachi Fuzoku Shiryokan** (see pg. 194) where a pre-earthquake downtown street has been re-created.

Back to the large intersection, cross the street towards a big modern building called "ABAB," and turn down the small street on the right hand side. Walk straight towards the railroad tracks where you'll find the **Ame-yoko** shopping arcade.

This walk should have taken you all day, in which case you'll be ready for dinner. In the Ueno area, you should try **Honke Ponta** (see pg. 81) for *tonkatsu,* or **Yansando** for Korean *yakiniku.* Or take a short taxi ride to the tofu restaurant **Sasanoyuki** (see pg. 87) or **Bon** (see pg. 73) for *shojin-ryori.*

• **Fukagawa–Kiyosumi Gardens–Tsukudajima** [M-25]

Take the Tozai Line to Monzennaka-cho (ride the front of the train going toward Kiba). Exit from the ticket booth, turn left and take the stairs to street level. To the right of the exit is the red gate to **Fukagawa Fudo Temple**. This

In Tsukudajima, back alleys like this one still exist in the shadow of modern tower blocks. © 1984 Tobias Pfeil

temple, a branch of the Narita Fudo Temple, was built in 1878 and reconstructed after the war.

Pass beneath the gate and follow the narrow shopping street to the temple. The street is lined with shops selling sweets and crackers. Try the *age-manju* at **Miyagetsudo.** After visiting the temple, turn left as you leave the grounds and walk straight until you reach the entrance to **Tomioka Hachimangu** shrine where sumo tournaments were held from 1684 to 1791. Behind the temple and to the right is a huge stone monument to the *yokozuna,* the grand champion sumo wrestlers. On the first, fifteenth, and eighteenth of each month the temple and shrine have a joint *ennichi* fair day where everything from fruit to toys to traditional undergarments are sold. The shrine holds a major festival every three years on August 19.

Walk through the shrine's main gate to Eita-dori, where a good *soba* restaurant, **Hoseian,** is located across the street and two doors down from an old *sembei* shop. Stop at Hoseian for lunch (Hours: 11:00 A.M.–3:00 P.M., 4:00 P.M.–8:00 P.M., closed Thu.), their tempura *soba* is great. After lunch start walking towards Kiyosumi Garden by following Eitai-dori to a big crossing. The cross street is Kiyosumi-dori which leads straight to the garden. Turn right on Kiyosumi-dori, walk straight, then cross a bridge and continue walking for about twelve minutes, until you see the thick foliage of the garden behind the wall on your left. Turn left at the next corner after passing a small playground, walk straight to the **Kiyosumi Garden** entrance.

Return to Kiyosumi-dori after visiting the garden, cross the street and take the #33 bus to **Tsukudajima** island. Get off the bus at Tsukishima-eki mae, six stops from the garden. You'll now be on the other side of the Sumida River.

In the Edo period, Tsukudajima was a tiny island, but has grown in size with reclamation projects started after World War II. The island is one of the few areas of town that suffered little damage in the 1923 earthquake and wasn't firebombed during the war. The narrow back alleys remain much the same as they were during the early part of the century. Wander around the streets behind the bus stop. Afterward, return to the bus stop and walk back, in the direction the bus came, to the first crosswalk. Cross the street and go straight until the road dead-ends. Turn left, then right to the **Tsukuda Kohashi,** a small bridge that crosses a swampy canal where old fishing boats are moored and wooden houses line the banks. Continue straight until you see the tall concrete wall built to protect the island from floods. Just before you reach the wall on the left will be a sign written in Japanese (住吉神社) directing you to **Sumiyoshi Jinja,** a shrine dedicated to the patron god of this traditional island home of fishermen.

Exiting from the shrine, walk towards the sea wall, turn to the left and you'll come to in an old house with the shop's name written on a square lantern in front. The shop sells *tsukudani* that are famous throughout Japan.

Walking past Ten'yasu, you'll see a large bridge that crosses the river. Walk through the underpass and turn left on the other side. Walk straight along the bridge to the first crossing and turn right, then left at the next street. There will be a sports center on the right-hand side of the next corner, and straight ahead is the Tsukishima neighborhood shopping arcade. The shopping area has a wonderful small-town feeling you won't find anywhere else in Tokyo.

After doing your shopping or browsing, return to the bridge and cross over to the Tsukiji district. At the end of the bridge turn right and keep straight until you see a beige building marked with a P for parking on the right. On the left-hand side, slightly before the parking building, is an orange brick apartment building on a corner. Turn left here. At the next signal turn right again and you'll reach **Teppozu Inari Shrine.** The shrine, built originally in 841, is famous for its miniature replica of Mt. Fuji built of lava. The "mountain" was, and still is, ascended by those too weak or too poor to ascend the real thing. The shrine's festivals are held in May and July. Leaving from the shrine's main gate, turn left and left again at the next street. Keep straight until you come to the main road, then turn right towards Hatchobori station on the Hibiya Line. From there you can go to Ginza, just a few subway stops away for a great meal (check the restaurant listings next to the Ginza map).

• **Goto Museum–Todoroki Ravine–Kuhonbutsu Temple–Okusawa Shrine–Jiyugaoka** [M-21]

If you're tired of big city life, take a short train ride to the suburbs for a glimpse at semi-rural Japan. This walking course starts off with a lovely museum. Take the Toyoko line from Shibuya Station to Jiyugaoka Station. Change trains here to the Tokyu Oimachi Line (you must change platforms, use the center staircase) and take the train to Kaminoge Station (four stops from Jiyugaoka). When you exit from the station, cross the main street and follow a street that is slightly to the left of the traffic light. At the second crossing turn right, and you'll see the beige-colored fence surrounding the museum. The **Goto Museum** is small but has an excellent collection of Asian art. The museum grounds are large and beautiful, with both a natural and landscaped garden, tea houses, a pond, statues, etc.

After the museum, return to Kaminoge Station and take the train back to Todoroki Station (walking takes about ten minutes). Exit the station past the photo developing booth, and turn left onto the street crossing the tracks. Then take a right, about fifty meters up, between a large tree and a tofu store. There you'll find a small spiral staircase that leads down to the banks of the Yazawa River in **Todoroki Keikoku** ravine. This is the only ravine in the Tokyo vicinity that has remained in its natural condition. The river itself is small and not particularly beautiful, but as you continue along the one-kilometer ravine the view improves somewhat. Across the river is a garden you can reach by a bridge. Further along you'll find a small waterfall called **Fudo no Taki,** where since the Edo period ascetics would come to stand beneath the falls and suffer. Nearby is a small stone statue of the young Kobo Daishi (744–835), founder of the Shinton sect of Buddhism.

Go up the stairs on the right side, of the waterfall, to **Todoroki Fudo Temple,** founded eight hundred years ago by Kogyo Daishi.

From there you should return to Todoroki Station , and take the train back to Kuhonbutsu Station . A short walk from the station is **Kuhonbutsu Temple,** a branch of Zojo-ji temple in Shiba, built in 1678, In the three halls opposite the main hall are nine statues of Buddha by the priest Kaseki that date from the same period. The temple yard is quiet (this is not a major sightseeing spot) and covered with huge trees.

Jiyugaoka, is a rather hip suburban community with boutiques, restaurants, coffee shops, etc. Have lunch or dinner at **Hana Kyabetsu,** a coffee-and-pancake shop serving over thirty kinds of pancakes (1-7-3 Jiyugaoka.

Tel: 3724-0310. Hours: 3:00 A.M.–11:00 P.M. daily), **Motomachi** (see pg. 88) for *okonomiyaki* or *teppan-yaki,* **La Jolla,** a Mexican restaurant with friendly atmosphere (1-24-8 Jiyugaoka. Tel: 5701-1737. Hours: 11:00 A.M.–2:00 P.M., 5:00 P.M.–10:00 P.M., closed Tue.)

Other Walks

In addition to the four walks we have already given, good walking tours can be made in other parts of town. Use the maps listed below each suggested course.

Yushima–Kanda: From Ochanomizu Station. See Yushima Seido Shrine, Amanoya (*amazake* shop), Kanda Myojin Temple, Yushima Shrine, *Akamon* (at Tokyo University), pass Ochanomizu Station again, Jimbocho (secondhand book district), Kanda (old restaurants), Akihabara (electronics district). [M-15 & 16]

Nihombashi–Ningyocho: Starting from either Nihombashi Station on the Ginza Line, or Ningyocho Station on the Hibiya Line. The area is full of old shops and great for wandering around. There is also the Suiten-gu shrine. [M-9 & 23]

OUTSIDE TOKYO

Whether you are just visiting Tokyo, but especially if you are living here, the urge to escape the city is bound to strike. Below we have recommended a few day trips and a couple of weekend excursions. Our space here is limited so we haven't given as many details as we would like. For further information, please contact the Tourist Information Center.

Kamakura

In 1185 the seat of Japanese government was moved from Kyoto to Kamakura under the new military rule of Minamoto no Yoritomo. For a brief two hundred years the capital city enjoyed the patronage of the ruling classes whose adherence to the Zen sect of Buddhism is attested by the more than sixty temples that remain in this small community today. Just under one and a half hours from Tokyo, the city has a number of fine restaurants and shops that make it a perfect day trip.

Details: Take the JR Yokosuka Line from Tokyo Station to Kita Kamakura Station. Don't miss Meigetsu Temple and Kencho-ji temple. Then to the east see the tomb of Shogun Minamoto no Yoritomo; the Kakuon-ji temple; the Zuisen-ji temple with its beautiful garden; the oldest temple in the area, Sugimoto-dera temple; and the beautiful bamboo gardens at Hokoku-ji temple. Next take the train to Kamakura Station, and leave by the west exit to visit Tsurugaoka Hachiman-gu shrine, Sasuke Inari Shrine, Zeni Arai

Benten, the Great Buddha statue, and the Hase-kannon Temple. For shops and restaurants walk along Komachi-dori, from the east exit of Kamakura station. An excellent, but expensive restaurant is **Shin Tanaka** (1-13-5 Komachi, Tel: 0467-25-3447. Hours: 11:30 A.M.–9:00 P.M. daily, *kaiseki* cuisine).

Nikko

Nikko is best known as the site of Shogun Tokugawa Ieyasu's mausoleum, the Tosho-gu shrine. Completed in 1636, the Buddhist-Shinto complex is Japan's best example of the lavish gold leaf and vermilion Chinese-style architecture favored by the military classes. In addition to the Tosho-gu shrine grounds there is the Nikko Museum, the botanical gardens of Tokyo University, and the beautiful Nikko National Park and Kegon Falls.

A recent added attraction is **Nikko Edo-mura,** a theme park focused on life in Japan during the Edo period of the seventeenth to nineteenth centuries, featuring *ninja* performances that delight small children (470-2 Karakura, Fujiwara-cho, Shioya-gun, Tochigi-ken. Tel: 0288-77-1777. Open daily 9:00 A.M.–5:00 P.M.).

Nikko is located to the north of Tokyo. Several package tours for day and overnight excursions are offered by travel agents. You can go on your own. With a rail pass take the JR Tohoku Shinkansen from Ueno Station, change at Utsunomiya to the local train to Nikko or take the Tobu Line to Nikko from Asakusa Station (a limited express train takes one hour, fifty-five minutes, reservations required; the rapid train takes two hours, ten minutes).

Mount Fuji

It is rare, indeed, these days to catch a glimpse of Fujisan through the smog. The tallest mountain in Japan, Mount Fuji was long held sacred by Shintoists. A pilgrimage to the top of the mountain was something one had to do once in a lifetime. Even today a trek up the peak is a popular weekend outing. Over 300,000 people do it every year.

There are a number of guided tours to Mount Fuji. To go on your own you can either take the Fuji Kyuko Bus from Shinjuku (daily departures in the morning from the Chuo Kosoku bus terminal at the west exit of Shinjuku station. The ride takes two and a half hours) or take the Chuo Line from Shinjuku Station to Kawaguchi-ko, then catch a bus from the station (Fuji Kyuko bus, Tel: 3374-2221). The bus will take you to the fifth station of the mountain. You can climb further up if you wish. It takes about six hours to reach the top and four to return. Along the route are plenty of places to stop, rest, eat or drink, even places to sleep. Quite often people will plan their ascent so as to arrive at the top in time to view the sunrise.

健康

HEALTH AND BEAUTY

HEALTH AND BEAUTY

ASIAN MEDICINE

Though Asian medicine has long been viewed with skepticism by Western health-care professionals, the holistic theories behind these "exotic" methods have found a new level of respectability. Recent studies on the relationship between stress and the increasing rate of illness have questioned the fundamental theories of western medicine and its increasingly specialized medicinal or surgical treatment for physical disorders.

While in the West the symptoms of a disease are often mistaken for the disease itself, Asian medicine tends to see the symptoms as a sign of imbalance in the body. Treatment aims at correcting imbalances by stimulating both the flow of energy and the body's own self-healing powers.

The major types of treatment are *hari* (acupuncture), *shiatsu* (pressure point massage), *kyu* (moxibustion or heat treatment) and *seitai* (a form of chiropractic). Each of the major organs has its own "pulse" showing activity, or lack of such, in that organ. Treatment is applied not only to the ailing organ but to the entire body. By inserting needles, or applying heat or finger pressure to a series of defined points on lines of energy called meridians, the body's energy flow is stimulated, blood circulation is improved, muscle fatigue and nervous aches and pains are relieved, while internal organs are generally "toned-up."

Treatment is not necessarily immediately effective, and several treatments over a period of time may be advisable. Western skeptics should note that the methods have been proven and used in China for over 4,000 years.

Hari—Acupuncture
ORIENTAL MEDICAL RESEARCH CENTER (Toyo Igaku Kenkyujo)   Kitazato Daigaku Byoin, 5-9-1 Shirogane, Minato-ku. Tel: 3444-6161.

For the first visit you must go between 8:00–10:00 A.M., Mon.–Sat. Go to the No. 1 reception desk and ask for *hari*. You will be given forms to fill out. Only a little English is spoken, but the doctors are great. [M-2]

DR. YUKIO KUROSU 1-1-32 Negishi, Taito-ku. Tel: 3841-2595. Hours: 9:00 A.M.–3:00 P.M. (until 6:00 P.M. on Tue. & Fri.), closed Sat., Sun., & hol.

English spoken. By appointment. [M-13]

KOJIMACHI REBIRTH Kur Haus Bldg., 2F. 4-2-12 Kojimachi, Chiyoda-ku. Tel: 3262-7561. Hours: 9:30 A.M.–9:00 P.M. (until 7:10 P.M. on Sat.), closed Sun. & hol.

Some English spoken. By appointment. They also offer massage and sauna therapy. [M-6]

TANI CLINIC Dainijusan Fuji Bldg., 5-4-10 Akasaka, Minato-ku. Tel: 3505-2771. Hours: 9:00 A.M.–5:00 P.M., closed Sun., Thu., & hol.

Acupuncture and Western Medicine [M-6]

DR. UCHI-IKE Sakamoto Bldg., 3F. 2-16-8 Dogenzaka, Shibuya-ku. Tel: 3464-4766. Hours: 8:00 A.M.–7:00 P.M. (9:00 A.M.–5:00 P.M. on Tue.), closed Sun. & hol.

Acupuncture and chiropractic techniques. Some English spoken. By appointment. [M-3]

Seitai—Chiropractic

TOKYO CHIROPRACTIC CENTER 3-5-9 Kita Aoyama, Minato-ku. Tel: 3478-2713. Hours: 9:00 A.M.–6:00 P.M., closed Thu., Sun. & hol.

English spoken. By appointment. [M-5]

WESTERN MEDICINE

While the care at Japanese hospitals may be fine, sometimes excellent, few foreigners will feel comfortable with the lack of English and the inability to make appointments. You simply have to go and wait your turn, which may take several hours. Care is inexpensive, however, for residents enrolled in the Japanese national health system. Under this plan, a patient pays only about 30 percent of the amount charged.

Private clinics tend to be favored by many. We haven't noted prices for the following clinics, but the cost for an initial visit usually runs from ¥6,000–¥8,000.

Clinics

TOKYO MEDICAL AND SURGICAL CLINIC 32 Mori Bldg., 2F. 3-4-30 Shiba-koen, Minato-ku. Tel: 3436-3028. Hours: 9:00 A.M.–5:00 P.M. (until 1:00 P.M. on Sat.), closed Sun.

Offers twenty-four-hour emergency service, general and specialist practice. English speaking. Probably the clinic of choice for most resident foreigners. [M-11]

NATIONAL MEDICAL CLINIC National Azabu Bldg., 5F. 4-5-2 Minami Azabu, Minato-ku. Tel: 3473-2057. Hours: 9:00 A.M.–7:30 P.M. (until 5:00 P.M. on Sat.), closed Sun. & hol.

English-speaking general practice. [M-2]

INTERNATIONAL CLINIC 1-5-9 Azabu-dai, Minato-ku. Tel: 3582-2646. Hours: 9:00 A.M.– noon., 2:30–5:00 P.M. (10:00 A.M.–noon on Sat.), closed Sun. & hol.

General practice. English, Russian, and Chinese spoken. [M-1]

TOHO FUJIN WOMEN'S CLINIC 5-3-10 Kiba, Koto-ku. Tel: 3630-0303. Hours: 1:00 P.M.– 6:00 P.M., Mon.–Fri. (until 4:00 P.M. on Sat.), closed Tue., Sun., & hol.

Inexpensive gynecological care by an English-speaking physician, Dr. Matsumine. [off Map]

KANDA DAINI CLINIC Umeda Bldg., 2F. 3-20-14 Nishi Azabu, Minato-ku. Tel: 3402-0654. Hours: 9:00 A.M.–noon, 2:00–4:00 P.M. (until 11:00 A.M. on Sat.), closed Sun. & hol.

Gynecological and obstetrical practice by English-speaking Dr. Makabe. [M-2]

DR. MICHIKO SUWA Hongoku Bldg., 3F. 5-25 Hiro-o, Shibuya-ku. Tel: 3444-7070. Hours: 9:30 A.M.–5:00 P.M., Mon.–Fri. (9:00 A.M.–noon on Wed. & Sat.), closed Sun.

Pediatrics, by an English-speaking female doctor trained in the States. [M-2]

Hospitals

Hospitals do not accept appointments, so you must show up, generally first thing in the morning, register at the reception area, and wait your turn. Hours for the hospitals and the different divisions within each are varied. Please call to confirm.

JAPAN RED CROSS HOSPITAL (Nisseki Iryo Center)   4-1-22 Hiro-o, Shibuya-ku. Tel: 3400-1311. [M-2]

ST. LUKE'S INTERNATIONAL HOSPITAL (Seiroka Byoin)   1-10 Akashi-cho, Chuo-ku. Tel: 3541-5151. [M-22]

ST. MARY'S INTERNATIONAL CATHOLIC HOSPITAL (Seibo Byoin)   2-5-1 Naka-ochiai, Shinjuku-ku. Tel: 3951-1111. [off Map]

TOKYO METROPOLITAN HIRO-O GENERAL HOSPITAL (Tokyo Toritsu Hiro-o Byoin)   2-34-10 Ebisu, Shibuya-ku. Tel: 3444-1181. [M-2]

NATIONAL CHILDREN'S HOSPITAL (Kokuritsu Shoni Byoin)   3-35-31 Taishido, Setagaya-ku. Tel: 3414-8121. [off Map]

Dental Care

TOKYO CLINIC DENTAL OFFICE   32 Mori Bldg., 2F. 3-4-30 Shiba-koen, Minato-ku. Tel: 3431-4225. Hours: 9:00 A.M.–6:00 P.M., closed Tue., Sun., & hol.
General dentistry and oral surgery. [M-11]

ISHII SHIKA   Onuki Bldg., 2F. 4-29-18 Nishi Gotanda, Shinagawa-ku. (Fudomae Station on the Tokyu Mekama Line). Tel: 3491-9004. Hours: 9:00 A.M.–5:30 P.M., closed Thur., first Sat. & Sun.
English-speaking. By appointment. [off Map]

Optical Care

TOKYO OPTICAL CENTER   Sone Bldg., 3F. 6-4-8 Ginza, Chuo-ku. Tel: 3571-7216. Hours: 10:00 A.M.–6:00 P.M., closed Sun. & hol.
Complete optical care. English spoken. [M-8]

INTERNATIONAL VISION CENTER   Kyowa Goban-kan Bldg., 3F. 3-3-13 Kita Aoyama, Minato-ku. Tel: 3497-1491. Hours: 10:00 A.M.–5:30 P.M., closed Sun. & hol.
Complete optical care. English spoken. By appointment only. [M-5]

Pharmacies

AMERICAN PHARMACY   Hibiya Park Bldg., 1-8-1 Yurakucho, Chiyoda-ku. Tel: 3271-4034. Hours: 9:30 A.M.–7:00 P.M. daily (11:00 A.M.–6:00 P.M. on hol.). [M-10]

THE MEDICAL DISPENSARY   32 Mori Bldg., 3-4-30 Shiba-koen, Minato-ku. Tel: 3434-5817. Hours: 9:00 A.M.–5:30 P.M. (until 1:00 P.M. on Sat.), closed Sun. & hol. [M-11]

NATIONAL SUPERMARKET PHARMACY   4-5-2 Minami Azabu, Minato-ku. Tel: 3442-3181. Hours: 9:30 A.M.–6:30 P.M. daily. [M-2]

ISUKURA YAKKYOKU   Suns Bldg., 2F. 1-7-2 Jingumae, Shibuya-ku. Tel: 3478-4382. Hours: 11:00 A.M.–6:30 P.M., closed Sun.
All kinds of Chinese medicine, specially mixed for the individual's particular ailment. [M-4]

NAGAI YAKKYOKU   1-8-10 Azabu-juban, Minato-ku. Tel: 3583-3889. Hours: 9:00 A.M.–7:00 P.M., closed Tue.
Natural Japanese and Chinese medicine. They can give consultations and prescriptions. Some English spoken. [M-1]

SENTO—PUBLIC BATHS

While a nice hot bath at the end of a long day is an appealing thought for most people, for the Japanese the love of bathing borders on the religious.

Until about twenty years ago most Japanese city dwellers bathed in *sento,* public bathhouses. More than just a place to wash, the *sento* was a social institution where, while scrubbing your neighbor's back, you could catch up on the local gossip. Though on a statistical average more Japanese families have color televisions than private baths, the regular bathhouse clientele now consists primarily of students and young people living in cheap apartments, or older people who just like the congenial bathhouse atmosphere. However, the idea of community bathing remains a pleasant one for most. Even today company or group outings are often planned around a visit to an *onsen* (hot-spring resort), where everyone soaks together in the steaming-hot pools.

Public baths are segregated by sex. You enter and pay the fee to the attendant who sits on a high platform overlooking both sides and doubles as a lifeguard. In most places you must bring all the bathing essentials: a towel, soap, shampoo, etc. Japanese generally use a small towel that, as the only concession to modesty, is draped nonchalantly in front of one's privates. After stripping in the locker room, you enter the tiled bathroom. Low along the wall will be a series of faucets (and sometimes shower heads). Sitting on one of the small stools, you thoroughly wash, scrub, and then rinse away remaining soap suds (as a foreigner you will always be under suspicion of breaking this rule). Only then do you climb into the communal bath and soak away your cares.

While few traditional bathhouses remain in Tokyo, we have listed some below, many of which are now located in modern buildings. You can often recognize a neighborhood bathhouse by its tall smokestack.

The entrance fee for basic bathhouses runs just over ¥300, at other specialized baths prices range from ¥600 to ¥2,000.

TSUBAME YU   3-14-5 Ueno, Taito-ku. Tel: 3831-7305. Hours: 6:00 A.M.–10:30 P.M., closed Mon.

This basic public bath has an *asayu no kai* (morning bath association) that gets together to bathe in the re-created mountain-grotto setting. [M-13]

GINZA YU   1-12-2 Ginza, Chuo-ku. Tel: 3561-2250. Hours: 3:00–11:30 P.M., closed Sun.

Another good, basic bathhouse. [M-8]

MITSUKOSHI YU   5-12-16 Shirogane, Minato-ku. Tel: 3441-9576. Hours: 3:30–11:00 P.M., closed Fri.

Standard public bath in a pre-war building. [M-2]

ASAKUSA KANNON ONSEN   2-7-26 Asakusa, Taito-ku. Tel: 3844-4141. Hours: 6:30 A.M.–6:30 P.M., closed Thu.

A truly classic bathhouse, the water is from a sodium chloride hot spring (great for rheumatism, nervous disorders, etc.) and is kept at a steady forty-five degrees Celsius. The walls are painted with the standard wall mural and every morning the *asayu no kai* meets for a friendly soak. The association has over a hundred members, most of them true bath-loving *Edokko.* [M-12]

AZABU-JUBAN ONSEN   1-5-22 Azabu-juban, Minato-ku. Tel: 3404-2610. Hours: 11:00 A.M.–9:00 P.M., closed Tue.

On the first floor is a *sento* with water from a hot spring. On the third floor is another spring

pool, a small sauna, a food shop, and a large tatami recreation room where amateur performances by mostly retired Japanese are given on Sundays from 2:00 or 3:00 P.M. until 5:00 P.M. [M-1]
BAIN DOUCHE Lions Station Plaza B1. 1-5-4 Kojimachi, Chiyoda-ku. Tel: 3263-4944. Hours: 4:00–10:30 P.M., closed Sun. & hol.

This small (but rather new and clean) bath is located two minutes from the moat of the Imperial Palace. Stop off here for a bath after jogging around the Palace course. [M-6]
PARU ONSEN Okazaki Bldg., 2F. 2-14-13 Shibuya, Shibuya-ku. Tel: 3409-4882/3. Hours: 10:00 A.M.–11:00 P.M., closed Thurs.

Has a jacuzzi bath, *shiatsu*, and massage. [M-3]
HEIWAJIMA KUR HAUS 1-1-1 Heiwajima, Ota-ku. Tel: 3768-9121. Hours: 10:00 A.M.–10:00 P.M. daily.

Huge, modern facilities with thirteen different kinds of hot-spring baths, a swimming pool, an athletic gym, a restaurant, etc. A bit like a bath wonderland. (Take east exit of JR Omori Station, and from bus stop No. 9 take bus to Leisureland Heiwajima.) [off Map]

Massage and Sauna

One of the great things about living in Tokyo are the neighborhood massage services. You will find their little postcard-sized advertisements in your mailbox. For the most part these are legitimate services, and when called either a man or a woman (often dressed in a charming white doctor's coat) will come around and give you a good working over. Away from home you can find massage services at health clubs, hotels, and some of the private bathhouses. A massage will cost from ¥4,000 to ¥6,000.

Most of these facilities also have baths, many have saunas.
SANWA MASSAGE Imperial Hotel, 4F. 3580-5449. Hours: 10:00 A.M.–9:00 P.M. daily.

Massage and pressure shower. [M-10]
KORAKUEN SAUNA (for men) Isetan Kaikan Bldg., 4F. 3-15-17 Shinjuku, Shinjuku-ku. Tel: 3352-2443. Hours: 11:00 A.M.–10:30 P.M., closed Wed.

Sauna and massage. [M-7]
LADIES SAUNA (5F in same building as above). Tel: 3356-2734. Hours: 10:00 A.M.–8:30 P.M., closed Wed.

Sauna, massage, and special body treatment. [M-7]
GREEN PLAZA SHINJUKU 1-29-2 Kabukicho, Shinjuku-ku. Tel: 3207-5411. Open twenty-four hours, until midnight on Sun.

Located in a large capsule hotel, instead of checking into a capsule after a very late night on the town you could come here and sweat off the hangover. Not exactly an upmarket establishment. [M-7]
KOJIMACHI REBIRTH (see **Acupuncture**) Women's sauna, men's massage.

SPORTS FACILITIES

Health and fitness are rather recent fads in Japan and a wealth of new sports facilities have been built to prove it. There are numerous public and private facilities. The public ones are often inexpensive (generally ¥300–¥500 per visit) and overcrowded; the private ones are usually for members only. Some of the larger hotels have facilities open to visitors with a fee that can run upward of ¥5,000.

Swimming pools follow the same rules. Most private pools belong to hotels or members-only sports centers. Hotel pools run upward of ¥4,000 per day, although some offer special evening discounts. During the summer many of the hotels offer a special summer membership for use of their outdoor pools.

The following hotels have sports facilities and allow visitors: Hotel New Otani (indoor & outdoor pool), Hotel Century Hyatt (indoor pool), Miyako Hotel (indoor & outdoor pool), Capitol Tokyu (outdoor pool), Hotel Okura (indoor & outdoor pool), Tokyo Prince Hotel (outdoor pool), Shinagawa Prince Hotel (indoor pool), and Holiday Inn (outdoor pool). Public and private outdoor pool opening dates vary each year.

TOKYO METROPOLITAN GYMNASIUM   1-17 Sendagaya, Shibuya-ku. Tel: 5474-2111. Hours vary according to the season, but basically 9:00 A.M.–9:00 P.M., closed the third Mon.

A huge complex including an indoor pool, work-out facilities, jogging track, etc. [M-29]

KOMAZAWA OLYMPIC PARK   1-1 Komazawa-koen, Setagaya-ku. Tel: 3421-6121.

An enormous sports complex originally built for the Tokyo Olympics. Includes an outdoor swimming pool (summer only), a training and workout gym (9:00 A.M.–5:00 P.M.), cycling courses, etc. Most facilities are closed on Mon. [off map]

TOKYO KOSEINENKIN SPORTS CENTER   4-7-1 Okura, Setagaya-ku. Tel: 3416-2611. Hours: noon–8:30 P.M. daily, from 11:00 A.M. on Sat., Sun., & hol.

Gym, sauna, and outdoor swimming pool (summer only). (From Shinjuku take the Odakyu Line to Seijo-gakuen Station. From there, the "Toritsudai Eki-yuki" bus takes about 10 min., and stops in front of the center.) [off Map]

NATIONAL GYMNASIUM SWIMMING POOL (indoor)   2-1-1 Jinnan, Shibuya-ku (in Yoyogi Park). Tel: 3468-1171.

There are three pools here; the Olympic pool and a small outdoor children's pool are open in the summer. The second indoor pool is open all year. Hours vary, closed the second and fourth Tue. of every month. [M-4]

MEIJI JINGU POOL (outdoor & indoor)   5 Kasumigaoka, Shibuya-ku (in Meiji Shrine Outer Garden). Tel: 3403-3456. Open June–Sept., Mon.– Sat. 10:00 A.M.–5:45 P.M. (enter by 5:00 P.M.), from 9:00 A.M. on Sun., from July 1-15 until 7:15 P.M. (enter by 6:30 P.M.), and from July 16–Aug. 31 until 8:45 P.M. (enter by 8:00 P.M.). [M-29]

MINATO-KU SPORTS CENTER   3-1-19 Shibaura, Minato-ku. Tel: 3452-4151. Hours: 9:15 A.M.–8:00 P.M., closed Mon.

The Minato Ward office-operated sports center includes an indoor pool, gym, basketball and tennis courts, etc. Hours for each area vary so call ahead. Located near Tamachi Station. [off Map]

NAUTILUS CLUB   Akasaka Branch: Akasaka DS Bldg., B1. 8-5-26 Akasaka, Minato-ku. Tel: 3405-1177. [M-5]

A growing chain of clubs in the Tokyo area, some have pools and others offer aerobics. We have given the address for the Akasaka Branch which has a pool. Other branches are in: Ichigaya, Ochanomizu, Aoyama, Suidobashi, Ikebukuro, Shibuya, and Shinjuku.

CLARK HATCH (men only)   Azabu Towers, 2-1-3 Azabu-dai, Minato-ku. Tel: 3584-4092. Hours: 7:00 A.M.–10:00 P.M., 8:30 A.M.–8:00 P.M. on Sat., Sun., & hol.

Fully equipped gym plus sauna. They supply gym clothes, towels, etc. [M-1]

SWEDEN HEALTH CENTER (women only)   Sweden Center, 5F. 6-11-9 Roppongi, Minato-ku. Tel: 3404-9739. Hours: 8:30 A.M.–9:00 P.M., 10:00 A.M.–5:00 P.M. on Sat., Sun., & hol.

Sauna, gym, dance classes, and massage offered. [M-1]

DO SPORTS PLAZA HARUMI   5-6-1 Toyosu, Koto-ku. Tel: 3531-8221. Hours: 10:00 A.M.–10:30 P.M., Mon.–Sat., open for visitors.

A huge sports center with swimming pool, gym, squash courts, jogging track, bowling alleys, golf driving range, sauna, massage, etc. [off Map]

DO SPORTS PLAZA SHINJUKU   Sumitomo Bldg. Annex, 2-6-1 Nishi Shinjuku, Shinjuku-ku. Tel: 3344-1971. Hours: 10:00 A.M.–8:30 P.M., Mon.–Fri.

Gym, sauna, diving pool, indoor track. Same charge system as the Harumi branch listed above. [M-7]

SUN PLAZA INDOOR POOL Sun Plaza Bldg., B2. 4-1-1 Nakano, Nakano-ku (near the north exit of Nakano JR Station). Tel: 3388-1151. Hours: July & Aug. open daily, noon–9:40 P.M. Mon–Fri., and from 10:00 A.M. on Sat. & Sun.; Sept.–June, open Sat. & Sun. noon–6:00 P.M. [M-26]
TOKYO SWIMMING CENTER (indoor & outdoor) 5-4-21 Komagome, Toshima-ku (JR Sugamo Station). Tel: 3915-1012. Hours: Indoor pool open all year (outdoor pool open from June through Aug.), 12:30 A.M.–8:00 P.M. Mon.–Sat., until 6:00 P.M. on Sun. & hol.
Members only. [off Map]

Jogging Courses
IMPERIAL PALACE COURSE (approx. 5 kilometers) This popular jogging and cycling course takes you around the moats of the Imperial Palace. You can start anywhere in the palace area. The two closest stations are Nijubashi-mae Station on the Chiyoda Line and Hanzomon Station on the Hanzomon Line. [M-10]
YOYOGI PARK COURSE (approx. 2.4 kilometers) You can start near the JR Harajuku train station or Shibuya Kokaido Concert Hall, then run around the NHK Broadcasting Center and the Yoyogi National Stadium. [M-4]

Cycling Courses
PALACE CYCLING COURSE (2.5 kilometers) Open Sun. 9:00 A.M.–5:00 P.M. only. You can borrow a bicycle behind the police box in the Kokyo-gaien Garden (Imperial Palace Outer Garden, Nijubashi-mae Station on the Chiyoda Line). The course starts from the moat of the east garden and the entrance of Kitanomaru Park. [M-10]
MEIJI-JINGU CYCLING ROAD (1.5 kilometers) Open Sun. & hol. Borrow a bicycle near Nihon Seinen-kan hall (Gaien-mae Station on the Ginza Line). The cycling road is lined with trees and goes around the park's sports facilities. [M-5]
TAMAGAWA SEISHONEN CYCLING COURSE (18 kilometers) This is a great course along the Tamagawa river passing soccer and tennis courts and parks. Borrow a bicycle at the service station on the other side of Tamagawa Ohashi (Tamagawa Bridge). You will need to show your passport. (Take the Tokyu Mekama Line from Meguro to Yaguchi Watari Station, about 30 min.) [off Map]

BEAUTY CARE
Hair care
Hair care is good in Tokyo, but many hairdressers do not know how to work with non-Japanese hair. Following are a few of the salons that have a good reputation in the foreign community. Shampoo, cut, and blow dry will run from ¥6,000–¥10,000.

MOD'S HAIR La Foret, 3F. Tel: 3475-0051. Hours: 11:00 A.M.–8:00 P.M. daily. [M-4] Printemps Ginza, 2F. Tel: 3564-4848. Hours: 10:00 A.M.–8:00 P.M., closed Wed.
Associated with Mod's Hair in Paris, the staff at this salon often do the hair for local fashion shows. The salon is run by Tamura Tetsuya who speaks English. [M-8].
PEEK A BOO Beruea Garden Bldg., B1. 4-2-11 Jingumae, Shibuya-ku. Tel: 3402-8214. Hours: 10:00 A.M.–6:00 P.M., closed Tue. [M-5]
ALLEN EDWARDS 2-17 Azabu-juban, Minato-ku. Tel: 5484-1167. Hours: 10:00 A.M.–8:00 P.M., Sun. & hol. until 7:00 P.M., closed Tue.
Tokyo branch of well-known Beverly Hills hairdresser. [M-1]
Y.S. PARK Roppongi: 5-10-31 Roppongi, Minato-ku. Tel: 3423-2244. [M-1] Omotesando: 4-29-3 Jingumae, Shibuya-ku. [M- 4] Tel: 3746-2244. Hours: 10:00 A.M.–8:00 P.M. daily.
M.M.K. HAIR INTERNATIONAL Roppongi TK Bldg., 4F. 5-2-6 Roppongi, Minato-ku. Tel: 3423-1661. Hours: 9:00 A.M.–6:00 P.M., closed Sun.
Salon run by three hairdressers with long experience working in the international community. [M-1]

Skin Care

NAGAI YAKKYOKU HIFU KOSO BIGANSHITSU   1-8-10 Azabu-juban, Minato-ku. Tel: 3583-1393. Hours: 10:00 A.M.–5:00 P.M., closed Tue.

On the second floor above Nagai Yakkyoku Pharmacy. A great place for inexpensive skin care, this shop, connected with the pharmacy downstairs, specializes in natural treatments for problem skin. You must have a skin test then return for a treatment. [M-1]

STUDIO V SKINCARE   Manshon 31 Bldg., 2F. 6-31-15 Jingumae, Shibuya-ku. Tel: 3406-8081. Hours: 11:00 A.M.–8:00 P.M. daily.

A wide range of reasonably priced skin-care options are offered by this Harajuku shop. Sothys brand products are used. Waxing. Reasonably priced. [M-4]

PARIS BEAUTY SALON CARITA   Paris Bldg., 2F. 3-5-30 Kita Aoyama, Minato-ku. Tel: 3478-5005. Hours: 10:00 A.M.–6:00 P.M. daily.

Very formal, elegant salon offering excellent skin and hair care. Manicure, pedicure, facials, and full body treatments. Quite expensive. [M-5]

MIRROR MIRROR   Jingu Mansion, 3F. 3-5-33 Kita Aoyama, Minato-ku. Tel: 3404-5852. Hours: 10:00 A.M.–7:00 P.M., closed Tue. & Wed.

Total skin care, manicures, pedicures, waxing, etc. By appointment. Small and quiet shop. On the expensive side. [M-4]

暮

THE BASICS

THE BASICS

PLANNING
Climate

The climate of Tokyo is somewhat similar to that of New York, only less extreme. All four seasons are clearly distinguished, a matter of great pride to the Japanese who for some reason believe this to be a feature unique to their country. Here are some generalizations:

Spring: pleasant through May. In June the month-long rainy season begins.

Summer: hot and sticky through September. In August and September typhoons are common.

Autumn: late September through mid-November are pleasant, crisp, and cool.

Winter: lasts from mid-November through March. Generally not too severe, snow falls occasionally and strong winds are common. December and January are cold but clear and sunny.

The best time to visit is in May or mid-October through mid-November. The inside of buildings and travel facilities such as buses and trains are climate-controlled. They tend to overdo it, so it's a good idea to carry around a sweater to wear inside during the summer, and in winter be sure you'll be able to remove a layer or two of clothing.

When to Travel

Aside from climatic considerations, Japanese domestic tourism patterns are something to think about. The Japanese tourist's reputation precedes him overseas and the stereotype is no less applicable within the country.

The Japanese travel frequently, to see the cherry blossoms bloom in Kyoto or the maple leaves turn red in the fall. National parks are visited at a yearly statistical average of over two times per person. Throughout the year famous temples and museums are besieged by tour groups of farmers and schoolkids on class excursions who love nothing more than a group photo with a foreign face in the center. During the major holiday seasons and on public holidays that fall next to a weekend, transportation outside of Tokyo is often booked months in advance, as are hotel rooms. If you're planning a trip out of town, try to book your hotel and tickets ahead of time. The major holiday seasons are:

Shogatsu—the Japanese New Year celebration, begins a few days before January 1 and lasts about a week. Tokyo closes down for the first three days of the year as most citydwellers return to their home towns.

Golden Week—from Green Day (the ex-emperor's birthday) on April 29 through Children's Day on May 5. This is another period of mass exodus from the city to the countryside or overseas destinations.

Obon and School Vacations—the two coincide. Schools let out from mid-June until late August. *Obon* is a three-day holiday from August 14–16 when people return to their home towns to honor the spirits of their ancestors.

Mid-February—not exactly a holiday, but during this time high school seniors from all over Japan come to Tokyo to take their college entrance examinations. It is next to impossible to find a hotel room or to extend your stay in a room.

Special Deals—Before You Go

The following is a list of special deals and information sources to check before you leave for Japan.

Japan National Tourist Organization "JNTO" This is a good source of general information on Japan as well as any specific information you might need—all free of charge. Ask your travel agent or JAL for the address of the nearest JNTO office. In Tokyo their main office is in the Tokyo Kotsu Kaikan Bldg., 2-10-1 Yurakucho, Chiyoda-ku. Tel: 3216-1901. [M-8]

Japan Rail Pass Foreign tourists visiting Japan for sightseeing purposes can apply for a rail pass at overseas JAL (Japan Air Lines) offices and at authorized travel agencies. The pass is valid for unlimited travel on the Japan Railways (JR) system. There are two kinds of passes: Ordinary and Green (First Class). The passes are for 7, 14, or 21 days. Passes for children aged 6–11 are half-price.

The passes can only be purchased overseas. At the time of purchase, you will receive vouchers that can be exchanged for passes at designated locations in Japan. Most Japan Travel Bureau (JTB) offices will redeem the passes. They can also be redeemed in Narita Airport at the Narita Travel Center in the arrival lobby. Tel: 0476-32-8852.

The vouchers must be exchanged within three months from the date of issue. If you are planning to travel around Japan at all, these passes are a great bargain. The price of a one-week ticket is only slightly higher than that of a single round-trip bullet-train ride to Kyoto.

Packing and Supplies

Just about anything your heart desires can be bought in Tokyo. That includes the items on the following list (with the exception of large-sized shoes). Please note that these are just suggestions given for the sake of preparedness.

Shoes All smart tourists already know they should pack comfortable walking shoes. In Japan, however, there are a few more considerations. First, sidewalks are often uneven and temple paths are frequently made of gravel; good shoes tend to be quickly destroyed. Also, you'll be taking your shoes off at unexpected times: in some offices, in homes, in temples, shrines, some museums, and at the tea ceremony. Shoes that slip easily off and on will save you a great deal of trouble. To avoid unnecessary embarrassment, socks with holes should be left at home. In the winter, thick socks are advisable. Japanese shoe sizes run small, women's shoes up to 24–24.5 (U.S. 7.5–8, British 7–8). A few stores carry larger sizes but don't expect to find anything fashionable.

Tissues and/or Hankies Most Japanese carry hankies or little packages of tissues. They are used to dab off perspiration in the summer, in lieu of toilet paper and towels in public restrooms, and as napkins in many restaurants. Hankies and tissues can be bought at station kiosks.

Flashlight Lighting in temples and museums is not always what it should be. If you want to see that lovely eighth century Buddha, you may just have to help light it yourself.

Instant Coffee If you're planning on staying in Japanese-style lodgings, *ryokan,* but can't do without a morning cup of coffee, bring a small jar of instant coffee or buy one here. *Ryokan* usually don't have coffee, but there will be a jar of hot water in each room for making tea.

Bath Towel Japanese public-baths do not supply towels, and *ryokan* provide only small handtowels. It's not a bad idea to bring an extra one with you.

Visas

Visas are required for citizens from countries that do not have a reciprocal visa-exemption agreement with Japan. The visa must be obtained before arriving in Japan.

Visa exemption for travelers not engaged in commercial activities are granted to citizens of the following countries:

- **For 180 days:** Austria, Bangladesh, Ireland, Germany, Liechtenstein, Mexico, Switzerland, and the United Kingdom.
- **For 90 days:** Argentina, Bahamas, Belgium, Chile, Columbia, Costa Rica, Cyprus, Denmark, Dominica, El Salvador, Finland, France, Germany, Greece, Honduras, Iceland, Iran, Israel, Italy, Lesotho, Luxembourg, Malaysia, Malta, Mauritius, New Zealand, Norway, Pakistan, Peru, Portugal, San Marino, Singapore, Spain, Surinam, Sweden, Tunisia, Turkey, Uruguay, U.S.A., and Yugoslavia.
- **For 14 days:** Singapore.

Visas are required for citizens from all other countries, including Australia. They can be obtained by writing to or visiting a Japanese embassy or consulate abroad.

Tourist Visa   A "Short-term Stay" visa is good for tourism, conferences, amateur sports, business trips, cultural, religious, or press activities; basically anything that's legal and you don't get paid for in Japan.

Duration   United States citizens: for 15–90 days, multiple entry, valid for 5 years. Australian citizens: for 60 days, multiple entry, valid for 12 months.

Extensions   Visas can usually be extended twice, giving most a maximum stay of up to 180 days. Applications must be made at least 10 days before the expiration date of your current visa. You may be required to prove that you can afford the extended stay. You will also need to apply for an **Alien Registration Card** by the ninetieth day.

Documentation   You will need 2 passport-size photos, your passport, a return ticket, and proof of financial independence, i.e., travellers checks, or sufficient cash. The visa usually takes 2–3 days to process.

- **Other Visas**

Visas for non-tourist purposes or longer stays are many and varied. The procedure is fairly complicated, usually requiring extensive documentation and one to two months of processing. You will normally have to have some kind of sponsoring organization. For further information check with the nearest Japanese consulate or write for one of the pamphlets listed below.

Working in Japan   It is illegal to work in Japan without a working visa. If you arrive in Tokyo and want to find a job, you will have to come on a tourist visa, find a sponsoring company here, then leave the country to make the application at an overseas consulate. You can buy inexpensive open-ended plane tickets that will allow you to leave Japan for a nearby country and return. Cheap tickets from Japan to Korea or Hong Kong will cost around ¥40,000–¥60,000.

Alien Registration Cards   If you are planning to stay for more than 90 days, you are required to apply for an Alien Registration Card by the ninetieth day. Immigration is very strict and failure to obtain your card in a timely fashion can result in deportation. If you run a few days over, they will usually accept your profuse apologies and a written *gomen nasai* (I am truly sorry) note that explains why you failed to apply. Applications can be made at the Tokyo Immigration Office. You will need three passport-size photos, a passport, and an address.

Tokyo Immigration Office   Daisan Godo Chosha Bldg., 2F. 1-3 Otemachi, Chiyoda-ku. Tel: 3213-8111

ARRIVAL

Arriving at Tokyo's Narita airport is one of the least pleasant parts of travel to Japan. The airport is located sixty kilometers from the city and protests by radicals and local farmers have resulted in strict security measures such as car searches and baggage checks of all those entering the airport grounds.

Formalities

A visa may be required before arrival. You must also fill out a quarantine form and an Embarkation/Disembarkation card. Your airline should have these two forms on board.

Customs

Customs inspection on arrival is fast and efficient. Officials are generally easy on foreign travelers, unless of course you've given them reason to act otherwise. There are separate lines for residents and nonresidents. Carts are available and can be used to carry your luggage to your chosen means of transportation.

An oral declaration is sufficient in most cases. Unaccompanied baggage must be declared in writing.

Customs Exempt Items: Personal effects and professional equipment to be used during your stay. Travelers over twenty years of age can bring in:

- 3 bottles of alcoholic beverages (a bottle is approximately 760 cubic centimeters)
- 500 grams of tobacco (400 cigarettes, 100 cigars)
- 2 ounces of perfume
- Gifts, souvenirs, watches, etc., are given duty-free entry irrespective of their quantity and value, provided that the total market value of all articles brought in other than alcoholic beverages, tobacco products, and perfume is not more than ¥200,000.

If you are planning to live in Japan for over a year, household effects including automobiles and boats may be imported, but the items must be exported upon leaving Japan.

Prohibited Items:
- Narcotic and stimulant drugs, and any utensils for drug use.
- Counterfeit, altered, or imitated coins, paper money, banknotes, or securities.
- Any books, drawings, or items considered damaging to the public (especially any portrayal of genitals and pubic hair).
- Articles infringing on patents, trademarks, copyright, etc.
- Pistols, revolvers, and all types of ammunition.

Restricted Items:
- Swords and other types of weapons require special permission.
- Plants and animals must be presented to the quarantine inspector prior to customs examination.

Currency:
- An oral declaration of currencies in your possession is requested.
- Up to ¥5,000,000 may be taken out of the country.

Passenger Service Facility Charge

All passengers departing from Narita are subject to a service charge of ¥2,000 per adult and ¥1,000 for children over two and under twelve years of age. Buy a ticket from one of the machines just before passport control. The charge is not levied on passengers arriving and leaving the same day.

Transportation to Tokyo

There are a number of ways to get into town from Narita Airport:

Limousine Bus   Tickets to TCAT, the Tokyo City Air Terminal [M-23], can be purchased in the arrival lobby. The bus stops right outside the terminal. There are a number of buses with different destinations so be sure you go to the correct stop. Your bags will be loaded onto the bus and you can reclaim them upon arrival at TCAT. Take a taxi from there to your hotel. Buses from TCAT to Tokyo Station or to some of the major hotels are also available. The closest subway station is Suitengu-mae on the Hanzomon Line, which is connected to the terminal by an underground passage.

- Price: ¥2,700. Departure to TCAT every 10–15 minutes (Buses departing from TCAT to Narita leave at 10-minute intervals). Travel time is one hour, but can be considerably longer in heavy traffic.

Limousine Bus to Other Destinations   There are special buses to Yokohama and Haneda Airport, as well as buses making the rounds of major hotels in Tokyo. Departure times are irregular.

Trains–Narita Express   This is the fastest link between Narita Airport and Tokyo. Excellent for the trip out to Narita, but since all seats are reserved and there is no standing room, coming in from the airport during peak times could leave you waiting around at the station for a hour or so. The train makes 23 round trips per day at intervals of approximately 30–40 minutes. You are advised to consult a detailed timetable.

Keisei Lines The Keisei private railroad company operates trains from their Keisei-Ueno Station [M-13] to Narita Airport. The trains are differentiated by speed and by how many stops are made along the way:

• Keisei Skyliner, ¥1,740. Travel time: 60 minutes with departures every 40 minutes.

• Keisei Limited Express, ¥940. Travel time: 75 minutes with departures every 20 minutes.

Taxi To central Tokyo the cost is around ¥30,000 and takes 1–1.5 hours depending on traffic.

Hired Car A car and driver to central Tokyo will cost about ¥55,000. The limousine bus company offers this service. You can order a car at the bus counter in the airport arrival lobby or call (03) 3747-0305.

Rental Cars Driving in Tokyo is one of the cultural experiences we suggest you do not attempt. Streets are narrow, crowded, and confusing. Most signs are in Japanese only. If you need a car, both Hertz and Avis have Tokyo affiliates. The cars can be reserved overseas and you can pick them up at the airport. You will need an international driving license or a Japanese one.

• Avis-Nissan Rent-a-Car: 2-3-2 Akasaka, Minato-ku, Tokyo. Landick Akasaka Bldg. 2F. Tel: 3583-0911

• Hertz-Nippon Rent-a-Car: Jinnan Bldg., 4-3 Udagawa-cho, Shibuya-ku, Tokyo. Tel: 3469-0919.

Cost for rental cars starts at about ¥5,500 for 6 hours (1300 cc subcompact).

Haneda Airport

The newly rebuilt Haneda Airport operates domestic flights and the international flights of Taiwan's China Airlines. The airport is located close to the city and a taxi ride to the center of town takes around forty minutes (about ¥6,000).

Monorail The monorail from Hamamatsu-cho Station [M-11] in Tokyo to Haneda is great if you have little baggage. Departures are every 10–20 minutes. Travel time: 23 minutes. Price: ¥460.

DETAILS
Money

The Japanese unit of currency is the yen coin. Denominations are ¥1, ¥5, ¥10, ¥50, ¥100, and ¥500. Bills are ¥1,000, ¥5,000, and ¥10,000. Money can be changed at the airport, in banks, or hotels. Exchange rates fluctuate daily. It is a good idea to figure the approximate exchange value of your currency for ¥1,000 which will be your basic bill of use in Tokyo.

Japan is essentially a cash-based society. Although this is changing somewhat, many places will only accept yen in cash and nothing but yen can be used. Travelers checks should be cashed in at banks. Restaurants will sometimes take only one or two credit cards, if any.

Japanese banks give excellent but painfully slow service. If you need to transfer money internationally it can take three days to a week. Before arrival, try to find out if your local bank has a branch or affiliate in Tokyo.

Tipping, Service Charges, Taxes

There is no tipping in Japan. If you leave your change on the table, the waitress will probably pursue you down the street to return your *wasure-mono* ("forgotten thing"). Most hotels and restaurants do include a ten- to twenty-percent service charge on the bill. Taxes are calculated at ten percent on hotel rooms when the room rate plus service charge is more than ¥15,000. A ten-percent tax is also charged on restaurant meals that come to more than ¥7,500 per person.

There is a national sales tax, called a "consumption tax," of three percent applied to most purchases. This tax is expected to increase in the future.

Business Hours

Business is generally done on a 9:00 A.M.–5:00 P.M. schedule, but with overtime being a favorite leisure activity of the Japanese, people can often be found in their offices at late as 7:00 or 8:00 P.M. Sundays are holidays for all but major stores, boutiques in busy areas, and some restaurants. Calling ahead is always a good idea. General business hours are:

- **Banks:** 9:00 A.M.–3:00 P.M. Mon.–Fri., closed Sat., Sun., and holidays.
- **Government Offices:** Generally open from 8:30–9:00 A.M. to 4:00–5:00 P.M. Mon.–Fri.
- **Post Offices:** Main offices: 9:00 A.M.–7:00 P.M. Mon.–Fri. Branches: 9:00 A.M.–5:00 P.M., closed weekends and holidays, but open twenty-four hours a day for international airmail and special delivery.
- **Department Stores:** 10:00 or 11:00 A.M.–7:00 or 8:00 P.M. daily, except one weekly holiday that varies with each store.
- **Most Shops:** 10:00 or 11:00 A.M.–6:00 or 7:00 P.M. daily.
- **Japanese Restaurants:** Lunch: 11:30 A.M.–2:00 P.M., dinner: 5:00–9:00 P.M.

Metric

Although the metric system is used in Japan for most things, traces of the traditional system of measurement can still be found. Rooms are commonly measured by how many *tatami* mats fill the floor space (six to eight is usual), and saké bottles that used to be one *sho* are now one point eight liters. You will not need these traditional measurements, but for those who don't know the metric system, here is a brief conversion chart:

1 centimeter (cm) = .39 inches	1 inch = 2.55 centimeters
1 meter (m) = 3.28 feet, 1.1 yards	1 foot = 0.31 meters
	1 yard = 0.93 meters
1 kilometer (km) = 0.62 miles	1 mile = 1.6 kilometers
1 gram (g) = 0.035 ounces	1 ounce = 28 grams
1 kilogram (kg) = 35.27 ounces, 2.2 pounds	1 pound =450 grams
1 metric ton (t) = 1.1 U.S. ton	
1 liter (l) = 0.26 gallons	1 U.S. gallon = 3.75 liters

Temperature: an easy formula for changing centigrade (C) to Fahrenheit (F) is:

$$C = (2 \times C) + 30 = F$$

Taking 30 degrees centigrade as an example gives:

$$30°C = (2 \times 30°C) + 30 = 90°F$$

Electricity

In Japan the power supply is 100 volts with alternating current (AC). Eastern Japan, including Tokyo, is on 50 cycles, western Japan on 60. Most hotels have adapters for small appliances such as electric shavers and hair dryers.

Food and Drink

In general, standards of hygiene are high and everything is safe to eat and drink. If, however, you're a picky eater, here are a few things to watch:

Water: If you don't like drinking heavily chlorinated tap water, you can find bottled mineral water at most stores and many restaurants. Imports such as Perrier are also available. Another alternative is club soda, but when ordering in restaurants be sure they understand that you want plain soda, or you might end up with a drink concocted of green sugar syrup and soda water. Ask for *purein soda* or *tansan*.

Drinks: Cold drinks are usually served pre-sugared. This includes fruit juices, milk, iced coffee, and tea. To order without the sugar syrup say *gamu nuki*. It may not be possible, as the drinks often are bought premixed.

Toast and Sandwiches: Bread almost always comes in inch-thick slices and very white. Brown bread, like brown rice, has not caught on here. Sandwiches are standardized: thin slices of trimmed white bread with a combination of nearly invisible slices of cheese, ham, cucumber, lettuce, tomato, mustard, and mayonnaise. To order that something be left out of your sandwich use the word *nuki* after the appropriate noun, e.g., *tomato nuki*.

Vegetarians: In Japanese you are *saishoku-shugi sha*.

Japanese Toilets

Foreigners always laugh at those illustrated *How to Use a Western Toilet* signs pasted on almost every Western-style toilet in Japan. Funny that one would need instructions. It is even funnier when you find dusty tennis shoe logos imprinted on a public toilet seat (admittedly a rare occurrence). But don't laugh too hard. Foreigners have been known to use Japanese-style toilets in all sorts of curious ways (one woman used it backwards for two months).

Japanese toilets are essentially small holes sunk in the floor or on a raised platform in the stall. One end of the receptacle will be covered with a small shield. The rules are: facing the shield, stand astride the hole and squat. Men are permitted to stand if they promise to use good aim. Other useful tips:

- Public restrooms are occasionally unisex. Women should just look the other way as they pass the men's urinals on the way to the stalls.
- Toilet tissue and towels are often not supplied in the truly public restrooms. Bring your own.
- To determine if a stall is occupied, do not yank on the door. Give a polite knock. A knock back means it's full.
- In Japanese toilets are called *toire*.

Safety

Part of Japan's good PR is its low crime rate. Aside from the occasional Yakuza (Japanese Mafia) brawl, some white-collar crime, and family suicides, there's not much trouble. Lost items are usually turned in and women can walk home safely at night. It is all part of the system and one of the best parts of it.

But things are changing. Crime statistics, though far from those of the United States, are on the rise. Crime and criminals are found in all large cities and tourists make good targets. Don't let your survival instincts relax too far. Here are a few suggestions:

- Have your name and address on your wallet, purse, camera equipment, etc., so it can be turned in if found.
- Carry your passport or Alien Registration Card at all times. The police do not usually stop tourists but if they do and you are without your identification you may be taken to the police station and kept until someone brings them down for you.
- When crossing the street, look to the right. Also, since pedestrians do not

necessarily have the right-of-way, crossing at designated crosswalks is advisable. If you jaywalk in front of a police station they can announce on a loudspeaker that you're doing a no-no.

• For women—If you are harassed it will probably be by an amicably inebriated businessman who wants to practice his English on you. They are easily discouraged.

• If you have problems, the following telephone numbers will put you in touch with emergency services:

Police: 110   Ambulance: 119

COMMUNICATIONS
Mail

Most hotels can handle overseas letters and packages. If you must mail a package internationally or send a registered letter, be sure to find a main post office. Post boxes have two slots, a red one on the left for regular-sized letters and postcards going to inland destinations, and a blue one on the right for everything else (foreign mail, express mail, etc.). Restrictions on size and weight of parcels vary with each country, but generally anything up to 10 kilos in weight and 125 centimeters in length is accepted. Most post offices sell boxes in three sizes (small, medium, large) for shipping. **The Tokyo International Post Office** is located at:

2-3-3 Otemachi, Chiyoda-ku, Tokyo. Tel: 3241-4891. [M-35]

• **General Delivery**

If you don't know where you'll be staying and expect to receive mail, you can have it delivered:

c/o Poste Restante, Central Post Office, Tokyo, Japan. [M-10]

General delivery or Poste Restante is called *kyoku dome* or *tomeoki* in Japanese. Your mail will be kept for thirty days, then returned to sender. Most embassies also provide this service.

Telegrams and Cables

Hotels, post offices, telegraph offices, JR stations, and the Bullet Trains handle domestic telegrams in English. The phone number for the domestic telegraph office is 115.

International telegrams can be sent from your hotel or KDD offices. Call: KDD (Kokusai Denshin Denwa), International Telegraph Office, 2-3-2, Nishi Shinjuku, Shinjuku-ku, Tokyo. Tel: 0057. [M-35]

Public Telephones

Telephones come in a variety of colors, shapes, and sizes. Some take coins (¥10 and ¥100) only, some take coins and prepaid telephone cards, and some take only prepaid telephone cards. Public telephones that can used to make international phone calls are appropriately labeled. On some of the newer phones that have a liquid crystal display you have to press the "start" button in order to begin.

Telephone cards come in denominations of ¥500 and ¥1000 (the more expensive the card, the more bonus calls you get). When you insert the card in the slot, a digital readout shows how many ¥10 units remain. If the card expires in the middle of a conversation, you may insert a new card or coins if the machine will take them. (By the way, Japanese phones do not give change for ¥100 coins.) Telephone cards are sold at telephone offices, some station kiosks, inside some telephone booths, and at various shops.

To use the phone, pick up the receiver, insert your card or coin, then dial. A ¥10 coin pays for one minute on a local call; the rates go up from there according to distance. A warning tone will sound when the time paid for has expired.

There are three Japanese companies offering international direct-dialing service. Since rates and service areas differ, you may wish to call the following toll-free numbers for further information:

KDD   0057   ITJ   0120-44-0041   IDC   0120-03-0061
Dial prefixes for each company are:
KDD   001   ITJ   0041   IDC   0061

This is to be followed by the country code, area code, etc. Rates, which are calculated in six second units, are about twenty percent cheaper after 7:00 P.M. on weekdays and on weekends, and forty percent cheaper during the late night hours from 11:00 P.M. to 8:00 A.M.

Phone Numbers   A typical Tokyo number is written (03) 3456-7890. The first part, (03), is the area code and is not needed when dialing from within the city. Long-distance, intercity, and some suburban calls will require the prefix.

Finding a phone number can be difficult and finding someone's home number is next to impossible unless you can read Japanese. There are English directories, but listings, though constantly improving, are limited. Unless the place is well known, it is essential to know the address of businesses and restaurants. The local directory assistance number is 104, but the service, which costs ¥30 a shot, is in Japanese only. However, NTT does operate an **Information For Foreigners** service at 5295-1010.

GETTING AROUND
Trains and Subways

Tokyo is blessed with one of the world's best public transportation systems. Trains and subways are fast, clean, convenient, and safe at all hours. Most stations have signs in English and maps of the total system showing all stops and transfer points. Subway and train lines are named and color coded. All systems connect at some point with the Japan Railway's (JR) Yamanote Line that encircles the city. There are three major systems in Tokyo:

Teito Rapid Transit Authority Includes the major subways lines: Ginza Line (orange), Hibiya Line (gray), Marunouchi Line (red), Chiyoda Line (green), Yurakucho Line (yellow), Tozai Line (turquoise blue), and the Hanzomon Line (purple).

Tokyo Metropolitan Subways "Toei" Includes the Toei Asakusa Line (pink), Toei Mita Line (blue), and the Toei Shinjuku Line (chartreuse).

Japan Railways (JR) The nationwide rail system includes local and long distance lines such as the Shinkansen "Bullet Trains."

The major JR lines in Tokyo are:

• Yamanote Line (green)—The loop train that encircles the inner urban area. The 35-kilometer loop has 29 stops and takes about one hour to make a complete circuit.

• Chuo Line (orange)—From Tokyo Station this line runs west through Kanda, Ochanomizu, Shinjuku, and ends in Takao. Rapid-service trains (marked by red kanji characters reading *kaisoku* or *tokkai*) skip certain stops.

• Sobu Line (yellow)—Runs east from Mitaka to Chiba, doubling as a local service for the Chuo Line (change trains at Ochanomizu).

• Keihin Tohoku Line (blue)—Runs north from Tokyo Station to Omiya and south, passing through Yokohama, to Ofuna.

Tickets: Bought at the station. Vending machines take ¥10, ¥50, ¥100, ¥500 coins, and some give change for ¥1,000 bills. The ticket collector in the booth by the wickets will change small bills. Destinations are often written only in Japanese, but in general the lowest-priced ticket will take you up the line for two or three stops, the next price should be enough for four or five stops, and so on. Children under six ride free, under twelve for half price (use the lower row of buttons which have the reduced fare written on them). If you are unsure of which is the correct ticket, simply buy the lowest fare (usually ¥120–¥170) and have some change ready to pay the difference when you exit from the ticket booth. This additional required fare can be adjusted by the ticket collector in the office or booth, but there are also ticket adjusting machines which are relatively easy to use. Tickets must be turned in as you exit.

Transfers: The same ticket can be used for transfers within the same system or line. For example a JR Yamanote Line ticket can be used on the JR Chuo Line, a ticket for the Toei Mita Line will allow you to transfer to the Toei

Shinjuku Line, etc.; intersystem transfers are more complicated. While it is possible to buy special intersystem transfer tickets, everything is written in Japanese. Since all you would save is ¥20–¥30 and the bother of buying a new ticket, it's probably easier just to buy the second ticket, or, in the case of a transfer that doesn't require exiting from the ticket booth, simply pay the difference when you get off. Fare adjustment machines are usually located near the exit gates.

Hours: Subways and trains operate from 5:00 A.M. to midnight. Rush hours are 7:30–9:30 A.M. and 5:00–7:00 P.M. If you want to witness the almost terrifying spectacle of thousands of commuters being crushed into trains, visit Shinjuku Station during these hours. If you do not enjoy pain, avoid rush hour whenever possible.

Stations and Exiting: Stations can be confusing, especially the larger ones and especially during the rush-hour sea of commuters. Don't panic. Find a ticket booth and speak slowly to the station attendants. Some stations have numerous exits and the differences between them are often drastic. If possible, find out ahead of time which exit you should take. Otherwise ask at the station before exiting from the ticket booth. Landmarks are usually the best thing to ask and look for. Train station exits are often marked North (*kita guchi*), South (*minami guchi*), East (*higashi guchi*), West (*nishi guchi*) and Central (*chuo guchi*). Subway station exits are usually numbered and alphabetized.

Maps: There is a transit map at the back of this book. English subway maps are also available at most hotels and can always be found at the Tourist Information Center.

Subway and Train Etiquette: Crowd behavior in Japan is sometimes rather curious. A sweet little old lady who just spent five minutes bowing good-bye to her friend on the platform will rush up jabbing her packages or umbrella into your back and scurry on the train to get a seat. Don't take it personally.

And, like anywhere in the world, women do occasionally meet an adventurous groper on a crowded train. Try preventive intimidation.

If you're next to the door on a crowded train, you might want to step out to avoid being crushed by the stampede of exiting passengers. If you're trying to get off from the middle of a crowded car, don't be shy and polite—just push, everybody else does.

Silver seats are for the elderly and the handicapped.

Lost and Found: If you're lost, ask a platform attendant or go to the nearest ticket booth. Tell them where you want to go. They may not speak English, but they should understand the name of your destination. If you lose something, call the appropriate Lost and Found office listed at the end of this chapter.

Taxis

There are more than 40,000 taxis cruising Tokyo daily. All are equipped with clever automatic doors on the passenger (left) side, some are equipped with coin-operated massage cushions, and a few have installed small color televisions. For ¥100 you can watch television until you arrive at your destination.

To stop a taxi simply wave discreetly. Taxis do not stop when you whistle or shout. Taxi stands are located at most hotels, department stores, and close to major intersections. A red light on the front dashboard of the passenger side indicates the taxi is free, a green light means it is occupied, and no lights or a printed sign means it's off duty.

You won't have much trouble getting a taxi except in bad weather, sometimes during rush hour, late Friday and Saturday nights, and during December. If you are desperate, try holding up two fingers. This is not an obscene gesture but means you are willing to pay double the fare. If that doesn't work, try three fingers. If that does not work, you may prefer the obscene gesture.

Drivers are generally pleasant, helpful, and honest. Rude drivers do exist but contrary to the belief of many foreigners, they are just as rude to Japanese passengers.

Fares: Taxi fares start at ¥680 for the first two kilometers and increase in increments of ¥90 for each additional 347 meters. Waiting time is charged at ¥90 per stop over 125 seconds. Between 11:00 P.M. and 5:00 A.M. there is an extra charge of thirty percent. If you need a receipt say *"Ryoshusho kudasai."*

Giving Directions: See pages 8–10, **How to Use This Book**. Some listings in this book have the name and address written in Japanese, and most correspond to one of the maps in the back of the book. Show both to your driver. Remember that if the driver didn't understand you the first time, he probably will not understand you any better if you shout the second time. Check the pronunciation guide in the back and try again.

Buses

If you read some Japanese or have lived here for a while, buses can be great for filling in the gaps of the train and subway system. They are, however, quite confusing and not recommended for the casual tourist. If you want to brave the system, here are the general rules for Tokyo bus travel: get on at the front door and deposit your money in the fare box next to the driver. The average fare is ¥180–¥200. Children pay half fare. Fare machines can change ¥50, ¥100 and ¥500 coins, and many take ¥1,000 bills. To stop the bus, push the button located above your seat. Stops are announced by the driver or by a prerecorded message. Exit by the back door. As on trains and subways, "Silver Seats" are for the elderly and the handicapped.

Bus Tickets: For a saving in bus fare or simply for convenience, bus tickets (*kaisuken*) can be purchased from the driver or at offices in major bus terminals.

Bus Routes: Bus routes are extremely complicated. (Sorry, but we are not giving any.) Most buses begin and end at train stations, so if you know the Japanese kanji for the stations, you can find a bus that at least will end up at a place where you can take other transportation. You can always ask the driver *"Kono basu wa _____ e ikimasu ka?"* (fill in the blank with the name of your destination).

Getting There

It may sound obvious, but the first thing you have to do to get somewhere is to figure out where you're going. With the exception of major buildings, in Tokyo that means three things: which district, what is the closest landmark or major crossing, and finally the name and address of the building. Unlike most major cities, Tokyo street names are given only to major roads. Addresses alone are not much help either. While in some parts of town, the numbering is very systematic, in others numbers seem arbitrarily distributed in a deliberate attempt to induce insanity.

A typical address is written 1-4-7 Roppongi, Minato-ku, Tokyo, 106, or sometimes 4-7 Roppongi 1-chome, etc.

1 is for the *chome* or sub-district, 4 is for the block (or a variation of one), 7 is the building number, Roppongi is the district, Minato-ku is the city ward, Tokyo is the city, and 106 is the postal code.

Here is a list of suggestions to get you where you're going:

1. Get the address, phone number, and the name of the district. Have someone draw a map.
2. Find out what the nearest landmark or major crossing is, and the directions to the place from there.
3. Get a description of the building if possible.
4. If you're traveling by train or subway, find out which exit is closest.

Use the maps in the back of the book as a reference source. If you need further assistance, someone at your hotel or the staff at the Tourist Information Center can probably help. Instructions written in Japanese are always helpful, but be sure you have them written in English as well, so you know where you are going.

Getting Lost

The best place to go for help is a neighborhood police box called a *koban*. If you cannot find one, ask someone on the street. If they do not know, ask someone else. If they do know, ask someone else all the same. People will often give you directions without knowing the place simply to avoid having to say no (not considered a nice thing to do in Japan). If two people give you the same directions, there is a good chance that the directions are correct. Shop clerks or people who look like they belong in the neighborhood are the best bet. Half of the people on the street commute to Tokyo and generally do not know much more than you do. Another possibility is the TIC-sponsored English-language Travel Phone (see below).

Lost and Found

Here is a list of the various Tokyo Lost and Found offices called *Wasure-mono Annai-jo* in Japanese.

Metropolitan Police Board: 1-9-11 Koraku, Bunkyo-ku. Tel: 3814-4151. Hours: 8:30 A.M.–5:15 P.M. Mon.–Fri., closed Sat., Sun., & hol. After three to five days all lost items go here.

Japan Railways: Tokyo Station Lost Properties Office, Tel: 3231-1880. Ueno Station, Tel: 3841-8069.

Teito Rapid Transit Authority (Subways): Ueno Station Office, Tel: 3834-5577.

Tokyo Metropolitan Buses, Streetcars, and Subways: Lost and Found Office of Kasuga Common Government Office, 1-35-15 Hongo, Bunkyo-ku. Tel: 3818-5760.

Taxis: Tokyo Taxi Kindaika Center, 7-3-3 Minami Suna, Koto-ku. Tel: 3648-0300.

TOURIST SERVICES

We've tried to tell you everything you might possibly want to know—but for further information:

Tourist Information Center "TIC"   This is a branch of the Japan National Tourist Organization that acts as an information service for foreigners. The English-speaking staff will provide information on touring Tokyo and on travel throughout Japan (all free). They also have information on current cultural events and useful publications like "The Tourist's Handbook." Other services are:

• Home Visit System—they will arrange a visit to a Japanese home.
• Travel Phone—provides English travel assistance. In Tokyo call: 3502-1461.

- Teletourist Information–recorded information on current cultural events. In English: 3503-2911. In French: 3503-2926.
- The TIC Tokyo Office is at: 1-6-6 Yurakucho, Chiyoda-ku, Tokyo. Tel: 3502-1461/2. Hrs: 9:00 A.M.–5:00 P.M. Mon.–Fri., until noon Sat., closed Sun., & hol. [M-10]

Japan Guide Association–will put you in contact with a licensed tour guide. You must then negotiate with the guide over price, etc. Tel: 3213-2706.

Japan Travel Bureau–offers tickets and information on domestic travel at various locations in Tokyo. They recommend their "Foreign Tourist Department" at Nittetsu Nihombashi Bldg., 3F. 1-13-1 Nihombashi, Chuo-ku. Tel: 3276-7771. Hours: 9:30 A.M.–6:00 P.M., closed Sat., Sun., & hol. [M-9]

Japan National Tourist Organization (JNTO)–for any information on Japan. Tokyo Kotsu Kaikan Bldg., 2-10-1 Yurakucho, Chiyoda-ku. Tel: 3216-1901. Hours: 9:15 A.M.–5:15 P.M. (until 12:30 P.M. on Sat.), closed Sun. & hol. [M-8]

Foreign Customer Liaison Office–Yurakucho Seibu department store offers a variety of services for foreign tourists. (Tel: 3286-5482/3) [M-8]

LANGUAGE

LANGUAGE

Japanese may not be the easiest language to learn for the average English speaker, but it could well be the most gratifying. Where else in the world could just one sentence constructed with merely passable fluency bring such accolades from the natives regarding the speaker's linguistic genius? Despite their admitted, though gradually disappearing, complex towards Westerners, many Japanese still remain convinced that their language is impenetrable to *gaijin* (foreigners). Many are the stories one hears of tall blue-eyed Westerners attempting to have conversations with locals in perfect Japanese, only to be rebuffed with "Sorry, I don't understand English."

In many situations you can usually get away with using the multitude of English and other foreign words that the Japanese continue to import into their language at an alarming rate. However, don't forget that even borrowed words must be pronounced in the Japanese way, or your attempts will simply be met with blank stares.

PRONUNCIATION

Correct pronunciation is the key to being understood, and its importance cannot be stressed too much. Japanese, being purely phonetic, is quite an easy language to pronounce.

For speakers of standard British English it goes something like this:

Short Vowels

---

       a—as the u in cup
       e—as the e in pen
       i—as the ee in feet, but clipped shorter
       o—as the o in song
       u—as the oo in book, but often so short as to be almost unpronounced

---

Long Vowels

> aa—as the a in father
> ee—as the ai in air
> ii—as the ee in feet
> o—as the ou in thought
> uu—as the u in flute

In other words, a long vowel has the same quality as a doubled short vowel. Combinations of vowels adhere absolutely to the above pronunciation rules. The letter "y" in Japanese is treated as a consonant and is never pronounced like the English "eye" which would be "ai."

Consonants

The pronunciation of Japanese consonants never varies. For example, "g" is always as used in the word "game," never as in "gin." Most consonants conform fairly well to the same sounds in English, with the following notable differences:

> f — halfway between f and h
> l/r — as is well known, Japanese makes no distinction in sound between the two but has a touch of "d" thrown in for good measure
> v — pronounced b

Because Japanese is a syllabic language consonants are always broken up by vowels (with the exception of "n," which can be followed by another consonant). However, in the spoken language double consonants do exist, and must be given double value. *Motto* (more) should be approached in a manner similar to that used in the pronunciation of "got to" and not "grotto".

Nonexistent Sounds

> si — becomes *shi*
> ti — becomes *chi*, or sometimes *tei*
> tu — becomes *tsu*
> th — usually *s, sh* or *z*, so that "thing" sounds like *shingu* and "that" sounds like *zatto*
> di/zi — becomes *ji* so that "this" sounds like *jisu*
> w — except *wa*. More often it becomes *u*, so that "woman" sounds like *uuman*
> y — before i or e, when it either disappears or becomes *i*, so that "yen" sounds like *en* and "yellow" sounds like *ieroo*

INTONATION

Unlike English (or most Western languages for that matter), Japanese has little rise and fall in pitch. Its flatness may be disconcerting at first, but as with pronunciation this can be crucial to being understood. Take the word *hashi,* which written with different but identical sounding characters can mean bridge, edge, or chopsticks. Of course you don't eat your rice with a bridge, and nine time out of ten times context will tell you which meaning is intended, but each of these words, is pitched slightly differently, albeit practically flat. Even in words which combine long and short vowels (e.g., Kyoto) the stress is normally not on the long vowel, but evenly distributed. It is worth noting, however, that the short *i* and *u* are often all but unpronounced. For example, the famous Japanese percussionist Yamashita Tsutomu used to write his name in roman letters "Yamash'ta Stomu."

ORIGIN OF KANJI

Kanji, Chinese characters, were imported in the sixth century, a period when Japan went overboard in its enthusiasm for continental culture, including not only Buddhism but also art and music. Most characters have at least two possible readings when used in Japanese. One is an approximation of the original Chinese pronunciation of the sixth century, while the other is a native Japanese word. The complexity of the use of kanji is possibly the biggest obstacle to learning Japanese. After you have learned several hundred (some 2,000 of them are approved by the government for teaching in school and use in the press) you begin to develop the ability to guess at the possible meaning of the more advanced kanji. Most of them, however, have to be memorized.

The numbers one to ten may give you some idea of the difference:

	Chinese reading	Japanese reading
1	*ichi*	*hitotsu*
2	*ni*	*futatsu*
3	*san*	*mittsu*
4*	*shi*	*yottsu*
5	*go*	*itsutsu*
6	*roku*	*muttsu*
7**	*shichi*	*nanatsu*
8	*hachi*	*yattsu*
9	*ku (or kyuu)*	*kokonotsu*
10	*juu*	*to*

*often pronounced *yon* because the word *shi* also means "death"
**often pronounced *nana* (because *shichi* can be awkward)

When counting aloud "one, two, three, . . . " the Chinese derived readings are used. If, on the other hand, you are in a shop and want three of an object whose name you don't know in Japanese, you would point to it and say *"Mittsu kudasai."* Actually, there are hundreds of different ways to count, using generic numerators indicating the shape or type of thing being counted. However, since these will probably only increase your confusion, they may safely be left for later. Also, remember that Japanese has no plural form. Never add an 's' to a Japanese word to indicate more than one. It sounds hideous and invites misunderstanding.

HIRAGANA AND *KATAKANA*

In addition to kanji, Japanese has two sets (wouldn't you know it!) of *kana* (phonetic syllabic signs). In comparison with kanji both are almost alphabetic in their simplicity. Although a native script of sorts did exist before the importation of kanji, the Chinese characters were used to standardize Japanese writing. However, since it was extremely unwieldy to use this pictorial script to represent sounds in Japanese, a set of angular-looking, purely phonetic abbreviations called *katakana* were developed during the early Heian period (794–1185).

Parallel to this, *hiragana,* an identically pronounced but visually more flowing phonetic system, was adapted from the calligraphic style of kanji.

Today *katakana* is used almost exclusively for rendering foreign words into Japanese, as well as for telegrams and governmental edicts. *Hiragana* is much more widely used, for writing common words, and for verb endings, etc. (in conjunction with kanji).

The *kana* alphabet, when written with roman letters, looks like this: (H=*hiragana*, K=*katakana*).

	H	K		H	K		H	K		H	K		H	K
a	あ	ア	i	い	イ	u	う	ウ	e	え	エ	o	お	オ
ka	か	カ	ki	き	キ	ku	く	ク	ke	け	ケ	ko	こ	コ
sa	さ	サ	shi	し	シ	su	す	ス	se	せ	セ	so	そ	ソ
ta	た	タ	chi	ち	チ	tsu	つ	ツ	te	て	テ	to	と	ト
na	な	ナ	ni	に	ニ	nu	ぬ	ヌ	ne	ね	ネ	no	の	ノ
ha	は	ハ	hi	ひ	ヒ	fu	ふ	フ	he	へ	ヘ	ho	ほ	ホ
ma	ま	マ	mi	み	ミ	mu	む	ム	me	め	メ	mo	も	モ
ya	や	ヤ				yu	ゆ	ユ				yo	よ	ヨ
ra	ら	ラ	ri	り	リ	ru	る	ル	re	れ	レ	ro	ろ	ロ
wa	わ	ワ	(wi)	ゐ	ヰ				(we)	ゑ	ヱ	wo	を	ヲ
n	ん	ン												

(*wi*) and (*we*) are in parentheses because, representing sounds that have ceased to exist in Japanese, they have fallen out of usage. The above table includes all the written forms you will need to know to write any sound in Japanese. In addition the *ka, sa, ta,* and *ha* rows can be "voiced" to produce *ga, za, da, ba,* etc., by adding two slash marks at their upper right corners (e.g., が). Similarly *ha* becomes *pa* by adding a small circle .

Learning kanji is obviously a time-consuming job, but with a little application *hiragana* and *katakana* can be mastered in the space of a couple of weeks.

RESPECT/POLITE LANGUAGE (*KEIGO*)

Respect language is one of the most difficult aspects of Japanese to master. Even young Japanese have a hard time with it. When speaking Japanese, the words you use can differ considerably depending on your relative status and/or familiarity with the person to whom you are speaking.

We don't suggest that you attempt to come to grips with *keigo,* but it is just as well to be aware of its existence. Even between men and women, language can differ greatly, especially when speaking politely.

In Japanese, personal pronouns such as "I" and "you" are often omitted, but the range of interchangeable words available is quite astonishing. Normally, the word for the personal pronoun "I" is *watashi* for women, and *boku* or *ore* for men, but when being deferential both become *watakushi.* The verb "to go" is *iku,* which becomes *ikimasu* or *mairimasu* or *ukagaimasu* as your status becomes lower.

However, don't worry about any of this too much. If anything, err on the impolite side. As long as your pronunciation is good and clear, and your attitude is not patronizing, no one is going to be offended.

As we said at the beginning of this section, you can often get by using English words pronounced in the Japanese way. Just remember that consonants are always to be followed by vowels, and speak slowly. You'll be surprised how often the message will get through. "*Ekusukyuuzu mii, ai donto no hoea ai amu. Kyan yuu puriizu teru mii hau tsuu fuaindo za posto ofisu?* Make sense? Try this, "Excuse me, I don't know where I am. Can you please tell me how to find the post office?"

COMMON WORDS AND PHRASES
Imported Words

Getting back to those borrowed words from foreign languages, here is a sample list of some of the more frequently used.

•Food/Drink	*Tabemono/Nomimono*
hors d'oeuvres	*odoburu*

sandwich	*sando-itchi* (*sando* for short)
coffee	*kohii*
bread	*pan* (from Portuguese)
stew	*shichuu*
curry and rice	*kareeraisu*
cola	*kora* (generic term)
hamburger (with bun)	*hanbaagaa*
hamburger (patty)	*hanbaagu (suteeki)*
beer	*biiru*
hot cocoa	*kokoa*
on the rocks	*onzarokku* (or just *rokku*)

•Shopping   ***Kaimono***

cigarettes	*tabako* (tobacco)
shirt	*shatsu*
radio/cassette player	*rajikase*
radio	*rajio*
television	*terebi*
personal computer	*pasokon*
word processor	*waapuro*
glass (for drinking)	*gurasu, koppu*
vodka	*uokka*
glass (windows, etc.)	*garasu*
panty hose	*pansuto* (panty stockings)

•Names and places   ***Namae/Chimei***

Hollywood	*hariuddo*
Beatles	*biitoruzu*
England/Britain	*igirisu*
Vienna	*uiin*
Bach	*bahha*
Van Gogh	*gohho*
Russia	*roshia*
Germany	*doitsu* (from the German word *Deutsch*)
Moscow	*mosukuwa*
Los Angeles	*rosanzerusu, rosu*

•Others

Women's Lib	*uuman ribu*
spaghetti western	*makaroni uesutan*
hotel	*hoteru*
building	*biru*
strike (industrial etc.)	*sutoraiki* (*suto* for short)

platform (trains, etc.)	*homu*
temporary work	*arubaito* (*baito* for short, from the German word *arbeit*)
mass communications (media)	*masukomi, media*
door	*doa*
studio	*sutajio*
artist's studio	*atorie* (from the French word *atelier*)
petit(e)	*puchi*
stadium	*sutajiamu*
almond	*aamondo*
Almond (chain of coffee shops)	*amando*
freebie	*saabisu* (service)
cashier	*reji* (cash register)
taste (in clothes, etc.)	*sensu*
physical proportions	*sutairu* (style)
apartment (small and cheap)	*apaato*
apartment (less small and cheap)	*manshon*
underground (avant-garde)	*angura*
black and white	*monokuro* (monochrome)
sensitive	*naiibu* (naive)
bartender	*baaten*
soundtrack	*santora*

Basic Vocabulary

Here is a collection of Japanese phrases that you should find useful. Don't forget about pronunciation or your efforts may be wasted.

•**Greetings**	***Aisatsu***
How do you do?	*Hajimemashite.*
How are you (are you well)?	*(O)genkidesu ka?* (The "O" may be added for extra politeness.)

It's been nice working with you.	*Otsukaresama deshita.* (There is actually no English equivalent for this phrase expressing communal commiseration of fatigue. It is commonly used at the end of a day's work in place of *sayonara.*)
Good morning.	*Ohayo gozaimasu.*
Good day (from mid-morning to late afternoon).	*Konnichiwa* (often pronounced *chiwa*).
Good evening.	*Konbanwa.*
Goodnight.	*Oyasumi nasai.*

Goodbye.	*Sayonara.*
Excuse me (I'm sorry).	*Gomen nasai,* or *Sumimasen.*
Excuse me (attracting attention).	*Sumimasen.*
Thank you.	*Arigato.*
Thank you very much.	*Domo arigato.*
Don't mention it.	*Do itashimashite.*
Please (go ahead).	*Dozo.*

•General

Yes (noting agreement).	*So desu.*
Yes please.	*Onegai shimasu.*
No thank you.	*Kekko desu.*
I don't want any.	*Irimasen.*
I've had enough.	*Mo ii desu.*
No (I disagree).	*Chigaimasu.*

Hai for yes and *ie* for no are usually given in phrase books, but are actually used mainly in situations where only a yes or no answer is expected. *Hai* is also used as polite confirmation that you have heard what the speaker is saying (or to indicate acceptance of an order), though not necessarily noting agreement with what has been said.

My name is_____.	_____ to iimasu.
Do you speak English (Japanese)?	*Eigo (Nihongo)wa wakarimasu ka?*
I don't understand.	*Wakarimasen.*
I understand.	*Wakarimasu.*
Where is_____?	_____wa doko desu ka?
a little	*chotto, sukoshi.*
all, everything	*zenbu*
something	*nanika*
anything	*nandemo*
nothing	*nanimo*

•Telephone   *Denwa*

Hello (on phone).	*Moshi-moshi.*
Is Fred there?	*Fureddo wa imasu ka?*
Just a moment, please.	*Sukoshi omachi kudasai.*
He (She) is out now.	*Ima dekakete imasu.*
About what time will he be back?	*Nanji-goro modorimasu ka?*
About 2:30.	*Niji-han goro.*
I'll call back later.	*Ato de kakenaoshimasu.*
Can you have him call me back?	*Orikaeshi denwa itadakemasu ka?*
Please tell him_____called.	_____kara denwa ga atta koto o tsutaete kudasai.
My number is_____.	*Denwa bango wa_____desu.*

•Counting—*Suuji*

Numbers one through ten were listed previously. The following examples should give you all you need to work out any number you require. Most irregularities have been noted. Above 1,000 the next unit is 10,000. After that all units proceed in multiples of 10,000.

10	*juu*	15	*juugo*
11	*juuichi*	16	*juuroku*
12	*juuni*	17	*juunana, juushichi*
13	*juusan*	18	*juuhachi*
14	*juuyon, juushi*	19	*juuku, juukyuu*

20	*nijuu*	21	*nijuuichi*	200	*nihyaku*
30	*sanjuu*	34	*sanjuuyon*	300	*sanbyaku*
40	*yonjuu*	46	*yonjuuroku*	400	*yonhyaku*
50	*gojuu*	53	*gojuusan*	500	*gohyaku*
60	*rokujuu*	67	*rokujuushichi*	600	*roppyaku*
70	*shichijuu, nanajuu*	78	*nanajuuhachi*	700	*nanahyaku*
80	*hachijuu*	89	*hachijuukyuu*	800	*happyaku*

100	*hyaku*	900	*kyuuhyaku*
1,000	*sen*	9,000	*kyuusen*
10,000	*ichiman*	90,000	*kyuuman*
100,000	*juuman*	900,000	*kyuujuuman*
1,000,000	*hyakuman*	9,000,000	*kyuuhyakuman*
100,000,000	*ichioku*	900,000,000	*kyuuoku*

•Time—*Jikan*

1 min.	*ippun*	1 hour	*ichijikan*
2 min.	*nifun*	2 hours	*nijikan*
6 min.	*roppun*	6 hours	*rokujikan*
10 min.	*juppun*	10 hours	*juujikan*
24 min.	*nijuuyonfun*	24 hours	*nijuuyojikan*

1:00	*ichiji*	5:00	*goji*	9:00	*kuji*
2:00	*niji*	6:00	*rokuji*	10:00	*juuji*
3:00	*sanji*	7:00	*shichiji*	11:00	*juuichiji*
4:00	*yoji*	8:00	*hachiji*	12:00	*juuniji*

2:05   *niji-gofun*
3:30   *sanji-sanjuppun / sanji-han* (half-past)
4:45   *yoji-yonjuugofun*

January	*ichigatsu*	July	*shichigatsu*
February	*nigatsu*	August	*hachigatsu*
March	*sangatsu*	September	*kugatsu*
April	*shigatsu*	October	*juugatsu*
May	*gogatsu*	November	*juuichigatsu*
June	*rokugatsu*	December	*juunigatsu*

1 day	*ichinichi*	11	*juuichinichi*	21	*nijuuichinichi*
2 days	*futsuka*	12	*juuninichi*	22	*nijuuninichi*
3	*mikka*	13	*juusannichi*	23	*nijuusannichi*
4	*yokka*	14	*juuyokka*	24	*nijuuyokka*
5	*itsuka*	15	*juugonichi*	25	*nijuugonichi*
6	*muika*	16	*juurokunichi*	26	*nijuurokunichi*
7	*nanoka*	17	*juushichinichi*	27	*nijuushichinichi*
8	*yoka*	18	*juuhachinichi*	28	*nijuuhachinichi*
9	*kokonoka*	19	*juukunichi*	29	*nijuukunichi*
10	*toka*	20	*hatsuka*	30	*sanjuunichi*

Sunday	*nichiyobi*	Thursday	*mokuyobi*
Monday	*getsuyobi*	Friday	*kinyobi*
Tuesday	*kayobi*	Saturday	*doyobi*
Wednesday	*suiyobi*		

1 week	*isshuukan*	1 month	*ikkagetsu*
2 weeks	*nishuukan*	2 months	*nikagetsu*

today	*kyoo*	this week	*konshuu*	this month	*kongetsu*
yesterday	*kino*	last week	*senshuu*	last month	*sengetsu*
tomorrow	*ashita*	next week	*raishuu*	next month	*raigetsu*

the day after tomorrow	*assatte*
the day before yesterday	*ototoi*
daytime	*hiruma*
night	*yoru*
now	*ima*

weekend	*shuumatsu*
(National) holiday	*saijitsu*
at about 1:00	*ichiji goro*
around July	*shichigatsu goro*
for about 1 hour	*ichijikan gurai*
for about 1 week	*isshuukan gurai*
later	*ato de*
I'll come back later	*ato de kimasu*
an hour ago	*ichiji-kan mae*

•Shopping — *Kaimono*

How much is it?	*Ikura desu ka?*
How much for all these?	*Zenbu de ikura?*
Do you take credit cards?	*Kurejitto kaado wa tsukaemasu ka?*
Do you have a larger (smaller) size?	*Motto okii (chiisai) no wa arimasu ka?*
Can I try it (them) on?	*Shichaku dekimasu ka?*
What other colors do you have?	*Hoka ni, donna iro ga arimasu ka?*
I'll (just) take this.	*Kore (dake) kudasai.*
It's not really me.	*Chotto imeji ga chigaimasu.*
Do you have _____?	_____ *wa arimasu ka?*

•Restaurants

I'd like to make a reservation.	*Yoyaku onegai shimasu.*
one person	*hitori*
two people	*futari*
three people	*sannin*
four people	*yonin*
five people	*gonin*
six people	*rokunin*
seven people	*shichinin*
ten people	*juunin*
We'd like the course for____yen.	_____ *en no kosu de onegai shimasu.*
The name is _____.	*Namae wa _____ desu.*
rice wine	*sake*
cold (only for saké)	*hiya*
hot (only for saké)	*atsukan*
saké flask	*tokkuri* or *ochooshi*
saké cup	*ochoko*
one flask (or bottle for other drinks)	*ippon*

two flasks	*nihon*
one cup (or glass)	*ippai*
two cups	*nihai*
I don't drink	*nomemasen*
May I have some tea (water) please?	*Ocha (omizu) kudasai.*
One more flask of saké	*Osake moo ippon.*
tastes good	*oishii*
tastes bad	*mazui*
The check (bill) please.	*Okanjo onegai shimasu.*
That was a lovely meal, thank you.	*Gochiso-sama deshita.*

•Hotel

Have you got a room?	*Heya aiteimasuka?*
How much with tax?	*Zeikomi de ikura desuka?*
Until _____	_____*made*

•Traveling

	Ryoko
taxi	*takushii*
airport	*kuukoo*
station	*eki*
ticket (train)	*kippu*
ticket (plane)	*kokuuken*
map	*chizu*
Does this train go to Shinjuku?	*Shinjuku wa kore de ii desu ka?*
Which platform for the train to- _____?	_____ *yuki wa nanban sen desu ka?*
Where is the entrance (exit)?	*Iriguchi (deguchi) wa doko desu ka?*
north	*kita*
south	*minami*
east	*higashi*
west	*nishi*
central exit	*chuuo guchi*
right	*migi*
left	*hidari*
straight on	*massugu*
I want to go here (pointing at map etc.)	*Koko e ikitai.*
Can I walk there?	*Aruite ikemasu ka?*
What your address?	*Juusho o oshiete moraemasu ka?*

What is the nearest station?	*Ichiban chikai eki wa doko desu ka?*
Can you give me a landmark?	*Nanika mejirushi o oshiete kudasai.*
I'm in the vicinity, but I can't find the place.	*Chikaku made kite imasu ga basho ga wakarimasen.*

The above is only a small selection, and any selection is going to be inadequate. If you intend to stay you will probably be buying dictionaries and/or textbooks anyway, or even taking a language course. Thousands of foreigners learn Japanese these days, some very well. If your interest is a sincere one you will find that even a superficial knowledge of Japanese will broaden your horizons tremendously. *Ganbatte kudasai.* Good luck!

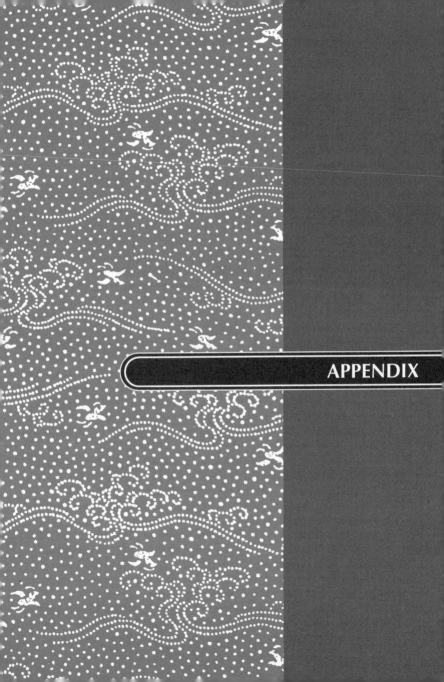

APPENDIX

APPENDIX

CALENDAR

Festivals (*matsuri*) have been an integral part of Japanese life for centuries. Tied to Shinto religious beliefs, festivals are like huge community parties given in honor of the local god. *Matsuri* are multi-function events. The purpose is to give thanks, to ask for future favors and protection from misfortune, to celebrate the joy of life, and to promote and reinforce group solidarity.

Japan was traditionally an agricultural society, and many festivals were rituals connected with planting and harvest seasons in the spring and autumn. In cities, the major festival time was the summer, a season of plagues and epidemics which frequently occurred in the crowded urban areas. Though the original purpose of most festivals is now often forgotten, *matsuri* are still joyous, occasionally raucous celebrations. Hundreds of thousands of people turn out for the more famous ones, while the small neighborhood festivals are more casual, family affairs.

Flower-viewing seasons have also been included in the calendar. Edo-period guides to the city listed the best spots for viewing the various seasonal attractions; where to view snow, cherry blossoms, fireflies, or autumn foliage. Much of the Edo scenery has disappeared, but a few of the famous sites have survived. We've included as many as possible.

The festivals listed in the calendar represent only a fraction of the hundreds held in and around the city. Because many festivals correspond to the lunar calendar, dates vary from year to year. The local tourist publications and TIC will usually have specific information on upcoming events. A few of the temples, shrines, and gardens listed in this section are not covered elsewhere in the book or on the maps. In such cases we have listed the nearest station, but for further information please ask TIC. All other locations are listed in the **Sightseeing** chapter under the appropriate headings.

January:

1

Ganjitsu—New Year's Day (national holiday).
From the stroke of midnight through the first few days of the year, people visit Buddhist temples and Shinto shrines to pray for good fortune during the coming year. It's great fun to go at midnight: bonfires are built and stalls sell *amazake* (sweet saké), food, astrology books, and *hamaya* (good luck arrows). It's the only night of the year that the trains and subways don't stop.
The most popular places to visit are: **Meiji Shrine, Senso-ji temple, Yasu-kuni Shrine, Hie Shrine, and Kanda Myojin shrine.**

1–7

Shichi Fukujin Meguri—Pilgrimage to the Seven Gods of Good Fortune. Since the late Edo period people have spent the first week of the New Year visiting the shrines of the Seven Gods of Good Fortune. There are several courses you can take, but the most popular is along the Sumida River. Each of the temples customarily gives away a small image of a god.
(1) **Tamon-ji temple**—for Bishamon-ten, the god of treasure. (2) **Shirahige Shrine**—for Jurojin, god of longevity. (3) **Mukojima Hyakkaen Garden**—for Fukurokuju, god of wealth and longevity. (4) **Chomei-ji temple**—for Benzai-ten, goddess of fortune. (5) **Kofuku-ji temple**—for Hoteison, god of good fortune. (6) **Mimeguri Shrine**—for Ebisu, god of commerce and wealth and Daikoku-ten, god of wealth.

2

Kokyo Ippan Sanga—Visit to the Imperial Palace. One of two times during the year that the emperor and empress appear before the people in the inner gardens of the palace. Enter by the **Nijubashi bridge,** 9:00 A.M.–3:30 P.M. (Nijubashi-mae Station, Chiyoda Line) [M-10]

6

Dezomeshiki—Grand Parade of Fire Brigades. Since the Edo period, men in traditional firefighter's uniforms perform acrobatic stunts on tall ladders at this festival. The parade is held in **Chuo-dori Hiroba** in Harumi from 10:00 A.M.

8

Dondoyaki—A bonfire is built from pine-and-straw New Year's decorations in a rite called Dondoyaki to pray for good fortune in the coming year. Gathering around the fire, children beat the ground with bamboo stakes shouting *"Dondoya."* When the fire dies down, pounded rice cakes, *mochi,* are roasted on the stakes and eaten to insure good health during the year. Held from noon–3:00 P.M. at **Torigoe Shrine** (Kuramae Station, Toei Asakusa Line). [M-24]

2nd Sun.

Kagami-biraki—This ceremony brings the New Year's festivities to an end. *Kagami-mochi,* a round two-layer rice cake used as an offering to the gods, is cut and eaten in a red-bean soup called *oshiruko.* This is usually done in people's homes, but a large ceremony is also held at the **Kodokan** judo hall. After a judo match, a Shinto priest divides an enormous *kagami-mochi* which is then mixed in the *oshiruko* soup and served to the audience. The ceremony starts at 10:00 A.M. [M-30]

15

Seijin no Hi—Adult's Day (national holiday). A day to honor all 20 year olds, who are now legally permitted to drink and smoke. It is one of the rare occasions for which young women wear kimono. At **Meiji Shrine** a traditional bow-and-arrow shooting ceremony is performed by the Ogasawara school of classical etiquette (based on *Bushido*). The ceremony called *Momoteshiki* is held on the grass near the Homotsu-kan at Meiji Shrine from 1:00 P.M. [M-4]

Mid-Jan.

Hatsubasho—The first sumo tournament of the year is held for fifteen days at the **Kokugikan.** [M-24]

February:

3 or 4

Setsubun—Bean-throwing ceremony. To purify the home against potential evil, people scatter roasted beans from inside to out shouting, *"Oni wa soto!"*

(Go out, devils!), and from outside in *"Fuku wa uchi!"* (Come in good luck!). The ceremony is also held at temples and shrines, where famous personalities partake in the festivities. Ceremonies are held at **Kanda Shrine, Zojo-ji temple,** and **Hie Shrine.** At **Senso-ji temple,** in addition to the bean throwing, a classical dance called *Fukuju no mai,* representing the dance of the seven gods of fortune is also performed. (Ask TIC for schedule.) At **Nishiarai Daishi Temple** a memorial for *daruma* dolls (see **Daruma ichi** on March 3–4) that brought good fortune to their owners during the previous year is held where nearly a hundred thousand *daruma* are burned while Buddhist sutras are chanted. The *daruma* service starts at 11:00 A.M., and the bean throwing from 3:00 P.M.

Early February

Tako-ichi—Kite fair. Small kites called *yakkodako* in the shape of a man are sold as fire-prevention charms for the home. At **Oji Inari Shrine** 10:00 A.M.–7:00 P.M. (Oji Station, Keihin Tohoku Line).

8   **Hari-kuyo**—A memorial service for pins and needles used and broken during the previous year. A custom since the Edo period, women bring the pins and needles to the shrine and bury them in radishes, tofu, etc. Held at Awashimado in the precincts of Senso-ji temple. [M-12]

11   **Kenkoku Kinen no Hi**—National Foundation Day (national holiday).

14   **Valentine's Day**—with an unusual Japanese twist. Only girls give to boys and only chocolate. A boon for candy manufacturers, the chocolates go on sale at least one month before.

25–Mar. 15   **Shiraume Matsuri**—Plum-blossom-viewing festival. Held at **Yushima Tenjin Shrine,** one of the famous Edo period plum viewing spots, the festival includes special ceremonies and entertainment on Saturday and Sunday. [M-13 & 16].

     Plum blossom viewing is also good at **Jindai Shokubutsu-en** [Take the 51 or 58 bus from Mitaka Station, Chuo Line to Jindai Shokubutsuen)

March:

3   **Hina Matsuri**—Girl's Day. *Hina* dolls representing imperial court figures are displayed on tiered shelves at home and in some public places during this festival for little girls. From mid-Feb. to this day, a *hina* doll fair is held in Asakusa-bashi.

3–4   **Daruma-ichi**—*Daruma* fair. A *daruma* is a legless doll originally painted with blank eyes. A wish is made and one eye is painted in. If the wish comes true, the other eye is painted. The dolls come in a wide range of sizes and are sold on the temple precincts during the festival. Over two hundred thousand people usually attend. Held at **Jindai-ji temple** in Chofu, 9:00 A.M.–7:00 P.M.

18   **Kinryu no Mai**—Golden Dragon Dance. A 15-meter-long, 75-kilogram golden dragon is carried by young men through the temple precincts. The festival celebrates the discovery of the small golden statue of Kannon (Goddess of Mercy) by the three Hinokuma brothers in the Sumida River in A.D. 628. The statue is now in **Senso-ji temple** and the festival is held there. The dance is performed two or three times during the day. [M-12]

21   **Shunbun no Hi**—Vernal Equinox Day (national holiday).

27–28   **Sentaikojin Matsuri**—Festival for the kitchen god. **Kaiun-ji temple** is dedicated to the god who protects the kitchen. On the festival day, small images of the god in a miniature shrine are given away. It is said that when you receive this charm, you must return home without visiting anyone along the way. The festival is held from 6:00 A.M.–5:00 P.M. (Aomonoyoko-cho Station, Keihin Kyuko Line).

April:
Early–mid-Apr.

Ohanami—Cherry-blossom viewing. A major rite of spring, almost everyone in town turns out to frolic beneath the pink blossoms at one of the famous spots in the city. Festivities often last until late in the evening and involve singing, dancing, and lots of saké drinking. The famous spots are: **Chidorigafuchi Park** along the palace moat [M-17], **Yasukuni Shrine, Korakuen,** and **Aoyama Bochi.** The two most lively spots for enjoying *ohanami* are **Ueno Park** and **Sumida Park** in Asakusa.

Mid–late Apr.

Ohanami (Yaezakura)—Cherry-blossom viewing. A late blooming cherry, *yae*, can be seen if you missed the early ones. At **Shinjuku-gyoen Garden.** Also *tsutsuji* (azalea) viewing at **Nezu Shrine.**

8   **Hana Matsuri**—Birthday of Buddha. Commemorative services are held at a number of temples. Entertainment includes a *daimyo gyoretsu* (parade of lords). At **Gokoku-ji temple** (Gokoku-ji Station, Yurakucho Line), **Senso-ji temple, Zojo-ji temple** and **Honmon-ji temple** (Ikegami Station, Tokyu Ikegami Line).

17   **Ueno Toshogu Taisai**—Toshogu Shrine is dedicated to Tokugawa Ieyasu, founder of the Edo-period samurai government, who is worshipped as a Shinto deity. Traditional music and dance are performed and ceremonies are held in his honor. At **Toshogu Shrine** in Ueno park from 10:00 A.M. [M-13]

29   **Midori no Hi (Green Day)**—Ex-Showa emperor's birthday (national holiday). The Golden Week holiday starts from this day.

End of Apr.–beg. of May

Ohanami—Wisteria-blossom viewing. At **Kameido Tenjin Shrine.** [M-41]
Ohanami—Peony-viewing. At **Nishiarai Daishi temple.** [M-43]

May:

3   **Kempo Kinembi**—Constitution Memorial Day (national holiday).

4   **Kokumin no Kyujitsu**—"People's Holiday" (national holiday)

5   **Kodomo no Hi**—Boy's Day (national holiday).
Theoretically for all children, the emphasis is on the little boys who everyone hopes will grow up big and strong like the carp. A symbol of strength and manhood, carp banners (*koinobori*) are flown from homes where little boys live. Samurai dolls are also displayed in the house.

5   **Kurayami Matsuri**—This festival dates back over 1,800 years. Starting off with fireworks at 4:00 P.M., over three hundred people carry *mikoshi* (portable shrines) through the streets. Things get pretty wild as people chant and push their way along. Much more energetic than your typical downtown festival. **Okunitama Shrine** is slightly out of the way but worth the trip. It's 30–40 minutes outside Shinjuku in Fuchu on the Keio Line.

5   **Suitengu Taisai**—A typical neighborhood festival. Portable shrines are carried by adults and children. Festival music and dancing are performed, and street stalls set up. The festival is held at **Suiten-gu shrine** in Ningyocho, 8:00 A.M.–10:00 P.M. [M-23].

Mid May

Kanda Matsuri—The Kanda Festival, one of the three big Edo festivals, is held to commemorate the Tokugawa victory at Sekigahara in 1600. Over seventy portable shrines are paraded through the streets, geisha perform classical dances, and a *shishimai*, or lion's-mask dance, is performed. The main festival is held in odd-numbered years. At **Kanda Shrine** for 3–4 days including Sat. & Sun. around the 14th or 15th. [M-16].

Mid May   **Natsubasho**—The summer sumo tournament is held for fifteen days at the **Kokugikan**. [M-24]

3rd Sat. and Sun.

Sanja Matsuri—Another of the three big Edo festivals, this one in honor of the three fishermen who found the image of Kannon in the river. Lots of ritual dances, music, over one hundred portable shrines, and huge crowds. At **Asakusa Shrine** next to Senso-ji temple. [M-12]

31-Jun. 1   **Ofuji-san Ueki-ichi**—Mount Fuji Potted-Plant Fair. The summer opening of Mount Fuji for climbing has been celebrated since the Edo period. The mountain has a semi-religious connotation for the Japanese and climbing Mount Fuji was something people tried to do once in their life. But for those with legitimate excuses for not climbing the real thing, a small replica of Fuji-san has been built 1890 at **Sengen Shrine** in Asakusa. Potted plants and flowers are also on sale at over three hundred booths. Goldfish, wind chimes, and a good luck snake charm made of straw are other big items. At Sengen Shrine in Asakusa. (Asakusa Station, Ginza Line, Toei Asakusa Line)

June:
Fri.–Sun. in early June

Kappa-matsuri—A *kappa* is a legendary water imp that looks something like a turtle with a plate on its head. The plate is full of water, and if the water runs out, the *kappa*, known for being mischievous, loses its power. In this festival, portable shrines are carried out into the waters of Tokyo Bay by young men. A good show of macho energy. At **Ebara Shrine** from noon on Sunday. (Shinbaba Station, Keihin Kyuko Line)

2nd Sun.   **Torigoe Jinja Taisai**—A nighttime festival where the heaviest portable shrine in Tokyo (four tons) is carried around the streets by lantern light. At **Torigoe Shrine,** 7:00 A.M.–9:00 P.M. [M-24]

10–16   **Sanno-sai**—Another of the big Edo festivals. It is somewhat smaller now, with only 50 portable shrines and 200–300 street stalls. There is a *gyoretsu* parade of people in traditional costume, folk-dancing, and tea-ceremony demonstrations. The *gyoretsu* is always held on Saturday. At **Hie Shrine,** 9:00 A.M.–6:00 P.M. [M-6]

Mid Jun.   **Ohanami**—Iris viewing. Best at **Horikiri Shobuen** (Horikiri Shobuen Station, Keisei Line) [M-42], the **Meiji Shrine Gyoen** and **Korakuen**.

July:
1   **Suijo-matsuri**—Water festival. A group of festival boats travels down the **Sumida River** from Yanagi Bridge near the Torigoe Shrine to Tokyo Bay. On arriving at the bay, *katashiro* (small paper dolls) are thrown into the sea by Shinto priests. The *katashiro* carry away bad luck and misfortune. Held at **Torigoe Shrine.** [M-24]

6–8   **Asagao-ichi**—Morning-glory Fair. In Edo, the morning glory was loved for its medicinal properties and for blooming only in the morning. For this fair, over 120 merchants set up stalls, many selling "the morning flower." At **Iriya Kishibojin.** (Iriya Station, Hibiya Line) [M-40]

7   **Tanabata-matsuri**—This festival celebrates the only day of the year that, according to ancient Chinese legend, the weaver princess (Vega) and her lover the cowherd (Altair) can cross the Milky Way and meet. People write their wishes on strips of colored paper called *tanzaku,* hang them on bamboo branches, and float them down a river the next day. Many shrines.

9–10	**Hozuki-ichi**—Ground-cherry Fair. A visit to Senso-ji temple on the tenth of July is equal to 46,000 visits at other times. The main souvenir of the fair is *hozuki,* a ground-cherry tree with red lantern-shaped blossoms. At **Senso-ji temple** from early morning to midnight both days. [M-12]
13-14	**Tsukuda Bon-odori**—A special Buddhist prayer-dance has been held here for 300 years as a memorial service to the spirits of the ancestors of the people of the neighborhood. The dance has been designated an Intangible Cultural Asset. At **Tsukuda Itchome** from about 7:30 P.M. to 9:00 P.M. [M-25]
13–16	**Obon**—A summer festival when people return to their hometowns to make offerings and give prayers to the souls of departed ancestors. During this time Bon-odori folk dances can be seen all over town.

Last Sat. of Jul.

Sumidagawa Hanabi-taikai—Sumida River fireworks display. Originally a festival to celebrate the summer "opening" of the river, the fireworks are the main thing today. The best place to watch is from between the **Kototoi Bridge** and the **Shirahige Bridge** or at the **Komagata Bridge,** all in Asakusa. This is the biggest of Tokyo's fireworks displays, but from the end of July through the beginning of August there are nearly two dozen other displays throughout the city and in nearby suburbs. [M-12]

August:
Early–mid Aug.

Tokyo Takigi Noh—Two Noh dramas and one Kyogen farce are performed by firelight in a memorial for the souls of those killed in World War II. It has been held since 1970. At **Hie Shrine,** 5:30 P.M. to 8:30 P.M. Tickets for the performance are available one month in advance, or may be bought the day of the performance. [M-6]
3 days, including one Sun. near the 7th

Tsukudajima Sumiyoshi Jinja-matsuri—This major festival, held every three years, is famous for preserving Edo traditions. There is a dragon dance on the first day, on the second day portable shrines tour the neighborhood, and on the third day the whole neighborhood visits the shrine. The next ones are due in 1996 and 1999. At **Sumiyoshi Shrine.** [M-25]
3 days around the 15th

Fukagawa Hachiman-matsuri—Another of the big Edo festivals, 100 portable shrines are carried by porters who run 8 kilometers to the shrine while the crowd dashes water on them. A *honmatsuri* (major festival), is held every three years, the next one in 1998. At **Tomioka Hachiman-gu shrine.** [M-25]

16	**Omen Kaburi**—In a traditional event from the Edo period, 25 believers in Buddha cross a 65 meter bridge, wearing masks representing various Buddhist saints. The ceremony dramatizes the Buddhist teaching that Amida will come with 25 saints to escort the dying to the Western Paradise. Held every three years, the next ones are in 1996 and 1999. Performance are given three times a day at 11:00 A.M., 2:00 P.M., and 5:00 P.M. at **Kuhonbutsu Joshin-ji temple.** [M-21]
25	**Kameido Tenjin-matsuri**—*Honmatsuri* is held every four years to propitiate the shrine's spirit. The main event is 200 Shinto priests parading in Heian period costumes by lantern light. The next festivals are in 1997 and 2001. At **Kameido Tenjin Shrine.** [M-41]

September:

10–21   **Dara Dara-matsuri**—*Dara dara* means "long" in Japanese and this annual festival of the **Shiba Daijin-gu shrine,** being unusually long, has been so named. A ginger market is set up and *chikibako,* small boxes, are sold as special souvenirs. It's said that if you put *chikibako* in a chest of drawers, you will have more kimono. The festival is especially popular from the 13th–17th. The major festival is held on even-numbered years. At Shiba Daijin-gu shrine from noon to 9:00 P.M. [M-11]

15   **Keiro no Hi**—Respect for the Aged Day (national holiday).

Mid Sep.   **Akibasho**—Autumn sumo tournament, the last held in Tokyo for the year at **Kokugikan.** [M-24]

21   **Nezugongen-matsuri**—Another famous Edo-period festival, a portable shrine from that period is still carried around the neighborhood. Shinto music and dance are performed. The Edo-period shrine is presented only on even-numbered years. At **Nezu Shrine.**

23   **Shubun no Hi**—Autumnal Equinox Day (national holiday).

25   **Ningyo Kuyo**—During this ceremony, childless couples make an offering of dolls to Kannon (the Goddess of Mercy) and pray that the goddess blesses them with children. Connected with this ceremony is a memorial service for old and worn-out dolls given to the temple (people don't like to throw them away). The dolls are burned in a huge pile and sutras are chanted for them. At **Kiyomizudo Temple** in Ueno Park, 2:00 P.M.–3:30 P.M. [M-13]

October:
1st Sat. and Sun.

   Furusato Tokyo-matsuri—Hometown Tokyo Festival. A huge city-wide festival to celebrate "Metropolitan Citizen's Day" on the first of the month. The Miss Tokyo Contest is held at this time, as well as a vast range of traditional cultural events, including folk and Shinto dancing, and music. A large market is set up with folkcraft and food products from all over Japan. At **Hibiya Park, Ueno Park, Senso-ji temple,** and many other places in Tokyo.

1–Nov. 15   **Geijutsu-sai**—A major city-wide cultural festival. Contact TIC for details.

1st Sat.   **Kiba no Kakunori**—Young men in Edo-period worker's costumes put on a spectacle as they perform acrobatic stunts on floating timbers, just like the real lumber workers used to do in the Edo period. At **Kurofune Bridge** (Monzennaka-cho Station, Tozai Line).

1st Sat.   **Fukagawa no Chikaramochi**—Another event from the Edo period, this one was for carriers of rice bags and saké casks to show their strength and ability. Now, strong young men perform acrobatics to traditional Edo music. At **Rinkai Park** (Monzennaka-cho Station, Tozai Line).

10   **Taiku no Hi**—Health-Sports Day (national holiday).

Mid–late Oct.

   Ohanami—Chrysanthemum viewing. Displays of chrysanthemums are given at various spots around the city. Best are at **Yasukuni Shrine, Senso-ji temple,** from the end of October at **Korakuen,** and from the beginning of November at **Hibiya Park** and **Meiji Shrine.**

11–13   **Oeshiki**—All temples of the Nichiren sect of Buddhism hold a memorial service in commemoration of the death of founder Nichiren. The main temple Honmon-ji at Ikegami (where Nichiren died in 1282) has the largest festival of all. On the night of the twelfth, Nichiren followers chant prayers and march to the temple carrying lanterns and huge paper-flower decorations. At **Ikegami Honmon-ji temple.** (Ikegami Station, Tokyu Ikegami Line)

16–18	**Kishibojin-sai**—A lighted lantern service is held once a year for Kishibojin, the Goddess of Children. A popular souvenir is a folkcraft toy called *susukimimizuku*, a small horned owl made of straw. At **Soshigaya Kishibojin Temple,** 9:00 A.M. to 11:00 P.M. (Kishibojin-mae Station, Toden Arakawa Line)
27–Nov. 3	**Kanda Furuhon-ichi**—Kanda Secondhand Book Fair. Over a million secondhand books are put on sale at 30-percent off along the streets of the Kanda old book shop district. At **Jimbocho Intersection.**
30–Nov. 3	**Meiji Reidai-sai**—In commemoration of the November 3 birthday of the Meiji emperor, classical court dance and music (*bugaku* and *kagura*), and classic martial arts are performed. Two special archery events are given, one on horseback with the riders in classical costumes. Other events include Noh drama and martial arts. At **Meiji Shrine.** [M-4]

November:

3	**Bunka no Hi**—Culture Day (national holiday)
	Tori no Ichi—Cock Festival. According to legend, the festival started when a group of samurai who had offered a *kumade* (bamboo rake) to the shrine, returned to give thanks for their victory. Since that time, the *kumade* has been considered a bringer of good luck. At the fair, bargaining for the rakes is customary, as is noisy hand-clapping by the two parties when a price is finally agreed upon. At Asakusa **Otori Shrine** [M-43]. The date of this fair is determined by the Chinese calendar and varies each year. Check with TIC.
15	**Shichi-Go-San**—Three-five-seven. This is a ceremony for five-year-old boys and three- or seven-year-old girls. The children, usually dressed in full kimono, are taken to visit the shrines. At **Meiji Shrine, Yasukuni Shrine, Kanda Shrine, Asakusa Shrine,** and **Hie Shrine.**
23	**Kinro Kansha no Hi**—Labor Day (national holiday)

December:

14	**Gishi Sai**—A memorial service for the famous Forty-seven Ronin is performed at the **Sengaku-ji temple** where they were buried after being forced to commit *seppuku* for avenging the death of their master. It was on this day in 1702 that they killed Kira Kozukenosuke in revenge. At **Sengaku-ji temple,** 7:00 A.M.–11:00 P.M. [M-36]
15–16	**Boro-ichi**—Trash Market. This fair has a history of over 400 years. About 600 booths are set up selling mainly nursery trees and plants, but also New Year's decorations and daily necessities, used clothing, and farm tools. At Boro-ichi Street, 9:00 A.M.–10:00 P.M. (Setagaya Station, Tokyu Setagaya Line)
17–19	**Hagoita-ichi**—Battledore Fair. Traditional battledores, *hagoita*, are sold in a variety of sizes with prices ranging from ¥500 to ¥300,000. At **Senso-ji temple,** 8:00 A.M.–2:00 A.M. [M-12]

Mid–Late Dec.

	Gasa-ichi—This market sells New Year's decorations made of pine, bamboo, and rice-straw ropes. At **Senso-ji temple** from early morning to midnight [M-12].
23	**Tenno Tanjobi**—Emperor's Birthday (national holiday)
31	**Joya no Kane**—At the stroke of midnight, on the last day of the year, every temple bell throughout the country begins to toll simultaneously. The bells toll

108 times to clear us of our 108 evil human passions. The general public are allowed to strike the bells at **Zojo-ji temple** and **Kan'ei-ji temple**.

CHRONOLOGICAL TABLE

150,000 B.C. **PRE-CERAMIC CULTURE**

10,000–300 B.C. **JOMON PERIOD** Jomon unglazed pottery. Hunting and gathering society.

300 B.C.–A.D. 300 **YAYOI PERIOD** Introduction of rice cultivation, bronze then iron, probably from China via Korea.

A.D. 300–710 **YAMOTO PERIOD** The country is ruled by warring clans. The Yamato clan takes control around A.D. 400. The early Yamato state rulers were the legendary ancestors of Japan's imperial family

538 (or 552) Buddhism and Chinese writing introduced from Korea.

593–622 Imperial regent Prince Shotoku Taishi promotes Buddhism and Chinese-based social and political reforms.

630 First official embassy to T'ang China

645 Taika coup d'état. The Soga family, having ruled behind the throne since 587, loses power to a coalition of influential families.

646–794 **NARA PERIOD** First permanent capital built in Nara on the Chinese model. Esoteric Buddhism influences the arts. The first official histories written: *Kojiki* (Record of Ancient Matters, 712), and *Nihon Shoki* (Chronicle of Japan, 720). Poetry is compiled in *Man'yoshu* (759).

781 Buddhist monasteries become a powerful threat to the imperial court. Nara is abandoned.

794–1185 **HEIAN PERIOD** The capital is moved to Heiankyo (present day Kyoto) and the great age of imperial court culture begins. In the later half of the period, Japanese arts and culture begin to develop independently of the formerly pervasive Chinese influence. Native writing scripts, *hiragana* and *katakana,* come into use.

850–1160 The Fujiwara clan dominates the court through intermarriage with the royal family and a series of regencies.

941 The court, intent on its pursuit of the arts, gradually loses control of the provinces to increasingly powerful provincial military families.

1000 Writing of the *Makura no Soshi* (Pillow Book) by Sei Shonagon.

1013 Writing of the literary classic *Genji Monogatari* (The Tale of Genji) by Lady Murasaki Shikibu.

1167 The provincial Taira clan rises to power. Taira no Kiyomori, the family head, becomes grand minister and dominates the Kyoto Court.

| 1180–85 | The Genpei War is started by a dispute over imperial succession and becomes a struggle between the Taira and Minamoto military clans for political control of the country. The Taira are defeated in 1185 by Minamoto forces under the leader Yoritomo. |

1185–1336   **KAMAKURA PERIOD**   Minamoto no Yoritomo establishes a military (*buchi* or *samurai*) government in Kamakura near Tokyo; court rule is ended, and Japan enters an age of feudal society; *bushi* ethics and the sword cult strengthen; Zen Buddhism influences the arts; the tea ceremony flourishes.

1192	Title of Shogun granted to Minamoto no Yoritomo.
1203	After the death of Yoritomo, the Hojo clan rules as regents to the shogunate.
1274 and 1281	Both Mongol invasions are repelled by timely typhoons.
1333	A power struggle between the senior and junior branches of the imperial family results in the Ashikaga clan's rise to power as supporters of the retired emperor Godaigo (senior branch).
1334	Kemmu Restoration. Go-Daigo takes Kyoto. The Hojo clan loses power and the Kamakura shogunate is ended as Go-Daigo reestablishes imperial rule.

1336–92   **NAMBOKUCHO PERIOD**   The succession dispute continues with rival northern and southern courts.

1336–1568   **MUROMACHI PERIOD**   Control of the government taken from Go-Daigo by Ashikaga Takauji, who assumes the title of shogun and begins to rule from Kyoto. The central government remains weak and the provinces remain under the control of constantly warring military rulers. The arts flourish as *bushi* and court aesthetics are blended. Noh and Kyogen dramatic forms are developed; Zen and the tea ceremony grow in importance and influence the arts of flower arranging, pottery, calligraphy, etc. *Suiboku-ga* (monochrome ink painting) becomes popular.

1457	Ota Dokan, a minor provincial daimyo, builds the first Edo castle.
1467–77	The Onin War fought over succession in the shogunate splits the Ashikaga following into factions. Fighting levels half the city of Kyoto and destroys the power of the shogunate. A stage of decentralized feudalism begins, with the country divided into small domains, tightly controlled by provincial military leaders. The court in Kyoto loses its source of land income and sinks into poverty.
1543	The Portuguese appear; Christianity and Western firearms are introduced. As trade develops and the use of firearms increases, the former balance of land-based wealth and power is disrupted. By the sixteenth century, there is a trend toward unification of the country as the powerful daimyo begin to expand their territory.

1568–1603   **AZUCHI-MOMOYAMA PERIOD**   Civil war ends the Ashikaga rule. Under a series of powerful military leaders the country is reunified. Throughout Japan, urbanized castle towns develop as the provincial daimyo consolidate their power. The arts become baroque in style, with palaces adorned in gold, lacquer, and primary colors. The art of screen painting (often on a gold ground) developed by the Kano school of art begins to flourish.

1590   Toyotomi Hideyoshi completes the unification of Japan, rules from Osaka. Tokugawa Ieyasu is given the Lands of Musashi (present Kanto province) and Edo Castle.

1582–98   Nationwide survey of the land, giving all rights to the overlord and registering the fields in the names of peasant cultivators. The survey institutionalizes the division of peasant and samurai and hastens the separation of the samurai from the land.

1592 and 1592   Invasions of Korea by Toyotomi Hideyoshi. After his death, the troops withdraw from Korea.

1600   The Battle of Sekigahara becomes a struggle for power after Hideyoshi's death, from which Tokugawa Ieyasu emerges victorious.

1603–1868   **EDO PERIOD**   The capital is moved to Edo (present day Tokyo) under the Tokugawa clan which begins over 250 years of peace. The country is closed to outside influences and strictly class controlled with the samurai at the top, followed by farmers, artisans, and merchants. The samurai role changes from soldier to bureaucrat and the agrarian foundations of feudal society are undermined as the economy becomes money-based and the merchant class becomes an economic power. Popular culture develops in the pleasure quarters of the city. *Bunraku,* Kabuki, and *ukiyo-e* flourish.

1603   Tokugawa Ieyasu takes the title of shogun.

1612   Official silver mint opened in Ginza.

1612–23   Mass persecution of Christians.

1639   Foreigners expelled (except a small colony of Dutch traders isolated on a southern island), the country is closed and a ban is placed on Japanese traveling abroad.

1657   Great Edo Fire.

1783–88   Crop failures throughout Japan lead to a period of great famine.

1804–29   Bunka-Bunsei Era; flourishing of the arts and popular culture in Edo.

1830–44   Tempo Era; domestic political and economic problems become serious; the government tries a series of reforms, but continues to fall into debt while the merchant class prospers.

1853   Arrival of Commodore Perry from the U.S., followed by the opening of two Japanese ports.

1867   The fifteenth and last shogun, Tokugawa Yoshinobu, accepts a proposal returning power to the emperor but keeping the position of prime minister within the Tokugawa clan.

| 1868 | The Meiji emperor, Mutsuhito, is enthroned. |

1868–1912   **MEIJI ERA**   A coalition of powerful daimyo and members of the nobility seize power from the Tokugawa clan. With the Meiji Restoration administrative power is returned to the emperor, the shogunate is abolished, and the Tokugawa clan is excluded from the new government. The emperor is moved from Kyoto to Edo, now renamed Tokyo (the eastern capital). With national security threatened by the western powers, a program for rapid modernization and Westernization is undertaken.

1868	Meiji Restoration.
1876	The wearing of swords is abolished.
1877	During the Satsuma Rebellion samurai resistance to the new government is crushed.
1881–85	In preparation for constitutional government, the Diet and cabinet system are established.
1889	Adoption of the new constitution.
1894–95	Sino-Japanese War over control of Korea; Japan defeats China and annexes Taiwan.
1899	Treaties with foreign powers revised and extra-territoriality is ended.
1902	Anglo-Japanese alliance treaty.
1904–05	In the Russo-Japanese War, Japan wins the southern tip of Manchuria and Sakhalin island.
1910	Annexation of Korea.
1912	Death of the Meiji emperor.

1912–26   **TAISHO ERA**   Under the reign of the new Taisho emperor the problems of a rapidly modernizing society emerge. By the 1920's the total population reaches over 55 million, the population of Tokyo alone is over 2 million. Japan sides with the Allies during World War I and sits as victor at Versailles.

1914	Japan joins the Allies in WWI.
1923	Great Kanto Earthquake strikes in the Tokyo and Yokohama area; approximately 143,000 persons are killed by the Earthquake, the tidal wave, and the fires that follow.
1925	Universal Manhood Suffrage Bill made law; the suppressive Peace Preservation Law is passed by the Diet.
1925	Death of the Taisho emperor.

1926–88   **SHOWA ERA**   The military grows in power as the country swings from a fascination with the West; nationalist sentiments rise. Japan becomes an imperialist power in Asia, and meets growing international disapproval siding with the Axis powers in WWII; the defeat and subsequent occupation of Japan by the United States finds the country destroyed; rebuilding follows the pattern of a Western capitalist economy.

1931	Manchurian Incident; Japan sets up a puppet state in China.
1933	Japan quits the League of Nations after being admonished for its actions in China.
1937	War with China breaks out again and becomes a part of World War II.
1937	Signing of the Tripartite Alliance with Germany and Italy.
1941	General Tojo Hideki becomes prime minister; attack on Pearl Harbor in Hawaii.
1945	The United States drops atomic bombs on Hiroshima and Nagasaki; Japan surrenders to the Allies.
1946	The Allied occupation of Japan begins with General MacArthur in charge.
1947	New constitution is made law; the emperor loses his "divine" status; the army, navy, and air force are abolished and Japan renounces war forever.
1951	Peace conference held in San Francisco. Japan signs a general peace treaty with 48 nations.
1952	Occupation of Japan ends.
1953	U.S.–Japan security treaty signed permitting the United States to maintain military bases in Japan.
1956	Japan becomes a member of the United Nations.
1960	Mass demonstrations over the renewal of the United States security treaty.
1964	Tokyo Olympic Games.
1970	Osaka Expo and the launching of Japan's first satellite.
1972	The United States returns Okinawa to Japan; winter Olympic games are held in Sapporo; Lockheed scandal; Prime Minister Tanaka Kakuei resigns.
1983	Former Prime Minister Tanaka found guilty of bribery; charges appealed.
1986	Tokyo Summit; landslide victory for the ruling Liberal Democratic Party.

1988 · HEISEI ERA

1988	Prime minister Nakasone Yasuhiro forced to resign over influence peddling scandal involving job placement company Recruit. "Bubble economy" comes to an abrupt end, throwing Japan into the worst economic recession since WWII. Emperor Hirohito takes ill; entire country plunges into voluntary "abstinance," (*jishuku*).
1989	Emperor dies on January 7, ending the Showa Era. New era is named Heisei.
1993	Liberal Democratic Party defeated at polls for the first time since taking power in 1955. Hosokawa Morihiro becomes prime minister. In sumo, Akebono (Hawaiian Chad Rowan), becomes first non-Japanese elevated to sumo's highest rank of *yokozuna*. Professional soccer in the form of "J-League" formed, and gains instant popularity to rival baseball.
1994	Hosokawa government toppled by unstable coalition between liberals and conservatives.
1995	Great Hanshin Earthquake levels much of Kobe and wreaks havoc on the Kansai area. Over 6,000 people are killed. Yen exchange rate against U.S. dollar rises above ¥90 for the first time.

INFORMATION, SERVICES, AND REFERENCE
• Airline Reservations

Aeroflot Soviet Airlines (SU)	Tel: 3434-9671
Air France (AF)	3475-1511
Air India (AL)	3214-1981
Air New Zealand (TE)	3287-1641
Alitalia Airlines (AZ)	3580-2181
All Nippon Airways (ANA)	3272-1212
British Airways (BA)	3593-8811
Cathy Pacific Airways (CX)	3504-1531
Civil Aviation Administration of China (CA)	3505-2021
China Airlines (CI)	3436-1661
Continental Air Micronesia (CO)	3592-1631
Canadian Air (CP)	3281-7426
Delta Air Lines (DL)	5275-7000
Egypt Air (MS)	3211-4521
Finnair (AY)	3222-6801
Garuda Indonesian Airways (GA)	3593-1181
Iran Air (IR)	3586-2101
Iraqi Airways (IA)	3264-5501
Japan Air Lines (JAL)	3457-1111
Japan Air System (JAS)	3438-1155
KLM Royal Dutch Airlines (KL)	3216-0771
Korean Air Lines (KE)	3211-3311
Lufthansa German Airlines (LH)	3580-2111
Malaysian Airlines System (MH)	3503-5961
Northwest Orient Airlines (NW)	3432-6000
Pakistan International Airlines (PK)	3216-6511
Pan American World Airways (PA)	3508-2211
Philippine Airlines (PR)	3593-2421
Qantas Airways (QF)	3593-7000
Sabena Belgian World Airlines (SN)	3585-6151
Scandinavian Airlines System (SK)	3503-8101
Singapore Airlines (SQ)	3213-3431
Swiss Air Transport (SR)	3212-1011
Thai Airways International (TG)	3503-3311
United Airlines (UA)	3817-4411
UTA French Airlines (UT)	3593-0773
Varig Brazilian Airlines (RG)	3211-6751
Virgin Atlantic Airways (VS)	3499-8811

• Flight Information
HANEDA Tel: 3747-8010
NARITA Tel: 0476-34-5000

• **Business Assistance**—While most large companies will have an interpreter, an interpreter in Japan is worth the high cost. At least you know you're getting the whole story. A number of companies offer interpreting and secretarial services:

TEMPUSTAFF Aoyama Suzuki Garasu Bldg., 5F. 3-5-14 Kita Aoyama, Minato-ku. Tel: 3405-5507.
JAPAN CONVENTION SERVICE Nippon Press Center Bldg., 2-2-1 Uchisaiwai-cho, Chiyoda-ku. Tel: 3508-1211.
SIMUL INTERNATIONAL Dai-kyu Kowa Bldg., 3F. 1-8-10 Akasaka, Minato-ku. Tel: 3586-8911.
SUMMIT SERVICE Imperial Bldg., 4F. 2-3-15 Ebisu Minami, Shibuya-ku. Tel: 3760-1251.

• Business Centers

These companies provide temporary office space and support staff.
INTERNATIONAL EXECUTIVE OFFICE 4-6-10 Yotsuya, Shinjuku-ku. Tel: 5379-1331.
JARDINE BUSINESS CENTER ABS Bldg. 2-4-16 Kudan Minami, Chiyoda-ku. Tel: 3239-2811

• Courier Service

DHL 1-37-8 Higashi Shinagawa, Shinagawa-ku. Tel: 5479-2580.
WORLD COURIER Kawashima Hoshin Bldg., 5F. 2-2-2 Shimbashi, Minato-ku. Tel: 3508-9281.
FEDERAL EXPRESS Shin Tokyo Bldg., 1F. 3-3-1 Marunouchi, Chiyoda-ku. Tel: 3201-4320.
CITY SERVICE for deliveries within Tokyo 2-11-5 Kyobashi, Chuo-ku. Tel: 3562-5665.

• Cultural Organizations

AMERICA-JAPAN SOCIETY, INC. Marunouchi Bldg., 3F. 2-4-1 Marunouchi, Chiyoda-ku. Tel: 3201-0780.
AMERICAN CENTER ABC Kaikan, 2-6-3 Shiba-koen, Minato-ku. Tel: 3201-0780.
ASIA CENTER OF JAPAN 8-10-32 Akasaka, Minato-ku. Tel: 3402-6111.
BRITISH COUNCIL 1-2 Kagurazaka, Shinjuku-ku. Tel: 3235-8031.
INSTITUTE FRANCO-JAPONAIS 15 Ichigaya Funagawara-cho, Shinjuku-ku. Tel: 5261-3933.
INTERNATIONAL HOUSE OF JAPAN 5-11-16 Roppongi, Minato-ku. Tel: 3470-4611.
ITALIAN INSTITUTE OF CULTURE 2-1-30 Kudan Minami, Chiyoda-ku. Tel: 3264-6011.
JAPAN FOUNDATION Park Bldg., 3 & 4F. 3-6 Kioi-cho, Chjiyoda-ku. Tel: 3263-4503.
TOKYO GERMAN CULTURE CENTER 7-5-56 Akasaka, Minato-ku. Tel: 3584-3201.

• Directory Assistance

Tokyo   Tel: 104
International   Tel: 0051

• Domestic Help and Babysitting

TOKYO DOMESTIC SERVICE CENTER 6-10-42-314 Akasaka, Minato-ku. Long-established maid and baby sitting service. Tel: 3584-4769.
TOKYO MAID SERVICE Nara Bldg. 2F. 1-54 Kanda Jimbocho, Chiyoda-ku. Tel: 3291-3595
BABY ROOM Tel: 3265-1111. Baby sitting service at the New Otani Hotel.
HOMEAID Tel: 3781-7536. Maids, babysitters, and party help.

• Economic Organizations

JAPAN CHAMBER OF COMMERCE Tokyo Shoko Kaigisho Bldg., 3F. Marunouchi, Chiyoda-ku. Tel: 3213-8585.
JETRO (Japan External Trade Org.) 2-2-5 Toranomon, Minato-ku. Tel: 3582-5511.
KEIZAI KOHO CENTER Japan Institute for Social & Economic Affairs. 1-6-1 Otemachi, Chiyoda-ku. Tel: 3201-1415.

• Embassies

Afghanistan	3407-7900	Myanmar	3441-9291
Algeria	3711-2661	Nepal	3705-5558
Argentina	3592-0321	Netherlands	3431-5126
Australia	3453-0971	New Zealand	3467-2271
Austria	3451-8281	Nicaragua	3499-0400
Bangladesh	3442-1501	Nigeria	3468-5531
Belgium	3262-0191	Norway	3440-2611
Bolivia	3499-5441	Oman	3402-0877
Brazil	3404-5211	Pakistan	3454-4861
Bulgaria	3465-1021	Panama	3499-3741
Canada	3408-2101	Papua N. Guinea	3454-7801
Chile	3452-7561	Paraguay	3447-7496
China	3403-3380	Peru	3406-4240
Colombia	3440-6451	Philippines	3496-2731
Costa Rica	3486-1812	Poland	3711-5224
Cuba	3449-7511	Portugal	3400-7907
Czechoslovakia	3400-8122	Qatar	3446-7561
Denmark	3496-3001	Romania	3479-0311
Dominica	3499-6020	Russian Federation	3583-4224
Ecuador	3499-2800	Saudi Arabia	3589-5241
Egypt	3770-8021	Senegal	3464-8451
El Salvador	3499-4461	Singapore	3586-9111
Ethiopia	3585-3151	South Africa	3265-3366
Finland	3442-2231	Spain	3583-8531
France	3473-0171	Sri Lanka	3585-7431
Germany	3473-0151	Sudan	3406-0811
Ghana	3409-3861	Sweden	3582-6981
Greece	3403-0871	Switzerland	3473-0121
Guatemala	3400-1830	Tanzania	3425-4531
Guinea	3769-0451	Thailand	3441-7352
Honduras	3409-1150	Tunisia	3353-4111
Hungary	3798-8801	Turkey	3470-5131
India	3262-2391	U.A.E.	3478-0659
Indonesia	3441-4201	Uganda	3469-3641
Iran	3446-8011	U.S.A.	3224-5000
Laos	3408-1166	U.K.	3265-5511
Lebanon	3580-1227	Uruguay	3486-1888
Liberia	3441-7138	Venezuela	3409-1501
Libya	3477-0701	Viet Nam	3466-3311
Malaysia	3280-7601	Yemen	3499-7151
Mexico	3581-1131	Yugoslavia	3447-3571
Mongolia	3469-2088	Zambia	3445-1041
Morocco	3478-3271		

• Emergency

Police   Tel: 110   Fire & Ambulance   Tel: 119

• Film Processing

IMAGICA   Used by professional photographers in Tokyo.
Ginza: 3-2 Ginza, Chuo-ku. Tel: 3535-6037.
Aoyama: 3-11-14 Kita Aoyama, Minato-ku. Tel: 3407-4850.
Shinjuku: 3-1-4 Nishi Shinjuku, Shinjuku-ku. Tel: 3346-1681.

TOKAN 5-27-3 Shimbashi, Minato-ku. Tel: 3437-2816. Hours: 9:00 A.M.–5:30 P.M., closed Sun. & hol. Overnight service with pick-up at many hotels.
CHAMP Tama Bldg. 1F. 1-3-18 Akasaka, Minato-ku. Tel: 3585-2855. Same-day processing, in by 10:00 A.M., out by 5:30 P.M.

• Furniture Rental
INTERFORM 4-19-20 Shirogane-dai, Minato-ku. Tel: 3441-3201. Leases and sales, quality new and used furniture (some modern Italian), excellent service.
TOKYO LEASE Tel: 3585-5801. For not-very-nice but inexpensive leased furniture.
OVERSEAS CORPORATION Tatsu Bldg., 1-18-2 Ginza, Chuo-ku. Tel: 3562-2061.
BETTER HOMES 7-7-8 Roppongi, Minatu-ku. Tel: 3405-4431.

• Housing—For less expensive housing, it's best to check with a real estate agent in the area where you want to live. The *Tokyo Journal* has listings.
KEN CORPORATION Sonic Bldg., 2-12 Nishi Azabu, Minato-ku. Tel: 3478-3821. Good for more expensive, Western-style housing.
SUN REALTY Homat Royal Bldg., 1-14-11 Akasaka, Minato-ku. Tel: 3584-6171. Also good for more expensive housing.

• Libraries
NATIONAL DIET LIBRARY 1-10-1 Nagatacho, Chiyoda-ku. Tel: 3581-2331. Hours: 9:30 A.M.–5:00 P.M., closed Sun., hol., & the fourth Wed. You must fill in a form to request a book, then wait about fifteen minutes, and you must be over twenty years old.
METROPOLITAN CENTER LIBRARY 5-7-13 Minami Azabu, Minato-ku (in Arisugawa Park). Tel: 3442-8451. Hours: 9:30 A.M.–8:00 P.M.; Tue.–Fri.; until 5:00 P.M. on Sat., Sun., & hol.; from 1:00 P.M.–8:00 P.M. on Mon. Closed the first Thurs. and third Sun. of the month.
METROPOLITAN HIBIYA LIBRARY 1-4 Hibiya-koen, Chiyoda-ku. Tel: 3502-0101. Hours: 10:00 A.M.–8:00 P.M., until 5:00 P.M. on Sat., Sun. & hol., closed first Thurs. & fourth Sun., and the fourteenth. If you stay in Tokyo more than one month you can borrow books, but you'll need a certificate from your hotel verifying this.
MING-YU INTERNATIONAL LIBRARY 4-8-8 Ginza, Chuo-ku. Tel: 3561-1181. Hours: 9:00 A.M.–5:30 P.M., closed Sat., Sun., & hol. This library is especially good for visual books.
WORLD MAGAZINE GALLERY Magazine House Bldg. 3-13-10 Ginza, Chuo-ku. Tel: 3545-7227. Hours: 10:00 A.M.–7:00 P.M., closed Mon. Magazines from around the world and a large video screen showing news and promotional videos.
AMERICAN CENTER Tel: 3436-0901. Hours: 10:30 A.M.–6:30 P.M., closed Sat., Sun., and hol.

• Lost and Found Offices—*See* The Basics.

• Printers—For quick printing of business cards.
HOTEL OKURA EXECUTIVE SERVICE SALON Hotel Okura Main Bldg., 5F. 2-10 Toranomon, Minato-ku. Tel: 3586-7400. Hours: 8:30 A.M.–6:30 P.M., closed Sun., & hol.
NAGASHIMA INTERNATIONAL PR OFFICE Imperial Hotel Main Bldg., Mezzanine., 1-1 Uchisaiwai-cho, Chiyoda-ku. Tel: 3504-1111. Hours: 9:00 A.M.–5:30 P.M., closed Sat., Sun., & hol.
PRINTBOY 1-23-20 Shibuya, Shibuya-ku. Tel: 3498-4661. Hours: 10:00 A.M.–7:00 P.M. daily. A great, design-it-yourself print shop. Minimal English spoken.

• Professional and Community Service Organizations
AA ALCOHOLICS ANONYMOUS Tel: 3971-1471.
TOKYO ENGLISH LIFE LINE "TELL" Tel: 5481-4347. Hours: 9:00 A.M.–1:00 P.M., 7:00 P.M.–11:00 P.M. English-language counseling service.

JAPAN HELPLINE Tel: 0120-461-991. Help when there are language problems in emergency situations.
JAPAN HOTLINE Tel: 3586-0110 and also Information Corner Tel: 045-671-7209. General Information on city life.
AMNESTY INTERNATIONAL Dai San Yamatake Bldg., 3F. 2-3-22 Nishi Waseda, Shinjuku-ku. Tel: 3203-1050.
FOREIGN CORRESPONDENTS' CLUB OF JAPAN Yurakucho Denki Bldg., 20F. 1-7-1 Yurakucho, Chiyoda-ku. Tel: 3211-3161.
INTERNATIONAL FEMINISTS OF JAPAN CPO Box 1780, Tokyo 100. Tel: 3904-2646. Hours: 7:00 P.M.–10:00 P.M.
TOKYO GAY SUPPORT GROUP Tel: 3453-1618. Write to CPO Box 1901, Tokyo 100-91.

• Repairs
Luggage:
WAKAO BAG Kobayashi Kopo 201, 2-3-21 Minami Aoyama, Minato-ku. Tel: 3404-3925. Hours: 9:00 A.M.–6:00 P.M., closed Sun. Luggage and leather goods repair.
Shoes:
MR. MINIT Found at major department stores (Mitsukoshi, Tokyu, Seibu, Daimaru, etc.). They fix while you wait.
TOKYU BUNKA SHOE REPAIR Tokyu Bunka Kaikan, 1F. 2-21-12 Shibuya-ku. Tel: 3407-7131 (ext. 313). Hours: 10:00 A.M.–6:00 P.M., closed Sun.
FUKUSHIMAYA 6-1-5 Roppongi, Minato-ku. Tel: 3402-8673.
Electrical:
YAMAMURA MUSEN 2-12-2 Higashi Azabu, Minato-ku. Tel: 3582-0064. Hours: 9:00 A.M.–6:00 P.M., closed Sun. & hol. English spoken.
ASAHI DENKA Tel: 3443-2280. Repairs all electrical brands.
QUICK BOY Tel: 3794-9292. Shoes, bags, umbrellas. Free delivery.

• Shipping/Removal
GLOBAL INTERNATIONAL Haraken Bldg., 3F. 1-8-1 Tamagawa-dai, Setagaya-ku. Tel: 3707-0471. A reliable and efficient company.
NIPPON EXPRESS CO., LTD. Sankin Bldg., 5F. 8-9-4 Ginza, Chuo-ku. Tel: 3572-4301. They will ship anything, by sea or air.
PURCELL INTERNATIONAL FORWARDING JAPAN Yanagi Homes Nihombashi #309, 18-3 Nihombashi Koami-cho, Chuo-ku. Tel: 3666-2981. Handles everything but mail.
AKABO KUMIAI DESPATCH CENTER Tel: 3866-8151. A mini-truck service for moving in Japan.
YAMATO UNYU (Takkyu Bin) Tel: 3541-3411. Can send packages from shops displaying the "Black Cat" sign. This company also does moves.

• Tailor
RICKY SARANI 3-3-12 Azabu-dai, Minato-ku. Tel: 3582-9741. Hours: 10:00 A.M.–7:00 P.M., closed Sun. & hol. Tailoring for men and women, also tuxedo rental.
KODA YOFUKU KOBO 3-24-1 Shimbashi, Minato-ku. Tel: 3433-4074. Hours: 10:00 A.M.–7:00 P.M., closed Sun. & hol. Alterations and mending.

• Tourist Services—*See* The Basics.

• Travel Agents
TOPPAN TRAVEL SERVICE Toppan Yaesu Bldg., 2-2-7 Yaesu, Chuo-ku. Tel: 3276-8121. Hours: 9:00 A.M.–5:00 P.M., until noon on Sat., closed Sun. & hol. English-speaking.
TOZAI TRAVEL Daini Maejima Bldg., 5F. 1-9 Yotsuya, Shinjuku-ku. Tel: 3355-1661. Hours:

9:30 A.M.–5:30 P.M., until noon on Sat., closed Sun. & hol. English-speaking, good for cheap tickets.

• Tuxedo and Formal Rental
RICKY SARANI (*see* **Tailor**)
DAIMARU DEPARTMENT STORE   10F. Tel: 3212-8011.
TOKYO ISHO   3-21-8 Nishihara, Shibuya-ku. Tel: 3485-6101.

Instruction
• Japanese Language—There are hundreds of language schools in Tokyo. Some are very good, but others are basically unprofessional organizations set up to provide "cultural visas" to supposed students. The entries on the following list have been recommended by the Japan Foundation and are primarily for serious full-time students. For details concerning prerequisites, course offerings, and cost please contact the schools directly. For other part-time schools check listings in the *Tokyo Journal.*

SOPHIA UNIVERSITY   Department of Comparative Culture, Sophia University, Ichigaya Campus, 4 Yonban-cho, Chiyoda-ku. Tel: 3238-4000. They also have a special summer session with various courses on Japan.
INTERNATIONAL CHRISTIAN UNIVERSITY   Japanese Dept., Division of Languages, College of Liberal Arts. Admission Office, I.C.U. 3-10-2 Osawa, Mitaka-shi. Tel: (0422) 33-3131. Summer Program: (0422) 33-3501.
THE JAPANESE LANGUAGE SCHOOL, THE INTERNATIONAL STUDENTS' INSTITUTE
3-22-7 Kita Shinjuku, Shinjuku-ku. Tel: 3371-7265.
NAGANUMA SCHOOL OF THE JAPANESE LANGUAGE   16-26 Nanpei-daimachi, Shibuya-ku. Tel: 3463-7261.
NICHIBEI KAIWA GAKUIN   1-21 Yotsuya, Shinjuku. Tel: 3359-9621.
KUMON JAPANESE LANGUAGE PROGRAM   Gloria Miyamasuzaka Part 3, 1F. 1-10-7 Shibuya, Shibuya-ku. Tel: 3407-5378. Particularly good for reading and writing.

• Orientation Companies
WELCOME FUROSHIKI   Tel: 3352-0765. A free welcoming and orientation service. They will visit your hotel or home.
OAK ASSOCIATES   Tel: 3354-9502. This company offers short orientation seminars for visiting executives, full orientation packages for corporations, and a placement service.

• Japanese Arts, etc.—For courses in tea, *ikebana,* calligraphy, and martial arts, see the corresponding chapters in the main text. A variety of other classes are offered in Tokyo, but most require Japanese-language ability. The following schools do accept students who can't speak Japanese.

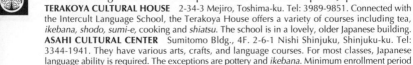

TERAKOYA CULTURAL HOUSE   2-34-3 Mejiro, Toshima-ku. Tel: 3989-9851. Connected with the Intercult Language School, the Terakoya House offers a variety of courses including tea, *ikebana, shodo, sumi-e,* cooking and *shiatsu.* The school is in a lovely, older Japanese building.
ASAHI CULTURAL CENTER   Sumitomo Bldg., 4F. 2-6-1 Nishi Shinjuku, Shinjuku-ku. Tel: 3344-1941. They have various arts, crafts, and language courses. For most classes, Japanese language ability is required. The exceptions are pottery and *ikebana.* Minimum enrollment period is three months.

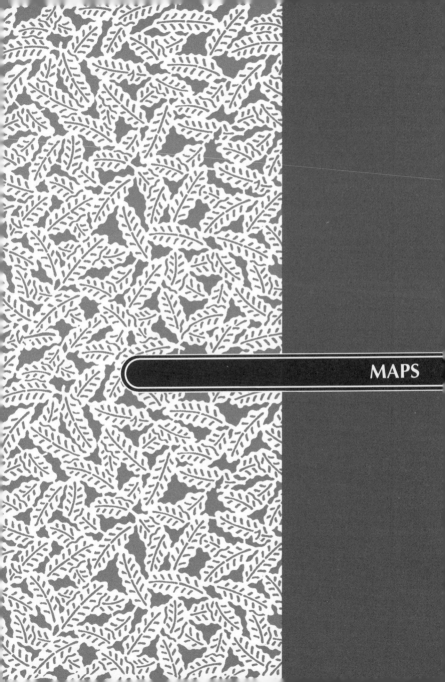

MAPS

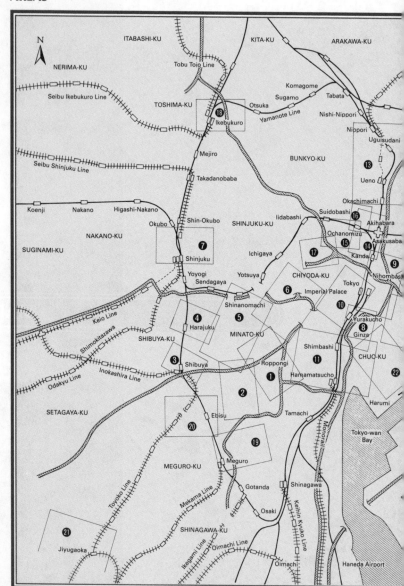

N

ITABASHI-KU

KITA-KU

ARAKAWA-KU

NERIMA-KU

Tobu Tojo Line

Komagome

Sugamo

Tabata

Seibu Ikebukuro Line

TOSHIMA-KU

Otsuka

Nishi-Nippori

Yamanote Line

Nippori

Uguisudani

Mejiro

Seibu Shinjuku Line

BUNKYO-KU

13

Takadanobaba

Ueno

Okachimachi

Koenji

Nakano

Higashi-Nakano

Suidobashi

16

Shin-Okubo

Iidabashi

Akihabara

Okubo

SHINJUKU-KU

Ochanomizu

15

Asakusaba

NAKANO-KU

7

14

SUGINAMI-KU

Shinjuku

Ichigaya

17

Kanda

9

Yoyogi

Yotsuya

Nihombas

Sendagaya

CHIYODA-KU

Tokyo

Keio Line

Shinanomachi

6

Imperial Palace

10

Shimokitazawa

4

5

Yurakucho

Harajuku

8

SHIBUYA-KU

MINATO-KU

Shimbashi

Ginza

3

Shibuya

Roppongi

11

CHUO-KU

Inokashira Line

1

Hamamatsucho

22

Odakyu Line

2

SETAGAYA-KU

Ebisu

Tamachi

Harumi

20

19

Tokyo-wan
Bay

Meguro

Toroko Line

MEGURO-KU

Mekama Line

Gotanda

Shinagawa

21

Osaki

Jiyugaoka

SHINAGAWA-KU

Oimachi Line

Haneda Airport

Keihin Kyuko Line

Ikegami Line

Oimachi

TOKYO AREA MAP

The twenty-five maps in the first part of this section cover the important districts of the city. Following them in the next part are small maps of locations not found on the major maps. The maps have not been drawn to uniform scale, and their directional axes vary, but the outlines of each district have been clearly marked on the Tokyo Areas map and can be consulted to gain a fair perspective.

Map entries are marked by numbers or symbols. Next to each map is a list of the entries with the corresponding map entry number and the page number where the entry is mentioned in the text. When two or more shops are located in the same building, one number is used for all. Map entries are divided by categories, e.g., accommodation, eating out, sightseeing.

Abbreviations or words in parentheses have sometimes been used to describe the type of shop, particularly when the name of one location is identical to that of another.

Tokyo is rarely an easy city to navigate, and even the native residents heavily rely on landmarks, well known streets, and crossings when trying to find a place or location for the first time. Common landmarks have been marked on the maps. If you get lost, or are taking a taxi, you may have success when you ask for one of these.

• Sightseeing

Names on the list are the standard Japanese names, but on the maps we have used the English where it will be easier to understand at a glance. Buildings found in our contemporary architecture section are listed here as well.

• Key

× police box
⛩ shrine
卍 temple
⊠ police station
〒 post office

[M-1] ROPPONGI

* See Roppongi inset map on page 305.

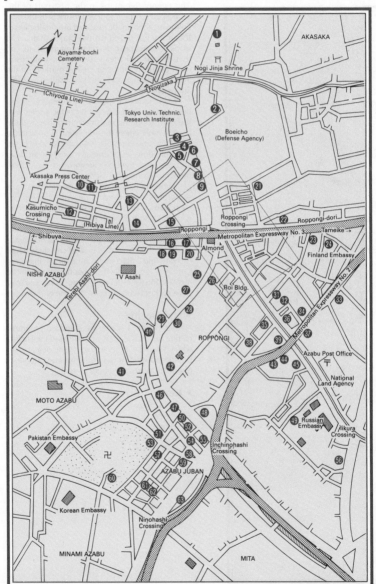

[M-2] NISHI AZABU—HIRO-O

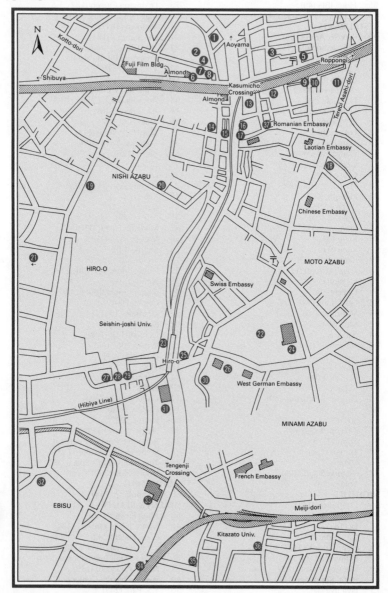

N

Kotto-dori

Aoyama

← Shibuya

Fuji Film Bldg.

Almond

Almond

Kasumicho Crossing

Roppongi

Terebi Asahi-dori

Romanian Embassy

Laotian Embassy

NISHI AZABU

Chinese Embassy

MOTO AZABU

HIRO-O

Swiss Embassy

Seishin-joshi Univ.

Hiro-o

(Hibiya Line)

West German Embassy

MINAMI AZABU

Tengenji Crossing

French Embassy

EBISU

Meiji-dori

Kitazato Univ.

*Roppongi Inset Map (see page 303)

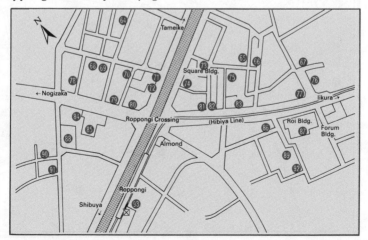

[M-3] SHIBUYA

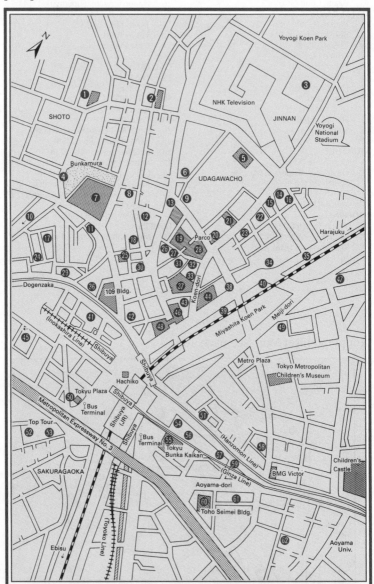

[M-4] HARAJUKU

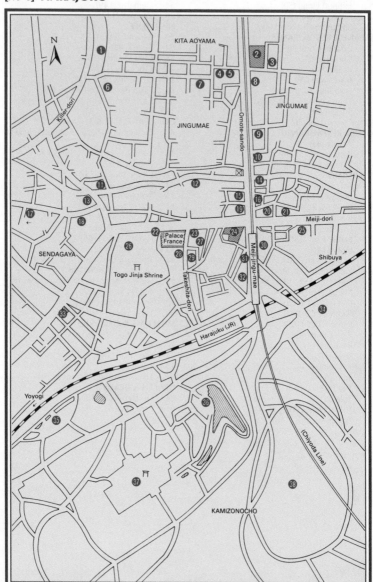

KITA AOYAMA

JINGUMAE

JINGUMAE

Killer-dori

Omote-sando

SENDAGAYA

Togo Jinja Shrine

Palace France

Takeshita-dori

Meiji-jingu-mae

Meiji-dori

Shibuya

Harajuku (JR)

Yoyogi

(Chiyoda Line)

KAMIZONOCHO

[M-5] AOYAMA

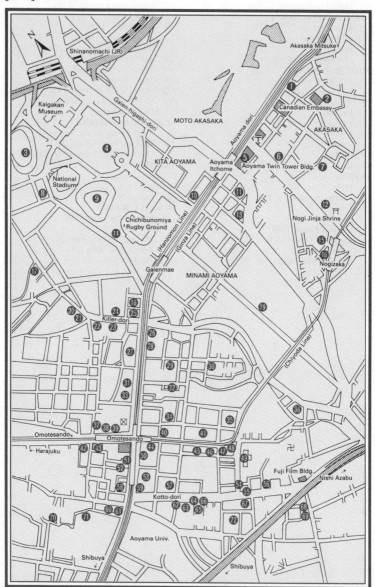

Shinanomachi (JR)

Gaien-higashi-dori

Kaigakan
Museum

MOTO AKASAKA

Akasaka Mitsuke

Canadian Embassy

AKASAKA

Aoyama-dori

KITA AOYAMA

Aoyama
Itchome

Aoyama Twin Tower Bldg.

National
Stadium

Chichibunomiya
Rugby Ground

(Hanzomon Line)

(Ginza Line)

Nogi Jinja Shrine

Gaienmae

MINAMI AOYAMA

Nogizaka

Killer-dori

(Chiyoda Line)

Omotesando

Omotesando

← Harajuku

Fuji Film Bldg.

Nishi Azabu

Kotto-dori

Aoyama Univ.

Shibuya

Shibuya

[M-6] AKASAKA—NAGATACHO

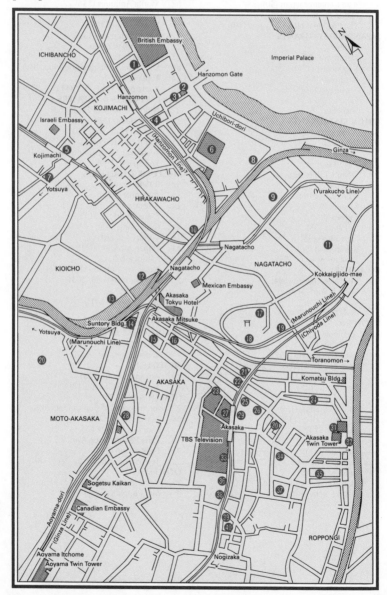

[M-7] SHINJUKU

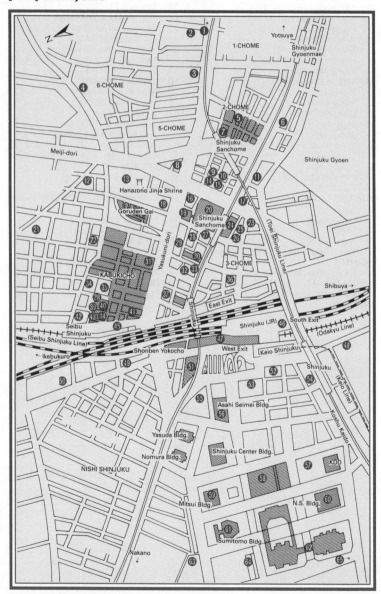

[M-8] GINZA

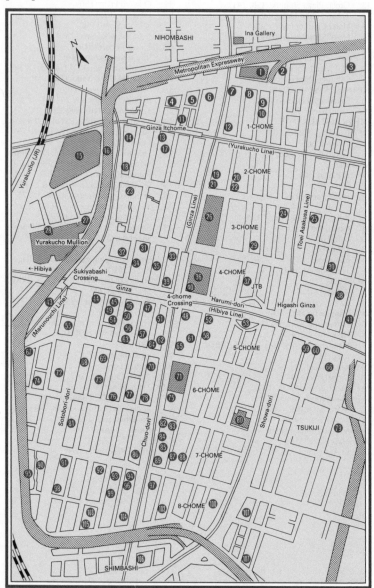

NIHOMBASHI

Ina Gallery

Metropolitan Expressway

Yurakucho (JR)

Ginza Itchome

(Yurakucho Line)

1-CHOME

2-CHOME

(Ginza Line)

3-CHOME

Yurakucho Mullion

← Hibiya

Sukiyabashi
Crossing

Ginza

4-chome
Crossing

4-CHOME

JTB

Harumi-dori

Higashi Ginza

(Marunouchi Line)

(Hibiya Line)

5-CHOME

(Toei Asakusa Line)

Sotobori-dori

6-CHOME

Chuo-dori

Showa-dori

TSUKIJI

7-CHOME

8-CHOME

SHIMBASHI

(continued on page 319)

[M-9] NIHOMBASHI—KYOBASHI

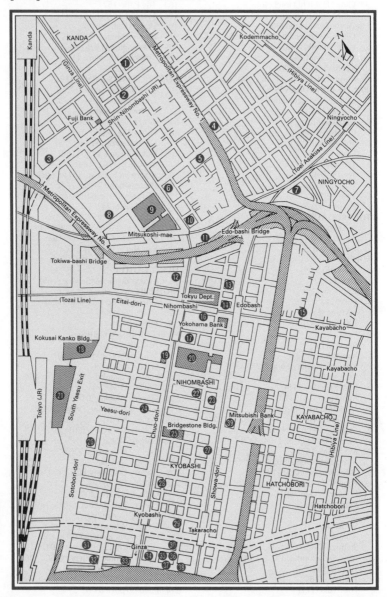

(continued from page 317)

[M-10] YURAKUCHO—HIBIYA—MARUNOUCHI

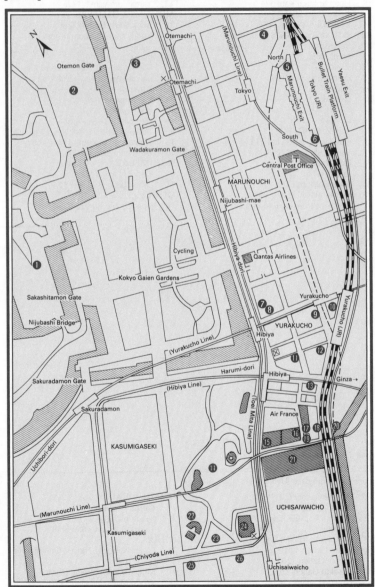

ACCOMMODATION
21   Imperial Hotel (46)
3   Palace Hotel (47)
4   Tokyo Marunouchi Hotel (48)
6   Tokyo Station Hotel (47)

RESTAURANTS
9   Kocho (72)
17   L'Alfresco (95)

SHOPPING
20   Hayashi Kimono (138)
21   Imperial Hotel Arcade (107)
20   International Arcade (107)
26   NEC Showroom (114)
18   Sakai Kokodo Gallery (128)
10   Sogo Dept. (104)

CONCERT HALLS & THEATERS
19   Geijutsu-za (168)
17   Hibiya Chanter Cine 1 & 2 (175)
24   Hibiya Kokaido (168)
22   Hibiya Yagai Ongakudo (168)
25   Ino Hall (168)
19   Miyuki-za (174)

15   Nissei Gekijo (168)
16   Scala-za (174)
12   Subaru-za (174)
7   Teikoku Gekijo/Imperial Theater (169)
16   Tokyo Takarazuka Gekijo (169)
10   Yomiuri Hall (169)

MUSEUMS & GALLERIES
8   Idemitsu Art Gallery (191)
7   Teikoku Gekijo/Imperial Theater (169)
5   Tokyo Station Gallery (200)

TRADITIONAL ARTS
21   Toko-an (206)

SIGHTSEEING
14   Hibiya Koen (218)
1   Kokyo/Imperial Palace (221)
2   Kokyo Higashi Gyoen (219)

HEALTH & BEAUTY
11   American Pharmacy (239)
21   Sanwa Massage (241)

OTHERS
23   Metropolitan Hibiya Library
13   Tourist Information Center (263)

[M-11] SHIBA—TORANOMON—SHIMBASHI

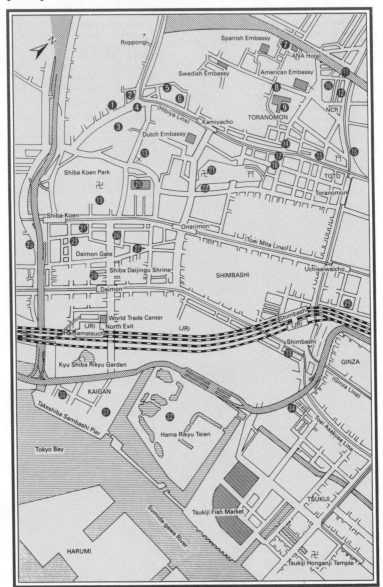

Roppongi

Spanish Embassy ⑦

ANA Hotel

Swedish Embassy

American Embassy ⑪

② ⑤ ⑧ ⑩
① ⑥ ⑫
④ ⑨
③ (Hibiya Line) ⑨ NCR
Kamiyacho TORANOMON

Dutch Embassy

⑬ ⑭

Shiba Koen Park ⑰ ⑮ ⑯
⑱
卍 ㉑ TOTO
⑳ Toranomon
⑲ ㉒

Shiba-Koen

Onarimon

㉔ (Toei Mita Line)

⑳ ㉕ ㉖
Daimon Gate ㉗ Uchisaiwaicho

Shiba Daijingu Shrine SHIMBASHI

㉘

Daimon

World Trade Center ㉙

(JR) North Exit (JR)

Hamamatsucho Shimbashi

JR

Kyu Shiba Rikyu Garden ㉝ Shimbashi

GINZA

(Ginza Line)

㉚ KAIGAN

㉛ ㉜ ㉞

Takeshiba Sambashi Pier

Hama Rikyu Teien Toei Asakusa Line

Tokyo Bay

Sumida-gawa river

TSUKIJI

Tsukiji Fish Market

卍

HARUMI Tsukiji Honganji Temple

ACCOMMODATION

7	ANA Hotel Tokyo (48)
9	Hotel Okura (49, 107)
27	Shiba Park Hotel (49)
31	Shiba Yayoi Kaikan (49)
29	Shimbashi Dai-ichi Hotel (47)
23	Tokyo Grand Hotel (49)
20	Tokyo Prince Hotel (49)

RESTAURANTS

26	Crescent (94)
22	Daigo (73)
32	Hamarikyu Teien Teahouses (97)
9	Tokalin (92)
10	Zakuro (82)

SHOPPING

6	Art Plaza Magatani (136)
9	Hotel Okura Arcade (49, 107)
11	Inachu Japan (126)
18	Ishida Biwa-ten (129)
17	Japan Sword (124)
1	Nodazen (125)

CONCERT HALLS & THEATERS

24	ABC Kaikan Hall (168)
4	Iikura La Foret 800/500 (168)
25	Meruparuku Hall (168)
16	Toranomon Hall (169)
33	Yakult Hall (169)

MUSEUMS & GALLERIES

30	Gatodo Gallery Takebashi (204)
34	Nakagin Capsule Tower Bldg. (207)
21	NHK Museum of Broadcasting (196)
2	NOA Bldg. (207)
8	Okura Museum (191)
15	Photo Gallery International (202)
14	Polaroid Gallery (202)
5	Reiyukai-Shakaden (207)
30	Shigeru Yokoto Gallery (204)
28	Tolman Collection (204)

TRADITIONAL ARTS

9	Chosho-an (206)

SIGHTSEEING

32	Hama Rikyu Teien (219)
3	Tokyo Tower (222)
19	Zojo-ji (214)

HEALTH & BEAUTY

13	The Medical Dispensary (239)
13	Tokyo Clinic Dental Office (239)
13	Tokyo Medical & Surgical Clinic (238)

[M-12] ASAKUSA

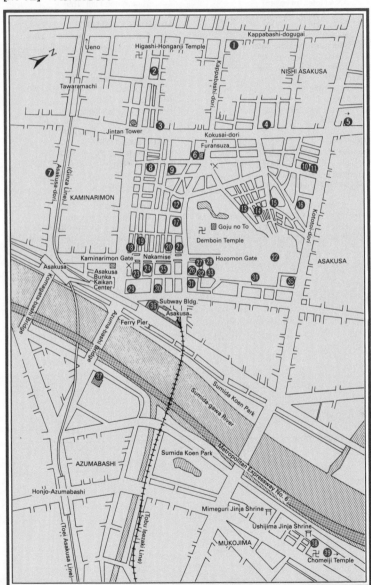

[M-13]   UENO

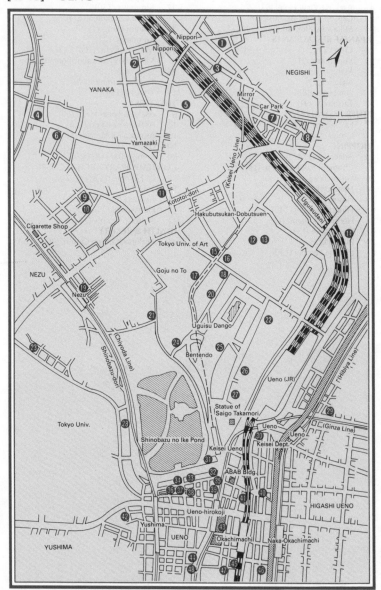

[M-14] AKIHABARA

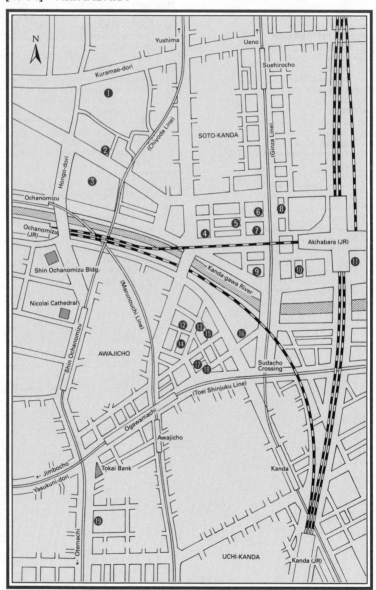

[M-15] OCHANOMIZU—JIMBOCHO

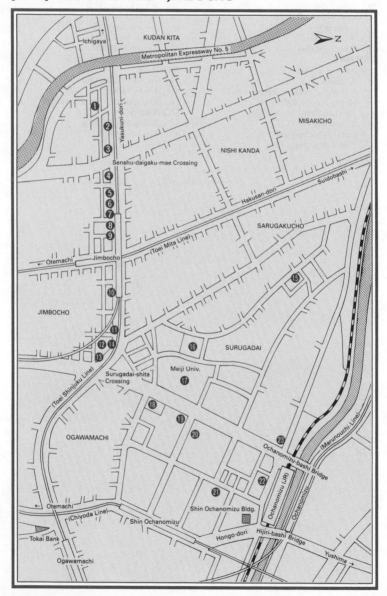

[M-16] YUSHIMA

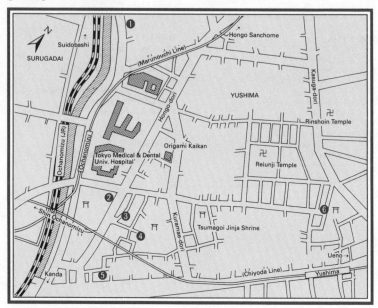

RESTAURANTS
1 Dusit Thien Doung (93)
5 Kandagawa Honten (86)
SHOPPING
3 Amanoya (141)
SIGHTSEEING
4 Kanda Myojin Shrine (215)
2 Yushima Seido (222)
6 Yushima Tenjin (216)

[M-17] KUDAN

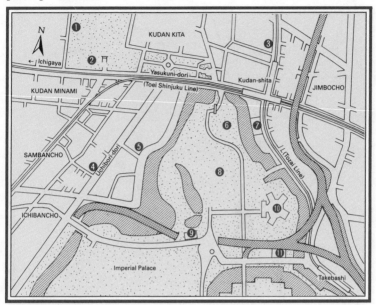

ACCOMMODATION
5   Fairmont Hotel (53)
3   Hotel Grand Palace (53)
4   Hotel Kayu Kaikan (48)
7   Kudan Kaikan Hotel (53)

NIGHTLIFE
7   Kudan Beer Garden (183)

CONCERT HALLS & THEATERS
7   Kudan Kaikan Dai Hall (168)
6   Nihon Budokan (223)

MUSEUMS
9   Crafts Gallery of the Museum of
    Modern Art (192)
11 Tokyo National Museum of Modern
    Art (192)
10 Science Museum (146)
1   Treasure House of the Yasukuni Shrine
    (195)

SIGHTSEEING
8   Kitanomaru Koen (218)
2   Yasukuni Jinja (215)

[M-18]   IKEBUKURO

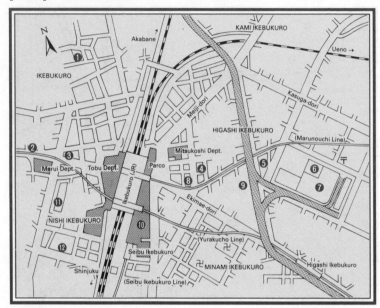

ACCOMMODATION
12   Hotel Metropolitan (51)
4   Hotel White City (58)
1   Ikebukuro Center City Hotel (51)
2   Kimi Ryokan (55)
6   Sunshine City Prince Hotel (51)

SHOPPING
10   Art Vivant (148)
8   Bic Camera (116)
3   Camera no Kimura (116)
10   Seibu Dept. (126)
7   Sunshine City (106)
9   Tokyu Hands (106, 151)
5   Toyota Auto Salon Amlux (114)

CONCERT HALLS & THEATERS
7   Sunshine Gekijo (169)
11   Tokyo Geijutsu Gekijo (169)

MUSEUMS & GALLERIES
10   Sezon Museum of Art (193)
7   The Ancient Orient Museum (195)

[M-19] MEGURO

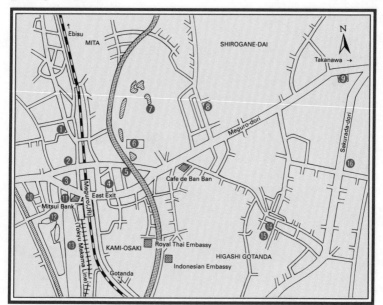

ACCOMMODATION
13 Gajoen Kanko Hotel (53)
1 Hotel Sanjoen (52)
12 Meguro Gajoen (53)
9 Miyako Hotel Tokyo (52)

JAPANESE RESTAURANTS
14 Hannyaen (72)
9 Issa-an (84)
11 Tonki (81)

OTHER RESTAURANTS
8 Ozawa (97)

NIGHTLIFE
10 Meguro Club (186)

SHOPPING
2 Antique Gallery Meguro (137)
5 Ikeda (138)
16 Matsuzakaya Camera (117)
3 Pioneer Showroom (114)

MUSEUMS & GALLERIES
15 Hatakeyama Museum (191)
8 Nani-Nani (207)
6 Tokyo Metropolitan Teien Museum of
Art (192)

SIGHTSEEING
7 National Park for Nature Study/Shizen
Kyoikuen (202)

[M-20]   DAIKANYAMA—EBISU

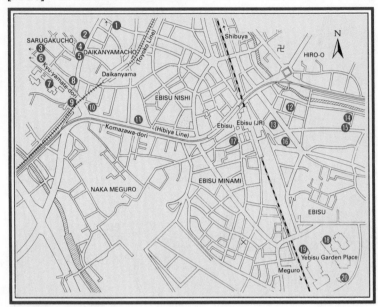

ACCOMMODATION
20   Westin Tokyo, The (53)

JAPANESE RESTAURANTS
1   Ichikan (75)
5   Kai (90)

OTHER RESTAURANTS
12   Il Boccalone (95)
3   Madame Toki's (94)
14   Ninnikuya (96)
7   Pachon (94)
17   Piga Piga (93, 183)
2   Tableaux (97)

NIGHTLIFE
11   Soul Bar Standard (180)
10   Yakochu (180)
19   Yebisu Beer Station (183)

SHOPPING
9   Dep't East (112)
16   Good Day Books (148)
4   Kamawanu (136)
18   Mitsukoshi Dept. (103)
8   Pink House (111)
15   Scandal Boy (113)
6   Shimada Junko (110)

GALLERIES
7   Hillside Gallery (203)
7   Hillside Terrace (206)
13   Studio Ebisu Photo Gallery (203)

[M-21] JIYUGAOKA

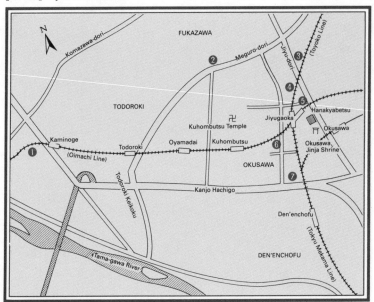

JAPANESE RESTAURANTS
3   Motomachi (88)
4   Okaju (80)
SHOPPING
6   Aikobo (118, 150)
7   Den-en (143)
2   Kinokuniya International (143)
5   Natural House (143)
MUSEUMS
1   Goto Art Museum (191, 231)

[M-22]   TSUKIJI—HARUMI

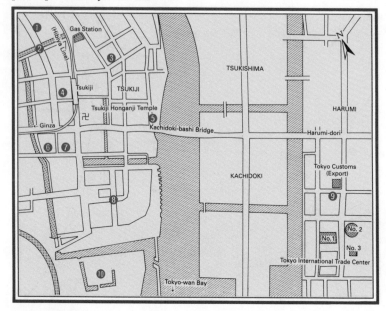

ACCOMMODATION
6   Ginza Marunouchi Hotel (47)
JAPANESE RESTAURANTS
5   Tentake (86)
7   Tsukiji Edogin (75)
4   Tsukiji Tamura (72)
SHOPPING
2   Kashiwaya (122)
1   Onoya Shoten (133)
8   Tsukiji Fish Market (74, 108)
MUSEUMS
9   Furniture Museum (196)
SIGHTSEEING
10   Hama Rikyu Teien (219)
HEALTH & BEAUTY
3   Seiroka Byoin/St. Luke's International
    Hospital (239)

[M-23]   NINGYOCHO

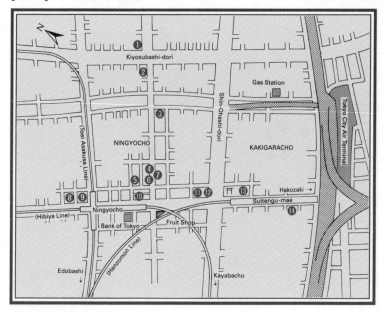

ACCOMMODATION
3   Hotel Kitcho (54)
JAPANESE RESTAURANT
5   Homitei (90)
SHOPPING
4   Bachi-ei Gakkiten (129)
9   Iseryu Shoten (127)
6   Iwai Shoten (122)
11   Kotobukido Kyogashi-tsukasa (139)
10   Kyosendo (133)
12   Shigemori Eishindo (140)
8   Ubukeya (125)
7   Yanagiya(140)
THEATERS
1   Meiji-za (168)
MUSEUMS & GALLERIES
14   Infomusu (200)
2   Kurita Museum (194)
SIGHTSEEING
13   Ṣuitengu (216)

[M-24]   ASAKUSABASHI

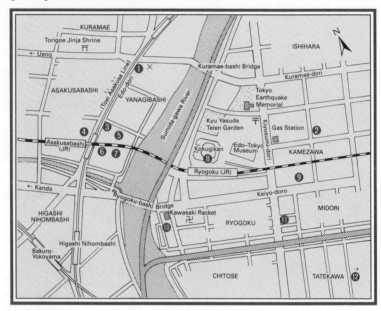

SHOPPING
12	Ito Oke-ten (125)
11	Kikuya (133)
4	Koundo (121)
6	Kyugetsu (120)
1	Musashiya Shoten (119)
7	Sakura Horikiri (121)
9	Tokyo Hyakka Funabashiya (150)
3	Wholesale Market (120)

SPORTS: SUMO
10	Kasugano-beya (171)
2	Kokonoe-beya (171)
8	Kokugikan Sumo Stadium (171)
5	Takasago-beya (171)

MUSEUMS
8	Sumo Museum (196)

[M-25] FUKAGAWA—TSUKUDAJIMA

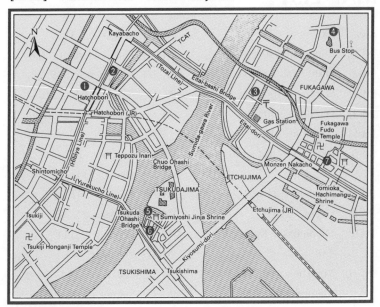

ACCOMMODATION
2   Holiday Inn (54)
SHOPPING
1   Naohei (125)
6   Tanakaya (142)
5   Ten'yasu (142)
GALLERY
3   Sagacho Exhibit Space (204)
SIGHTSEEING
4   Kiyosumi Teien (219)

MAP LIST

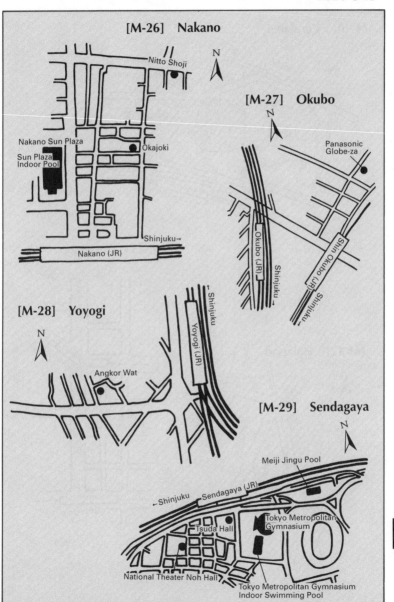

[M-26] Nakano

Nitto Shoji

N

Nakano Sun Plaza

Sun Plaza Indoor Pool

Okajoki

Shinjuku→

Nakano (JR)

[M-27] Okubo

N

Panasonic Globe-za

Okubo (JR)

Shin Okubo (JR)

Shinjuku→

Shinjuku→

[M-28] Yoyogi

N

Angkor Wat

←Shinjuku

Yoyogi (JR)

[M-29] Sendagaya

N

Meiji Jingu Pool

←Shinjuku Sendagaya (JR)

Tokyo Metropolitan Gymnasium

Tsuda Hall

National Theater Noh Hall

Tokyo Metropolitan Gymnasium Indoor Swimming Pool

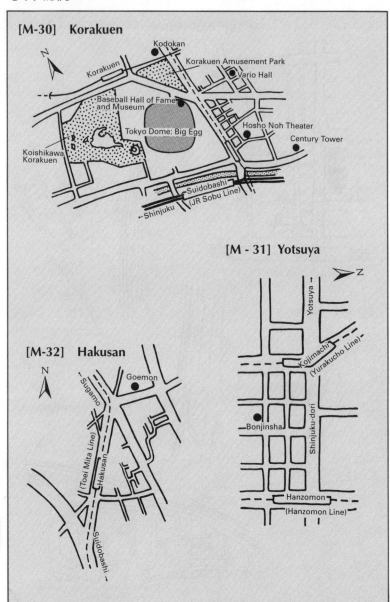

[M-30] Korakuen

N

Kodokan

Korakuen

Korakuen Amusement Park

Vario Hall

Baseball Hall of Fame and Museum

Tokyo Dome: Big Egg

Hosho Noh Theater

Century Tower

Koishikawa Korakuen

Suidobashi (JR Sobu Line)

←Shinjuku

[M - 31] Yotsuya

Z

↑Yotsuya

Kojimachi (Yurakucho Line)

Shinjuku-dori

Bonjinsha

Hanzomon (Hanzomon Line)

[M-32] Hakusan

N

←Sugamo

Goemon

(Toei Mita Line)

Hakusan

Suidobashi

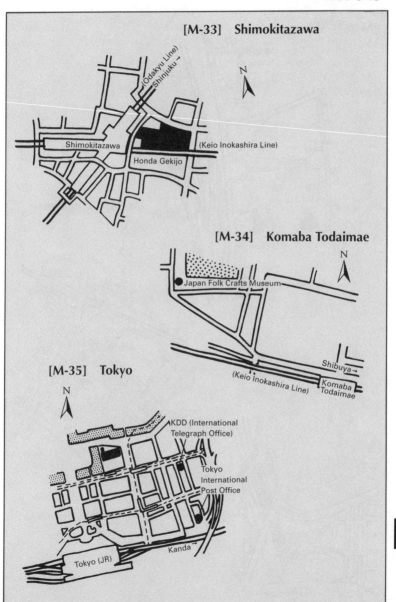

[M-33] **Shimokitazawa**

(Odakyu Line)
Shinjuku →

N

Shimokitazawa

(Keio Inokashira Line)

Honda Gekijo

[M-34] **Komaba Todaimae**

N

Japan Folk Crafts Museum

Shibuya →

(Keio Inokashira Line)

Komaba Todaimae

[M-35] **Tokyo**

N

KDD (International Telegraph Office)

Tokyo International Post Office

Kanda →

Tokyo (JR)

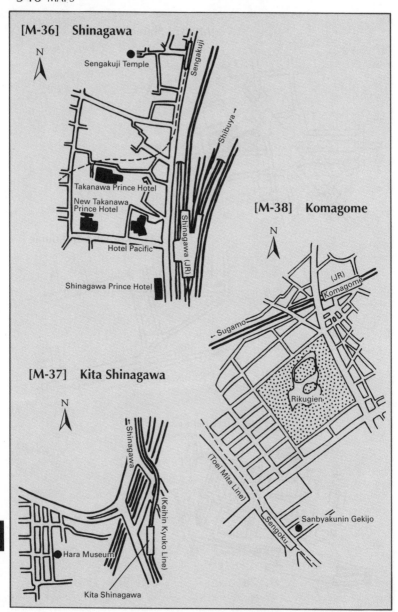

[M-36] Shinagawa

N

Sengakuji Temple

Sengakuji

Shibuya →

Takanawa Prince Hotel

New Takanawa Prince Hotel

Shinagawa (JR)

Hotel Pacific

Shinagawa Prince Hotel

[M-37] Kita Shinagawa

N

Shinagawa

(Keihin Kyuko Line)

Hara Museum

Kita Shinagawa

[M-38] Komagome

N

(JR) Komagome

← Sugamo

Rikugien

(Toei Mita Line)

Sengoku

Sanbyakunin Gekijo

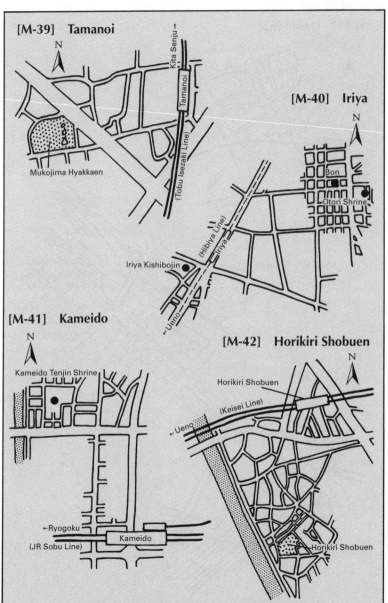

[M-39] Tamanoi

N

Kita Senju →

Tamanoi

(Tobu Isezaki Line)

Mukojima Hyakkaen

[M-40] Iriya

N

Bon

Otori Shrine

(Hibiya Line)

Iriya

Iriya Kishibojin

← Ueno

[M-41] Kameido

N

Kameido Tenjin Shrine

← Ryogoku

(JR Sobu Line)

Kameido

[M-42] Horikiri Shobuen

Horikiri Shobuen

(Keisei Line)

← Ueno

Horikiri Shobuen

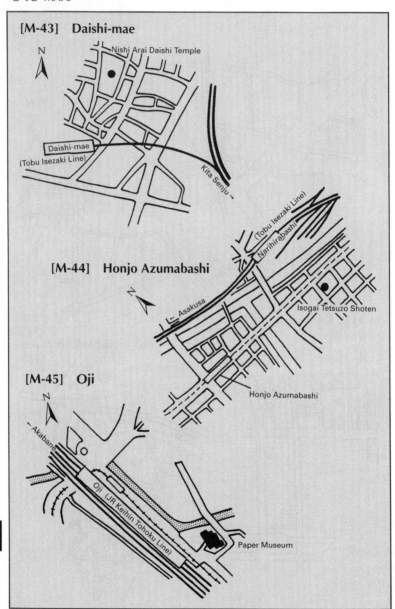

[M-43] Daishi-mae

N

Nishi Arai Daishi Temple

Daishi-mae
(Tobu Isezaki Line)

Kita Senju –

[M-44] Honjo Azumabashi

(Tobu Isezaki Line)

Narihirabashi

N

Asakusa

Isogai Tetsuzo Shoten

[M-45] Oji

N

– Akabane

Oji (JR Keihin Tohoku Line)

Honjo Azumabashi

Paper Museum

PHOTO CREDITS

P. 18   Tsuzuki Kyoichi

P. 29   Courtesy of Shiseido Co., Ltd.

P. 44   Bipod: Leslie Martin and Sally Schwager

P. 62   Bipod: Leslie Martin and Sally Schwager

P. 71   Tobias Pfeil

P. 100   Bipod: Leslie Martin and Sally Schwager

P. 135   Tobias Pfeil

P. 151   M. Yoshida

P. 156   Hayashi Eitetsu

P. 167   Nakafuji Takehiko

P. 178   Bipod: Leslie Martin and Sally Schwager

P. 185   Tobias Pfeil

P. 188   Sekiya Masaaki. ("Uji-an" teahouse, designed by Isozaki
           Arata)

P. 193   Yamamoto Tadasu

P. 199   Courtesy of Hara Museum of Contemporary Art.

P. 210   Bipod: Leslie Martin and Sally Schwager

P. 216   M. Yoshida

P. 229   Tobias Pfeil

P. 236   Bipod: Leslie Martin and Sally Schwager

P. 246   Bipod: Leslie Martin and Sally Schwager

ACKNOWLEDGMENTS

The *Tokyo City Guide* and its authors owe their thanks to a vast number of people who gave advice, recommendations, support, and enthusiasm to this project. A special thanks is owed to the following people: Mori Akira, Hara Saburo, Ichimura Suzuko, Inagaki Jiro, Hashimoto Yoshio, Ohashi Atsushi, Shimada Masae, Watari Koichi, Robin Thompson, Nick Bornoff, Baby and Marcy, Richard Greer, Mihara Yoshiyuki, Hasumi Yuko, Matsui Takeyoshi, Utsunomiya Sotaro, Leonard Koren, the staff at TIC, Matsui Yoichi, Nose Chieko, Tsunoi Naoko, Arai Mieko, Hotta Aki, and Jeannie-Kay and Walter Shill.

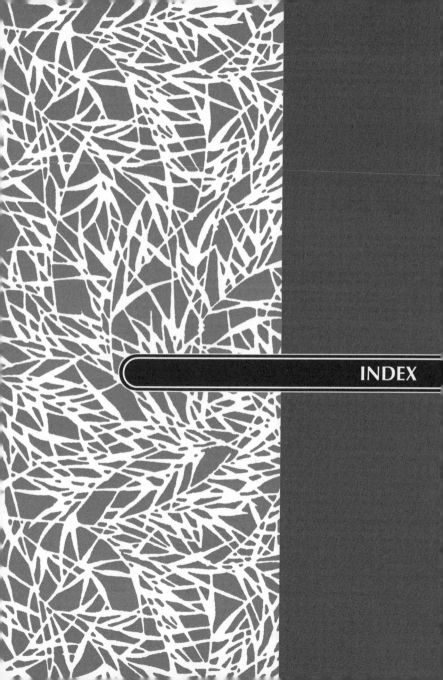

INDEX

Other Titles in the Tuttle Library

MODERN JAPANESE PRINTS POSTCARDS
by Norman and Mary Tolman

JAPAN: The Art of Living Postcards Sets 1 and 2

JAPAN COUNTRY LIVING POSTCARDS: Spirit ·
Tradition · Style

JAPAN: An Invitation Postcards
(Set 1) Beauty and Splendor, (Set 2) Culture and Tradition

KARHU'S CLASSIC KYOTO POSTCARDS
by Clifton Karhu

BEAUTIFUL JAPAN: A SOUVENIR *photographed by*
Narumi Yasuda

THE BOOK OF TEA *by Kakuzo Okakura*

ZEN FLOWERS: Chabana for the Tea Ceremony
by Henry Mittwer

DOWN THE EMPEROR'S ROAD WITH HIROSHIGE
Edited by Reiko Chiba

HIROSHIGE'S TOKAIDO IN PRINTS AND POETRY
Edited by Reiko Chiba

PAINTED FANS OF JAPAN: Fifteen Noh Drama
Masterpieces *by Reiko Chiba*

SESSHU'S LONG SCROLL: A Zen Landscape Journey
Introduction and notes by Reiko Chiba

THE SEVEN LUCKY GODS *by Reiko Chiba*

INRO AND OTHER MINIATURE FORMS OF
JAPANESE LACQUER ART *by Melvin and Betty Jahss*

NETSUKE: Japanese Life and Legend in Miniature
by Edwin C. Symmes, Jr.

THE WONDERFUL WORLD OF NETSUKE: With One
Hundred Masterpieces of Miniature Sculpture in Color
by Raymond Bushell